Architects of American Air Supremacy

Gen Hap Arnold and Dr. Theodore von Kármán

Dik A. Daso, Maj, USAF

Air University Press
Maxwell Air Force Base, Alabama

September 1997

Library of Congress Cataloging-in-Publication Data

Daso, Dik A., 1959–
    Architects of American air supremacy : Gen. Hap Arnold and Dr. Theodore von Kármán / Dik A. Daso.
        p.   cm.
    Includes bibliographical references and index.
    1. Aeronautics, Military—Research—United States—History. 2. Arnold, Henry Harley. 1886–1950. 3. Von Kármán, Theodore, 1881–1963. 4. Air power—United States—History. I. Title.
    UG643.D37   1997
    358.4′00973—dc21

97-26768
CIP

ISBN 1-58566-042-6

First Printing September 1997
Second Printing August 2001

Disclaimer

for
Lindsey and Taylor
providers of motivation and inspiration

Contents

Photographs

Foreword

The United States Air Force is the most technologically advanced service in the world. Stealth, precision, global range, and space systems are only a few of the hallmarks of USAF technology. Airborne laser weapons, super-accurate sensors, and hypersonic aircraft are already in the early stages of development. Creations such as these are not the product of stagnant minds or idle hands.

It was in 1944 that General of the Army Henry H. "Hap" Arnold established the Army Air Forces (AAF) Scientific Advisory Group (SAG) under the direction of Dr. Theodore von Kármán. The SAG meticulously created the first science and technology forecast ever accomplished in military history. The study predicted many of the developments in aviation technology which, today, most Americans take for granted. Some of the more outstanding of these are supersonic flight, precision weaponry, accurate radar, and the development of intercontinental ballistic missiles (ICBM).

In *Architects of American Air Supremacy*, Dik Daso tells the story of the founding of the scientific and technological base of today's USAF. But this work is much more than simply a history of technology. The SAG was a culminating point reached only after many years of building interpersonal relationships, developing industrial bonds, and tapping the wisdom of America's most influential scientists. In large measure this book reflects the symbiotic nature of the military and the society which it serves. This book is an introduction to the very nature of the USAF—a service founded in aviation science and technology and built by great commanders, innovators, and dedicated men and women in the service of their nation.

RONALD R. FOGLEMAN
General, USAF
Chief of Staff

About the Author

A native of the Cleveland area, Dik Daso is a 1981 USAF Academy graduate of Cadet Squadron 31, "The Grim Reapers." His flying career began as a T-38 Talon instructor pilot at Laughlin Air Force Base, Texas. He then flew two tours in the RF-4C Phantom, stateside and in Korea. He also flew the F-15 Eagle for a short tour before finishing his master's of arts in American revolutionary period history at the University of South Carolina (USC) in Columbia. He taught military and world history at his alma mater during the 1992–93 school year. A unique set of circumstances allowed him to return to USC, home of the Gamecocks, where he completed his doctorate in military history in March 1996. During 1995, he served as the historian for the most recent Air Force science and technology study, *New World Vistas*, where he edited the "Ancillary" volume (14) of the study. He has also published articles in the USAF professional magazine, *Airpower Journal*.

Currently, Dik Daso is a member of the Air and Space Operations Directorate in the Air Staff at the Pentagon in Washington, D.C.

Preface

This study highlights elements of technology with which Henry H. Arnold and Theodore von Kármán were directly involved. Very little is included covering specific air operations during World War II, although technology was certainly vital to them. Little is included concerning scientific achievement outside of the framework of the Army Air Forces, although the effect of military technological development on the civilian world, during and particularly after the war, is indisputable. More significantly, the evolution of American science itself, from empiricism to a more German, theoretical approach to problem solution, is only indirectly addressed through the evolution of airpower. The biographical approach, emphasizing scientific and technological elements in Arnold's and Kármán's lives, is essential because the interaction of personalities, as well as their institutions, is inexorably linked to the development of American airpower. The importance of the personalities involved precludes a purely technological history of the airplane or the Air Force as a system within itself. For in the end, it was two men using their broad experience and innovative ideas, who created the blueprint with which American air supremacy has been built.

A major theme of this study is how people influence each other. Consequently, decisions affecting institutions are molded, not just by experience but also by personal influences. This is a history of ideas. It is an examination of how the Air Force has come to believe itself a military service with its base firmly anchored in advanced technology and how those beliefs originated. Additionally, it is the story of how airpower technologies evolved through World War II. Scientists had a hand in technological development, but not the only hand. Government officials directed and funded scientific and technological research. University professors, a large part of the scientific community, accomplished much of the essential research. This posed an interesting problem for Kármán because, traditionally, American science had revolved around

xvii

utilitarian values rather than theoretical understanding of both practical and scientific problems.[1] Industry provided the brawn required to mount the massive buildup of World War II military forces. But interaction of all of these, shaped by perceptions, vision, and interpersonal experiences, directed the actual evolution of airpower.[2] Underlying the major themes in this study is the realization that an integral part of this technological evolution was frequently the result not of superior planning or wisdom, but of good fortune, or dumb luck and happenstance.

The Army Air Corps, while led by Arnold, had actually jettisoned "conservatism toward technological change" long before the end of World War II.[3] Arnold's utilization of scientists, but particularly his association with Dr. von Kármán, propelled the Army Air Forces into a new era by forcing a shift in traditional paradigms concerning the airplane and its potential. Kármán's detailed suggestions, manifest in his 1945 science and technology forecast reports were supported by postwar Air Force leadership and eventually institutionalized by the independent Air Force, forming the scientific and technological orientation of today's massive USAF airpower system. Arnold's selection of Kármán to write the first Air Force science and technology forecast ensured that the Air Force maintained a strong branch of German style theoretical methodology in problem solution in addition to a branch that continued using purely empirical methods.

An examination of technological advances during this period shows that Arnold's command was characterized by three distinct technology-related periods. All three periods were determined by events and pressures dictated by a combination of America's political, social, and economic involvement during the interwar years as well as during Word War II.

Also, an attempt has been made to level the previously heroic characterizations of both Arnold and Kármán, showing that each had personal flaws that influenced their judgment, as well as other's perceptions of them, in sometimes unexpected ways. In many respects, these men were simply reacting to the events of their time, using their life experiences and relationships to untangle the web of crisis resulting from world war. Their personal flaws along with their perceived flaws of others constitute a crucial piece of the story of airpower's evolution before, during, and after World War II.

I shall not discuss many interesting areas of Air Force history since they have been covered by others. Operational events, to a large extent, have been left to other writers. Several recent works have admirably addressed operations, although much is yet to be done. Doctrine as an independent subject has been admirably examined by Dr. I. B. Holley Jr. and R. Frank Futrell, but, although related to the evolution of technology, doctrine is not examined independently here. Holley's conclusions about the organizational shortfalls in the Army Air Forces from the First to the Second World War are, perhaps, too simplistic in the largely unexplored area of science and technology. Benjamin S. Kelsey has addressed the foundations of Army Air Corps production and procurement in *The Dragon's Teeth: The Creation of United States Air Power for World War II* and suggests that the foundations for America's massive production efforts were established well before the beginnings of the Second World War. Holley has also produced a masterful assessment of procurement of aircraft in the Army Air Forces. The "nuts and bolts" of this complex piece of the Air Force puzzle is meticulously dissected in his monograph, *Buying Aircraft: Matériel Procurement for the Army Air Forces*, prepared for the Army Center of Military History. Politics of the interwar period, also an important element of this study, have been admirably examined in Jeffrey S. Underwood's, *The Wings of Democracy: The Influence of Air Power on the Roosevelt Administration, 1933–1941*, a crucial step forward in the military historiography of the period. Herman S. Wolk's study, *Planning and Organizing the Post War Air Force, 1943-1947*, is excellent for administrative matters. He is currently revising and expanding the work for the upcoming 50th anniversary of the Air Force. At this time, however, it does not include anything more than a cursory look at the administration of scientific elements. Ronald Schaffer's, *Wings of Judgment: American Bombing in World War II*, addresses the issues of ethics and morality as it applied to American World War II bombing campaigns. This approach seems to have increased relevancy, particularly in the recent controversy over the Smithsonian's *Enola Gay* exhibit.[4]

A separate word must be said about the available biographical works on Arnold and Kármán. Arnold's biography was written by Thomas M. Coffey and published in 1982. Contributions for the project were made by many of Arnold's closest associates and friends so that it is hardly without bias. Exhaustive personal interviews and correspondence formed the backbone of his research, and the problems of memory are present at times. An excellent summary of Arnold's personality, authored by Maj Gen John W. Huston, USAF, Retired, can be found in *The Proceedings of the Eighth Military History Symposium*, held at the USAF Academy in 1978. His article, "The Wartime Leadership of 'Hap' Arnold," is not so much about leadership as it is about the determination and drive behind leadership. Another short biography by Flint O. DuPre, is merely a summary of Arnold's own *Global Mission*, published in 1949. As is frequently pointed out, some dates are wrong and some names are misplaced, but *Global Mission* is still the best account of Arnold's personal life and his private relationships that is available.[5]

Theodore von Kármán has been the subject of two biographical efforts and many biographical articles. The most recent of these, *The Universal Man: Theodore von Kármán's Life in Aeronautics*, by Dr. Michael H. Gorn, traces the professor's life in its entirety. Paul A. Hanle also chronicled Kármán's life in *Bringing Aerodynamics to America*, which leans more toward his European accomplishments and the European scientific climate in the early 1900s. Together, these two works are an excellent set. The research in these two volumes reaches far above that of the Arnold works, perhaps a reflection of the tendency of American historians to shy away from military topics.[6]

If the current trend continues, however, military history may be on the brink of a necessary reshaping. Gorn, for example, has authored a study of the science and technology forecasting process in the US Air Force titled *Harnessing the Genie: Science and Technology Forecasting for the Air Force, 1944–1986*. His emphasis is an evaluation of the evolution of this process, rather than the story of its origins. Yet even this work is now incomplete as the Air Force has just completed its latest science and technology forecast, *New World Vistas*, delivered to the secretary of the Air Force and the chief of staff exactly 50 years after the first one was delivered in December 1945.[7]

The photos within this study reflect research done over the past two years. Many of these photos have not been seen since the end of World War II. Many more have never been published in any historical works. With a subject that continually bounces up against technological devices of one kind or another, it is often easier to show than to tell the reader what exactly they are reading about. The appendices include a brief career summary for General Arnold, including his West Point records, and Kármán's two summary reports, *Where We Stand* (includes Parts I and III, which have never been published) and *Science: The Key to Air Supremacy*. Rather than a detailed analysis of the documents, they have been included in their entirety.

In addition, I have been fortunate to conduct several interviews with individuals who participated in many of the events that occurred from 1930 to 1950. From early jet assisted takeoff (JATO) participants to original Scientific Advisory Group (SAG) members, their contributions have been indispensable. Unfortunately, I have been forced to depend upon others for material in foreign archives, particularly those in the Public Records Office and other British aviation repositories.

In the end, this project adds the story of an intricate scientific and technological evolutionary process to all major works in fields which examine Air Force aviation. No single volume contains more than brief glimpses into the origins of the ideas behind American military airpower as it relates to the development of a technological system driven by social, political, personal, and military influences. These brief glimpses require clarification and expansion. I believe this study serves to fill that void.

dad
18 September 1997
Pentagon, Washington, D.C.

Notes

1. Perhaps the best discussion of the American propensity to pragmatism can be found in, Edward W. Constant II, *The Origins of the Turbojet Revolution* (Baltimore: Johns Hopkins University Press, 1980). The quiet battle that took place in American science during the 1930s and 1940s between the theoretical engineers and the practical engineers is an underlying current in this study. It is my intention to demonstrate how the interaction of each of these scientific schools affected the development of airpower largely through personal and institutional values, beliefs, and interactions.

2. John M. Staudenmaier, *Technology's Storytellers* (Cambridge, Mass.: MIT Press, 1985). One thing becomes clear in this book, approaches to the history of technology vary tremendously from author to author. The Society for the History of Technology has acted as a clearinghouse for these over the past several decades but only recently has there been an explosion of works in this field.

3. Alex Roland, "Science, Technology, and War," *Technology and Culture* 36 (supp.), no. 2 (April 1995): S83-S99.

4. The following are listed in the order mentioned in the text: Richard G. Davis, *Carl A. Spaatz and the Air War in Europe* (Washington, D.C.: Center for Air Force History, 1993); I. B. Holley Jr., *Ideas and Weapons: Exploitation of the Aerial Weapon by the United States During World War I* (Washington, D.C.: Office of Air Force History, 1953). Holley addresses the interwar period more directly in "Jet Lag in the Army Air Corps," in *Military Planning in the Twentieth Century: The Proceedings of the USAFA 11th Military History Symposium, 1984 USAF Academy*, ed., Harry R. Borowski (Washington, D.C.: Office of Air Force History, 1986); however, the element of American utilitarian methodology versus German theoretical approach to problems is not directly addressed; Robert Frank Futrell, *Ideas, Concepts, and Doctrine*: vol. 1, *Basic Thinking in the United States Air Force, 1907–1960* (Maxwell AFB, Ala.: Air University Press, 1989); Benjamin S. Kelsey, *The Dragon's Teeth: The Creation of US Air Power, World War II* (Washington, D.C.: Smithsonian Institution Press, 1982); I. B. Holley Jr., *Buying Aircraft: Matériel Procurement for the Army Air Forces* (Washington, D.C.: Center for Military History, United States Army, 1964); Jeffery S. Underwood, *The Wings of Democracy: The Influence of Air Power on the Roosevelt Administration, 1933–1941* (College Station, Tex.: Texas A&M University Press, 1991); Herman S. Wolk, *Planning and Organizing the Post War Air Force, 1943–1947* (Washington, D.C.: Office of Air Force History, 1984); and Ronald Schaffer, *Wings of Judgment: American Bombing in World War II* (New York: Oxford University Press, 1985). Michael S. Sherry, *The Rise of American Air Power: The Creation of Armageddon* (New Haven: Yale University Press, 1987), is a sweeping approach to explain the growth of American air forces from both political and intellectual directions.

5. The following are listed in the order mentioned in the text: Thomas M. Coffey, *HAP: The Story of the U. S. Air Force and the Man Who Built It, General Henry H. "Hap" Arnold* (New York: Viking Press, 1982); John W. Huston, "The Wartime Leadership of 'Hap' Arnold," in Alfred F. Hurley and Robert C. Ehrhart, eds., *Air Power and Warfare: The Proceedings of the 8th*

Military History Symposium, United States Air Force Academy, 18–20 October 1978 (Washington, D.C.: Office of Air Force History, 1979); Flint O. DuPre, *Hap Arnold: Architect of American Air Power* (New York: MacMillan Co., 1972); and Henry H. Arnold, *Global Mission* (New York: Harper and Brothers, 1949).

6. Michael H. Gorn, *The Universal Man: Theodore von Kármán's Life in Aeronautics* (Washington, D.C.: Smithsonian Institution Press, 1992); Paul A. Hanle, *Bringing Aerodynamics to America* (Cambridge, Mass.: MIT Press, 1982).

7. Michael H. Gorn, *Harnessing the Genie: Science and Technology Forecasting for the Air Force, 1944–1986* (Washington, D.C.: Office of Air Force History, 1988).

Acknowledgments

This project, in its entirety, has benefited from the efforts of many dedicated individuals. Dr. Michael H. Gorn, from the Office of Air Force History, has provided welcome encouragement and keen, yet compassionate, criticism. His singular knowledge of Theodore von Kármán, and his enthusiasm for the same, has been of prime importance during this project. Additionally, my graduate committee consisting of Professor Owen Connelly, Professor Alex Roland, and particularly Dr. S. Paul Mackenzie have helped me maintain focus, condense, rebuild, and discard in places where pride of ownership frequently formed a barrier between logic and irrationality. Pointed comments by Maj Gen John W. Huston, USAF, Retired, Col Murray Green, USAF, Retired, Mr. Herman Wolk, and Dr. Daniel Mortensen were not only appreciated but also saved several obvious errors. Those which remain are solely my own.

A number of individuals gave of their time in personal interviews. Among these, is Professor William R. Sears, a long time Kármán associate and one of his most gifted pupils. His impersonation of his Hungarian professor added both humor and penetration to that complex man. Professor "Homerjoe" Stewart kindly welcomed me into his home on short notice and shared his personal experiences with the JATO project and the early days of the Jet Propulsion Laboratory. Additionally, Dr. H. Guyford Stever and Gen Bernard Schriever, USAF, Retired, provided details on the early Scientific Advisory Board and early US missile development where they had been lacking before. Dr. Ivan Getting and Mr. Chester Hasert, both original Scientific Advisory Group members (1944–1945), shared personal stories and experiences that enriched my understanding of the infant SAG as well as added color to the experience of Operation Lusty, the scientist's invasion of Europe.

During the research phase of this project, many archivists were held hostage by my continual questioning, "stacks" requests, and fax queries. Among these are the archivists of the Library of Congress Manuscripts Division, home of the Arnold Collection; the National Air and Space Museum, both in Washington, D.C., and at Silver Hill, Maryland; the California Institute of Technology Institute Archives, now housed in the new Beckman Center basement; the West Point Archives; and the National Archives at College Park, Maryland. Particularly meritorious efforts were made by John Bluth at the Jet Propulsion Lab in Pasadena, California, Bonnie Ludt at the Caltech Archives, and too many members of the Library of Congress staff to name.

I am indebted to the USAF Historical Research Agency and Col Richard Rauschkolb's meticulous staff. A research grant from that institution got this project off to a fine start. The archives at Maxwell Air Force Base, Alabama, offer a wealth of personal papers and unit histories that are essential material for any work in the airpower field. Also at Maxwell AFB, I owe many thanks to Col Phillip S. Meilinger, dean, School of Advanced Airpower Studies, who read early versions of the history and offered careful criticism and candid advice.

More personally, I owe a great debt to Robert Arnold, General Arnold's grandson, who spent the better part of a weekend showing me his personal collection of Arnold memorabilia and papers. From him I received a unique look into Arnold's family life as well as a new appreciation for California wine.

Finally, I owe a special thanks to Mr. Duane J. Reed, USAF Academy Special Collections. As an Air Force Academy cadet I respected his judgment and wisdom on any airpower history matter. Today, as an Air Force major, I realize how his dedication to cadet education through the years has impacted personal and professional lives throughout the USAF. It was during a 1993 discussion in his office at the Air Force Academy Special Collections Branch, that the concept for this project crystallized.

Chapter 1

Genesis

When the Wright Brothers accomplished America's first powered airplane flight on 17 December 1903, they would have been hard pressed to believe that in less than one century, manned aircraft would refuel in midair, travel at hypersonic speeds, carry tons of cargo in warehouse-size holds, or serve as the primary means of international world travel. Their airplane was a device that had only one purpose, to lift a man into the sky. Today, aircraft perform too many functions to count, using so many different designs that even knowing them all is a monumental undertaking. But how is it that we have come so far, so fast? Important answers lie in the complex relationship between the American military and the society in which it exists. Individuals, both military and civilian, make decisions based upon perceptions and experience as much as upon the presumed capability of a particular technology. In the case of the Army and the air weapon, this was particularly true.

This is a story of genesis. It is simple to argue that, today, American airpower is a decisive factor on the modern world battlefield. Air supremacy demonstrated against Iraq in the 1991 Gulf War bolsters the case. During World War II, this would have been a much more difficult, even impossible, argument to make. It was during that war, under the leadership of Gen Henry H. "Hap" Arnold, that the Army Air Forces (AAF) earned the recognition and respect of the entire world. In retrospect, this was largely due to American industrial strength. Mass production of weapons to meet the needs of the armed forces reached a fevered pitch during World War II. Forever after, this symbiotic relationship has existed in reality, although not officially in the lexicon until 1960, as the "military-industrial complex."

But the state of today's Air Force cannot be attributed to General Arnold or any one individual. It is possible, however, to trace the origins of American air supremacy directly to Arnold's understanding of airpower and the intuitive powers of

1

Theodore von Kármán, a transplanted Hungarian aeronautical scientist, who drafted a plan making that vision a reality. This is the story of how these men, both assisted by the experience of lengthy, diversified professional careers, came together and created that blueprint, *Toward New Horizons*, and finalized it on 15 December 1945.

Henry Harley "Hap" Arnold

Henry H. Arnold, a man of vision and determination, was there almost from the beginning. Born 25 June 1886, he learned to fly in 1911 and, with Lt Thomas D. Milling, started the Army's first flying school that same year. By accident, Arnold ended up in Washington, D.C. during the First World War where he was influential in building a war economy for airplane production in 1917. Although generally accepted as "too little, too late," these efforts provided Arnold invaluable experience utilized with great effect in the Second World War. Between the wars, Arnold was involved with a variety of traditionally "unmilitary" uses for the Army's airplanes—forest fire watching, "New Deal" reform support, US mail delivery, and air shows. He was keenly aware of the links between politics and public opinion to the survival of the Army's air forces. At the same time, Arnold found himself in the middle of radical changes in aviation technology. He led 10 Martin B-10 bombers from Washington, D.C., to Fairbanks, Alaska, demonstrating the capability of the Army's new all-metal monoplane. He handled publicity well and frequently used it to the advantage of the Army Air Forces.[1]

Although a dynamic public personality, his military methods have often been called into question. He was never a very good student (see appendix A for his West Point record), although his military performance record at the military academy would have been considered excellent until his senior, or first class, year. During his active duty career, he seemed, at times, harsh and abrupt. He sometimes made hasty decisions but was capable of rescinding those which, in different light, appeared flawed. His loyalty was called into question by his superiors. Nevertheless, as World War II approached, circumstances delivered Gen Hap Arnold command of the Army Air Corps.

Nathan F. Twining, who worked on Arnold's staff from 1940 to 1942, and became the first Air Force officer to hold the chairmanship of the Joint Chiefs of Staff said, "There was some lost motion in those early days, but Arnold straightened that out before the war was over."[2] He did this, in large degree, by strength of his own will and certainty in his decisions. His father's influence, summarized on a photo he scribed for his son Harley in 1903, was ever apparent. "Fully comprehend what is required of you," it read, "and act with promptness and fidelity." Others, such as the Wright Brothers, reinforced in Arnold that "the 'will to do' in many cases may make the impossible, possible."[3] Laurence S. Kuter, a member of Arnold's trusted advisory council, once wrote that it was very unwise to utter the words, "It can't be done," around the general. Those were fighting words.[4]

Many descriptive adjectives have been used by contemporaries, superiors, and subordinates in describing Arnold: go'er, do'er, strong and courageous, tough and rough, turbo-supercharged, a steam engine, and leading at a very fast pace.[5] Gen Emmett "Rosie" O'Donnell, USAF, Retired, one of Arnold's advisory council, recalled that, "when confronted by a problem, he solved the problem and didn't try to look for some ideal way to do it. He hit it head on. He was a great red-tape cutter."[6] He had a classic type-A personality. Two additional traits: impatience and remarkable vision toward the future, are most important in understanding Gen Hap Arnold as an airpower pacesetter.

"I have been impatient all my life," the general wrote in 1942, "and will probably be impatient to get the caisson rolling faster when I go through the gates of Arlington but that's my make-up, and that's that."[7] He was unable to tolerate delay and was restless. He was unable to sit in one place for very long, unless in a high-level meeting, and was always in the middle of one project or another.[8] He rejected opposition and was intolerant. His disdain for "can't do" attitudes was well known.[9] He was, above other definitions, restively eager for things to happen. Arnold wanted any task to have happened yesterday; no fiddling around, particularly during war. His driving personality, mixed with the pressures of high command during World War II, contributed stresses which probably exacerbated the heart condition that ended his life in January 1950. Occasionally, his enthusiasm to accomplish tasks resulted in duplication of effort by staff officers who had been "tagged" or "Hey, you'd" in the hall by Arnold.[10] Occasionally, when dissatisfied or just to make a point, Arnold resorted to a verbal eruption that was not soon forgotten by the recipient.[11]

To admit that Arnold was impatient is one thing, to suggest that his impatience was deleterious would certainly be incorrect. The United States military, facing a war on two fronts separated by six thousand miles, could not have been in a more precarious position. Airplanes, pilots, and mechanics could not have appeared fast enough to diminish the immediate threat of catastrophe. Gen Hap Arnold's "impatience" was exactly what the Army Air Corps needed during the early years of American involvement, both before and during World War II.[12] In 1944 Arnold also demonstrated that his vision for the future was as important to the Army Air Forces as his impatience had been before the war began. His flying experience as well as his familiarity with the Washington bureaucratic system in two world wars was nothing less than a miraculous combination at exactly the right time.

Theodore von Kármán

Theodore von Kármán, Hungarian, Jewish, and one of Europe's finest scientific minds, came to America to escape the radically changing social and political climate in Germany where he had been teaching during the 1920s. Enticed by the deep pocket of the Guggenheim Fund, Kármán was convinced that his work could be best accomplished in the pleasant surroundings of Pasadena, California, at the California Institute of Technology (Caltech). After severing his official ties with Germany, Kármán became a vital scientific voice during the expansion of American airpower.

He, too, had been molded at an early age by his father's influence. Although Kármán had demonstrated remarkable mathematical aptitude in his youth, his father insisted upon his study of humanities and the arts. Kármán was formally educated in strict German style, and in his young adulthood he enjoyed the festive atmosphere of Hungarian and Parisian cafés. Kármán applied his aeronautical knowledge in untraditional ways, attacking real world situations like soil erosion and construction-related stress problems by using fluid flow dynamics equations. His theoretical brilliance, tempered with intuitive practicality, which he credited to his father's pedagogical advice, was harnessed in America through a remarkable circle of acquaintances and a unique convergence of circumstances. This was true despite the tendency of American scientists to ignore theoretical science resulting in pragmatic and empirical solutions to engineering problems.[13]

But Kármán was not the only European scientist who emigrated to the United States. Albert Einstein, Enrico Fermi, Eugene Wigner, Leo Szilard, James Franck, and Edward Teller, for example, had also decided that the US offered a safer, more open climate for their scientific work.[14] But Kármán brought with him an international reputation as the finest aeronautical mind of his generation. He also brought the unique ability to see through the complexities of a problem, envision a simplified solution, communicate the solution to his younger associates, and then, knowing the situation would be resolved, move on to the next pressing problem. The seeds of his wisdom, having been planted in the minds of his colleagues and students, were then free to grow and bear fruit. His expertise in aeronautics and his success in problem solving became well known to Army Air Forces leadership, not only by direct contact, but through the advice and recommendation of influential Kármán associates. His enthusiasm and scientific intuition was accessible just when Gen Hap Arnold and his air forces needed that wisdom most.

The Evolution of Airpower

This is the story of the evolution of a technology, more correctly, a technological system: airpower. It is this process that is examined here. Used throughout the work is the single word *airpower* as it has become conventional to do within Air

5

Force circles. *Airpower*, the word, represents a unification of instrument and function and summarily implies much more than just "airplane" coupled with "power" as it did at the beginning of World War II. By 1944, Arnold was using the two-word term *air power* in describing the totality of his air forces, which included much more than just combat airplanes used in war.[15]

In the early days, airplanes were a curiosity. By the end of the Second World War, the airplane, in all its different forms, was only a small part of an intricate system. Since the creation of the Menlo Park invention factory by Thomas A. Edison, technological systems have been a reality. Initially, early systems included only physical components—pieces of the machine itself. From 1876 through 1925, systems developed into more than just machines but also included organizations, people, and other nonphysical attributes. "Large systems," according to Thomas P. Hughes, consisted of "energy production, communication, and transportation, which composed the essence of modern technology."[16]

The air forces developed all of these elements and many others specific to accomplishing aerial combat missions during World War II. These included a variety of industrial production efforts, massive chains of military logistics support, overseas and continental air bases, munitions production of all kinds, radar detection webs, technical training schools, steel mills, research and development facilities (civilian and military), as well as cooperative efforts between Allies.

In fact, the Army Air Forces were participants in what Hughes has called, "the twentieth century's most characteristic activity—technological system building."[17] The development of this complex military airpower system, in America at least, functioned often as much as a result of personality interactions, perceptions, and trust, as it did due to the available technologies, or "gadgets," themselves. The air war effort, in all its different facets, became so massive that, to many, even General Arnold, it frequently seemed incomprehensible.[18]

Notes

1. The Army Air Forces did not officially come into being until 1941. Before then, from 1920 to 1926, it was the Army Air Service. From 1926–1941, it was the Army Air Corps. On 18 September 1947, the Air Force was officially born. Throughout this study, I will attempt to use the appropriate title for the appropriate time period. Frequently, the term *air forces* refers to the air force in use at that time, regardless of the official name, to minimize confusion.

2. Gen Nathan F. Twining, USAF, Retired, oral history interview (OHI) number 206, 3 November 1967, United States Air Force Academy (USAFA), Special Collections, Colorado Springs, Colo., 40–42.

3. H. H. Arnold, "Sunday with the Wrights," 1925–1926, Library of Congress, box 227; also located in the Murray Green Collection (MGC), USAFA, Special Collections, Colorado Springs, Colo. In the Green notes, he described the photograph in notes taken while at the Arnold Ranch in Sonoma, Calif.

4. Laurence S. Kuter, "The General vs. The Establishment: Gen H. H. Arnold and the Air Staff," *Aerospace Historian*, September 1973, 186. The advisory council was a very interesting organization that Arnold initiated early in his tenure as commander of the Army's air forces. It included several officers who were assigned directly to Arnold and who had no other function but to organize tasks and help out the "thinking process" for the general. Arnold wrote to Carl "Tooey" Spaatz on the occasion of their change of command that it was one of the most valuable tools he ever had. A more detailed study of the advisory council is not offered here but would be a valuable examination for the future.

5. Thomas D. Milling, oral history interview, Columbia University Oral History Review (CUOHR), MGC; Benjamin S. Kelsey, interviewed by Murray Green, 9 June 1971, MGC; Twining; and Thomas M. Coffey, *HAP: The Story of the U.S. Air Force and the Man Who Built It, General Henry H. "Hap" Arnold* (New York: Viking Press, 1982), 202.

6. Gen Emmett "Rosie" O'Donnell, USAF, Retired, oral history interview, 2 December 1967, USAFA/OHI, USAF Historical Research Agency (AFHRA), Maxwell AFB, Ala., K239.0512-1476.

7. Henry H. Arnold to Carl A. Spaatz, letter, 19 August 1942, MGC.

8. Laurence S. Kuter, "How Hap Built the AAF," *Air Force Magazine* 56, no. 9 (September 1973): 88–93.

9. "Reminiscences of Friends and Family: Carl A. Spaatz," CUOHR. Here Spaatz explains General Arnold's impatience.

10. Maj Gen Franklin Carroll, interviewed by Murray Green, 1 September 1972, MGC; James H. Doolittle, oral history interview, 22 December 1977, USAFA/OHI, 20–21; Kuter, "The General vs. The Establishment," 189.

11. Edward Bowles to Murray Green, letter, 18 March 1971, MGC.

12. Murray Green and many other of Arnold's associates have suggested that Arnold's impatience was the key to his personality. This is certainly

true. What is more important is that he apparently had the right personality for the situation.

13. Hugh L. Dryden, oral history interview, CUOHR, AFHRA, 38. Dryden said that the difference between American scientists and German scientists was, "If the calculations didn't make practical sense, then the Americans didn't build it. However, if that is what the formulas said, then the Germans decided to build it that way." The definitions of technology, applied science, pure science, basic (fundamental) research, and applied technology are elusive, but 50 years ago they were not only different than they are now, they often had less delineation than does today's lexicon. Arnold and Ira C. Eaker wrote in their book *Winged Warfare* (New York: Harper and Brothers Pub., 1941), 215, "Research has been defined as a systematic investigation of some phenomena . . . by the experimental method, to discover facts or coordinate them as laws. This is a dry definition which fulfills the requirement of the scientist." It appeared that Arnold understood American science perfectly.

14. Thomas P. Hughes, *American Genesis: A Century of Invention and Technological Enthusiasm* (New York: Penguin Books, 1989), 389.

15. Arnold, speech before the National Advisory Committee for Aeronautics (NACA) employees in Cleveland, Ohio, 9 November 1944, film, in the possession of Mr. Robert Arnold, Sonoma, Calif.

16. Hughes, 24–35, 184–85. For further study of the evolution of technological systems in America, see Hughes's notes 1–4, 487–88. I have adopted his simple definition of "technological systems" for this study; additionally, Martin van Creveld's, *Technology and War: From 2000 B.C. to the Present* (New York: Free Press, 1989), 153–234, pt. III, "The Age of Systems," offers a broad examination of the growth of military systems of all kinds from 1830 to 1945.

17. Hughes, 184–87, 381–98. Quote on 383. Hughes offers an excellent study of the evolution of a variety of systems in America and considers many of the driving influences behind them.

18. Henry H. Arnold to Frank M. Andrews, letter, 29 March 1943, found in Frank M. Andrews Papers, box 1, correspondence "A," Library of Congress, Washington, D.C. See chapter two for the discussion.

Chapter 2

Educating an Airpower Architect

Henry Harley "Hap" Arnold was not supposed to enter the Army.[1] His older brother, Thomas, was to attend West Point and continue the Arnolds' family tradition of American military service that began during the War for Independence. Henry Harley, Hap's namesake and great-great-grandfather, had been a private in the Pennsylvania militia. Another relative, Peter Arnold, fought with Gen George Washington's army. Thomas G. Arnold, his grandfather, had been a nail maker and fought at the Battle of Gettysburg during the Civil War. Herbert, Henry's father, had been a physician during the Spanish-American War and served in Puerto Rico in 1898. Despite the military legacy, and after attending Penn State during the year prior to the West Point admission tests, Thomas rejected his parents' persistent urging to attend West Point. So Henry Arnold, then called Harley, inherited the opportunity to carry on the family's military heritage, which he did with great distinction.[2]

Cadet Arnold entered the military academy the same year the Wright Brothers flew at Kitty Hawk, North Carolina, but horses, not airplanes, were his first love. He, along with many West Pointers in the class of 1907, yearned for a cavalry assignment. The dashing uniforms, the thunder of the charge, and the perceived class distinction between cavalry and every other branch of the Army, except the Engineering Corps, did not escape observation by members of the Corps of Cadets.[3] One of the youngest cadets ever admitted to West Point at 17 years and one month, Arnold found a niche at the tradition-laden institution. He became a founding member and, eventually, the leader of the "Black Hand." This covert spirit squad was responsible for many of the most spectacular student pranks ever accomplished in West Point's history. Harley, called "Pewt" and "Benny" by his friends, had a fiery tongue and was frequently late for class. He earned far fewer demerits, however, than most classmates during his first three years at "The Point" (see appendix A). While leading the

West Point Archives

Class of 1907

Courtesy Robert Arnold

**"Pewt" Arnold, West Point
sophomore, 1905**

legendary "Hand" during his first-class year, he amassed over one hundred "ticks," nearly double his single year high, but still less than many of his friends. His future wife, Eleanor "Bee" Pool, recalled that her first visit with Harley at The Point was through the window of his room. He had been confined to quarters for a disciplinary infraction.[4]

Arnold also channeled his spirit into sports. He saw frequent playing time as a second string varsity football running back, put the shot for his class track and field team, and excelled at polo. Academically, Harley had an uncanny memory. He "specked" (memorized) several pages of

10

logarithmic tables, which was impressive but did not raise his final class standing any higher than 66 out of 111. His standing would have been much lower were it not for generally high military discipline marks. Cadet Arnold's last weeks at the military academy were, perhaps, typical for the soon-to-be lieutenant. During cavalry drill (cadets still rode horses regularly in those days), Arnold was awarded demerits for chewing tobacco during formation, an act strictly forbidden. Not only did this infraction keep him from many of the graduation festivities, but some believed that it provided the necessary leverage for the authorities in charge of graduation assignments to issue Arnold a ticket straight into the infantry. The cavalry, Arnold wrote, "was the last romantic thing left on earth."[5] His graduation standing was too low for engineering school, and after a brief but high-powered struggle, arranged by his father and fought by the new lieutenant against his congressman, his senator, and the adjutant general of the Army, he accepted his commission and assignment as an infantryman. In later reflection, his wife, Bee, summarized the situation. "Those with brains got the engineers, but I don't think that Hap was the engineering type at all."[6]

Lieutenant Arnold "volunteered" for an assignment in the Philippine Islands. The secretary of war, the only man in the Army who could change his assignment, was in the islands overseeing the establishment of new Army posts, and Arnold hoped to plead his case personally. He never got that opportunity. For the next two years Arnold worked hand in hand with engineering corpsmen already mapping various islands and never saw the secretary of war.

The Airplane—More Than a Curiosity

In 1909, his unit was transferred to Fort Jay on Governors Island, New York. There Arnold became aware of the airplane as more than just a curiosity. Although he had seen the Bleriot airplane briefly while in France on his roundabout return from the Philippines, both the Wright Flyer, purchased in 1908 by the Army, and a Glenn Curtiss machine landed at Governors Island during his tour. Still trying to escape the infantry, Lieutenant Arnold took the entrance tests for the

11

Arnold's pilot training class, Dayton, Ohio, May 1911. John Rogers, USN, (above center) was the first naval officer to fly a Wright machine. Tommy Milling (above right and below) was Arnold's best man when he married Eleanor "Bee" Pool, 10 September 1913.

Ordnance Department, which held the most promise for early promotion (the lowest rank allowed in this division was first lieutenant). While waiting for the results of the exams, Arnold received a letter from the War Department which offered him the opportunity of a lifetime; the chance to learn how to fly.[7]

Against the advice of his commander, but recognizing an opportunity to free himself from infantry ties, he accepted orders for flight instruction. Arnold recalled his commanding officer's warning, "Young man, I know of no better way for a person to commit suicide!"[8] The young second lieutenant considered those words a challenge. By April 1911, Arnold was in Dayton, Ohio, to begin flying lessons at Simms Station, the home of the Wright Brothers' flying school. Arnold joined Lt Thomas DeWitt "Tommy" Milling for an introduction to the flying machine given by the Wrights at their factory. Together, Arnold and Milling spent hours learning how the delicate machine was assembled, disassembled, greased, tightened, and repaired. Sharing the experience of becoming new aviators, the two young lieutenants developed a fast friendship. Arnold was grateful for the time spent in the factory because, although the Army had decided to train pilots, it had not begun training mechanics or crew chiefs. In 1911, every pilot was also a mechanic of sorts.

Orville and Wilbur Wright normally taught these ground lessons personally, but Arnold's flight instructor was a Wright employee named Al Welsh. In fact, it does not appear that Arnold ever took a flying lesson with Orville or Wilbur Wright. Between 3 May and 13 May, Arnold flew every one of his first 28 lessons with Welsh. An average flight lasted eight minutes. In practical terms, Arnold became a "pilot" on the day of his first solo, May 13, a Saturday. Technically, his civilian airplane pilot certificate (*Fédération Aeronautique Internationale* [FAI]) was awarded on 6 July 1911. He did not receive his "official" military aviator rating until 22 July 1912, as reflected in War Department General Order No. 40.[9]

Following initial flight qualification, Arnold and Milling crated up the Army's two newest Wright Flyers and followed them by train to College Park, Maryland, the home of the first Signal Corps flight school. The hours spent on the Wright factory floor began to pay off. Arnold and Milling assembled

Library of Congress

Al Welsh (left), a Wright Brothers employee, flew Arnold's first 28 instructional flights. Welsh died in a flying accident in 1913.

Air Force Historical Research Agency

The Wrights instilled Arnold's "will to do" when it came to airpower. This early "bulb" exposure was taken of Orville (left) and Lieutenant Arnold after an early evening flight at College Park, Maryland, July 1912.

the craft themselves in preparation for the opening of the flight school. The only two Army pilots were now its only flight instructors as well. Not only did they become skilled pilots but they became skilled airplane mechanics and dedicated crew chiefs as well. They even created the first "dash-1," the airplane technical manual, which included a picture of the craft with each of the parts meticulously labeled by hand.

Flight then was still a fair weather game. As winter approached the Washington area, the aviators boxed up their planes and moved to

The first airborne radio took as much room as the pilot (1912).

Arnold and Milling standardized the nomenclature for parts of the airplane. It was the first military aviator's technical manual—today's "Dash-1."

Barnes Farm, near Augusta, Georgia, hoping for more temperate weather. Although the flyers endured the only blizzard to hit Augusta in 15 years, much flying and training, including wireless radio work, photography, and even bomb dropping was accomplished before returning to College Park in May 1912.[10]

For the rest of that year, tragedy seemed to stalk the flying community. Wilbur Wright died of typhoid fever on 30 May. Al Welsh died in a plane crash in June. In July, Arnold crashed off the coast of Massachusetts in a new Burgess/Wright "tractor" airplane. It was in that crash that Arnold received the scar on his chin that showed distinctively for the rest of his life. Two more Army aviators, Lewis C. Rockwell and Corp Frank Scott, were killed in September (Scott was the first enlisted man to perish in an aircraft accident). In November, it was Arnold who would once again face the hazards of early flight.[11]

The month of October was one of achievement rather than disaster. Arnold was awarded the first Mackay Trophy for the most outstanding military flight of the year. Arnold and Milling had been challenged to fly a triangular route between Fort Meyer, College Park, and Washington, D.C., and pinpoint a "troop concentration." In winning the award, Arnold had completed the reconnaissance course and reported the strength and location of the simulated enemy troop concentrations to the event judges. In one respect the "contest" was really not a contest at all. Milling, the only other participant, had become ill immediately after takeoff and was forced to withdraw. The flight did, however, demonstrate an actual

The first Mackay Trophy, awarded to "Lieutenant Henry H. Arnold, 29th U.S. Infantry, 9 October 1912." The three-foot-tall trophy resides in the National Air and Space Museum, Washington, D.C.

16

mission for Army aviation, something the Army air arm was still struggling to define (as demonstrated by the variety of missions practiced while bivouacked in Georgia). Perhaps because of these circumstances, Arnold did not take himself or his accomplishment too seriously. The young lieutenant wrote Bee that "It [the trophy] certainly is handsome. I figure that it will hold about four gallons so I cannot see how you can fill it with anything but beer."[12]

At the end of the month, Arnold, Milling, and the rest of the College Park airmen traveled to Fort Riley, Kansas, to participate in Army ground force exercises. Arnold's enthusiasm for flying was temporarily doused by a nearly fatal airplane flight on 5 November 1912. Lieutenant Arnold and an observer, Lt A. L. P. Sands, were inexplicably thrown into a spin toward the ground. Arnold righted the craft and missed a violent crash by only a few seconds and tens of feet. The

On 5 November 1912 at Fort Riley, Kansas, a photographer happened to be present to document aerial maneuvers scheduled for that day.

A.L.P. Sands (left) and Arnold (right) were scheduled for an observation flight. Takeoff and the majority of the flight were normal.

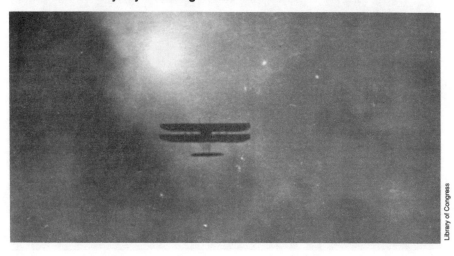

Just after this high-altitude photo was taken, Arnold's plane entered a spin as he began his landing pattern.

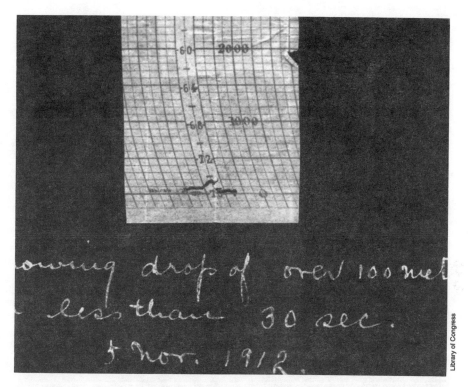

A crude recording device, a barograph, captured the 100-meter altitude loss in less than 30 seconds, which shattered Arnold's confidence in airplanes at the time.

onboard altitude-measuring device, a barograph, clearly recorded a drop of 300 feet in 10 seconds, ending up just above the ground zero line. It was too close a call for Arnold. He was so rattled that he immediately requested three weeks leave and temporarily removed himself from flying status. "From the way I feel now," he explained, "I do not see how I can get in a machine with safety for the next month or two." By then, Arnold had earned several aviation firsts: winning the first Mackay Trophy, setting several altitude records, and, somewhat more dubiously, accomplishing the first successful spin recovery in an airplane.[13]

Those few weeks of "grounding" grew into a few months, and then a year as deskbound Arnold served as the assistant to the officer in charge of aviation in the Office of the Chief

Signal Officer, Brig Gen George P. Scriven. When the young
lieutenant married Eleanor Pool in September 1913, he was
effectively removed from the active flying roster. At that time,
Army flyers were not permitted to marry and remain on flying
status. Although this requirement softened by World War I,
Arnold was relegated to ground duties until November 1916.[14]

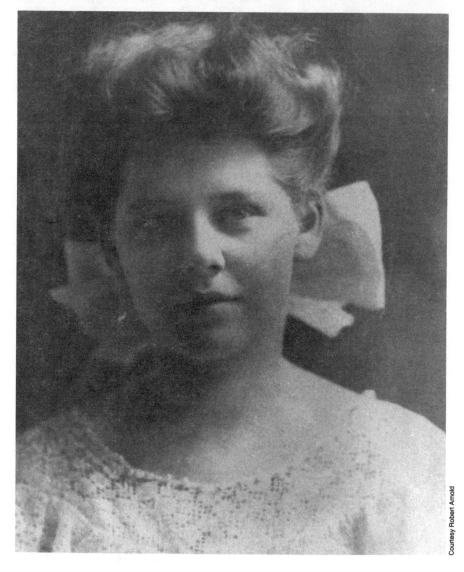

The young socialite, Eleanor "Bee" Pool.

Although back in the infantry, Arnold never wavered in his belief in the importance of airpower. He recalled that in 1913, flyers fought a constant uphill battle for acceptance as well as for modern equipment. "At that time," Arnold said, "we in the Air Service looked to foreign countries for engines that might give us better performance."[15] Even as a lieutenant, Arnold looked for the best technology available, regardless of its origin.

Not only did the lieutenant look for the best new technology, he constantly sought improvements for the machines the Army already had. As early as 6 November 1911, Arnold had written Orville Wright about his concerns that aircraft did not carry enough weight or climb fast enough for military use. Arnold suggested increasing engine power and propeller revolutions to maximize performance. Brother Wilbur responded with a detailed explanation of how to fine-tune the engines, both new and old, and explained that the propellers and chains "have a large factor of safety and if sudden jerks are avoided, will easily carry 25% more power than our present motors give."[16] But Arnold was not satisfied with the response. On 18 November, he again wrote the Wrights. "Could we put a 60 or 70 H.P. [horsepower] engine in the standard machine and put 2 or 3 more teeth in the engine sprocket? This would give us much more power when it was needed but for ordinary flying we could fly on less than the maximum power of the motor."[17] Arnold was always pushing for improved equipment and maximum aircraft capability, whether it was available or not.

After his nearly fatal spin, Arnold continued his inquiries, initially with a different emphasis. "If machines are inverted and given the sand test, what factor of safety should be required? . . . What other tests could be given for determining the factor of safeties [sic] of any important parts?"[18] His concern with aircraft safety began after his spin and never wavered during his career.

Before long, Arnold was back to inquiries about performance and design directed at the Wrights. "As it is desired by this office to incorporate a stress test of some kind in our specifications for machines," he wrote, "we would greatly appreciate it if you would send to us . . . the chart showing the travel of the center of pressure for various speeds and weights." Or, "Will you kindly tell me what, if any, are the objections to having the propellers turn in the opposite direction to what they turn now in your machines." And, "The light scout machines have caused more or less controversy, but I think the Signal Corps is at last persuaded as to the necessity of having them even though there is no one capable of flying them but Milling."[19] The Wrights always answered his letters in detail, but it seemed each response generated two more questions.

Arnold's constant inquisitive attitude about aircraft was a result of his pilot training and mechanical skills. He was not an aeronautical expert, however, and did not always understand the science behind or the engineering problems associated with his queries. Changing prop direction, for example, would have required the Wrights to reverse nearly everything internal to the machine. Yet he was never fully satisfied with a machine as it stood. As a pilot he wanted safer aircraft capable of higher altitude, better load capability, greater range, and faster speed. As a mechanic he wanted interchangeable parts, peak engine performance, and substantial margins of safety in construction. Lieutenant Arnold wanted the best available equipment for the Air Service, and he did what he could to get it.

Just as important as his understanding of up-to-date aircraft technology were his experiences while serving in the bureaucracy of Washington. During this period he was involved in quelling unrest among aviators who were forced to fly substandard planes along the Mexican border even as ripples of revolution swept through that country in 1913. Arnold's impossible job was to remedy their complaints. Most of these concerned the safety of the air machines, and compromises were made by both the staff and the aviators before a final resolution was reached. Arnold testified before Congress—a rare occurrence for a lieutenant—during early debates over an independent Air Force and tried to explain the high casualty rates being suffered due to outdated and poorly maintained equipment. He also instructed the Signal Corps staff about the possibilities for airplanes in combat.[20] Soon Arnold found himself back in the infantry and stationed in Manila. But this introductory experience in Washington was not wasted over his lengthy career.

From December 1913 through 1915, Lieutenant Arnold participated in practice ground attacks on different Philippine Islands. During one of these exercises, Arnold watched a young lieutenant plan and execute a flawless attack at Bataan. Arnold was so impressed that he told Bee upon his return that he had met a future Army chief of staff. This young man would become Arnold's friend, commander, and staunch supporter nearly a quarter century later: his name was George Catlett Marshall. Lieutenant Arnold was gaining experience and contacts that no other Army officer could match over a 50-year career. His experiences outside of the flying world became as valuable to future air forces as his personal aviation experiences. Then, as unexpected as his orders to join the Wrights in Dayton had been, he received orders to requalify into the Aviation Section of the Signal Corps.

Although George Marshall had once impressed Arnold with his tactical skill on maneuvers in the Philippines, Arnold impressed Marshall by utilizing American scientists to improve the Air Corps. Here they visit Randolph Field during the war.

USAF Museum

23

Return to D.C.

Nineteen fifteen was a watershed year for science, technology, and engineering. Albert Einstein offered the "theory of relativity" publicly, Alexander Graham Bell made the first transcontinental phone call (New York to San Francisco), and the Panama Canal was completing its first full year in operation. The establishment of the National Advisory Committee for Aeronautics (NACA) in 1915, marked the beginning of the second major phase of American aeronautical development: turning infant theory and experimentation into a tangible program of inquiry.[21]

Although joint Army-Navy aeronautical committees had existed before the NACA, they had no official status and even less authority over the progress of aeronautical science. The need for a committee with legitimate power to direct research and offer advice became apparent the following year while the Army was providing air support for Brig Gen John J. Pershing's punitive expedition into Mexico. One plane was lost before the operation even began, while another crashed a few days later leaving only six of the original eight for operations. The craft in use, the Curtiss JN-3, had insufficient power to climb over the mountains and insufficient strength to withstand unpredictable winds and storms. Replacements were not immediately available.[22]

Even as the punitive Mexican expedition was under way, and having quelled the airmen's dissent, Arnold was adjusting to his new assignment. As the supply officer at the newly established Aviation School at Rockwell Field near San Diego he held the new "junior military aviator" rating and wore a fresh set of captain's bars. Arnold arrived in May, but his requalification training did not begin until 18 November 1916. He completed training in six days when he soloed again for the first time in over four years.[23] Soon he was off to Panama as commander of a squadron there. In Panama he was supposed to find an acceptable location for an air base before bringing his squadron to assist in the defense of the Canal Zone. No consensus could be reached on a location between the Americans—both Army and Navy—and the Panamanians, and he was sent back to Washington to take up the matter

In 1916, after regulations prohibiting married officers from flying were relaxed, Arnold was sent to North Island, California, to regain his flying qualifications. Captain Arnold served as supply officer until November when he began flying again after nearly four years on the ground.

National Archives

USAF Museum

His checkout took all of a week.

directly with Gen Leonard Wood, commanding general of the Atlantic Department. Arnold heard the news of America's entry into the Great War on the ship to Washington on 6 April 1917. He knew he would not be back to Panama any time soon.[24]

By August, Col Henry Arnold (temporary) was permanently assigned to his wartime post in Washington, D.C., as executive officer of the Air Division (the furthest up the chain of his "dozen-jobs-in-one"). He had pressed for an assignment to Europe but was denied a transfer to the combat zone. Again, his assignment offered experience in the administration and, more importantly, the buildup of American air forces, which would pay off two decades later. Arnold rapidly became an indispensable aid to his superiors, who had little knowledge of air matters. While stuck in Washington, Arnold saw firsthand the immense problems facing the Air Division: lack of trained mechanics, lack of pilots, lack of funding, and lack of an aircraft production system, which Arnold considered the biggest headache of the war. Arnold spent most of his time traveling around the United States checking on aircraft production and development and keeping his superiors informed of the slow progress being made in these areas.[25]

All of these problems resulted from America's policy of neutrality which, until February 1917, was publicly supported by President Woodrow Wilson. To build the American military, in any form, was to abandon neutrality as a policy. Not until German unrestricted U-boat warfare threatened American overseas trade with continental Europe did public opinion shift dramatically to one of active intervention. The interception of the Zimmermann telegram, a memo from Berlin to Mexico City seeking a military alliance against the United States, added insult to injury, but interventionist politics already ensured funding for the military. Still, this funding came too late to build a fully functional Air Service.[26]

Arnold continued searching for improvements in planes and weapons. He teamed up with a task force of civilian scientists and produced the first "guided missile," dubbed the "Flying Bug," which was a beautiful, woodcrafted minibiplane. Early versions were simply made of paper maché. It housed a two-stroke Ford engine and carried a "warhead" of 200–300 pounds of explosives. The Bug had no wheels and was launched from a wagon-like contraption that ran on a long section of portable track. The "missile" engine was started at one side of the track. When the engine was fully revved, the mechanical counter was engaged and the Bug was released. When it reached flying speed, it lifted off and flew straight

Arnold at his War Department desk during WWI, the youngest colonel in the Army.

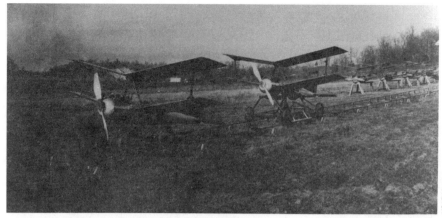

The "Flying Bug" was America's first guided missile. During the development of the weapon, Arnold met such notables as "Boss" Kettering, the "Bug's" inventor, Elmer Sperry, Henry Ford, and Dr. Robert Millikan. The "Bug" was launched from a wagon-like carrier and was to fly directly ahead toward the enemy. After a predetermined number of engine revolutions had occurred, a cam fell into place that allowed the wings of the small biplane to fold up. The "Bug" would fall from the sky, and its 250-pound payload would explode.

The team was composed of civilians and members of the other services as well. Arnold is at the far left.

ahead, climbing to a preset altitude controlled by a supersensitive aneroid barometer. When the Bug reached its altitude, the barometer sent signals to small flight controls that were moved by a system of cranks and a bellows (from a player piano) for altitude control. A gyro helped maintain the stability of the craft, the barometer helped maintain altitude, but only the design of the wings assured directional stability. The Bug flew straight ahead until the mechanical counter had sensed the calculated number of engine rotations required to carry the weapon the intended target distance. A cam fell into place and the wings folded, looking much like a diving falcon swooping down on its prey. The Bug was rarely as deadly, and certainly not as fast, as a falcon.[27]

On the Bug team were Lawrence and Elmer Sperry, who had spearheaded the Navy's "aerial torpedo" project a few months earlier, Orville Wright, Robert Millikan, and, the primary

Not all tests were successful.

"The Bug."

"The Bug."

engineer, Charles Kettering. Most test flights were accomplished at McCook Field, near Dayton, Ohio. An early test nearly ended in disaster as the errant missile flying wildly out of control narrowly missed crashing into the reviewing stands. After witnessing the initial test of the Bug, Arnold recalled that the gadget flew "like a thing possessed of the devil."[28] Lateral controls added shortly after these tests rectified the control problem, which was the result of overdependence upon the dihedral of the wings for lateral stability. More important than the gadget itself were the members of the team, particularly Millikan, who would play a vital scientific consultant role in the 1930s and during the Second World War. Arnold never forgot his experiences in production, administration, scientific experimentation, or testing. Nor did he forget the men who had helped create the fledgling force from an unfertilized embryo.

Arnold did, finally, make it over to Europe. He was certain that General Pershing would want to bring the Bug into

USAF Photo

Generals Pershing and Arnold in San Diego after the Great War.

Arnold inspects the first "Liberty" engine produced for combat use.

The DH-4 was used well after the First World War. Arnold never forgot the lesson of obsolete surplus after the war. Shown here is Mason Patrick's personal DH-4B.

combat as soon as possible and went to convince him. Officially his orders were to sail by mid-October and become familiar with training organization methods in France and combat operations at the front.[29] His trip was not a success. He immediately fell victim to Spanish flu, which was rampant on the East Coast. After recovery, he made it to the Western Front during November but only shortly before the armistice went into effect. Because the weather was so terrible, however, he flew no combat missions. The Bug project died shortly thereafter.[30]

Arnold later recalled the importance of many advances that occurred in aviation during the war years. Some of the most significant were oxygen masks with communications devices all in one, air-to-ground radio communication sets, automatic cameras, armored pilot seats, increased firepower for strafing, the Bug, and improved aeronautical medical research equipment. Additionally, the establishment of the NACA held promise for the future of airplane research and development. Aircraft production, however, never reached acceptable levels. For example, even though Liberty engines were produced in great quantity, the United States never figured out how to build enough aircraft for the engines. By the end of the war, 1,213 American built DH-4 aircraft had made it overseas, but only about 600 had been sent to the front.[31] Arnold had witnessed the production bottlenecks firsthand and would remember the consequences of a failed production arrangement when he was in a position to do something about it.

Publicity and Planning

After returning from Europe and no longer being needed in D.C., Arnold received orders back to Rockwell Field. There he assumed the post of district supervisor, Western District of the Air Service. From January to June 1919, Arnold supervised the postwar demobilization of the Western Division. Even while dealing with massive reductions in the size of the Army, Arnold promoted aviation as best he could. He held air shows and ordered his "low flying team" to perform for California crowds. At one of these events, Arnold "decorated" movie star Mary Pickford with a banner making her an "Honorary Ace." The positive publicity generated by

District Supervisor, Western District of the Air Service, Rockwell Field, 1919.

Library of Congress

events such as these was desperately needed in the immediate postwar years.[32]

Arnold was well aware that public opinion was a powerful tool in maintaining support for the Air Service. When Rockwell Field closed temporarily, Arnold was transferred to San Francisco as air liaison officer for the Ninth Corps Area. A witness to the rapid drawdown, Arnold was determined to do what he could to bolster support for airpower. On his own initiative, Arnold established "fire patrols" over the western region that not only saved thousands of acres of timber, but millions of dollars as well. His activities caught the public's attention. A peacetime use for military airplanes kept the shrinking service in the air, at

Library of Congress

The Rockwell Field Low Flying Team included a young Lt James H. Doolittle (second from right).

Library of Congress

They frequently performed for stars like Mary Pickford, "Honorary Ace" of the day.

Their formations thrilled the California crowds.

least for a while.[33] "Arnold the politician" was developing during these early days in San Francisco.

During the years 1919 to 1924 Arnold's working relationship with other Army officers began taking shape. William "Billy" Mitchell's zealous approach to creating an independent Air Force taught Arnold how not to tackle a political hot potato. Arnold recalled that Mitchell had warned him away from outspoken methods Mitchell had been using. Mitchell realized that he was financially able to survive expulsion from the Army, but most of his followers did not come from wealthy backgrounds. Carl "Tooey" Spaatz and Ira C. Eaker served under Arnold during his next tour, again at Rockwell Field. These men became Arnold's right- and left-hand men over the next two decades. Eaker coauthored three books with Arnold, and Spaatz succeeded Arnold's command and become the first chief of staff of the independent Air Force in 1947. The amazing "Jimmy" Doolittle

USAF Museum

Brig Gen William "Billy" Mitchell stands under the Barling Bomber with the development team. Mitchell was instrumental in getting Arnold back into the flying game in 1916.

Library of Congress

Arnold and Spaatz in November 1919. Arnold often reminded Spaatz, who changed the spelling of his name 10 years after this photo was taken, of the importance of civilian scientists to the Air Forces.

Arnold and Ira C. Eaker at Los Angeles in 1932. Together these two were an unbeatable public relations team.

Library of Congress

caught Arnold's attention after pulling off a dangerous flying stunt for a gathered crowd of onlookers. Arnold grounded the young second lieutenant for one month but later called on him to command the famous raid on Tokyo.[34]

While Arnold successfully pressed for publicity out west, Billy Mitchell held most of the headlines everywhere else. On 21 and 22 July 1921, Mitchell's bombers sank the German battleship *Ostfriesland*, considered unsinkable by most naval officers. The wild publicity that followed marked the event as the Air Service's first major victory over the Navy in terms of service roles and missions. The seeds of strategic bombing had been sown.

Another one of Mitchell's ideas was the "Barling" bomber, a six-engine behemoth capable of carrying a 10,000 pound payload. Although it seemed logical to build this monster in support of a "strategic" bombing mission, its performance was so poor that it could not fly over the mountains between Dayton and Washington while fully fueled. The Appalachians exceeded its service ceiling.

But the Barling was not a total loss. Valuable wind tunnel data, parts design, and other aeronautical engineering problems were addressed and solved during the Barling's development. In that way, the Barling influenced the design of the B-17 and B-29, which were the American backbone of true

The Barling Bomber in flight. This six-engine behemoth did not even have enough power to fly over the Appalachian Mountains.

strategic bombing in World War II. Although Arnold found the Barling operationally worthless, he realized that sometimes "the full-scale article must be built to get the pattern for the future."[35]

In the fall of 1924, Arnold was recalled to Washington by Gen Mason Patrick, then chief of the Air Service. Patrick, a classmate of "Blackjack Pershing," had been so impressed with Arnold's California performance that he had added a commendation to Arnold's military record (201 file). Before joining Patrick's staff, however, Arnold attended the Army Industrial College in Washington. His World War I experience with aircraft production had been less than satisfying, and now Major Arnold knew why. The Army planners were determined to utilize the American auto industry as the primary contractor to manufacture airplanes in time of crisis. Arnold lobbied for a different approach. He argued that the aircraft industry should remain the major contractor while using the auto industry for small parts and other subcontracting jobs. This short "college" assignment was one of the most valuable of his career, one which he said "was to stand me in good stead in later years."[36] Not only did Major Arnold have a plan for future buildups in his mind, but he realized that his civilian industry contacts from earlier tours would be essential if a sizable production scheme had any hope of success. Glenn Curtiss, Elmer Sperry, Donald Douglas, and Larry Bell were only a few of those contacts.

During 1925 and much of 1926, Arnold served as Patrick's chief of information. In this function he was able to keep his eyes and ears open to new developments in foreign and domestic aviation, in both the civil and military arenas. In a failed effort, he attempted to keep Billy Mitchell out of trouble by urging him to temper his language and writings while campaigning for an independent Air Force. Mitchell, causing too much trouble, was "exiled" to Fort Sam Houston in San Antonio, Texas, in February 1925. Mitchell was not gone long. When he returned to face a military court-martial, Arnold was his Washington liaison officer. By Christmas 1926, with Mitchell "martyred," Arnold considered resigning but gained the resolve needed to endure his own punishment.[37] In the turbulence of Billy Mitchell's trial and under the threat of a court-martial of his own (the official charge was violation of the Articles of War and was made by Mason Patrick) for misappropriation of government supplies in an effort to sway legislators in support of Mitchell's viewpoint, Arnold was himself "exiled" to Fort Riley, Kansas, the Army's largest cavalry post.[38]

It was at Fort Riley in 1927 that Arnold made his choice to remain a military officer. Beyond the malice of his superiors, both personally and toward aviation, Arnold believed that he had suffered numerous career setbacks. He had never been assigned to the cavalry, even after repeated requests. He had been denied any opportunity to participate in the American war effort in Europe. He had testified on Mitchell's behalf despite warnings from his superiors that by siding with Mitchell he was jeopardizing his career. Additionally, the national economic picture was very good. The New York Stock Exchange was higher than it had been on the same date for the previous five years. Cotton and coffee hit all-time highs in the market, and General Motors reported record profits during the week of 23–30 July 1927.[39] Additionally, Arnold had reached his 20th year of military service, which entitled him to half-pay and full benefits if he were to retire.

John K. Montgomery, then president of American International Airways (a branch of Pan Am), had offered the major a lucrative position as the first president of Pan Am Airlines.[40] On 24 July, Arnold replied, "As much as I would like to tell you that I will resign and take up work with the company, I hesitate doing it on account of the obligations which I have with my family." Further, Arnold suggested that he might take four months leave to work for Pan Am and then make his final decision.[41] This leave was apparently never taken even though Montgomery had called Jack Jouett, a mutual military friend of Arnold's, now stationed in Washington, to expedite the leave request.[42] Thus, family concerns were foremost on Arnold's mind at the time his final decision was made. Remarkably, Maj Henry Arnold and his family remained in the Army.

Arnold never mentioned his family as a motive in his recollections. "I couldn't very well quit the service under fire," he said.[43] One of Arnold's biographers, Thomas Coffey, suggested that the frustrated major had many things to accomplish in the Air Corps, many ideas to test.[44] At that moment, however, there was no chance that Arnold would ever hold a position that would allow him to "test" anything. He had been banished within the Army. His reputation preceded him when he was sent to the "worst post" in the country as punishment for his clear violation of official regulations. Henry Arnold was lucky he was still an Army aviator at all.

Still, Arnold made the most of his time at Fort Riley. He indoctrinated cavalry officers in the uses of airpower. He wrote children's stories about pilots and flying and named the hero after his middle son, "Bill Bruce." In all, he wrote six "Bill Bruce" books from 1926 to 1928 and earned about two hundred dollars for each one. His unit delivered President Calvin Coolidge's vacation mail for a time. On one occasion he met, flew, and dined with Will Rogers, the famous satirist.[45]

He completed this tour and even attended the Army Staff College despite the protests of the college's commandant,

Arnold (second from left) served under H. Conger Pratt (far right) at Wright Field in 1928 and 1929. Here Orville Wright, "Tooey" Spaatz, and "Benny" Foulois gather for a few moments.

who had served on the court that had tried Billy Mitchell. After his tour at the Army Staff College, Arnold took command of the Fairfield Air Service Depot near Dayton, Ohio, in the fall of 1928. In an expanded role during 1931, Arnold also served as executive officer to the chief of the Materiel Division at Wright Field, Brig Gen H. Conger Pratt. It was while in these assignments that Arnold developed his understanding of and a distaste for the Army research and development (R&D) system.[46] Arnold was sickened by the lack of progress he perceived at Wright Field. New in 1930, for example, the Douglas O-38 two-seat observation biplane was capable of only 130 miles per hour (MPH). "What the hell have we gained in twenty years?" he rhetorically asked his son Hank, "Nothing!"[47] These perceptions were etched deeply into his memory and stayed with him the rest of his career.

The O-38. "What the hell have we gained in twenty years. . . . Nothing!"

Caltech

By November 1931, Arnold assumed command at March Field near Los Angeles, California. Lieutenant Colonel Arnold's World War I associate, Dr. Robert Millikan, 40 miles away in Pasadena, was now Caltech's president. Winner of a Nobel Prize for physics in 1923, he was continuing his cosmic ray research in the face of a challenge to its validity by Karl Compton of Massachusetts Institute of Technology (MIT). Arnold had little understanding of the nature of these experiments, which involved moving a lead sphere to different altitudes and taking electronic measurements. Nonetheless, Millikan had no trouble convincing Arnold to lend him a Curtiss B-2 Condor bomber to complete his charged particle experiments. Arnold had his mechanics build a special "bomb" rack for the sphere, which was affixed to the Condor. These experiments were carried out from Canada to Mexico over a period of months. As part of this project, measurements

43

Dr. Robert A. Millikan. This portrait hangs in the Athenaeum, the faculty club at the California Institute of Technology.

USAF Photo

USAF Museum

Arnold loaned WWI acquaintance R. A. Millikan a Curtiss B-2 "Condor" bomber like this one for use in his continuing cosmic ray experiments while he was commander at March Field, California.

were also taken underground, in mines, and at a variety of elevations on the earth. One time Millikan transported the ball to Lake Arrowhead on top of a high mountain peak. Unfortunately, the ball was so heavy that it broke through the bottom of the rickety boat in which he was transporting the experiment. It sank to the bottom of the lake. Arnold recalled that the first time they met following the unfortunate mishap, he addressed the professor as "Admiral" Millikan.[48]

New Deal reforms, air shows, public relations campaigns, and exercises, as well as support of scientific research, kept Arnold's 1st Wing busy in the early 1930s. Even though the American economy had collapsed, Arnold did not forget the technical development of his airplanes. Military funding continued at forecast levels into 1934 but faded somewhat with the advent of Franklin D. Roosevelt's (FDR) reforms. Air shows at March Field were major public events in southern California as they had been at Rockwell Field a decade before. Movie stars and celebrities of all sorts visited the field on show days. The inevitable result was a page of favorable publicity in several newspapers in southern California the following day. But perhaps Arnold's most impressive accomplishment during this tour of duty was not accomplished at March Field or even with his own airplanes.

Arnold won his second Mackay Trophy as commander of a flight of 10 new B-10 bombers conducting a round-trip flight from Washington, D.C., to Fairbanks, Alaska. The first all-metal, low-wing monoplane, the Martin B-10 bomber, was the most technologically advanced airplane in the US inventory. After a solid month's preparation, Arnold took his planes on the near 18,000-mile round-trip flight with only one major foul-up and no aircraft losses along the way. Planning was meticulous. A poor showing would have been a catastrophic embarrassment, particularly since the Air Corps was still stinging from its lackluster performance while carrying the US mail in the spring of 1934.[49] The success of the mission brought Arnold a well-earned decoration, a trophy, and proof that long-range bombers could threaten once unpenetrable and isolated territorial boundaries, both those of potential enemies and those of the United States.

The B-10 was a major advance in aircraft technology.

Arnold presents Secretary of War Dern with a totem pole from the frontier. Arnold earned his second Mackay Trophy for the mission.

Arnold took 10 of the first all-metal monoplanes from Washington to Alaska and back. The positive publicity helped salve the wounds of delivering the mail but also opened the eyes of America to the long-distance capabilities of airpower.

But Arnold always pushed for improvement. His airplanes made the trip to Fairbanks, but now the route would have to be flown faster or higher. One of his favorite places to search for improvements in aeronautics was Caltech. There "Admiral" Millikan had gone a long way in fulfilling his dreams for American aviation. Caltech had the best wind tunnel facilities in the western United States. It had one of the finest academic faculties. The civil aviation industry was beginning to locate nearby in southern California. Caltech had definitely aroused the interest of the commanding officer at March Field.[50]

By March 1935, Millikan, Brigadier General Arnold, and Professor Theodore von Kármán, director of the Guggenheim Aeronautical Laboratory, California Institute of Technology (GALCIT) wind tunnels had become well acquainted. Kármán recalled that he had first seen Arnold as a major, perhaps on one of Arnold's inspection tours to the Los Angeles area while still assigned to Wright Field. From 27 December 1929, through 4 January 1930, Arnold was in the Los Angeles area on an inspection tour. Again, from 18 February through 7 March 1930, Arnold visited a variety of locations in southern California. After a brief trip to the north, Arnold returned to the Los Angeles area from 24 to 29 March. During these trips there was ample opportunity for Arnold to have visited Caltech and Robert Millikan. Although Kármán did not appear at Caltech until the first week in April 1930, later trips allowed them to meet. "Maj. Arnold," Kármán remembered, "came 'alvays' in the 'vind toonel' and asked me questions."[51] By 1930, Kármán, second in the field of aeronautics only to his former professor Ludwig Prandtl, had come permanently to Caltech from Aachen, Germany, enticed by a Guggenheim Fund stipend. Arnold's association with the Hungarian professor provided him with a lifelong, personal tutor in theoretical aeronautical science and its application to airpower. During the first half of the 1930s, both Arnold and Kármán developed a similar vision for military aviation: the United States needed a cooperative aeronautics establishment which coupled civilian scientific and industrial expertise with the practical needs of the Army Air Corps.[52] To Arnold, this collaboration meant better Air Corps airplanes. To Kármán, it meant great possibilities for Caltech and the west coast aviation industry. A decade later their vision would become a reality.

Notes

1. The origin of the name "Hap" is still a matter of dispute. Arnold's original West Point tag was "Pewt." Arnold's West Point diary, located at the USAF Academy Library, carries that name proudly across the front cover. The *Howitzer*, West Point's yearbook, also noted the nickname "Benny." In his youth, Arnold was called "Harley," his middle name, by family members. One account claimed that his "perpetual smile" while flying as a stunt double on an early motion picture led a Hollywood producer, who probably could not remember his name, to call him "Happy." This was then shortened. Another suggested that Hap, when angry, would involuntarily tighten his lips in an insidious smile. This famous smile deceptively portrayed Arnold as happy when he was, in reality, quite the opposite. Arnold's early letters to Bee were laced with a variety of pet names. For many years the nickname "Sunny" and "Sunny-Jim" were used. For a short time the tag "Billikens" was exchanged. Billikens was a cartoon character from 1910–1911 (resembling today's Grinch) which featured a tuft of hair and an insidious grin which seemed to reflect Henry's hairline and facial expression. It is most likely that "Hap" is short for "Happy," the name that Bee, his wife, used for him in many of their personal letters. The name "Hap" did not catch on in his military/personal correspondence until about 1930. Until then, many classmates still addressed correspondence to "Pewt," his West Point nickname, while to Bee he was most often "Sunny."

2. "Address by Brig Gen H. H. Arnold," Gladwyne, Pa., 30 May 1938, Papers of Ira C. Eaker, Library of Congress, Washington, D.C., box 38, Arnold speeches, 2; Mrs. Barbara Arnold, interviewed by author, 6 April 1995, Washington, D.C. Mrs. Arnold is the daughter of Donald Douglas and widow of the late William Bruce Arnold, General Arnold's son.

3. Maj Gen John W. Huston, USAF, Retired, to author, letter, 22 February 1996. General Huston is currently editing Arnold's wartime diaries and is an authority on General Arnold and his military career.

4. Gen H. H. Arnold, "Reminiscences of Friends and Acquaintances," USAF Academy, Special Collections, Colorado Springs, Colo. (hereafter, Friends of Arnold), Mrs. H. H. Arnold section; see also the *Biographical Register of the Officers and Graduates of the USMA at West Point New York*, supp. vol. 5, 1900–1910; *Official Register of the Officers and Cadets of the USMA*, June 1904; and *Howitzer*, 1907, the student yearbook. All of these are available at the West Point Archives.

5. The Henry H. Arnold Collection, Library of Congress, Washington, D.C., box 262A; West Point, *Howitzer*, 1907. See also Murray Green Collection (MCG), notes from the Columbia University Oral History Review (CUOHR); Henry H. Arnold, *Global Mission* (New York: Harper and Brothers, 1949), 7–8; a generally accurate but hard-to-find book by Flint O. DuPre, *Hap Arnold: Architect of American Air Power* (New York: MacMillan Co., 1972), 1–14, is a shorter version of *Global Mission*; Henry H. Arnold and Ira C. Eaker, *Army Flyer* (New York: Harper and Brothers, 1942), 40–41.

6. *New York Daily Tribune*, 13 June 1907. The article also displayed a marvelous, informal class picture of the graduates; see also Mrs. H. H. Arnold, interviewed by Murray Green, n.d., MGC, USAF Academy, Colorado Springs, Colo. Mrs. Arnold was known by all as "Bee." Arnold titled his letters to "Beadle," a pet name. In the early 1900s, "B-e-a" was the short form of "Bertha," a name Mrs. Arnold would have likely found unacceptable. Bee was also called "BeeBee" by her own family.

7. Arnold Collection, Library of Congress, box 3, folder 9. A copy of the flight log is also available at the National Air and Space Museum Archives, H. H. Arnold folder; see also *Global Mission*, 1–21.

8. Arnold, *Global Mission*, 15.

9. Arnold's ratings were FAI airplane pilot certificate no. 29, July 1911; military aviator, War Department 1912–1914, July 1912; expert aviator, Aero Club of America no. 4, September 1912; and junior military aviator, May 1916. Memorandum for Special Assistant to the JCS for Arms Control, 21 September 1970, Air Force Historical Research Agency (AFHRA), 168.7265-8. This document contains a study by the Office of Air Force History listing the first 22 military pilots and their license dates verified in published War Department General Order files at the Pentagon.

10. Arnold Collection, box 3, folder 9; Arnold, *Global Mission*, 30–38.

11. Arnold, *Global Mission*, 35–41.

12. Arnold to Bee, letter, 20 June 1913, MGC. Arnold loved to have fun and a drink was never out of the question in his early career. His father had

been rather strict about the use of alcohol and did not even permit it at Henry and Bee's wedding, a decision he later wished he had modified to allow champagne. Tommy Milling, Arnold's best man for the affair and a fellow pilot, smuggled some liquor up from the Arnold cellar during the reception anyway. It was interesting that, after the war, Arnold and Bee were both subjects of a Pabst Beer advertisement which showed them at their Ranch in Sonoma Valley, Calif. Robert Arnold, interviewed by author, 14–16 July 1995, Sonoma, Calif.

13. H. H. Arnold, second lieutenant, to commanding officer, Signal Corps Aviation School, letter, subject: Report from Fort Riley, 6 November 1912, AFHRA, 168.65-38. The first portion of the letter describes the progress being made with the various airplanes at Fort Riley. Observation techniques were discussed in addition to mention of a number of engine problems. Arnold's disclosure of the near-accident is added at the end of the report in a straightforward paragraph explaining the event. Letters from this period are also located in the Arnold Collection, box 3, folder 9. Theodore von Kármán explained a "spin" this way: "A spin is like a love affair. You didn't notice how you got into it, and it is very hard to get out of." Hugh Dryden, "Theodore von Kármán: 1881–1963," in *Biographical Memoirs* (New York: Columbia University Press, 1965), 361.

14. Arnold, *Global Mission*, 41–43; Arnold Collection, box 222, the Global Mission folder; also see National Archives, Arnold 201, 94, stack W-3; and CUOHR, B. Foulois. The safety statistics during the 1990–1991 flying year for the US Air Force showed that less than two major accidents (not necessarily even a fatality) occurred every 100,000 flying hours. This included combat operations in the Persian Gulf War. In 1913 the safety rate equivalent would have been 950 deaths per 100,000 flying hours not including major accidents where planes could not be repaired.

15. Gen Henry H. Arnold, USAF, Retired, interviewed by T. A. Boyd, 19 October 1949, El Rancho Feliz, Sonoma, Calif., transcript in MGC.

16. Arnold to Orville Wright, letter, 6 November 1911 and Wilbur Wright to Arnold, letter, 10 November 1911, Wright Brothers Papers, Library of Congress, Washington, D.C., box 9, H. H. Arnold folder. Hereafter cited as Wright Papers.

17. Arnold to W. Wright, letter, 18 November 1911, Wright Papers.

18. Arnold to O. Wright, letter, 27 January 1913, Wright Papers. The "sand test" was accomplished by flipping the aircraft over and loading the wings with sand until the wing spars began to crack. Thus, aircraft strength was determined by inverted sand weight which simulated the forces of lift on the wings themselves. This test is still used today in modified form, most recently to test the wing strength of the C-17.

19. Arnold to O. Wright, letter, 1 February 1913, Wright Papers; Arnold to O. Wright, letter, 23 February 1913, Wright Papers; Arnold to Mr. Wright, letter, 15 March 1913, Wright Papers. Orville tried to reassure Arnold that the scout ship was the "easiest machine that we build. Its high speed in landing is its only drawback. It is a very strong machine and has a larger

factor of safety than any of the other models." Wright to Arnold, letter, 22 March 1913, Wright Papers.

20. Maurer Maurer, ed., *The U.S. Air Service in World War I: Early Concepts of Military Aviation*, vol. 2 (Washington, D.C.: Office of Air Force History, 1978), 12–13, 19–20; Arnold, *Global Mission*, 41–43.

21. Although the NACA was founded as an "advisory" organization, loopholes in its organic legislation quickly opened the door to a more research-oriented function. This was the ultimate intent of the drafters of the 1915 rider to the Naval Appropriations Act. Dr. Alex Roland, interviewed by author, 15 February 1996; also see Alex Roland's book on the NACA, *Model Research: the National Advisory Committee for Aeronautics, 1915–1958*, vol. 1 (Washington, D.C.: National Air and Space Administration, 1985), preface and chap. 1, for further details.

22. Roger E. Bilstein, *Orders of Magnitude: A History of the NACA and NASA, 1915–1990* (Washington, D.C.: National Aeronautics and Space Administration, 1989), 1–15; and Howard S. Wolko, *In the Cause of Flight: Technologists of Aeronautics and Astronautics* (Washington, D.C.: Smithsonian Institution Press, 1981), 18; Robert Frank Futrell, *Ideas, Concepts, Doctrine*, vol. 1, *Basic Thinking in the United States Air Force, 1907–1960* (Maxwell AFB, Ala.: Air University Press, 1989), 19; and Wesley Frank Craven and James Lea Cate, *The Army Air Forces in World War II*, vol. 1, *Plans and Early Operations, January 1939 to August 1942* (Chicago: University of Chicago Press, 1948), 7. Maurer, 75–89. The Air Service sent a few ill-prepared planes with Pershing as aerial observation platforms. Before long, many of them were destroyed, and several pilots were killed due to crashes.

23. Washington Service Diary, 1917–1918, Arnold Collection, box no. 3, folder 13.

24. Arnold, *Global Mission*, 46–47.

25. Arnold Collection, box no. 3, folder 13.

26. Dik Daso, "Events in Foreign Policy: The End of American Neutrality, 1917–1918" (typed manuscript, University of South Carolina, 1994), 1–12, author's possession, Burke, Va.

27. Many photos are included as well as many of the original documents, which described the weapon and its construction. Interestingly, Elmer Sperry claimed that he had invented the "Bug" and quit the project in 1919 thoroughly disgusted with Kettering. The engine was designed by C. H. Wills, Ford's former chief designer. USAF Museum, "Kettering Bug" folder.

28. Arnold, *Global Mission*, 74–76; Thomas P. Hughes, *American Genesis: A Century of Invention and Technological Enthusiasm* (New York: Penguin Books, 1989), 130–34; Stephen L. McFarland, *America's Pursuit of Precision Bombing, 1910–1945* (Washington, D.C.: Smithsonian Institution Press, 1995); also Glenn Infield, "Hap Arnold's WWI Buzz Bomb," *Air Force Magazine*, May 1974, n.p.

29. John W. Huston to author, letter, 22 February 1996.

30. Arnold Collection, World War I Diary.

31. Maurer, 88; also Arnold, *Global Mission*, 63–64.

32. Arnold Collection, photo albums.

33. Arnold, *Global Mission*, 92–93.

34. Ibid., 91–98. For an excellent tribute to "Jimmy" Doolittle, one should review the Winter 1993 issue of *Air Power History*, which was dedicated to the life of the aviation pioneer.

35. Alfred F. Hurley, *Billy Mitchell: Crusader for Airpower* (Bloomington, Ind.: Indiana University Press, 1975), 64–70. For a highly detailed account of the trial, see Michael L. Grumelli, "Trial of Faith: The Dissent and Court-Martial of Billy Mitchell" (PhD diss., Rutgers, 1991); and Arnold, *Global Mission*, 109–12.

36. Arnold Collection, box 3, folder 17; Arnold, *Global Mission*, 113.

37. Arnold, *Global Mission*, 113–23; and Hurley, *Billy Mitchell*, 100–5.

38. Huston to author, letter, 22 February 1996. General Huston was kind enough to clear up the circumstances of Arnold's "exile" in this correspondence.

39. *New York Times*, 23–30 July 1927, various pages.

40. Maj H. H. Arnold to John K. Montgomery, letters, 15 and 24 July 1927, John K. Montgomery Papers, Caroliniana Library, University of South Carolina, Columbia. Hereafter cited as J. K. Montgomery Papers; also Arnold, *Global Mission*, 123–28.

41. Arnold to Montgomery, letter, 24 July 1927, J. K. Montgomery Papers.

42. Montgomery to Arnold, letter, 27 July 1927, J. K. Montgomery Papers. Included in this letter are the specifics of the salary and perks offered to Arnold: presidency of Pan Am; $8,000 per year salary; 300 shares of B stock (voting shares); and 1,200 more if he stayed on with the company.

43. Arnold, *Global Mission*, 122.

44. Thomas M. Coffey, *HAP: The Story of the U.S. Air Force and the Man Who Built It, General Henry H. "Hap" Arnold* (New York: Viking Press, 1982), 126.

45. Arnold Collection, Billy Bruce folders; recently, David K. Vaughan, "Hap Arnold's Bill Bruce Books," *Air Power History* 40, no. 3 (Winter 1993): 43–49.

46. Lois E. Walker and Shelby E. Wickam, *From Huffman Prairie to the Moon: The History of Wright-Patterson Air Force Base* (Dayton, Ohio: Air Force Logistics Command, 1986), 59–61, 149. Arnold had commanded the Rockwell Air Depot in California from 1922–1924. He also wrote the history of Rockwell Field while he was there. A copy of the manuscript is located in the AFHRA.

47. Col H. H. Arnold Jr., USAF, Retired, interviewed by Murray Green, MGC, 29–30 August 1972, Sheridan, Wyo. Lois E. Walker and Shelby E. Wickam, *From Huffman Prairie to the Moon: The History of Wright/Patterson Air Force Base* (Dayton, Ohio: Air Force Logistics Command, 1986), 218–19.

Arnold appeared to be getting used to the system during these two years. He directed projects on flame suppression from engine exhausts and contrail dissipation; the intent of both was to make American aircraft less visible to enemy gunners. Maj Gen Donald J. Keirn, Retired, interviewed by Murray Green, MGC, 25 September 1970, Delaplane, Va.

48. Bowman flew several of Millikan's experimental missions. His task was to orbit a particular area with a 500-pound lead ball at various altitudes up to 21,000 feet. Bowman felt certain that Millikan introduced Arnold to Kármán at Caltech. Brig Gen H. W. Bowman, Retired, interviewed by Murray Green, MGC, 23 August 1969, n.l; Arnold, *Global Mission*, 139. See Robert H. Kargon, *The Rise of Robert Millikan: Portrait of a Life in American Science* (Ithaca, N.Y.: Cornell University Press, 1982) for a fair description of the Karl Compton challenge.

49. Arnold, *Global Mission*, 133–47. For some unknown reason, Arnold allowed an inexperienced B-10 pilot to take one of the birds out on a flight. The pilot ended up in Cook's Bay, and the B-10 was swamped in 20–40 feet of icy water. Remarkably, the other crews were able to save the plane and drain the water from the fuselage. It cranked up on the first try and flew the rest of the way to Washington, D.C., much to Arnold's relief.

50. Since Clark Millikan, Robert Millikan's son, had joined the faculty at Caltech, Kármán used to differentiate the two by calling Robert, "Old Millikan," to everyone but Old Millikan himself. Dr. Sears is a former student, colleague, and friend of Theodore von Kármán, one of only a few who called him by his informal name, Todor. William Rees Sears, interviewed by author, Tucson, Ariz., 8 July 1995. For an excellent summary of the Guggenheim influence, see Richard P. Hallion, *Legacy of Flight: The Guggenheim Contribution to American Aviation* (Seattle: University of Washington Press, 1977).

51. Theodore von Kármán, oral history interview, USAF Academy, Colo., 27 January 1960; and Michael H. Gorn, *Universal Man: Theodore von Kármán's Life in Aeronautics* (Washington, D.C.: Smithsonian Institution Press, 1992), 81. Also in the NBC newsreel that covered the Rose Garden ceremony where Kármán was given the first Medal of Science by President John F. Kennedy, Kármán remembered Arnold and his inquisitive nature back in the early days (January 1963). Arnold's flight logs carefully documented his trips to California while he was at Fairfield Depot. On one trip, he spent nearly one month in the Los Angeles area during which he might have visited Caltech, Old Millikan, and later, Kármán. A copy of these logs is located in both the Library of Congress, Arnold Collection and the USAF Museum, Wright-Patterson AFB, Dayton, Ohio, Arnold file. The fact that Kármán ranks Arnold as a major would date their initial meetings to sometime before 1 February 1931 when he was promoted to lieutenant colonel.

52. Gorn, 116, 158.

Chapter 3

Conceptualizing the Future Air Force

In January 1936, Arnold was transferred back to Washington. Maj Gen Oscar F. Westover had taken over as chief of the Air Corps and had convinced Gen Malin Craig, chief of staff, that he needed Arnold as his assistant. Another candidate for that job was General Headquarters (GHQ) Air Force commander, Brig Gen Frank M. Andrews. Andrews and Westover had clashed regarding independence of the air arm. Westover, who had opposed separation from the Army throughout his career, and Arnold, perhaps having learned a lesson about bucking the system at too high a level, agreed that remaining part of the Army held definite advantages for the Air Corps, particularly in the area of logistical support. From that point, Andrews's career took a different path from Arnold's. By 1939, Andrews had moved over to the general staff under George Marshall, and Arnold held command of the Air Corps.

Arnold recalled that, "the entire family said good-by, in tears, to March Field." More than sunny California, Arnold hated leaving his position of operational command.[1] During his first two years back in Washington, Arnold handled a hodgepodge of administrative and public relations problems. But it was during these years as Westover's assistant that his views on science, technology, and the Army Air Corps (AAC) gained nationwide attention even in the midst of internal Air Corps turbulence.

On 1 March 1935, the GHQ Air Force had become a reality based on the recommendations of the Baker and Drum Boards. Those boards had recommended the formation of a general headquarters air force capable of organizing independent air operations as well as direct support of the ground forces. GHQ also supported the Army's responsibility for coastal air defense. The GHQ Air Force was the first manifestation of a truly independent air arm, including an independent mission, within the Army. Essentially, the Air Corps had become a branch of the Army, like cavalry and infantry. GHQ represented the combat arm of the service

After formation of the GHQ Air Force in 1935, Andrews (far left) visited Arnold at March Field, California.

while the Office of the Air Corps held responsibility for finances, training, and materiel. Neither branch, however, controlled tactical bases, which remained under the control of Army corps area commanders. During times of war, GHQ would be assigned directly to the battlefield commander. The dual command situation never proved effective or efficient and, although an improvement over earlier arrangements, was never totally satisfactory to aviation branch leaders.

Six months after the formation of the GHQ Air Force, an Air Corps study known as the Browning Board recognized the detrimental effect the dual structure was having on the Air Corps. Col William S. Browning's panel recommended a consolidation of Air Corps structure that would place the GHQ under the command of the Office of the Chief of the Air Corps.

Although this recommendation was adopted in practice it was not until June 1941 when the Army Air Forces were officially established, that the situation was finally resolved. Army Regulation (AR) 95-5, *Army Air Forces*, 20 June 1941, defined the function of each level of command. The chief of the Army Air Forces was also to act as deputy chief of staff for air (and by February 1942, a member of the Joint Chiefs of Staff) and in that capacity was directly responsible to the secretary of war and the Army chief of staff for all air operations. Unity of command was finally achieved within the Army Air Forces. Arnold used this to ensure, among other things, continued scientific and technological advances in his command.[2]

Even before restructuring took place, Arnold chaired a committee formed in 1936 to examine how best to create a "balanced air program." There was nothing unusual in his report; in fact, it followed very closely the recommendations made previously by the Drum Board. The numbers reflected in each report for personnel and planes were similar. Surprising today but realistic at that time, the forecast for airplanes required was only 1,399 in 1936 increasing to a meager 2,708 in 1941.[3] Although Arnold's report was primarily an attempt to reckon with depression budgets, no mention was made of scientific research or technological development. Rather, the program's primary concern was to save dollars in all areas except purchasing airplanes.

In September 1937, Arnold modified the conservative approach his "balanced air program" report had taken. While addressing the Western Aviation Planning Conference, Arnold summarized his philosophy for creating an aeronautical institution in America second to none.

> Remember that the seed comes first; if you are to reap a harvest of aeronautical development, you must plant the seed called *experimental research*. Install aeronautical branches in your universities; encourage your young men to take up aeronautical engineering. It is a new field but it is likely to prove a very productive one indeed. Spend all the funds you can possibly make available on experimentation and research. Next, do not visualize aviation merely as a collection of airplanes. It is broad and far reaching. It combines manufacture, schools, transportation, airdrome, building and management, air munitions and armaments, metallurgy, mills and mines, finance and banking, and finally, public security—national defense (emphasis in original).[4]

Arnold, in this statement, had issued the broadest description of the evolving technological system of airpower, even if he didn't make a distinction between empirical versus theoretical research. If the Air Corps had little money for research and development, then perhaps universities and industry could be persuaded to find some. After all it had been the Guggenheim Fund that had fostered aeronautical departments at several universities almost a decade earlier.[5] No matter the source, experimental research was the key to future airpower.

Arnold had very cleverly linked Air Corps development to civilian prosperity in the aviation industry, hoping that civilian institutions would pick up the fumbling research ball while the Air Corps was struggling just to acquire planes. His ideas reflected the "Millikan philosophy," that of bringing the center of aeronautical science in America to Caltech, which had shaped that university since the 1920s. This philosophy, coupled with Arnold's realization that airpower was a complex system of logistics, procurement, ground support bases, and operations, guided his vision for future growth.[6] Arnold's approach to airpower development was actually the first mention of what became the military-industrial-academic complex after World War II.[7]

In addition to bolstering industrial and public support for the technological advancement of the Air Corps, Arnold was continually forced to deal with the inherent administrative confusion caused by the establishment of GHQ Air Force the year before. In particular, responsibility for aeronautical research was not well defined between the branches, further slowing Arnold's efforts there. Nevertheless, the GHQ was the first crack in the foundation of Army control over airpower.[8]

As was all too frequent an occurrence in these early years of aviation, a tragic aircraft accident took the life of General Westover on 21 September 1938. Arnold was now the top man in the Air Corps. Arnold's experience in Army aviation had prepared him for the tasks ahead, and now he was in a position to tackle these problems.

When Arnold "shook the stick" and officially took command of the Air Corps on 29 September 1938, many military aviation projects were under consideration both at Wright Field and at the National Advisory Committee for Aeronautics facility at Langley: radar, aircraft windshield deicing, jet assisted takeoff (JATO) system (actually a rocket), and a host of aircraft and engine design modifications. Many of these projects were related to the brand new B-17, an aviation technology leap in itself.[9] Arnold wasted no time in calling the "longhairs" to a meeting at the National Academy of Sciences (NAS) under the auspices of the Committee on Air Corps Research to solve these problems.[10] It was no surprise that Arnold immediately accelerated Air Corps R&D efforts. In his first message as Air Corps commander, Arnold devoted a separate paragraph to the subject that reflected his public views on airpower. "Until quite recently," he said, "we have had marked superiority in airplanes, engines, and accessories. That superiority is now definitely challenged by recent developments abroad. This means that our experimental development programs must be speeded up."[11] But his views were already common knowledge to most airmen.

Assisting the "speeding up" process, Guggenheim Aeronautical Laboratory, California Institute of Technology (GALCIT) and the Massachusetts Institute of Technology (MIT) sent representatives to this NAS meeting. Vannevar Bush and Jerome Hunsaker, of MIT, grabbed the windshield deicing problem for their institution while openly dismissing JATO as a fantasy. Hunsaker called JATO the "Buck Rogers" job. Bush explained to Robert Millikan and Kármán that he never understood how "a serious engineer or scientist could play around with rockets."[12] Arnold knew that GALCIT had already demonstrated some success in that area. The condescending attitude held by the MIT elite did not go over well with General Arnold. From this meeting onward, Arnold thought of Bush as something less than forward looking, despite his excellent, even pioneering record in electrical engineering. The case of Vannevar Bush was a classic example of how a talented individual had been dropped from confidence because of personal perceptions.

On the other hand, Millikan and Kármán, representing GALCIT, eagerly accepted the JATO challenge, an attitude that Arnold no doubt appreciated. JATO represented potential funding for the struggling GALCIT Rocket Research Project, established in 1936. This project, also known as GALCIT

USAF Photo

Today, the Jet Propulsion Lab is a massive complex nestled in the foothills just north of Pasadena, California.

Project number 1, was established by Dr. Kármán and Dr. Frank Malina, and exists today as the Jet Propulsion Laboratory (JPL).[13] It was after this NAS meeting that the Arnold/Kármán association officially began. Arnold saw Kármán as a useful tool, a tap for recognizing undeveloped technologies. Kármán saw the Army Air Corps as a worthy recipient of his services. More importantly, however, the funding Arnold made available seemed bottomless and helped Caltech maintain its status as the leading aeronautical university in the country. Kármán was dedicated to helping the Army but was also dedicated to Caltech, the GALCIT, and Robert Millikan. Nonetheless, this alliance, above all others which Arnold held with scientists and engineers, proved one of the most significant and engaging collaborations in the early history of American airpower.

This meeting was just the beginning of Major General Arnold's push toward making science and technology an integral part of the Air Corps. He even invited Gen George C. Marshall to a luncheon with the visiting scientists. Marshall wondered, "What on earth are you doing with people like that?" Arnold replied that he was "using" their brain power to develop devices "too difficult for the Air Force engineers to develop themselves."[14] The realization that civilian help was the only way to ensure that the AAC had the best technology available was typical of Arnold. He didn't care where the devices came from, he only cared whether his Air Corps was utilizing them. By including Marshall in this circle of scientists, Arnold began winning support for advanced technology from the highest ranking Army officers.

Not only did Arnold utilize the advice of these scientists, he gathered information from civilian aviators as well. One in particular influenced Arnold's commitment to technology. In late 1938, Arnold had exchanged letters with Charles Lindbergh, who was touring Europe. In his correspondence, Lindbergh expressed concern over US lethargy in airplane development. "It seems to me," Lindbergh wrote, "that we should be developing prototypes with a top speed in the vicinity of 500 mph at altitude . . . the trend over here seems to be toward very high speed."[15] This revelation worried Arnold. In March 1939, Arnold established a special air board to study the problems Lindbergh had addressed. By April 1939, Arnold had convinced Lindbergh to accept an active duty commission as a member of the study group. This group, known as the Kilner Board, produced a five-year plan for research and development within the Air Corps. The report was shortsighted in many respects but did represent the immediate needs of the air arm. Jet propulsion and missiles, for example, were not even considered.[16]

Lindbergh's impact was immediate but short-lived. In a written recommendation for the NACA, Lindbergh gained support for an expanded aeronautical research facility to be located at Moffett Field, California. The funding was approved on 15 September 1939, the same morning Lindbergh spoke out against American participation in the European war on three major national radio networks. President Roosevelt tried to dissuade him from taking his views directly to the nation. "Lindy" was a skilled communicator. After his historic flight, the Guggenheim Fund had invested $100,000 to subsidize a national tour expressly designed to generate support for aviation. By the late 1920s, Lindbergh had toured over 80 cities and influenced millions of Americans. In many respects, Lindbergh became the American spokesman for aviation.[17] As such, his words carried an inordinate amount of influence. Fearing his effect on public opinion, FDR promised Lindbergh a new cabinet post if he remained silent concerning American participation in the European War. Arnold had been caught in the middle of the presidential offer but there was never any doubt in the general's mind that Lindbergh would turn down such an offer and speak his own mind. Arnold was right. Consequently, Lindbergh "resigned" his commission, but Arnold had already taken his earlier warnings to heart.[18]

Arnold's public campaigns reflected Lindbergh's warnings. In January 1939, while speaking to the Society of Automotive Engineers in Detroit, Arnold reemphasized that America was falling behind in aircraft development. He attributed this failing to an inadequate program of scientific research. "All of us in the Army Air Corps," he stated, "realize that America owes its present prestige and standing in the air world in large measure to the money, time, and effort expended in aeronautical experimentation and research. We know that our future supremacy in the air depends on the brains and efforts of our engineers."[19] His dedication to continuous research, experimentation, and development was more focused and more defined than it had ever been, and now he carried the message across the country.

Arnold's official correspondence reflected the same commitment to R&D. In a memorandum to the assistant secretary of war dated 2 March 1939, Arnold vigorously defended proposed funding for research and development.

The work of the large number of aeronautical research agencies in this country should be afforded government support and encouragement only through a single coordinating agency which can determine that the individual and collective effort will be to the best interests of the Government. The NACA is the agency designated by law to carry out basic aeronautical research and its own plant and facilities cannot cover all phases of development. Furthermore, there are many public or semi-public institutions whose students or other research personnel are willing and anxious to perform useful investigation that will contribute to a real advancement of the various branches of aeronautical science.[20]

As a member of the NACA Main Committee since taking over the Air Corps, Arnold attended the committee meetings regularly and was familiar with the workings of the group. More importantly, he was acquainted with the other main committee members who together read like a "Who's Who" in American aviation. Aside from Van Bush, Orville Wright, Charles Lindbergh, and Harry Guggenheim were all members of the main committee in 1939. Shortly after this memo was sent, Arnold established an official liaison between the NACA facilities at Langley Field and the Air Corps Materiel Division at Wright Field. Arnold assigned Maj Carl F. Greene to the post in an effort to tighten the relationship between the two organizations.[21] The attempt to consolidate R&D programs was valiant, but time was running short. Conflict in Europe assured that the relationship never matured.

Toward Production R&D

The expanding war in Europe indicated that a posture of readiness was prudent and necessary for the United States. From the day that Germany invaded Poland in September 1939, Arnold realized that all American production efforts would be needed just to build enough aircraft of designs already on line to create a fighting air force. "For us to have expended our effort on future weapons to win a war at hand," he wrote to General Spaatz in 1946, "would be as stupid as trying to win the next war with outmoded weapons and doctrines."[22] While the outcome of the war was in question, and even though the US was not yet directly involved, Arnold emphasized R&D only to improve weapons or aircraft by using technologies that were already on the drawing board. Essentially, from September 1939 until the spring of 1944, the majority of Army Air Force R&D efforts were dedicated to short-term improvements in existing technologies.[23]

By May 1940, FDR had called for a fivefold increase in aircraft production in America. Producing 50,000 planes each year seemed a tall order to everyone but Arnold, who had recommended an even greater number despite his staff's conservative estimates. Gen Lauris Norstad, USAF, Retired, a member of Arnold's Advisory Council, recalled the process that led to Arnold's recommendation.

The general had called all his top people together in Washington. "Gentleman, here is our opportunity to tell people in authority and to tell the country what we need. The president has asked for this figure. I am going to give you until tomorrow morning at 9 o'clock, and you think about how many airplanes we are going to ask for. It has to be real, but use your imagination. Don't hold yourselves back to restrictions of budgets under which we have been trained in the last few years." The following morning Arnold announced, "Gentleman, I am going to call on you to give me your figures. Again, I will tell you, be bold." The first officer suggested an additional squadron at Atlanta; the second asked for a squadron at Oklahoma City and so on. "Gentlemen, at the outside, even with replacements, this adds up to about 100 planes. To hell with you! I'm going over to the White House now, and do you know what I'm going to tell the President? I am going to tell the President that we need 100,000 airplanes." He did.[24]

Arnold's World War I production experience had demonstrated to him the expansion capabilities of American industry, a lesson he did not forget. Apparently FDR had learned a lesson from World War I as well. The Wilson administration's policy of neutrality had prevented any serious preparation for war until it was too late for American industry to gear up for mass production of any air weapons. FDR's decision to build planes, and lots of them, based largely upon the advice of his trusted advisor Harry Hopkins and Arnold, ensured that American industrial strength would make a decisive impact during the war. By July 1940, Arnold had begun his campaign of personal encouragement in the factories. The spirit behind his enthusiasm was a direct result of the lessons he had learned in the last war.

> I can remember the last World War—when in the beginning the American aircraft industry had a capacity of less than 100 planes a year. I saw one factory sign a contract eighteen months later to deliver 100 planes a day. . . . The American aircraft industry today is incomparably superior in

Arnold with Harry Hopkins in October 1943. Hopkins was an airpower advocate and had a positive influence on FDR concerning the evolution of that technological system.

every regard to the state it had reached even at the close of the last war. . . . So, make no mistake about it, we shall train the mechanics, we shall train the flyers, and we shall build the planes.[25]

Consequently, most of Arnold's time in the months prior to Pearl Harbor and in the early years of American involvement was spent touring factories, arranging training courses for new pilots, establishing bases of operations, haggling over congressional legislation, and encouraging the factory workers, who he believed were vital to the creation of real American air supremacy. He personally spent the time touring factories because he feared that aircraft production was well behind schedule. Arnold revealed his deep fears to Major General Andrews, now in command of the Panama Canal Zone, in January 1941.

> As you know we are leaning over backwards to give everything to the British. Very little is coming to us. . . . Engines are the neck of the bottle more than anything else and England has priority on engines. So, taking everything into consideration, aircraft production insofar as getting airplanes for U.S. units is more or less of a mess, and no matter what we do in this matter there will be no relief for several months in the future. . . . All I can say is that we hope to get planes to everyone—but at this writing it is only a hope.[26]

For General Arnold, R&D was not an immediate answer to American production woes in 1941. His faith in the power of the American mass production line was a direct result of his World War I experience.

The total production effort that followed these early letters of despair shocked everyone, including Arnold. By April 1943, the four star wrote back to Lieutenant General Andrews, now air commander in the European theater, "By God, Andy, after all these years it was almost too much—I don't imagine any of us, even in our most optimistic moments, dreamed that the Air Corps would ever build up the way it has. I know I damn well never did."[27]

Airplane production became one of the major reasons for American airpower's evolution into a massive technological system by 1944. Until the early years of World War II in Europe, the American aircraft industry was still in its infancy. The war forced it into early adolescence. Despite the many challenges inherent in the massive buildup of airplanes, Arnold still found time to push for a few untested technologies that showed exceptional promise while also pressing his field commanders to use "science" to advantage whenever possible.[28]

Propellerless Aircraft

The most spectacular of these technologies was the JATO program that Caltech had been working since the NAS meeting in November 1938. Since it was most desirable to build aircraft that carried heavy bomb loads, the problems of high-wing loading on initial takeoff became extremely important. "In many cases the maximum allowable gross weight of an airplane was limited solely by take-off considerations. One of the many methods . . . proposed for the

USAF Museum

A JATO rocket engine about 18 inches long.

elimination of this difficulty involved the use of auxiliary rocket jets to augment the available thrust during take-off and initial climb."[29] The net result was an increase in range for a desired payload. Frank Malina, Homerjoe Stewart, and the rest of the "suicide club" spent most of 1940 and the first half of 1941, developing the JATO system. By summer, Malina's team was ready to flight test the device. Capt Homer Boushey flew an Air Corps "Ercoupe" from Wright to March Field, the selected spot for the test, late in July 1941. After a failed static firing resulted in a spectacular explosion, the rockets were affixed to the underside of the Ercoupe's wings, near the wing roots. After the failed static firing, it was decided to accomplish an anchored test firing of the rockets physically attached to the plane. Although this test was more successful than the previous one, fragments of burning propellant and a small piece of a nozzle had still burned a forearm-sized hole in the underside of the Ercoupe tail. "Well, at least it isn't a big hole," one of the onlookers observed. A successful airborne confidence firing test of the rockets was completed on 6 August, but the big test was yet to come.[30]

USAF Museum

Capt Homer Boushey in the Ercoupe at March Field.

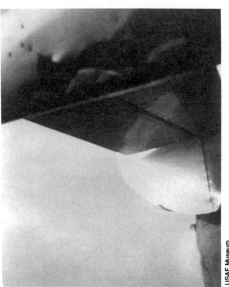

USAF Museum

The results of the ground test run were less than spectacular.

On 12 August, despite the ominous results of the previous tests, Boushey strapped into the Ercoupe, now loaded with six JATOs, three under each wing. William Durand, long-time friend of Kármán, NACA charter member, and chairman of the NACA's Special Committee on Jet Propulsion, had been invited to witness the JATO flight test. A test aircraft, a Piper Cub, piloted by Dr. Clark Millikan, idled next to the Ercoupe waiting for the soon-to-be rocket plane to release brakes. Both aircraft revved their motors and released their brakes. In a matter of only a few seconds, having reached the predetermined speed, Boushey ignited his rockets. In a cloud of smoke, followed shortly by the crack of the rocket ignition, the Ercoupe catapulted into the air and over the 50-foot banner that marked the calculated height after rocket ignition. The Piper Cub appeared to climb in slow motion. The JATO had been a remarkable success.[31]

JATO was so successful that Kármán decided that it would be possible to launch the Ercoupe on rocket power alone, sans propeller. To cover up the fact that the prop had been removed, the Ercoupe's nose was plastered with safety posters as if it were undergoing some form of repairs. One of the

Jet Propulsion Lab

NACA's William Durand (center) was present for the initial JATO tests. Later, he would be sworn to secrecy during development of the first American jet aircraft.

posters read, "Be Alert, Don't Get Hurt!" At least the JATO team had a sense of humor. Karman calculated that 12 JATO motors would be required to accomplish the first American rocket-powered airplane flight. On 23 August Boushey strapped in one more time. Kármán had calculated that at least 25 knots of ground speed would be needed for the test to work properly. But how to accelerate to the required speed without a working prop? A standard pickup truck fitted with a long rope pulled out on the runway in front of the propless Ercoupe. Boushey grabbed the rope like a rodeo bull rider and held on while the truck accelerated to the calculated 25 knots. Boushey released the rope, fired the rockets, now twice as loud and smokey, and hurtled 10 feet into the air on rocket power alone. He had enough runway left to make a safe landing straight ahead. Additional testing continued in both solid and liquid auxiliary propulsion for the next decade.[32] Arnold pushed this program because it demonstrated potential for increasing the combat range of his heavy bombers.

Although not initially the most spectacular of all the Air Corp's scientific and technological research programs, Arnold's direct involvement in bringing the British, "Whittle" jet engine to America, beginning in April 1941, illustrated his personal commitment to technology and its application to the American war effort. As in 1913, Arnold could have cared less where the technology came from; if it benefited the Air Corps, he wanted it. So it was with the "Whittle" engine and the development of American jet aircraft.[33]

Throughout 1938, Arnold had received Lindbergh's reports, which suggested that some German pursuit planes were capable of speeds exceeding 400 MPH.[34] He had also assigned Lindbergh to the Kilner Board in an effort to project R&D requirements for the Air Corps. Whether Lindbergh had been duped by the Nazis on preplanned factory tours during his visits to Germany turned out to be irrelevant. Lindbergh suggested that the Air Corps begin research that would lead to a 500-MPH fighter, and Arnold was convinced that he was right. Arnold's constant quest for better technologies and equipment forced a confrontation with George W. Lewis, director of aeronautical research at the National Advisory

The Ercoupe clears the 50-foot banner during the test run.

The second angle shows the test aircraft piloted by Clark Millikan.

Kármán calculates the number of engines required for a JATO-only takeoff.

Committee for Aeronautics. "Hap," at that moment not very happy, wanted to know, "why in the name of God we [in the Army Air Corps] hadn't got one [a 400-plus mph fighter]." Lewis replied, "Because you haven't ordered one."[35] Arnold was furious. A lengthy dialogue followed during which Arnold discovered that Lewis was well aware that the technology to build faster planes had existed for some time. Lewis had not suggested building one because it was not the NACA's function to dictate what the military should or should not build. To Arnold, the NACA was not acting like a true team player. The general might have even considered Lewis's attitude unpatriotic.[36] This incident overshadowed the many successful programs the NACA had undertaken during Arnold's tenure.

Having lost trust in the workings and leadership of the NACA, Arnold resorted to other civilian agencies in an effort to capitalize on "Whittle" jet engine information made available to

Jet Propulsion Lab

Twelve canisters were needed, the propeller was removed, and the nose was covered in safety posters. "What about tomorrow if I meet with an accident today?"

hin by Air Chief Marshal Sir Charles Portal in April 1941. Although the NACA took steps toward jet engine development directed by the 1941 Durand Board, formed in March 1941 at Arnold's request, importing the plans and an engine from Britain was the general's personal achievement.[37] In September, he took these plans and created a separate, supersecret, production team including Larry Bell, of Bell Aircraft, and Donald F. "Truly" Warner of General Electric (GE). GE was selected because of previous work done under the guidance of Sanford Moss on "turbosupercharging," a process similar to the turbojet concept.[38] The project military representative was Col Benjamin Chidlaw. This Bell/GE team was so secret that only 15 men at Wright Field knew of its existence. The contracts with GE had been handwritten and transmitted in person by Arnold's personal liaison, Maj Donald

Arnold is greeted by Dr. George Lewis during a November 1944 trip to Cleveland.

J. Keirn. Keirn recalled that the first GE contract was for a turboprop and was being built in Schenectady, New York, while the "Whittle" engine project was undertaken at West Lynn, Massachusetts. The three Durand Board engine teams—one at Westinghouse, a second sponsored by the NACA, and the first GE project—were unaware that Arnold had directed Chidlaw to get a jet in the air under absolute secrecy.[39] "Good Mother of God, General Arnold," Chidlaw asked bewildered, "How do you keep the Empire State building a secret?" Sternly, Arnold replied, "You keep it a secret."[40]

The supersecret engine was assembled at Lynn, Massachusetts under the project title, "Supercharger Type #1." At Larry Bell's factory, the airframe project received an old program number so as not to arouse any suspicion. The workers themselves were segregated from each other so that even the members of the team were not totally sure what they were building. The AAF officer who was to be the first American military man to fly a jet, Col Laurence Craigie, never revealed his mission even to his wife, who found out about it

Arnold departs for England in April 1941 on the "Clipper."

Courtesy Robert Arnold

in January 1944 with the rest of the country. Craigie recalled that "the only project I know of that was more secret was the atomic bomb."[41]

On 2 October 1942, the Bell XP-59A flew three times. The first two flights were piloted by Bob Stanley, a Bell test pilot and Caltech graduate, and the third was flown by Col Laurence Craigie, the first military man to fly the American jet plane. In actuality, the plane had flown for the first time during taxi tests on 30 September and again on 1 October, but Larry Bell insisted that the first flight was not "official" until the brass hats were present as witnesses.[42] The internal "cloak of secrecy" was so effective that the general NACA membership had heard only rumors of the technology. Only William Durand himself had been informed of Arnold's "Whittle" project but had been sworn to secrecy. The day the XP-59A flew, he was the only member of the NACA who knew of the existence of the plane. In fact, he was at Muroc the day of the "official" first flight.[43]

The "Super Secret" XP-59A team. Bell test pilot, Bob Stanley; program director, Col Benjamin Chidlaw; liaison officers, Maj Don Keirn and Maj Ralph Swofford; and Larry Bell.

It was not until 7 January 1944 that the rest of America, including Mrs. Craigie, found out about the flight. The *Washington Post* carried the inaccurate front page headline, "U.S. Making Rocket War Plane," which detailed the events of 15 months before.[44] The development of the XP-59A can legitimately be called the first Air Force skunk-works project.

America's development of the jet engine was a typical example of how Arnold utilized technological advancement in attempting to improve Army Air Forces capability. Once aware of a particular technology, he decided whether it was applicable to AAF airplanes or their combat capability. As late as January 1939, for example, Arnold had stated, "Because of the high efficiency and flexibility of operation of the controllable propeller as it exists today, it will be many years before any means of propulsion, such as rocket or jet propulsion, can be expected on a large scale."[45] But British

76

The British get a look at their modified "Whittle" engine, the A-I. GE engineers made a few modifiations to the original design that increased efficiency.

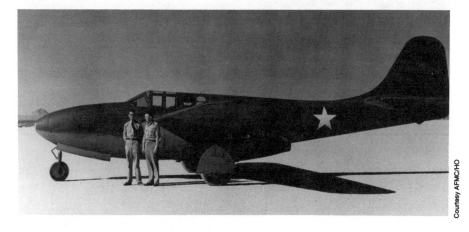

Bob Stanley and Col Laurence "Bill" Craigie flew the first three flights of the XP-59A "officially" on 2 October 1942 at Muroc.

Courtesy AFMC/HO

Larry Bell (left), Col Bill Craigie, and Dr. William Durand were all present for the "official" test flight.

engine developments, coupled with the underpinnings of early American turbojet concepts, and the promising work done at GALCIT Project no. 1 during 1940, convinced him that jets and rockets held significant potential for his air forces. Arnold always wanted the most advanced capabilities for his airplanes. But during this period, he wanted them within two years, no later.[46]

At Wright Field in 1945, Orville and the first military jet pilot, Bill Craigie, watch an F-80 fly at the AAF Fair. In only four decades, Orville had seen the evolution of their invention into an immense technological system.

Once convinced, he gathered trusted scientists, engineers, and officers together. Then, using the force of his personality, he directed what he wanted done with the technology. His teams were given considerable latitude in accomplishing the task and rarely failed to produce results.[47] Some who had served on these "Hap-directed" task forces had private reservations about specified tasks. "You never thought the things he asked you to do were possible," one Douglas Aircraft engineer recalled, "but then you went out and did them."[48] Colonel Chidlaw's XP-59A team was one glittering example.

The XP-59A was an exceptional program in that it violated Arnold's general tendency from late 1939 until mid-1944 to expend R&D efforts only on current production equipment. But Arnold saw the possibility for unbelievable capability from continuous research concerning jets. He envisioned aircraft capable of speeds exceeding 1,000 MPH and, despite criticism, completely believed in the future of jets. Arnold, having seen the British Gloster Meteor during its initial ground tests, realized that the first jets would not be the production models. Instead, he felt it more important to get a jet aircraft flying and then work on the modifications necessary to make it combat worthy. Perhaps he remembered the lesson of Billy Mitchell's "Barling" bomber, which had provided vital data and production techniques even though it was an operational failure. Additionally, Arnold was able to get a substantial jump on the program by promising the British an improved formula for high-speed, high-temperature turbine blades in return for all available British jet experimental data and an engine. As it stood, jet aircraft did not have the necessary range to be of much value to the AAF, which would soon be flying missions from England to Germany. Consequently, until the problem of limited range was solved, the production effort was not pushed as hard as that of combat-ready aircraft. For that reason, American jets did not contribute directly to World War II victory.[49] Arnold's push for the B-29 "Superfortress" can be better understood, however, in light of Arnold's perception of the importance of combat range to mission success. This was particularly true for operations in the Pacific, although the airplane was not designed specifically for that theater.

Radar, Bugs, and Aphrodite

Another Hap directed project was established while the XP-59A was under development. In May 1942, Arnold ordered the formation of the Sea-Search Attack Development Unit (SADU). This unit was composed of scientists from MIT, the National Defense Research Committee (NDRC), and operations personnel from the Navy and the Air Forces. Total control of all assets having to do with submarine destruction—research and development, production, even combat execution—fell to this organization. Arnold viewed this specific task with such high priority that he attached the unit directly under his command, eliminating all bureaucratic obstacles to mission accomplishment.[50] Having seen early "American-version" radars at Fort Monmouth as early as May 1937, General Arnold was satisfied with the potential that radar had demonstrated and pushed hard for combat capability in that area. The multicavity magnetron that made short-wave radar practical was a British invention. In April 1942, Dr. Edward L. Bowles, from the MIT Radiation Laboratory (RADLAB), was assigned as a special consultant for radar installations. Arnold's commitment and Bowles' expertise helped make the SADU an extremely effective unit. Arnold reminded Spaatz of the ultimate impact of SADU and the development of microwave radar in a letter after the war. "The use of microwave search radars during the campaign against the submarine was mainly instrumental in ending the menace of the U-boats. Germany had no comparable radar, or any countermeasures against it. In fact, for a long time the Germans were not even aware of what it was that was revealing the position of their subs so frequently."[51] As Arnold counted on Caltech for much of his aeronautical advice, he depended on MIT for similar advice concerning electronic advances, particularly radar.

In fact, it was German (and eventually Japanese) treachery in the conduct of the war, particularly with U-boats, that jolted Arnold into an attempt to rekindle an earlier pet project: the "Flying Bug." Although using the World War I surplus Bugs was considered until 1942, the idea was finally dismissed due to the relatively short range of the weapon (only 200 miles). Other projects, however, did result from this initial rekindling.

In the fall of 1939, Arnold wrote his old friend Charles Kettering, now vice president of General Motors, wanting to develop "glide bombs" to be used if war came. What he wanted was a device that could be used by the hundreds and that might keep his pilots away from enemy flak barrages. Arnold wanted the weapon to glide one mile for each thousand feet of altitude, carry a sizable amount of high explosive, have a circular error probable (CEP) less than one-half mile, and cost less than seven hundred dollars each. Kettering was convinced that it could be done fairly quickly. By December 1942 the GB-1 (glide bomb) was well under development, and by spring 1943 it was being used in Europe. Although the

USAF Museum

19 August 1940, Boss Kettering (left), Arnold, and William S. Knudsen discuss production plans. The massive effort, at times, surprised even Arnold.

GB-1 provided some protection to American airmen, it was highly inaccurate. Since the AAF held closely to the doctrine of precision bombing, the GB-1 was quickly shelved.[52] The GT-1, a glide torpedo, was somewhat more successful and saw some use in the Pacific theater. The development of the glide bomb series of weapons, which later included radio steering and television cameras, demonstrated one thing very clearly. General Arnold was not completely sold on precision bombing doctrine.

As the air war progressed, B-17 and B-24 bombers literally began to wear out. These surplus bombers occupied valuable space and even more valuable maintenance time. By late 1943, General Arnold had directed Brig Gen Grandison Gardner's Eglin Field engineers to outfit these "Weary Willies" with automatic pilots so that the airplanes, both B-17s and

The GB-1 was specifically designed to keep aircraft away from enemy flak belts.

Two were loaded on specially modified B-17s and, although ineffective, were a stepping stone to "smart bombs."

B-24s, could be filled with TNT or liquid petroleum and remotely flown to enemy targets. The idea behind Project Aphrodite was to crash the orphan aircraft into the target—a large city or industrial complex—detonating the explosives. General Spaatz utilized several of these "guided missiles" in August 1944 against targets in Europe. They were largely unsuccessful because they were easy to shoot down before they reached the target area. At Yalta, shortly after the first "Willies" were used in combat, the British vetoed further Aphrodite missions because of possible German retaliation to the undeniable "terror" nature of the weapon. "Weary Willies" were grounded after Yalta, much to General Arnold's disappointment.

Interestingly, Aphrodite was clearly a nonprecision weapon system. Yet, Arnold staunchly supported its development even before Germany launched V-1 and V-2 attacks against England in the early morning hours of 13 June 1944. Not only were Willies capable of carrying large amounts of explosives, using them as guided missiles assured that none would remain in American stockpiles. Arnold remembered the painful Liberty engine lessons from World War I production days. He didn't want B-17s flying a decade after this war was over as the DH-4 had done.[53]

The importance of Aphrodite was not its impact on the outcome of the war. Arnold had no great hopes for the ultimate effectiveness of these "area" weapons. Rather, Aphrodite demonstrated Arnold's willingness to supplement precision-bombing doctrine in an effort to save the lives of American airmen, particularly since he was feeling confident that the war in Europe was, essentially, under control by late spring 1944. In a staff memo, Arnold explained that he didn't care if the Willies were actually radio controlled or were just pointed at the enemy and allowed to run out of gas.[54] Aphrodite did provide an opportunity to test new automated piloting technology in a combat situation. Additionally, and more importantly, destroying "weary" bombers made room for new airplanes, which the prescient Arnold knew the air forces would need after the war ended.

Although Arnold was determined to rid the inventory of useless machines, in combat he generally preferred manned

USAF Museum

"Weary Willie" aircraft served a dual purpose, they eliminated useless surplus from the inventory and furthered development of remote piloted "missiles."

bombers to Willies. In November 1944, Arnold reminded Spaatz of the salvage rules for damaged aircraft. "The accelerated activities of our fighting forces in all theaters makes it increasingly important that we utilize our material resources to the maximum, not only for the sake of the economy, but also in order that the greatest possible pressure be brought to bear against the enemy."[55] The experienced Arnold realized that to win a war one side must "try and kill as many men and destroy as much property as you can. If you can get mechanical machines to do this, then you are saving lives at the outset."[56] At this point, though willing to try nonprecision methods on occasion, Arnold realized that technology had not surpassed the abilities of manned bombers in accuracy or guile for accomplishing that mission.[57]

Back to Buck Rogers

Having established and tested his working pattern, General Arnold began actively planning for the future of airpower. NACA methodology under George Lewis left Arnold feeling let down, particularly in the field of advanced aircraft research.[58] And although Wright Field had been vital to AAF production research and problem solving, personnel shortages made long-range studies a simple impossibility. Additionally, Arnold said he was irritated with the Materiel Division engineers' no-can-do attitude. Perhaps frustrated was a better description. Arnold once told a gathering of Materiel Division engineers "I wish some of you would get in and help me row this boat. I can't do it alone."[59] Finally, any request for formal assistance from Vannevar Bush—now chief of the Office of Scientific Research and Development (OSRD), even though it and its predecessor the National Defense Research Committee (NDRC) had played a vital role in weapons development during the war, particularly with radar and the atomic bomb—was not an option for Arnold. Bush's attitude toward the JATO Project had proven to Arnold that, although an excellent electrical engineer, Bush was no visionary. Bush once told Major Keirn, "Whittle" liaison officer, that the AAF "would be further along with the jet engine had the NDRC been brought into the jet engine business," sarcastically adding, "but who am I to argue with Hap Arnold."[60] The general and the OSRD chief held widely different views concerning military involvement in R&D. Bush believed that the military should be excluded from any type of research other than production R&D. Arnold was adamant in the belief that long-term R&D also required military input lest the civilian world drive the development and implementation of airpower doctrine and policy. Their personal differences likely began to develop during 1938 and 1939 when Bush held the reins at the NACA and Arnold served on its executive committee. It appeared that they just did not like each other.

Over the years, Arnold and Bush had come in contact while serving as members of the NACA and while working NDRC/OSRD affairs during the war. It was during these years that Arnold was introduced to Bush's views on civilian science and its relationship to military affairs. Bush believed that the highly technical nature of the World War II environment required the efforts of scientists and engineers to ensure ultimate military victory. So did Arnold. Bush realized that the backbone of American R&D was nestled in the armed services and their laboratories. So did Arnold. Unfortunately, during times of national emergency, Bush concluded that the military was forced to concentrate on production research as opposed to basic research. Although not "forced" into this, it was the choice General Arnold had made. In fact, many of Dr. Bush's ideas were similar to those Arnold had supported during the early war years. The friction that developed between these two men was rooted in Bush's views on civilian versus military control of long-term military R&D.[61]

In 1942, for instance, Bush had recommended the formation of a group to supersede the War Production Board that included "research people" having the authority to alter war production plans. This meant, of course, that the military might have to abdicate some measure of control over its doctrine (as reflected in the production decisions made by Bush's scientists). Further, Bush advocated formation of an independent civilian group of scientists and engineers to screen scientific ideas prior to any military involvement or implementation. "I feel sure," Bush said, "that new and valuable ideas are much more likely to come to fruition if they can develop their formative stages among groups of independent scientists and engineers *before* being subjected to the rigors of military association [emphasis added]."[62] What this meant, in short, was that after scientists filtered ideas, only those that they felt had merit would be passed along to military planners. In essence, Bush, as leading scientific advisor to the president, would have had a personal hand in directing military doctrine and planning. The idea that a civilian scientist, outside the boundaries of the military establishment, would hold such power was unacceptable to Arnold as well as other military leaders, particularly those in the Navy.

Bush's ideas for control of military R&D were not a secret. In fact, during the war he pressed so hard for acceptance of those ideas that Jerome Hunsaker, his closest working companion from MIT, cautioned him against continued attempts to force the issue of civilian "filtering" prior to military input. Hunsaker believed that the Army and Navy "would develop resistance of a vigorous nature" to squelch these concepts. To diffuse any possibility of conflict, Hunsaker, after admitting that he did not see how Bush's scheme could work, offered several options for future consideration concerning scientific advice in the decision-making process. "My advice," Hunsaker ultimately wrote, "is to let this matter rest for the present and not bring it up before your Council until something clear and specific can be presented for discussion."[63] Despite this advice, Bush remained a "separatist" concerning inputs from military leadership into the path for military R&D. These views effectively prevented him from having any serious impact on the future of Army Air Forces planning in any form.

Most of the research problems Arnold addressed during the war were related to the immediate needs of the AAF. The "Whittle" jet engine problem was, perhaps, the only exception. Arnold likely justified the project based on his acquisition of British plans and hardware that, essentially, brought the Air Forces up to speed with the rest of the world. While dealing with these short-term research problems, which always involved available technologies, Arnold had formed strong opinions about the major participants in the American scientific and research communities. Lack of faith in the NACA, exasperation with Wright Field, and the incompatibility of OSRD/NDRC philosophy with Arnold's convictions convinced him that, if he were to have an effective long-term plan for the AAF, an independent expert panel of free-thinking civilian scientists given initial direction by the AAF was the only answer. As he had said in different ways on several occasions, the future of American air supremacy depended on the brains and efforts of engineers and scientists.

Now that the European war was winding down and the air war was definitely won, Arnold once again turned his thoughts to the distant future of the Air Force. His call to action came in the form of a memo from an old friend and supporter of airpower, Gen George C. Marshall. On 26 July 1944, Marshall wrote, "The AAF should now assume responsibility for research, development, and development procurement."[64] The impatient General Arnold saw an immediate opportunity to act. Arnold had already decided that America's leading aeronautical scientist, Theodore von Kármán, whom he had known and trusted since the early 1930s, was the man he needed at the head of the Army Air Forces Long Range Development Program.[65]

Notes

1. Henry H. Arnold, *Global Mission* (New York: Harper and Brothers, 1949), 152–53; Herman S. Wolk, *Planning and Organizing the Post-War Air Force, 1943–1947* (Washington, D.C.: Office of Air Force History, 1984), 12–15.

2. Wolk, 20–31.

3. "Report of Special Board Appointed to Make Up a Balanced Air Program," 5 August 1936, Air Force Historical Research Agency (AFHRA), 145.93-96; see also Herman S. Wolk, 12–20.

4. Brig Gen H. H. Arnold, assistant chief of the Air Corps, address to the Western Aviation Planning Conference, 23 September 1937, AFHRA, 168.3952-119. This belief in research may have been the result of earlier association with Dr. Robert Millikan. In 1934, Millikan had warned military officials through the executive Scientific Advisory Board, established in the summer of 1933, that "research is a peace-time thing and . . . moves too slowly to be done after you get into trouble." Quoted in Michael S. Sherry, *Preparing for the Next War: American Plans for Postwar Defense, 1941–45* (New Haven: Yale University Press, 1977), 123.

5. Richard P. Hallion, *Legacy of Flight: The Guggenheim Contribution to American Aviation* (Seattle: University of Washington Press, 1977). This book summarizes the entire story of the Guggenheim influence on the early years of American aviation.

6. Henry H. Arnold, "Air Lessons from Current Wars," address, Bond Club, Philadelphia, Pa., 25 March 1938. Arnold emphasized the foundations of airpower as not just planes but also "the number of flyers, mechanics, and skilled artisans available . . . and the size and character of the ground establishments we lump under the general name 'air bases.'" Ira C. Eaker Papers, Library of Congress, Washington, D.C., box 58, Arnold Speeches. Hereafter cited as Eaker Papers.

7. Michael S. Sherry, *The Rise of American Air Power: The Creation of Armageddon* (New Haven: Yale University Press, 1987), 200–201.

8. Maurer Maurer, *Aviation in the US Army, 1919–1939* (Washington, D.C.: Office of Air Force History, 1987), 319–43.

9. Henry H. Arnold to Oscar Westover, letter, 18 May 1937, Murray Green Collection (MGC), Library of Congress, box 55. For a list of the NACA

projects, see the NACA Executive Meeting Minutes, National Archives Annex, College Park, Md.

10. Michael H. Gorn, *Universal Man: Theodore von Kármán's Life in Aeronautics* (Washington, D.C.: Smithsonian Institution Press, 1992), 84. Eaker verified that Arnold and his staff reviewed intelligence reports on the air battles of the Spanish Civil War. One of Arnold's 1938 speeches covered the Civil War in great detail and concentrated on the uses of airpower. Ira C. Eaker, transcript of oral history interview, 19 October 1978, Oral Interview Series, US Air Force Academy (USAFA), Colo.

11. Maj Gen H. H. Arnold, chief of the Air Corps, "A Message from the Chief to the Corps," 30 September 1938, National Air and Space Museum (NASM) Archives, Arnold Folder, Washington, D.C. This message was Arnold's first as chief following Westover's death.

12. Theodore von Kármán and Lee Edson, *The Wind and Beyond: Theodore von Kármán, Pioneer in Aviation and Pathfinder in Space* (Boston: Little, Brown and Co., 1967), 243; Kármán, oral history interview by D. Shaughnessy, 27 January 1960, USAFA Special Collections, 2.

13. There are detailed accounts of this meeting in the Robert Millikan Collection, Library of Congress, Washington, D.C., 9.15 (roll number 10). In a letter from Mason to Arnold, 5 January 1939, Mason summed up the results of the NAS meeting of the "longhairs."

14. Arnold, *Global Mission*, 165–66; see Sherry, *The Rise of American Air Power*, 186–88.

15. Charles Lindbergh to Henry H. Arnold, letter, 29 November 1938, AFHRA, 16865–40.

16. Wesley Frank Craven and James Lea Cate, eds., *The Army Air Forces in World War II*, vol. 6, *Men and Planes* (1955; new imprint, Washington, D.C.: Office of Air Force History, 1983), 178–80.

17. Leonard S. Reich, "From the *Spirit of St. Louis* to the SST: Charles Lindbergh, Technology, and Environment," *Technology and Culture*, April 1995, 365–67; see also Robert E. Herzstein, *Roosevelt and Hitler: Prelude to War* (New York: Paragon House, 1989), 226–31; and Jeffery S. Underwood, *Wings of Democracy: The Influence of Air Power on the Roosevelt Administration, 1933–1941* (College Station, Tex.: Texas A&M University Press, 1991), 111.

18. Charles A. Lindbergh, *Charles A. Lindbergh: Autobiography of Values* (New York: Harcourt Brace Jovanovich, Publishers, 1976), 190–92.

19. Maj Gen H. H. Arnold, "Performance and Development Trends in Military Aircraft and Accessories," speech given before the Society of Automotive Engineers, Detroit, Mich., 11 January 1939, AFHRA, 168.3952-119, 15–16.

20. Arnold to the assistant secretary of war, letter, 2 March 1939, AFHRA, 167.8-33.

21. NACA Letterhead, 1938, Kármán Collection; and NACA Executive Committee Meeting Minutes, National Archives, College Park Annex, College

Park, Md. Arnold served on the Executive (Main) Committee from October 1938 to April 1946.

22. Arnold's detailed comments are in response to a news article critical of Air Force leadership during the war. Arnold feared that the hostile tone might influence funding in the Congress and warned Spaatz to read it carefully. Arnold to Spaatz, letter, 9 November 1946, St. Francis College, Spaatz Papers, box 256.

23. H. H. Arnold and Ira C. Eaker, *Winged Warfare* (New York: Harper & Brothers, 1941), 239. Arnold summed up what would become his wartime R&D philosophy, "Sacrifice some quality to get sufficient quantity to supply all fighting units. Never follow the mirage, looking for the perfect airplane, to a point where fighting squadrons are deficient in numbers of fighting planes."

24. Gen Lauris Norstad, transcript of oral history interview, AFHRA, K239.0512-1116. By 1944, America was producing over 120,000 airplanes per year.

25. Message, Franklin D. Roosevelt, "Fifty Thousand Airplanes," to a joint session of Congress, 16 May 1940. Reprinted in Eugene Emme's, *The Impact of Airpower: National Security and World Politics* (Princeton, N.J.: D. Van Norstrand Co., Inc., 1959), 69–72; also H. H. Arnold, "The New Army Air Force," *Army Magazine*, 29 July 1940, AFHRA, 168.3952-122, 1939–1940. For a more detailed look at the lessons that might have been learned after the First World War, see I. B. Holley, *Ideas and Weapons: Exploitation of the Aerial Weapon by the United States During World War I; A Study in the Relationship of Technological Advance, Military Doctrine, and the Development of Weapons* (1953; new imprint, Washington, D.C.: Office of Air Force History, 1983), chapter IX.

26. Arnold to Frank M. Andrews, letter, 22 January 1941, Frank M. Andrews Papers, Library of Congress, Washington, D.C., box 1, corr. A. Hereafter cited as Andrews Papers.

27. Arnold to Andrews, letter, 29 March 1943, Andrews Papers, box 1, corr. A.

28. Arnold to Eaker, letter, 8 August 1943, Eaker Papers, box 50. "The more I think of our recent interchange of messages regarding German countermeasures against your bomber formations, the more I am convinced that you should have on your staff a free thinking technical man who is not tied down with current logistics, current modifications, and current procedure in any way. This man's main mission in life should be to sit there and weigh the information received . . . then advise you what action should be taken by you to outsmart the Germans. . . . This technician should also have a staff of two or three more scientists who would help him diagnose German moves and the motives behind them. At this writing, I have nobody in mind at all for this long-haired technical job, but if you think well of the plan I will rake up somebody and send him over to you, and I will also send the assistant scientists to sit there and help him." This philosophy carried over into his directions to Kármán's mission in the fall of 1944.

29. Clark B. Millikan and Homer Joe Stewart, "Aerodynamic Analysis of Take-Off and Initial Climb as Affected by Auxiliary Jet Propulsion," 14 January 1941, original report in the custody of Dr. Homer Joe Stewart, Alta Dena, Calif.

30. Dr. Homer Joe Stewart, interviewed by author, 21 July 1995, Alta Dena, Calif.

31. Stewart interview. Dr. Durand had been named chairman of the Jet Propulsion Committee on 24 March 1941. This committee, instigated by Arnold and created by Vannevar Bush, the NACA Main Committee chairman, became known as the Durand Board. See Alex Roland, *Model Research: the National Advisory Committee for Aeronautics, 1915–1958,* vol. 1 (Washington, D.C.: Scientific and Technical Information Branch, National Aeronautics and Space Administration [NASA], 1985), 189.

32. Stewart interview. Dr. Stewart confirmed the JATO story told in Kármán's autobiography, except to correct the fact that Boushey was a captain, not a lieutenant; Kármán and Edson, 249–51; photos from the JPL archives in Pasadena revealed the safety poster sayings.

33. The story of why America did not develop the jet engine earlier may be traced to its tendency toward utilitarian uses for "science." The story, a fascinating study in the evolution of American science, is expertly covered by Edward W. Constant II, *The Origins of the Turbojet Revolution* (Baltimore: Johns Hopkins University Press, 1980).

34. Charles Lindbergh to Arnold, letter, 29 November 1938, AFHRA, 16865-40.

35. John F. Victory, oral history interview, number 210A, October 1962, USAFA Oral Interviews, USAFA, Colorado Springs, Colo. Victory was the first employee of the NACA in 1915 and served as secretary throughout the period of this study.

36. Victory interview. The story is too long to reproduce but, essentially, Lewis sat at his desk in Washington and strictly adhered to the "advisory mission" of NACA. It was rare that the NACA offered to expedite research or offer data without being asked by the Army Air Corps first. Arnold certainly saw this attitude as an obstacle to rapidly expanding the size and capability of the air arm; Hugh L. Dryden, oral history interview, Columbia University Oral History Review (CUOHR), MGC, 23. Dr. Dryden substantiates the basis of the 500-MPH story.

37. Vannevar Bush to Jerome C. Hunsaker, 10 March 1941, Bush Papers, box 53, Hunsaker Folder, Library of Congress.

38. Maj Gen Frank Carroll, interviewed by Murray Green, 1 September 1971, Boulder, Colo., transcript in MGC, roll 12; also James O. Young, "Riding England's Coattails: The U.S. Army Air Forces and the Turbojet Revolution" (Edwards Air Force Base [AFB], Calif.: Air Force Flight Test Center History Office, 1995).

39. Maj Gen Donald J. Keirn, interviewed by Murray Green, 25 September 1970, Delaplane, Va., transcript in MGC, roll 12. Keirn proves

that there were two separate engine projects at GE at the same time; see also Roland, for Durand Committee discussion.

40. Gen Benjamin Chidlaw, interviewed by Murray Green, 12 December 1969, Colorado Springs, Colo., transcript in MGC, roll 12. The question of why the United States was so late entering the jet age is expertly examined in Constant II, 150–75 in particular. He cites the American tradition of empiricism as the reason that "radical" technologies were not produced ahead of more theoretically oriented countries like Germany and England.

41. Lt Gen Laurence Craigie, interviewed by Murray Green, 19 August 1970, Burbank, Calif., transcript in MGC, roll 12. Additional information on the "Whittle" can be found in the Arnold Collection, Library of Congress, box 47. Walt Bonney, representing Bell Aircraft Corporation, was tasked to answer a flood of calls which resulted after the *Washington Post* story was released on 7 January 1944. In his press release he emphasized the total secrecy of the project beginning in September 1941. Bonney did write a brief history of jet propulsion to placate the mass inquiries, but the secret nature of jet propulsion was protected. Walt Bonney, Bell Aircraft Corporation, 11 January 1944, NASM Archives, Jet Propulsion Folder. Arnold's, "Second Report of the Commanding General of the Army Air Forces to the Secretary of War," 27 February 1945, AFHRA, 168.03, tells the story from his perspective. "Never has a plane been built in this country under greater secrecy," 76; also Young; also Ezra Kotcher, "Our Jet Propelled Fighter," *Air Force,* March 1944, 6–8, 64.

42. Gen Laurence Craigie, USAF, Retired, and Gen Franklin Carroll, USAF, Retired, interviewed by Murray Green, MGC. Craven and Cate mistakenly state that Craigie was first to fly the jet; also see Daniel Ford, "Gentlemen, I Give You the Whittle Engine," *Air and Space,* October/November 1992, 88–98.

43. Roger E. Bilstein, *Orders of Magnitude: A History of the NACA and NASA, 1915–1990* (Washington, D.C.: NASA, 1989), 31–48; Roland, vol. 1, 191–192; also Dryden, CUOHR.

44. "U. S. Making Rocket War Plane," *Washington Post,* 7 January 1944, 1.

45. Maj Gen H. H. Arnold, "Performance and Development Trends in Military Aircraft and Accessories," speech given before the Society of Automotive Engineers, Detroit, Mich., 11 January 1939, 14. AFHRA, 168.3952-119.

46. Young, 12.

47. Laurence S. Kuter, "How Hap Arnold Built the AAF," *Air Force Magazine* 56, no. 9 (September 1973): 88–93.

48. F. W. Conant, CUOHR, in MGC. Conant worked for Donald Douglas during this period. Not to be confused with James B. Conant of MIT.

49. Brig Gen Godfrey McHugh, interviewed by Murray Green, 21 April 1970, Washington, D.C., transcript in MGC; Colonel F. Lyon to Arnold, letter, September 1941, in MGC ref: Arnold Papers, box 43, Library of Congress; Maj Gen Frank Carroll, interviewed by Murray Green, 1 September 1971, Boulder, Colo., transcript in MGC, roll 12; Arnold

interview with T. A. Boyd, range was a major factor in determining which weapons or aircraft to build. The problems for Germany, at least in home defense, did not involve worries about range; and Ford, 88–98.

50. Wesley Frank Craven and James Lea Cate, eds., *The Army Air Forces in World War II*, vol. 1, *Plans and Early Operations, January 1939 to August 1942* (1955; new imprint, Washington, D.C.: Office of Air Force History, 1983), 550.

51. Arnold to Spaatz, letter, 9 November 1946, Spaatz Papers, Library of Congress, box 256; Stimson Diaries, 1 April 1942, in MGC, roll 12, documents Bowles's assignment as special consultant; Spaatz to Arnold, letter, 1 September 1944; Arnold to Spaatz, letter, 12 September 1944, in MGC, roll 12; Arnold to Oscar M. Westover, letter, 18 May 1937, in MGC.

52. Arnold to Kettering, letter, 3 November 1939, reprinted in MGC, 638. This letter marked the beginning of controllable missile development which included powered and nonpowered bombs and missiles of all kinds; Arnold to Spaatz, letter, n.d., in MGC ref: Spaatz Papers, Library of Congress, box 8, record MM. "Obviously, this is an area weapon," Arnold wrote; Brig Gen Oscar Anderson, memorandum to George Stratemeyer, 2 April 1943, in MGC ref: Arnold Papers, box 137; also Craven and Cate, vol. 6, 253–62.

53. Lt Gen Henry Viccellio Jr., interviewed by Murray Green, 13 May 1970, San Antonio, Tex.; Arnold to Kenney, letter, 25 October 1944; Arnold's War Diary, October 1944–December 1945, Library of Congress. For a summary of Crossbow and Allied countermeasures, see Wesley Frank Craven and James Lea Cate, vol. 3, *Europe: Argument to V-E Day, January 1944 to May 1945* (1955; new imprint, Washington, D.C.: Office of Air Force History, 1983), 525–46. In Jacob Neufeld's, *Ballistic Missiles in the United States Air Force 1945–1960* (Washington, D.C.: Office of Air Force History, 1990). It is pointed out that Navy Lt Joseph P. Kennedy Jr. was killed while flying a Weary Willie mission, 10.

54. Lt Gen Fred Dean, interviewed by Murray Green, 20 February 1973, Hilton Head, S.C., transcript in MGC, roll 12; Arnold to Spaatz, letter, 22 November 1944, reprinted in MGC, roll 12.

55. Arnold Staff Memo, 2 November 1944, Arnold Papers, box 44, Library of Congress; Arnold to Spaatz, letter, 22 November 1944, in MGC, roll 12. To clarify the different "Willy" projects, "Weary Willy" aircraft were flown to the enemy battle lines, then the pilot set the automatic pilot and bailed out in friendly territory. "Willy Orphan" was totally radio controlled and was remotely launched and guided into enemy territory sometimes from a mother ship which followed it to enemy territory. Aphrodite was also totally radio controlled, normally from the ground.

56. Arnold, Bowles, Ridenour, telephone transcript, 9 August 1944, in MGC, roll 12.

57. The circular error probable for bombs dropped during World War II during American daylight missions was 3,200 feet for a 2,000 pound bomb. During Desert Storm, CEP for the same size bomb using precision guidance

was three meters for over 80 percent of the bombs dropped. Dr. Richard P. Hallion, Air Force historian, interviewed by author, 28 August 1995.

58. Roland, vol. 1, 192. Arnold did not give up on NACA altogether. In 1944 he pressured Donald Marr Nelson to push the construction of the Jet Engine Facility in Cleveland, Ohio. This facility became the test center for the engines that Arnold had kept secret in earlier years. Ironically, the facility was named after George Lewis, the research director most directly responsible for Arnold and Kármán's distrust.

59. Grandison Gardner, CUOHR, 11–13, 33. Gardner refers to Arnold's hesitation to use Wright Field engineers for important projects. Tactical research was even taken away from Wright Field and moved to Eglin AFB under command of Gardner for this very reason; also see Lt Gen Donald L. Putt, oral history interview by J. C. Hasdorff, 1–3 April 1974, Atherton, Calif. AFHRA, K239.0512-724, 24.

60. Maj Gen Donald J. Keirn, interviewed by Murray Green, 25 September 1970, Delaplane, Va., transcript in MGC, roll 12.

61. Vannevar Bush, "Organization of Defense Research," as sent to Harry Hopkins, 3 March 1941, Vannevar Bush Papers, General Correspondence, box 51, H. Hopkins Folder, Library of Congress, Washington, D.C. Vannevar Bush had been involved in conflicts with the military services before. Specifically, he had butted heads with Naval Vice Adm Harold G. Bowen, and in that case, had forced Bowen's removal from his position. Harvey M. Saplosky, *Science and the Navy: The History of the Office of Naval Research* (Princeton: Princeton University Press, 1990), 17–18.

62. Vannevar Bush, "Research and the War Effort," speech to the American Institute of Electrical Engineers, New York, 26 January 1943. Bush Papers, General Correspondence, box 174.

63. Jerome Hunsaker to Vannevar Bush, letter, 24 March 1942, Bush Papers, General Correspondence, box 53.

64. Marshall to Arnold and Gen Brehon B. Somervell, Army Services of Supply commander, letter, 26 July 1944, in MGC, roll 12.

65. Getting, interviewed by author, 9 November 1994. Dr. Getting believed that Arnold had consulted Dr. Edward Bowles before deciding upon Kármán to head the SAG. Arnold respected Bowles' opinion and had been impressed by this work on the SADU. He trusted his views on the direction for science and technology for the Air Force. Getting, however, gives too much credit to Bowles. This is understandable considering his World War II RADLAB association with Dr. Bowles.

Chapter 4

The European Influence

Theodore von Kármán

Near Budapest, Hungary, in the spring of 1881 von Sköllöskislaki Kármán Todor was born to Helen and Maurice von Kármán. Todor, "gift of God," was the couple's third healthy son and soon demonstrated remarkable mental skills marking him as the brightest of their offspring. Helen, who carried the bloodline of many gifted scientists, and Maurice, adept at social matters, offered a rich family backdrop during Todor's formative years. At age six, Todor showed off for visitors by multiplying six-digit numbers in his head with the speed of a present-day calculator. At 16, Todor was awarded the Eötvös Prize as the finest mathematics and science student in all of Hungary.[1] This was only the beginning of an academic, scientific, and engineering career which would have few equals in the first half of the twentieth century.

In the early 1900s, after a very successful secondary school life, Kármán took up studies with Professor Ludwig Prandtl, noted expert in fluid mechanics, at the Göttingen Mathematical Institute. Göttingen, steeped in German traditional education practices which separated teachers and students as well as theory from application, stifled Todor's social and mental spirit. He had become accustomed to the café lifestyle of Budapest and in 1908, bereft of motivation and money, he traveled to Paris; a journey which transformed his life. In March 1908, the daughter of a close friend, divorced and a likely love interest, dragged the young professor to an early morning aerial demonstration at a Paris airstrip. The flight he witnessed was performed by a craft which appeared like a "box kite made of sticks, wood and paper," and it intrigued him. From that moment, Kármán dedicated himself to the infant science of aeronautics—a different kind of fluid dynamics.[2] Following his new-found interest in the wind (or 'vind' as he pronounced it), Theodore von Kármán moved to Aachen, Germany, where he became the director of the Aachen Aeronautical Institute.

First Lieutenant Kármán served in the Austro-Hungarian Army during World War I.

Little, Brown and Co.

After only three short years at Aachen, Professor von Kármán found himself in the midst of World War I. In the summer of 1915, while German armies enjoyed success on the Eastern front, Kármán assumed the post of Director of Research of the Austro-Hungarian Aviation Corps at an aircraft factory near Vienna. At his post he did pioneering work on helicopters, machine gun/propeller synchronization, and fuel tank protection. This was his first real contact with military officials and air operations.[3]

After the war, Kármán was persuaded to serve as Minister of Education in the Károlyi government, a progressive, democratic regime. Count Mihely Károlyi sympathized with western ideas but could not hold power after harsh territorial terms were levied against Hungary. It was not long before the radical, Communist Béla Kun government took control, from

Little, Brown and Co.

Among other aeronautical projects, he made significant progress in the development of a "captive observation helicopter."

March to August 1919. Kármán succeeded in enacting several major educational reforms in the Hungarian system in this short period of time, most of which had been initiated under the Károlyi government. But he soon lost interest in government service after witnessing the harsh backlash of terrorism instituted during the brief administration of Adm Nicholas Horthy, which included the torture and execution of peasants, workers, and Jews. Béla Kun's hasty exit from the scene, and the turmoil which followed, convinced the young professor that his previous job at Aachen, not a political career, held the best opportunity for his continued aeronautical research. In the early autumn of 1919, after he was assured that his Aachen position was still available, Kármán moved to Vaals, Holland, a small village near the institute just across the German border. His mother and sister followed in 1921.[4]

During the early 1920s, Kármán rebuilt the aeronautical laboratory at the institute which had suffered five years of neglect and misuse during the war. His pioneering work on the nature of turbulence quickly surpassed Prandtl's and thereby raised the status of his laboratory and its experimental work. By building on the work of his mentor, Kármán established a rivalry between his institute and Göttingen which grew in intensity until Kármán's departure in 1930. From 1922 to 1924, Kármán hosted international conferences and held festive teaching sessions during which he advocated practical applications of what most German academics considered "pure science" at his home in Vaals. Both of these activities drew frowns from more traditional academics who still held to strict separation of student/ teacher relationships as well as the purity of the "formula" itself. By the mid-1920s, even Prandtl demonstrated these tendencies by withholding Kármán's name from a promotion list because of his Jewish/Hungarian ancestry.

By 1926, the Aachen Institute had reached the pinnacle of its potential within the German educational system. Enrollment had approached its apogee and could never have surpassed Göttingen which received greater state subsidies and, traditionally, enrolled the children of a great percentage of Germany's elite families. Uncontrolled inflation had eaten away at budgets and enrollment countrywide, but Aachen suffered disproportionately because of the lack of state support and influential familial attendance.[5]

American Opportunity

While Kármán's world was slowly disintegrating at Aachen, the scene in American aeronautics showed great promise. The Guggenheim Fund had begun selecting schools to receive significant aeronautical department stipends. The Guggenheims, both Harry and his son Daniel, "wanted to make aviation practical, safe, and of great value to the commercial development of this country."[6] Initially, these schools were concentrated on America's east coast. But after a diligent, well-argued case was made by Robert Millikan, Caltech also appeared on the list of seven universities which were to launch American aeronautics into competition with the Europeans.[7] The key to Millikan's case was Theodore von Kármán and his methodology. Although Harry Guggenheim himself favored Prandtl, Millikan was convinced that the younger, more vibrant and practical Kármán was a more appropriate addition to the Pasadena scene.[8]

Robert Millikan had been commissioned into the Army Signal Corps during World War I as the chief of the Science and Research Division. During this period, Millikan met Colonel Arnold who was serving as, among other things, assistant director of the Office of Military Aeronautics in Washington.[9] After the war, Millikan took the chairmanship of the Caltech Executive Council in 1921 (university president). His goals were to thrust Caltech science programs to national preeminence and to bring aviation interest and industry to southern California.[10] Millikan believed that science, "knowledge of the facts, the laws, and the process of nature," was vital to American destiny as long as it was applied properly to practical uses, such as aviation. Others held similar beliefs but it was Millikan, supported by Guggenheim Foundation money, who accelerated the building-up process at Caltech.[11] Daniel Guggenheim himself took an interest in Caltech, Millikan, and the possibility of luring a notable European away from the Continent. By 1926, Millikan had convinced Kármán to visit Caltech.

Even before informing the Guggenheims that Kármán was the first choice for the Caltech position, Millikan had begun what evolved into a lengthy courtship with the soft-spoken Hungarian scientist. Intrigued by the offer to visit Caltech, Kármán accepted a $4,000 stipend which Millikan had offered to act as a consultant for the new GALCIT wind tunnel, still in the planning stages. The money was more than many faculty at Caltech made in one year, indicating the seriousness which Millikan placed upon landing Kármán at the Pasadena school. In light of the financial problems facing German institutions, it was impossible for Kármán to refuse the opportunity. Over the stiff protest of his aging mother, Helen, Kármán, and his little sister, Pipö, set out to America in the early summer of 1926. Helen von Kármán was convinced that America was a haven for Europe's criminals and societal dregs and could not be convinced otherwise. Kármán had earlier committed to a trip to Japan and in an effort to escape that obligation, he doubled his consultation fee to $4,500 ($750/month). The Kawanishi Machinery Company didn't flinch at the demand and Kármán revised his arrival date to early in 1927, accommodating both opportunities. In 10 months, Kármán would earn nearly four times his annual salary at Aachen.[12]

After paying an introductory visit to the Guggenheim Mansion in New York, the Jewish-Hungarian professor and Pipö traveled to California by rail. For the next two months, Kármán modified the design which had been drafted by Millikan's son, Clark, and Professor Arthur L. "Maj" Klein, a young but impressive aeronautics faculty member. Kármán radically changed the tunnel design in structure, layout, and capability. The most significant advancement was placing the motor inside the tunnel, near the wind-producing propeller. This maximized efficiency by utilizing a short drive shaft, characteristic of the newest European wind tunnels. With the design complete and accepted by Robert Millikan over the design of his own staff, Kármán saw little reason to remain at Caltech any longer that fall. Tunnel construction would be well handled from then on by Caltech faculty members. Although Kármán continued acting as tunnel consultant, his function as the brains behind the concept had concluded. It was time for the young professor to move on. He traveled back east where he delivered several lectures at other Guggenheim schools; MIT and New York University (NYU), as well as the NACA and even for the Army Air Corps (AAC). His NACA speech must have had bittersweet impact as Max Munk, a fellow Prandtlite, had just been fired by George Lewis, the Aeronautical Research Director. Then he delivered Pipö to her ship bound for France. He traveled to Japan, arriving in January, to complete his obligation to the Kawanishi Company.[13]

In Kobe, Japan, Kawanishi representatives, aware of Kármán's strenuous travel schedule, had arranged for a minivacation at a Japanese resort hotel. Surrounded by excellent food, lovely women, and plenty of time to relax Kármán enjoyed this well-deserved interlude. By mid-January he was hard at work helping in the modification of yet another wind tunnel, this time for the Japanese. He appeared to have a particular fondness for Japanese culture and Japanese women. His photo album retained a large number of snapshots of his acquaintances, while his house (in Pasadena at least) was loaded with Japanese trappings and furniture.[14] While in Japan, he designed the first wind tunnel which was useful in Japanese airplane design. The Kawanishi Company had become an important manufacturer of Japanese World War II aircraft. Once again, in characteristic style, Kármán did not remain in Japan to see the wind tunnel project to its completion. He left in the late spring and returned to Aachen. Kármán had planted the seeds for improving Japanese wind tunnel design just as he had done over the years in Germany and more recently at Caltech.[15] His reputation as a project initiator was well developed by the time he arrived permanently in the US.

Although enthusiastic enough in 1926 to accept part-time research associate status, Kármán did not immediately commit to a move. For the next two years, Kármán divided his time between Caltech and Aachen. During this period, the young Hungarian began to feel the uneasy squeeze of German social and political upheaval. He had been abandoned to a certain degree by his former professor, Ludwig Prandtl, in the early 1920s. The situation had not improved by 1928. There were too many Jewish, non-German professors employed in Germany already. Hyperinflation had also lessened the financial support which the institution retained and enrollment continued to drop. Even Aachen showed little promise for great advancement and Kármán, despite protests from his mother, began to talk of a move west.[16]

Other incidents troubled Kármán in these years of radical changes in Germany. On one occasion, the professor was driving back home to his village in Holland. The street which crossed the German border had been blockaded, preventing his easy return. This condition existed for several days. One day, a heavy rain had made the road very slick and Kármán, not totally used to driving his new "Buick," slid helplessly into the wooden barrier. Surrounded by a quartet of German soldiers, Kármán was told that not only must he pay the fine for breaching the gate but also offer reparations for the damaged materials. "Instead of having to pay you," Kármán loudly announced, "you should pay me. I have abolished a needless barrier between two friendly nations."[17] This incident summarized both the attraction and the revulsion of Kármán's institute. Kármán supported international cooperation on matters of science and because of that view enrolled many foreign students in his aeronautical programs at Aachen. The diversity of the student body did not restrict the resultant appearance of nationalistic or anti-Semitic views. The academic leadership at Göttingen definitely did not favor such extra-Germanic relations.

On another occasion, one of the professor's most dedicated students appeared at work with a swastika adorning his jacket. Kármán called the graduate student to his office where he reminded him that citizens of a "civilized nation like Germany" did not wear those symbols, particularly since they were offensive to others. The student, ashamed, removed the insignia. The blanket of anti-Semitism spread beyond the student body. A Jewish student had been indicted by a campus fraternity on a particular matter. The report from the organization began, "Mr. _____, Hungarian Semite." While the hearing before the University Senate continued, some faculty members had agreed that the infraction had earned the abuses. Kármán questioned the right of the fraternity to tag the student by his origin as had been done. "I must ask whether in the German Republic, where there is an equality of races, is it right for a student fraternity to designate a student by his origin." The senate agreed that the indictment was anti-Semitic as well as nationalistic and chastised the fraternity for its approach to the problem. Kármán noted later, "At that time the majority of the Senate were still reasonable. A year later, the climate changed."[18]

By the end of 1928, Millikan had formally asked Kármán to move to Caltech as the full-time director of the GALCIT. His salary was to be $10,000 each year coupled with complete control of the laboratory, its function, and its entire budget. Added to the deal, in the spring of 1929, was the directorship of the Daniel Guggenheim Airship Institute in Akron, Ohio, which provided an additional $2,000 each year in salary for minimal consulting work which could be accomplished from

Caltech. Incidentally, this position was awarded to Kármán by Harry Guggenheim himself, over the head of the University of Akron's president, George F. Zook. Zook's first choice had been professor Jerome C. Hunsaker of MIT and the Goodyear-Zeppelin Corporation. These enticements were enough for Kármán but not for his mother and sister who strenuously protested the possibility of a move. But political events and social changes eventually convinced even Helen and Pipö that the Germany they once knew was now evolving out of control.[19]

In the summer of 1929, it was apparent that the political and social climate in Germany had irrevocably changed. The Aachen Institute had agreed to hold a symposium exploring the new science of supersonic aerodynamics. The details had been arranged two years before, while Kármán was in Kobe, Japan. The gathering of 70 notable scientists was to occur, by chance, on the "Day of Shame," the anniversary of the signing of the Treaty of Versailles, 28 June. One of the Aachen student associations found out that five visiting scientists were to be vested with honorary degrees. These men represented, unfortunately, countries which had fought against Germany in the First World War. Without a word to Kármán, the rector struck out the honorary degree ceremony from the program. In a rare fit of anger, Kármán denounced the rector in front of the senate. He implied that students did not make university policy and this occurrence showed how cowardly the rector's solution had been. One of Kármán's colleagues remarked, "You must honor their national feelings." His anger grew. "Students are here to learn," the professor indignantly replied, "not to make politics."[20] Nationalism and anti-Semitism were two political trends which Kármán feared. Perhaps he should have been more compassionate. After all, the Treaty of Trianon, signed one year after Versailles, evoked similar emotional responses in Hungarians who spent many years attempting to regain territory yanked form them by their supposed "friends" after World War I. In any case, Kármán clearly understood the power of nationalism and the possible consequences of uncontrolled nationalistic sentiments.[21]

In October 1929, Kármán finally agreed to Millikan's offer and promised to arrive in Pasadena by the spring of 1930.

Even after the collapse of the American stock market, Kármán's salary and contract provisions were secured and irrevocable. It was an agonizing decision for the professor, which he said had been made for political rather than professional reasons. Hyperinflation had crippled Aachen in the early 1920s. Economically the institute never fully recovered. Unemployment was rapidly rising as a result of the worldwide depression. Anti-Semitism was becoming more overt and German nationalism only compounded its impact. Even professors who had once been close friends and colleagues now were turning away from the "non-German" professor. There was little doubt, however, that despite the changing political climate, Kármán was not in physical danger. Despite his ancestry, his accepted excellence in aeronautics would likely have protected him from direct Nazi persecution. After all, it was Hermann Göring's staff who had queried Kármán about serving in a position as an Air Ministry consultant. It was the Air Marshal himself who once said: "Who is or is not a Jew is up to me to decide."[22]

In addition, the rivalry between Aachen and Göttingen was becoming less competitive because of the disparity in funding and enrollment between the universities. The atmosphere which he had seen in the United States was more than appealing, it was compelling. His salary was to more than triple in real terms. He was to hold total control over two aeronautics laboratories. He was to be the most honored aeronautical professor in the entire country, and it was all to happen immediately. Kármán saw the opportunity to escape the increasingly unpleasant political and social climate of Germany, improve his standard of living, expand his influence in a new world where his methods (both theoretical and practical) were praised rather than belittled. But he also realized that Caltech offered an opportunity to continue the professional rivalry between himself and Prandtl while at the same instant separating himself from his teacher's tremendous European influence. For Kármán it was Caltech or nowhere.[23]

Kármán had summarily declined a job offer from Dr. William Durand of Stanford University in the midst of his first American visit. This was significant because Durand was well respected worldwide as one of America's leading scientists. (In fact, Kármán had insisted that the Guggenheims publish a series of aeronautical texts to be used in all the Guggenheim schools. This six-volume set titled, *Aerodynamic Theory*, was edited by Dr. Durand and is still used today.) The reason he declined the Stanford position seems clear. He had just left an environment where he was "second string" to Prandtl. Clearly, the Stanford job would have placed him in a similar situation. Kármán looked upon Durand with a great deal of respect. In fact, he credited Durand with "bringing about a transition from purely empirical, practical engineering to a physically understood, scientific engineering" in America.[24] His final decision, although made in the face of growing political and social turmoil, allowed a much broader professional influence, an element of the move which Robert Millikan and the Guggenheims continually suggested. "I always had believed," Kármán agreed, "that the goal of my life was to eliminate the gap between scientific theory and application, and I had the impression that it would be a particular challenge to reach this goal in the United States."[25] Additionally, he could not overlook the personal benefits of salary (income tax was only one percent of earnings and Kármán frequently joked about that as the reason for his decision), comfort, or prestige. It would have been difficult for anyone to pass on such an offer.[26]

Practical Applications

Theodore von Kármán had always admired Sir Isaac Newton. Newton was the quintessential theoretical scientist as well as a practical engineer. Not only had Newton postulated the Universal Law of Gravity but had also, for example, designed a footbridge over a river near his alma mater, King's College, in Cambridge, England.[27] Kármán emulated Newton and, throughout his career in aerodynamic theory, maintained a strong interest in the actual engineering of his formulations as well as applications of his work to worldly problems.

Practical applications of Kármán's theories were reflected in a variety of traditionally nonaeronautical projects. Not including the professor's work in theoretical fluid dynamics, he helped redesign the ill-fated Tacoma Narrows Bridge which was destroyed by gusty northwestern winds on 7 November 1940. Kármán also used wind tunnels to study soil erosion and proposed methods of controlling these effects. He made calculations which helped in the construction of dams, most notably the Grand Coulee Dam. To repair cracks which had developed in the dam, Kármán suggested treating the structure like a "thin plate" resembling an aircraft fuselage panel, an approach new to civil engineering. After the suggested "stiffeners" were installed on the dam, the necessary resistance to "buckling stresses" was created, thereby saving the structure. While still in Europe, in an effort to learn more about aeronautics, Kármán had even taken a flying lesson which ended with a crash landing in a potato field.[28]

In fact, it was his application of fluid mechanics coupled with his theoretical understanding of science which impressed Millikan so much. Yet Kármán never believed that theoretical aerodynamics should be sacrificed at the expense of practical applications of the science. Together, knowledge of theory and ingenuity in application were synergistic, inseparable. Clark Millikan, for example, once suggested that Caltech aeronautics be divided into a "scientific" division and a more "applied" division, similar to the system which existed at Göttingen. "But I am not Prandtl," Kármán explained. That division never occurred.[29]

A story best illustrates the Kármán/Millikan professional relationship. Dr. William R. Sears, gifted Kármán student and also a professor at Caltech and Cornell for many years, remembered how Kármán's advice got him his first job at Caltech. In early 1939, Sears had been offered a position on the MIT aeronautics faculty but preferred to stay at Caltech if an opening was available. Sears notified Dr. Millikan of his desires but he required an answer in fairly short order. After a few weeks with no response, Sears called Dr. Millikan's secretary to set up an appointment to discuss the issue. There happened to be an immediate hole in "Old Millikan's" schedule, so Sears dashed from his GALCIT office down the stairs and out the building. There stood Kármán who, in his usual, curious way queried, "Bill, Vere are you going?"

Sears replied, "I'm going over to see Dr. Millikan."

"You vill see Old Millikan? Vhat vill you tell him?"

Sternly Sears explained, "I'm going to tell him that I want to know, right now, whether I am going to be kept here at Caltech to do what I want to do or if I will have to do it at MIT."

Kármán took the cigar out of his pocket, knocked the ashes off a little bit and said, "Ja. But I vould not say in those vords."

"Well what words would you use?" Sears asked.

"Now Bill, you tell Dr. Millikan this: Yes it is true that I am mainly interested in the theoretical aspects of the subject, but I am always guided by the need for applications."

"I can't say THAT!" Sears whined while rolling his eyes. Disappointed, he went to Dr. Millikan's office.

Millikan was seated at his desk and asked Sears to come and sit down. "Now Sears, what is it that you want to do?" Well, Sears told Millikan just what Kármán had suggested and after he had finished, Millikan leaned back in his chair with his fingertips touching and quietly announced, "I think we have a place for you here."[30]

This story emphasizes several important points. First, by the late 1930s, Kármán understood Robert Millikan perfectly. He knew that "Old Millikan's" goals for his institution were linked to commercial, industrial production (jets, wings, rockets, weather measuring devices, etc.). Kármán was also aware that pure scientists had more difficulty learning how to apply their trade to real-world problems. The need for applied scientists was part of Millikan's plan to make Caltech a leader in the national aircraft industry by getting research funding from companies like Boeing, Douglas, and the military.

The major role which Millikan played at Caltech during this time was that of a fund raiser. When possible, Millikan allowed his staff to stray from Caltech as long as there was a payback, in either funding or prestige, at some later time. Millikan's ability to bring in the "kilo-bucks and mega-bucks" was what kept Caltech going in the early years of aviation. Millikan's adroit manipulation and acquisition of staff and funding allowed Caltech's scientists to pursue "cutting edge, frontier issues." Caltech scientists examined supersonic and transonic flight and a small group had even begun pursuits in rocket propulsion by the end of the decade. Kármán, therefore, was not the only one at Caltech who realized the importance of practical applications of scientific theory. In fact, it was Millikan who offered Kármán the GALCIT job based on this very criterion.[31] In the long term it was an offer which benefitted not only Millikan's school but the United States as well.

But Millikan did not stop with Kármán. He enlisted the services of notable scientists throughout the 1930s. Two of these were C. C. Lauritsen, who ushered in the electrical industry to Caltech, and Thomas Hunt Morgan, leading geneticist in the US and eventual Nobel laureate for medicine in 1933. Millikan became a "pied piper" for American scientists assuring the university's success during tough fiscal times.[32] He even convinced Albert Einstein to lecture at Caltech from 1930 to 1932, on an associate basis. Kármán's acquisition, Millikan's Nobel Prize winning reputation, the newest possible facilities, as well as the standing of other academic staff members, over time made Caltech the most vital and most renowned of the Guggenheim-funded schools.[33] For two decades, Kármán served Caltech as the leading figure in aeronautics in America, and it was with Caltech that his loyalties remained strongest throughout his career.

By 1933, Kármán, who had held his position open at Aachen since his departure in 1930, was forced to make a final choice. The new Nazi Ministry of Education informed the professor that his leave of absence would no longer be continued. He was given the choice of resigning or resuming his teaching responsibilities during the following semester. In his resignation letter, he sarcastically and somewhat boastfully wrote, "I hope that you will be able to do for German science in the next years as much as you accomplished in this year for foreign science."[34] His final professional link to Germany was cut.

Loyalty aside, Kármán's varied interests were part of his universal appeal. While such well-knowns as Jerome Hunsaker (former naval aeronautical engineer, chair of MIT's aeronautical engineering department, and NACA member) and Vannevar Bush (chair of the NACA Executive Committee) had shunned jet and rocket engine R&D, Kármán was encouraging the study of "unconventional ideas."[35] Although solving theoretical problems was Kármán's strength, he was not afraid to challenge accepted theory or, when necessary, get his hands dirty during experimental evaluation. On at least one occasion, the professor climbed into his wind tunnel with a handful of modeling clay, and modified an airplane wing root which he suspected of causing high-speed turbulence. The modification became known throughout the world as "Kármáns," small wing fillets which minimized turbulence at high speeds. These wing modifications were vital to the stability of the final version of the Douglas DC-3, one of the world's most successful aircraft. His theories on high speed turbulence were instrumental in the successful penetration of the sound barrier, a barrier many believed would never be broken.[36] It was no accident and a certain irony that Kármán was so widely sought out that he contributed a great deal to aeronautics in Germany, Japan, and the United States. Even while at Caltech, his influence continued throughout the aeronautics world. His 1935 Volta Conference address, which treated the problem of drag in compressible fluids, reinforced the German scientist's ideas for the swept back wing which was incorporated into the eventual development of the ME-262—a project already ahead of the Allies' jet programs.[37]

Never one to believe others without logical evaluation, Kármán also felt that "to be always logical is horrible."[38] His thinking process set him apart from others who supported large working groups as the only avenue to problem solution. Kármán recounted an instance where, during a visit to a Midwestern industrial factory, he noticed a cartoon which defined "Teamwork vs. Individual Effort." In the frame titled "Individual Effort," five jackasses were pulling a bail of hay in five different directions. In the frame titled "Teamwork," were the same five asses pulling the hay in the same direction. Kármán could not help but remark that this illustration "might apply to jackasses but not to scientists." Although he found usefulness in study groups, he believed that individual creativity was often suppressed, sometimes because of the reputations of more respected members of the groups.[39] Essentially, younger members of groups were afraid to speak up for fear of having their own prestige crushed by a more experienced, more highly respected, and sometimes less

111

knowledgeable member. Kármán said, "In the long run I still think that the finest thoughts come not out of organized teams but out of the quiet of one's own world."[40]

A Gifted Teacher

This is not to say that the professor was a stereotypical, introverted scientist. He was also a gifted teacher. He was well prepared and organized for each lecture. The countless equations which covered his chalkboards were a thing of beauty. William Sears, once a Kármán student, recalled, "The lines were straight, properly aligned, and legible."[41] Kármán also had the ability to pass his knowledge to students outside the classroom environment, at any time and at any place. A former student and contributor to *Toward New Horizons*, Frank Wattendorf, related an incident which demonstrated the point. While still at Aachen, Wattendorf and Kármán frequently worked late at the professor's home. The last streetcar available for Wattendorf's return home left around midnight. One night, while walking to the station, Kármán envisioned a new approach to the problem at hand, creating a simplified physical concept of turbulence. Upon reaching the streetcar, the professor scribbled his new formula on the side of the car, explaining his thoughts as he went along. The patient conductor finally insisted that the men either board or depart as the hour was very late. Wattendorf, although he understood the basic process described during the lesson, could not recall the steps in the proper order. Unfortunately, the eager student could not see the writing which was now etched into the outside skin of the streetcar. After jumping off and then back on the car at each stop, he finally transferred the professor's work to his student notebook. The process was preserved after an all-night session in which Wattendorf refined the equations and graphed the final results of the computations.[42] Kármán had envisioned the final solution while his assistant, gaining valuable experience, crunched the numbers validating his professor's "happy thought."[43]

It was another of Kármán's students, Frank Malina, who summarized the unique abilities which the professor possessed and which the Wattendorf story neatly portrays.

First, he had the gift of "creative scientific conception at its highest level." Second, he was expert at "clarifying and reducing to clear and transparent form, material which had been before confused and hence only imperfectly comprehended." Finally, Kármán had the knack of "finding the essential physical elements in complicated engineering problems so that rational and simple approximate solutions could be obtained, which solutions could then be improved by successive approximation."[44] These "successive approximations" were completed by his students or his staff and, over time, earned him the reputation as an idea initiator or seed planter, a reputation he carried throughout his American career.

It was also common practice for Kármán to invite students and faculty members to his spacious Pasadena home for midweek gatherings consisting of Hungarian food and "shop talk." During the gathering, he mingled with his guests, Jack Daniels or plum brandy and a cigar in hand, spreading his enthusiasm for science. His home, regardless of the continent, was a true source of spiritual strength. His mother and sister were constant companions and confidants as well as a link to his rich European heritage, although more than one of Kármán's students believed that Pipö was more of a hindrance than a help in his day-to-day work.[45] The festive atmosphere was reminiscent of the café scene from which he had emerged almost 30 years before, often including famous Hollywood guests and high-ranking military officers but rarely including German beer, which he missed a great deal.[46]

The casual relaxation of the situation was ideal for learning. The professor's teaching method centered around a comprehensive, "broad based" belief that scientists should learn some engineering and engineers should learn some science. He had a unique ability to explain complex solutions in rather simple terms which was important to his belief that students learned by progressing "from the specific to the general," from localized phenomena to the overall interaction of all the phenomena in a generalized form. Kármán held the belief that: "Any difficult engineering problem would profit from going back to basics."[47] Additionally, he explained, "I do not consider science as a trade. I consider science much more

SAF Photo.

Kármán's home in Pasadena, California.

USAF Photo.

The separate "school house" located in the backyard where much of the casual learning took place.

as an art. Science is an organization of your impressions, of your experiences, visual, hearing, by logical methods."[48] Kármán also insisted upon open idea exchange, in the classroom or with colleagues, even if a solution appeared flawed. He resented, for example, Robert Goddard's insistence upon total secrecy during his early rocketry experiments because it resulted in duplication of effort and a time delay in eventual experimental success. Although Kármán considered him a genius, Goddard's suspicious nature limited the impact of his work. Additionally, Goddard was more interested in patents for his work than sharing his results through professional journals.

Perhaps some of Kármán's resentment was the result of an earlier attempt to include Goddard in the JATO project for the Army Air Forces. Frank Malina had gone to visit Goddard's lab where he was received politely but sent away without any new information. Later it was revealed in Goddard's diary that he intentionally withheld his research from Malina. "Kármán sent Malina to get information. I did not show him anything." To those at Caltech working in the field of rocketry, this made Goddard an inventor rather than a kindred scientist.[49] Yet, even under difficult circumstances, Kármán was able to point out absurdity or inconsistencies without destroying a relationship or squelching enthusiasm.[50] His teaching ability was undoubtedly one reason why Arnold, a man of somewhat basic academic ability, came to like and respect Kármán as he did. Kármán's wind tunnel lessons were at the heart of this respect.

Wanted: Idea Generator

More significantly, Kármán took exception with those who sought his advice and then refused to share the results of his wisdom. In 1930, while Kármán was testing the GALCIT wind tunnel efficiency rating, Eastman Jacobs, sent by NACA Research Director Dr. George Lewis, monitored the project closely. The 5.6 to 1 efficiency rating was roughly equal to the best wind tunnels available in Europe. Kármán, keeping true to his belief that all information should be openly shared, allowed Jacobs complete access to the results for his report to

Lewis.[51] In 1933, Clark B. Millikan, son of the Nobel laureate and Kármán's colleague at GALCIT, had requested data from a NACA experiment on boundary layer control (BLC); that is, air flow very close to the surface of an object moving through fluid. His request was flatly refused. Lewis' excuse was that the data was too preliminary. It had long been NACA policy to withhold preliminary test results from civil industry but the scientific community, until this instance, had been immune. This sequence of events forced the evolution of an antagonistic relationship between the GALCIT and the NACA which had an unexpected impact during the Second World War.[52]

Over the next five years, the level of cooperation did not improve. Twice during the period Kármán had proposed the construction of a supersonic wind tunnel. Twice Lewis had turned him down. Lewis' rationale for refusing Kármán's wind tunnel request was illuminating. Since the limiting airspeed of an aircraft propeller was approximately 500 MPH, to design a wind tunnel which produced wind speeds two or three times that speed was ludicrous. Of course the planes which Kármán had in mind were not to be powered by propellers. As early as 1932, Kármán had publicly discussed the possibility of building a 1,000-MPH aircraft. A Pasadena newspaper carried the headlines in October that year. "Kármán Caltech Workers Plan 1000 mph Rocket Plane: New Type Engine Would Suck Air in Front, Blow it Out Back." Kármán explained that the motor would consist of a small tunnel running the length of the aircraft. "It would draw air at the front, expand it at the center, and force it out under great pressure at the rear. . . . Such an engine would give the ship a speed of 1000 mph in the stratosphere."[53] Apparently, George Lewis was never briefed on the California newspaper article.

Driven by the belief that high-speed aircraft were a definite possibility, better wind tunnels became one of Kármán's greatest obsessions. In 1942, for example, he approached Vannevar Bush, head of the Office of Scientific Research and Development (OSRD), for fifty thousand dollars for a preliminary study leading to the next generation of supersonic wind tunnels. "Is this the best thing you can do for your country?" the chairman asked. Kármán attributed his rebuke to that of a good man holding "limited vision."[54]

Again in 1938, Clark Millikan resubmitted his request for Freeman's boundary layer data. Again, Lewis refused to release the results. These unreasonable and seemingly arbitrary refusals substantiated Kármán's picture of the NACA as a managed research team, void of individuality and lacking a spirit of cooperation.[55] Also in the late 1930s, GALCIT had been contracted by the NACA to research boundary layer air flow around concave and convex wing forms. Kármán's team proudly submitted their findings to Dr. Lewis. Lewis ridiculed the report as "nothing new" and merely a repeat of prior NACA experimentation. Since the NACA had not shared their data with the GALCIT, Lewis' claims held little merit with Kármán. Kármán told Lewis a story which reflected his opinion of the importance of the GALCIT report. There was once an explorer whose name was Columbus. He was challenged to find a new sea route to the Indies. Although he failed at his primary task, the work he accomplished was generally regarded as successful. From that time forward, Kármán had a disparaging impression of NACA, its policies, and its leadership.[56] The clash of personalities, in this case, Lewis versus Kármán, resulted in the clash of institutions, GALCIT versus the NACA.

In 1939, while Caltech scientists were working on the JATO problem, Arnold told Kármán of his belief that experimental research was the only way to get and keep American aeronautics on top in the world. Arnold wanted to know what type of equipment the Air Corps needed to begin the process. Kármán suggested a high-speed wind tunnel be built at Wright Field, one which required 40,000 horsepower to operate. This was the same tunnel Lewis had already refused at the NACA. At that time it was a revolutionary piece of equipment. Arnold immediately found funding for the project. When George Lewis heard of the Air Corps' attempt to invade the sanctity of NACA research, he flatly opposed any form of military R&D whatsoever. Further, if there was to be a 20-foot wind tunnel at all, the NACA would build it and would ensure it would be designed by the one man who could do the best job on its design.

"And who is that?" Arnold asked Lewis.

"Kármán."

"You're too late. He's designing the wind tunnel for me."[57] Arnold had zeroed in on Kármán's unique mastery of aeronautics as a tool for the Air Forces, a choice which Lewis unwittingly verified. The general could never conceal his grin, but this time he didn't even try. After the war, Arnold summarized his wartime perceptions on the deficiencies within the NACA.

> It is probable that the NACA, in following its directive to study the "problems of flight," concerned itself overly with the device, with the vehicle of flight. Either the scope of the NACA has been interpreted narrowly, or complimentary subsidization should have been established as fruitful and unexplored fields of research became apparent. The NACA's treatment of the "problems of flight" might be compared to the use of a government subsidy solely for the technical development of the automobile without paying any attention to roads and other complementary facilities. Those factors which enabled the airplane to operate over vast distances or which make it a vital element in the social and economic structure were neglected.[58]

Despite his reputation as a gifted research scientist, aeronautical engineer, and teacher, Kármán remained a man of humility. During his lifetime, he shared the company of Einstein, Henry Ford, Daniel Guggenheim, Ghandi, Jane Mansfield, Orville Wright, Pope Pius XII, Joseph Stalin, and President John F. Kennedy, a diversified lot to be sure. The ease with which he moved through these impressive social and political circles demonstrated that, although he was aware of his personal standing as a renowned scientist, he sought no status or reward for it. On one occasion, Kármán made a trip from Caltech out to Princeton University. One of his former students, Dr. Joseph Charyk, was a young faculty member there.

"Vile I'm there," Kármán casually asked, "I might see my good friend Einstein. Vould you mind calling him up and getting a date?"

"You know I can't call Einstein and get a date!" Charyk replied incredulously.

"Ja, just call him up and tell him I'd like to see him."

Charyk finally made the connection and Einstein warmly welcomed the professor during his Princeton visit. Dr. Charyk recalled his great fortune as he was invited to come along to meet the great physicist, a courtesy Kármán extended to his best students.[59] In the case of Einstein, Kármán showed remarkable interest in those who were experts in unfamiliar fields of study.[60]

In reality, Kármán was interested in everything surrounding him. True understanding was only achieved with an open mind. The professor once said, "The greatest progress in my lifetime has consisted of the elimination of what I call the scientific prejudices."[61] During his life he successfully breached barriers between engineers and scientists, work and leisure, art and science, students and teachers, home and classroom, thinkers and laborers, as well as "long hairs" and military men. While at Caltech, Kármán developed a similar vision to that held by Gen Hap Arnold; both realized the advantages of a cooperative aeronautics establishment between civilian scientists and military men working together on the same team. Arnold realized the potential impact which technological advancement held for his Air Forces. Kármán realized the potential gains for his university which Army funding would allow.[62]

General Arnold had once tried, illegally, to convince legislators to establish policy based upon Billy Mitchell's vision of an independent Air Force; and it earned him an all-expense-paid trip to middle-of-nowhere Kansas. By now, however, Arnold realized that it was only a matter of time before the dream of independence for the Air Forces would be realized.[63] Arnold's imagination went far beyond the thinkable present; it was clearly visionary. Men who served with Arnold during the war said that Arnold was the only prominent military officer to have possessed a broad enough view or a clear enough understanding of the potential capability of science to alter the complexion of the air service.[64] Arnold realized that the technical genius needed to fulfill his vision could only be found far beyond the military in the universities and in civilian industry despite the fact that he himself was not a person of deep scientific or engineering training. He needed an idea generator, a seed sower, a catalyst. He realized that scientists and engineers were the kind of people who were going to bring him the ideas he needed.[65] It was Kármán who best summarized this vision in terms the general appreciated. "You certainly know that I always admired your imagination and judgement," Kármán wrote after the war, "and I believe that you are one of the few men I have met who have the format to have at the same time your feet on the ground and your head over the clouds—even on the days when the ceiling is rather high."[66] If Kármán was to be a more permanent addition to Arnold's staff in Washington, one to provide the spark which might ignite the torch for the future of the Air Force, Arnold felt compelled to alert his long-time acquaintance, Nobel laureate and Caltech's president Robert Millikan, to Kármán's temporary departure from that university's staff.

Notes

1. I am indebted to Dr. Michael Gorn for his insights into Theodore von Kármán's personality and for his book, *The Universal Man: Theodore von Kármán's Life in Aeronautics* (Washington, D.C.: Smithsonian Institution Press, 1992), 3–5, from which much of this material was derived.

2. Theodore von Kármán and Lee Edson, *Wind and Beyond: Theodore von Kármán, Pioneer in Aviation and Pathfinder in Space* (Boston: Little, Brown and Co., 1967), 41–43; Gorn, 19–22.

3. Hugh L. Dryden, "Theodore von Kármán, 1881–1963," *Biographical Memoirs* (New York: Columbia University Press, 1965), 345–84; Gorn, 29–30.

4. Felix Gilbert, *The End of the European Era, 1890 to the Present* (New York: W. W. Norton and Co., Inc., 1970), 178–80; Kármán and Edson, 89–95. The Károlyi government came to power during what Kármán called the Chrysanthemum Revolution, reflecting the dense petalled red flower used as their symbol. "I remember that it was a rather friendly revolution," he later recalled; also Gorn, 31.

5. Gorn, 33–38. Although Gorn suggests that Aachen reached stature as great as Göttingen, this was really only true because of Kármán's standing in the scientific community. Enrollment, funding, and prestige advantages still belonged to Prandtl's institution. See also Paul A. Hanle, *Bringing Aerodynamics to America* (Cambridge, Mass.: MIT Press, 1982), 105–115. Hanle's work details the university system political interplay and implies a much deeper and divisive political agenda between the professors at Göttingen and other German universities. Kármán's non-German origins were detrimental to his advancement as the 1920s progressed.

6. Richard P. Hallion, interview for *New World Vistas*, 28 August 1995, tape, Bolling AFB, D.C.; also see Hanle, chap. 2. Hanle details Millikan's quest for Guggenheim funds.

7. Richard P. Hallion, *Legacy of Flight: The Guggenheim Contribution to American Aviation* (Seattle: University of Washington Press, 1977), 46–53; and James H. Doolittle oral history interview (OHI), 26 September 1971. For

an excellent summary of Millikan's influence at Caltech see Dr. Judith Goodstein, *Millikan's School: A History of the California Institute of Technology* (New York: W. W. Norton and Co., 1991).

8. Gorn points out that Prandtl's popularity in the US was largely the result of the wide range of publicity which Göttingen had received in America. Kármán, at this point in his career, was not universally known except to aeronautical scientists throughout the world; Hanle, chap. 5 is a detailed discussion of Prandtl and his methodology. Chapter 6 focuses on the differences and the interaction between Prandtl and Kármán. His primary source research is excellent. For the differences between the two scientists see particularly page 65.

9. Robert H. Kargon, *The Rise of Robert Millikan: Portrait of a Life in American Science* (Ithaca, N.Y.: Cornell University Press, 1982), 87–92; Theodore von Kármán, Columbia University Oral History Review; and Gorn, 81–82.

10. *The Guggenheim Aeronautical Laboratory of the California Institute of Technology (GALCIT): The First Twenty-five Years* (Pasadena, Calif.: Caltech, 1954); also Gorn, 39–40, 56; and Kármán and Edson, 124.

11. Kargon, 119; and Kármán and Edson, 151.

12. Kármán, 121; Gorn, 44; Hanle, 104.

13. Kármán and Edson, 124–25; "The Triple Alliance: Millikan, Guggenheim, and von Kármán," *Engineering and Science*, April 1981, 23–25; and Alex Roland, *Model Research: the National Advisory Committee for Aeronautics, 1915–1958*, vol. 1 (Washington, D.C.: National Air and Space Administration, 1985), 93–97.

14. Kármán Papers, photo collection. Of the dozens of photos taken during his trip to Japan, several show Kármán arm in arm with one, two, or three women. One small collection of photos is a series showing a Japanese woman in various stages of undress and, finally, nude. Apparently, this was a very relaxing trip for the young Hungarian.

15. Kármán and Edson, 121, 129–33. Kármán respected Kawanishi himself as a man of "liberal and visionary tendencies"; Gorn, 48–49.

16. Gorn, 41, 50–54; also Hanle, 115.

17. Kármán and Edson, 140.

18. Ibid., 142–43; Gorn, 51.

19. Kármán and Edson, 145; Gorn, 52–53.

20. Kármán and Edson, 144–45.

21. Gilbert, 178–80. In addition to reparations, the major sticking point for Germany concerning the Treaty of Versailles, Hungary's army was limited to 35,000 men and three-fourths of its territory and two-thirds of its population were ceded to Czechoslovakia, Yugoslavia, and Rumania. See Hanle, 120–22, for Prandtl's nationalistic tendencies.

22. Quoted in Kármán and Edson, 146. From Alan D. Beyerchen's *Scientists under Hitler* (New Haven: Yale University Press, 1977), chap. 1. It could be concluded that not even Kármán's longtime service and scientific excellence would have prevented his persecution and removal from his university post. Gilbert, 270–77, also offers a brief summary of the events surrounding Kármán's departure.

23. Gorn examines the continued rivalry between Kármán and Prandtl which existed in one form or another until the GALCIT was well established as a world leader in aeronautics in 1935. See Gorn, 61–64; also Hanle, 125, 134; and Kármán and Edson, 141.

24. Theodore von Kármán, *The Collected Works of Theodore von Kármán* 4 vols., *1953–1963* (London: Butterworths Scientific Publications, 1956).

25. William Rees Sears, *Stories from a Twentieth Century Life* (Stanford, Calif.: Parabolic Press, 1993), 75. There were to have been seven volumes. The final one covering unsteady airflow theory was never produced because of the onset of World War II; Robert Millikan to Guggenheim, letter, 9 July 1929, Guggenheim Fund Papers, Library of Congress, box 4; also Robert Millikan to Kármán, letter, 26 August 1929, Kármán Papers, 4.1; and Kármán and Edson, 141.

26. Chester Hasert, interviewed by author, 9 November 1994. The one percent interest story was part of this interview.

27. Kármán and Edson, 295–96; also Sears, 229. In fact, Kármán kept a separate Sir Isaac Newton file in his personal papers and displayed a slide of Newton during his introductory lecture on aerodynamics.

28. Kármán and Edson, 207–8; also Kármán, interviewed by Shirley Thomas, transcript, January 1960; Sears, 210–11.

29. Sears, 55.

30. Dr. Sears told this story, accent and all, during his 1995 interview. He insisted that the story showed how well Kármán understood Millikan and his philosophy for Caltech. For the published version of the story, see Sears, 92–93.

31. William R. Sears, interviewed by author, 8 July 1995, tape, Tucson, Ariz.; also Richard P. Hallion, AF Historian, interview for *New World Vistas*, 28 August 1995, tape, Bolling AFB, D.C.

32. Kármán and Edson, 147–48.

33. Richard P. Hallion, *Legacy of Flight: the Guggenheim Contribution to American Aviation* (Seattle: University of Washington Press, 1977), 187. Of the five original schools, Hallion gave separate consideration to Caltech and lumped all the others into one comprehensive chapter. Without a doubt, Caltech stood above the other schools in overall impact.

34. Kármán and Edson, 146.

35. Kármán, oral history interview, US Air Force Academy; see also Frank J. Malina, "Memoir on the GALCIT Rocket Research Project, 1936–1938," 6 June 1967, JPL (prepared for the First International Symposium on the History of Aeronautics, Belgrade, 25–26 September 1967); Robert Frank Futrell, *Ideas, Concepts, and Doctrine: Basic Thinking in the United States Air Force*, vol. 1, *1907–1960* (Maxwell AFB, Ala.: Air University Press, 1989), 219–20. Van Bush had stated, "I don't understand how a serious engineer or scientist can play around with rockets." There was a definite view that "science was very much against rocketry" during the late 1930s, said Kármán.

36. Kármán, interviewed by Shirley Thomas; Gorn, 58.

37. Ibid. Lt Gen Donald L. Putt, Air Force Historical Research Agency (AFHRC) oral history interview, K239.0512-724, 109. Putt described how,

during Lusty, Kármán was interviewing a German scientist, Dr. A. Buseman, who explained that his idea for the swept wing came from Kármán's Volta lecture. Kármán reportedly smacked his forehead as he recalled the substance of the lecture.

38. Kármán and Edson, 233. Kármán agreed with the German poet Goethe, who said, "some logic is desirable, but to be always logical is horrible."

39. Ibid., 307. It was thinking which eliminated the element of individuality, like George Lewis' firing of Max Munk in 1926, which Kármán was so much against.

40. Ibid., 247, 307; Kármán, interviewed by Shirley Thomas, transcript, January 1960; Lee Edson, "He Tamed the Wind," *Saturday Evening Post*, 3 August 1957, 77.

41. Sears, 211.

42. This story was recounted by Hugh Dryden, 353. Dryden was a personal friend and colleague of both Wattendorf and Kármán. He also served as Kármán's deputy during the first Scientific Advisory Group study, "Toward New Horizons: SCIENCE, the Key to Air Supremacy, Commemorative Edition, 1950–1992" (Wright-Patterson AFB, Ohio: Headquarters Air Force Systems Command History Office, 1992).

43. Kármán and Edson, 136–37.

44. As quoted in Dryden.

45. Sears, interviewed by author, 8 July 1995. Dr. Sears told the story of the "little" sister interrupting technical discussions with petty comments often placed well out of the context of the conversation. Kármán shrugged them off and continued to go about the business at hand after the interruption was over; Homer Joe Stewart, interviewed by author, 21 July 1995. "Homerjoe" echoed Sears' view that Pipö was at times an annoyance, but he also related that Kármán never allowed anyone to interrupt him while he was speaking to her.

46. Gorn, 55, 64. Part of the "festive" atmosphere was provided by a huge red banner with oriental writing all across it. Kármán hung this banner across the long empty upper wall across from his living room win-dows. He brought the banner back from one of his oriental adventures. The sign, as translated by one of his Chinese students (probably H. S. Tsien) read, "After the show, come eat at Joe's": not very philosophical but it looked good. Homer Joe Stewart, interview with author, 21 July 1995, Pasadena, Calif.; also Sears, 209.

47. Sears, interviewed by author.

48. Ibid., 211; Gorn, 35, 68; and Kármán, interviewed by Shirley Thomas, 5, 10.

49. Theodore von Kármán interviewed by Donald Shaughnessy, 27 January 1960, 5–6; for an objective approach to Robert Goddard see, J. D. Hunley, "The Enigma of Robert H. Goddard," *Technology and Culture* 36 (April 1995): 327–50.

50. Gorn, 68, 83, 157.

51. Kármán and Edson, 126–27; see Gorn, 166–67, note number 5. A summary of the NACA/GALCIT rivalry is located here.

52. Roland, vol. 1, 538.

53. "Kármán Caltech Workers Plan 1000 mph Rocket Plane," unknown newspaper, 21 October 1932. Kármán Papers, Caltech, 157.1.

54. Kármán and Edson, 230.

55. Ibid., 224–25; and Roland, vol. 1, 97–98, 548.

56. Sears, interviewed by author; also Kármán and Edson, 297; also Sears, 230–31.

57. Kármán and Edson, 226.

58. H. H. Arnold, "Science and Air Power," *Air Affairs*, December 1946, 193.

59. Dr. Joseph Charyk, interview for 50th Anniversary of the Scientific Advisory Board (SAB), 25 September 1994.

60. Kármán, interviewed by Shirley Thomas; Lee Edson, "He Tamed the Wind," *Saturday Evening Post* (3 August 1957), 69; Gorn, 107, 156. It would be interesting to know if Einstein and Kármán ever discussed military issues while at Caltech together. An interesting article by Ilse Bry and Janet Doe "War and Man of Science," *Science* 122 (11 November 1955): 912–13, presents Einstein's views on the responsibility of scientists to mankind. In this view offered in 1950, Einstein suggested that a "lamentable breakdown" in discipline had been caused by scientific zeal. Possible impact on human life and death had not been considered.

61. Kármán, interviewed by Shirley Thomas.

62. Gorn, 116, 158. It is also interesting that the professor and the general were just as comfortable with the Hollywood crowd as they were with members of the political and scientific hierarchy in America.

63. James H. Doolittle, oral history interview, USAF Academy (USAFA), 22 December 1977, 4.

64. Godfrey McHugh, interviewed by Murray Green, 21 April 1970, MGC, roll 12. McHugh was the administrative assistant to the Scientific Advisory Group at its inception in December 1944; and Gen Bernard Schriever, interview with author, 9 November 1994, National Academy of Sciences, Washington, D.C., Lt Gen Don Putt, USAFA/OHI, 1–3 April 1974; Jimmy Doolittle, USAFA/OHI, 21 April 1969; and Hugh Dryden, flight interview, February 1960, AFHRA, K146.34-41, 22–23.

65. Kármán and Edson, 268; and Dryden, CUOHR, 36; also, Gen Bernard A. Schriever, address given at the 50th Anniversary of the SAB, 9 November 1994, National Academy of Sciences, Washington, D.C. In, *New World Vistas, Ancillary Volume* (Washington, D.C.: USAF Scientific Advisory Board, 1996). Schriever quoted a letter from Arnold's son Bruce which he believed described the general perfectly; "He [Arnold] would be the first to admit that he was no genius, but he was an extremely innovative person and was able to utilize his imagination in a way that the crudest model could, in his eyes, become a successful product in the future."

66. Kármán to Arnold, letter, 7 December 1949, Kármán Papers, 124.

Chapter 5

The Blueprint

Although General Arnold had probably already decided on Kármán as the man he needed to create the long-range forecast for the AAF, he spent a great deal of time in conversation with Robert Millikan verifying his choice. Recall that Kármán had already been a special consultant to the Air Corps and to Arnold since 1940 at Wright Field during the construction of the high-speed wind tunnel, not to mention his participation in the JATO project. Millikan agreed that Kármán had the broad base of knowledge and experience to head such a study. Despite his friendship with Arnold, the prospect of losing the world's leading aeronautics professor to the Pentagon must have disappointed Millikan. But he realized that the Army Air Forces were in a scientific bind. He later pointed out that the cooperation which flowed from Caltech to the AAF may not have occurred "had it not been for the fact that you [Arnold] and I have had so many things in common, not only in the last war but in the inter-war period. It has been a very great delight, as well as profit, to me to be able to swap ideas with you and to try to assist in your problems."[1] Kármán, the primary subject of Millikan's letter, had problems of his own.[2]

In May 1944, Kármán had been advised that surgery was required for a nagging stomach ailment (he called it a "carcinoma" in his autobiography). The trouble had evidently started in the summer of 1941 when he visited the Mayo Clinic for a stomach problem. By mid-July, the surgery had been completed and Kármán was recuperating at the Westbury Hotel in New York City. He felt well enough to ask Clark Millikan for information on continuing programs at the GALCIT. Although, according to Dr. Robert Millikan, Kármán was supposed to have been at a "sanitarium" near Bolton Landing, Lake George, New York, for a month's recuperation, he was never there for more than two weeks at a time.[3]

As July turned to August, General Arnold called "Old Millikan" to set his plan for the future of the Air Forces into motion, including borrowing Kármán. On Thursday, 3 August, Millikan called Arnold with Kármán's address at Lake George. Arnold cabled Kármán (who was actually at the Westbury) at Lake George, New York. "Have been wanting to see you for some time but have just heard that you are ill." The message continued, "Hope it is nothing serious and am wondering what the chances are of your coming down sometime in the next couple of weeks."[4] The cable was forwarded to the professor immediately. Kármán responded the following day, Saturday, 5 August, "Please let me know [at] New York City Westbury Hotel whether my visit first of next week would be agreeable. Please give the time convenient to you. I am also at your disposal at any later date."[5] The new address was annotated in pen on the return message by Arnold's secretary. Acting with customary swiftness in matters of science and technology, Arnold arranged to meet the professor Monday or Tuesday morning on the tarmac at LaGuardia airport near Kármán's New York hotel. This spared Kármán an uncomfortable trip to Washington and gave Arnold a half-day break from his hectic Pentagon office.[6]

The LaGuardia meeting holds a somewhat legendary place in the history of Air Force scientific and technological development. Kármán recalled the details of the meeting but many of the dates of the events detailed in his autobiography for that fall were inaccurate. Nevertheless, when Arnold's plane arrived, jostled by the rough winds of a passing cold front, Kármán was transported by an Army staff car to the end of the runway where the general joined him after deplaning. Arnold dismissed the military driver and then, in total secrecy, discussed his plans for Kármán and his desires for the forecasting project. Arnold spoke of his concerns about the future of American airpower. How would jet propulsion, radar, rockets, and other "gadgets" impact that future?

"Vhat do you vish me to do?" Kármán asked.

"I want you to come to the Pentagon and gather a group of scientists who will work out a blueprint for air research for the next twenty, thirty, perhaps fifty years."[7] After promising to give all of the orders on Kármán's behalf (the professor insisted on that caveat), Arnold hopped back in his plane, the deal done. Kármán, flattered and excited, was impressed that

General Arnold had the vision to look far beyond the war years seeking university scientists for help. The timing of Arnold's request was not an accident.

Several key elements in wartime operations had been realized and only after D day was Arnold convinced that Allied victory in Europe was a foregone conclusion. The air war had become almost routine. At that point it was merely a numbers game: Allied air strength versus dwindling Axis air capability. The Normandy invasion had been carried out under the umbrella of complete air supremacy. The P-51 had been operating successfully with drop tanks for several months and results were positive. Once again, even though Arnold himself admitted the near-fatal mistake of waiting to develop the long-range capability of the P-51, range was the determinant of success. And most importantly, B-29 production had increased to near acceptable combat levels. This long-range, heavy bomber was Arnold's Pacific trump card. He had devoted a great deal of personal effort to ensure its development, despite initial severe engine problems. Only after he was confident that these production and procurement programs were succeeding did the general return to his pre-September 1939 "future-of-the-Air-Force" mode of thinking.[8]

Before the GALCIT chief joined Arnold in Washington, he had contractual work with General Electric (GE) to finish. On August 11, the same week he met with Arnold, he also met with Hans Kraft of the Turbine Engine Division, Steam Research Section at GE, Schenectady, New York. "It was really a great pleasure for me to see you in such good health again that we could do some real work, last Friday," Kraft wrote on 16 August.[9] For the rest of August and much of September, Kármán worked to close out his affairs with GE, feeling better every day. In the last week of September he relocated to the Raleigh Hotel in Washington. By October 1, he pronounced himself "completely recovered" in a return letter to Dr. William Sears, now employed at Northrop Aircraft.[10]

General Arnold and Dr. von Kármán were in "continual conference" after the LaGuardia encounter. Kármán recalled that he was "more impressed than ever with Arnold's vision."[11] Arnold insisted that Kármán examine everything and let "imagination run wild."[12] This challenge fit perfectly into Kármán's philosophy as the following example illustrates. On 3 April 1941, Kármán joined a number of consultants at Walt Disney Productions to evaluate the possible applications of animated cartoons to problems of national defense training. After viewing four specific examples of Disney's animation capability, which varied from full animation of entire processes to partial animation mixed with real instruction, Kármán offered this comment.

> When you have a process like airflow, for example, or the buckling of a structure, some animation is necessary. But from my point of view, what you call semi-animation is a great discovery, especially for instructional films. . . . I think the main thing is that students have imagination. You see, an animated film leaves nothing for the imagination. What we need in teaching is 20% animation, and 80% the student's imagination, and I think these films are marvelous for that.[13]

Kármán's philosophy was tailor-made for fulfilling Arnold's charge.

To ensure the accomplishment and excellence of this crucial task, Arnold imposed no completion deadline, a luxury later rescinded, and insisted that Kármán's group travel to all foreign countries and assess their aeronautics programs. He would then make a bold final report; a viable forecast for attaining future American air supremacy.[14]

Arnold stuck to his *modus operandi*. Planning for the establishment of the forecasting group itself was totally secret, almost "cloak and dagger."[15] Just as Arnold had secretly given the jet engine problem to the Bell/GE team in 1941, he now gave the critical task of forecasting the requirements for obtaining future air supremacy to Kármán and his scientists. To accomplish his mission, Kármán was officially designated as AAF consultant on scientific matters on 23 October 1944, one month after his arrival in the District of Columbia.[16]

Kármán was so hard at work ironing out the early details of organization that, at the other end of the country, his other boss, R. Millikan, was somewhat distressed that the professor had not communicated his personal status or intentions with Caltech from June through October. Millikan's concerns about his gifted professor were eliminated when Kármán finally telegramed on 2 October.

> Had several conferences with Arnold he will see you probably this week. I definitely recommend not to refuse his demand. Consider extremely important working out [here] for him. Program on scientific basis midway between negative attitude to new ideas and overoptimism concerning so called unlimited possibilities of science. Doing this job well also highly important for future of aeronautical research at Caltech. He told me you thought I am the right person. I strongly desire to devote about six months to this job. Feel well recovered but definitely inadvisable for me to plunge into administrative and st[r]enuous duties of ORDCIT and GALCIT for several months.[17]

This message illustrated that Kármán had his institution as well as the AAF in mind when he accepted Arnold's offer. Certainly, Caltech stood to benefit both financially and prestigiously having the great professor as chairman of the AAF study. Millikan, now placated, realized the potential gains and by the end of the month had even authorized other Caltech faculty to participate in the scientist's exploitation of Luftwaffe secret technology—better known as Operation Lusty (**LU**ftwaffe **S**ecret **T**echnolog**Y**). Kármán was free to serve the AAF but the element of potential long-term impact on Caltech and the GALCIT had not passed unnoticed.[18]

In addition to the institutional impact, Kármán worried about his personal financial affairs. After he had already committed to this Washington assignment, Kármán was informed about the military's strict "conflict of interest" laws. These laws required that all contractual obligations Kármán held with firms associated with government projects be terminated. For Kármán, of course, that was nearly all of his consulting obligations. General Arnold's legal staff "recommended" that the professor terminate all affiliation with Northrop Aircraft, General Electric, and his own Aerojet Engineering Corporation. Somewhat uncharacteristically, Kármán replied on the same day to the instructions issued by Col Robert Proctor, a member of Arnold's executive staff, and guaranteed compliance with the recommendations. It is interesting to note that, although Kármán was prohibited from active negotiations with Aerojet, he was permitted to retain his stock interest in the company which he founded with four other Caltech scientists.[19]

If there was much sincerity behind Kármán's good intentions concerning military affiliation and service, there was also a clear element of avarice. His concern with pay, certainly well founded in light of the requirements of government service, revolved around a California lifestyle which included an enormous home, two servants, a live-in family, and frequent parties and gatherings. This lifestyle was expensive. It must also be remembered that when he resigned from his position at Aachen in 1933, he also forfeited his pension and retirement benefits which had accumulated over three decades of service. His undeniable interest in the progress of rockets, particularly JATO-type projects, became a very lucrative part of his association with the AAF. Although difficult to prove that Kármán intentionally pushed projects toward Aerojet Engineering, it is undeniably true that the professor and his four investment colleagues benefitted from military contracts during and long after the war. By 1944, Aerojet held military contracts totaling more than 5.2 million dollars. Kármán once said, "As part of my participation in the military, my conviction is that even if the research and development is made for military purposes, the experience shows in civil aviation profits. So I believe that what will help in the military is not only for making war, but contributes very much to the progress of technology in general."[20] In this instance, "profits" likely was intended to mean, "benefits." But the monetary linkage Kármán saw between civil and military projects was undeniable. It was his Aerojet stocks which eventually provided him a small fortune from a relatively small $1,500 initial investment.[21]

In light of War Department legal requirements and his constant concern over future financial security, Kármán took steps ensuring his immediate financial stability. Perhaps at the direction of Robert Millikan, Kármán wrote a lengthy plea to Mr. James R. Page, chairman of Caltech's Board of Trustees, requesting continued pay at Caltech during his consultancy in Washington. He explained that government regulations required the termination of previous contracts to prevent potential ethical problems. On the other hand, legalities prevented the War Department from paying anything beyond $25.00 each day and no provision existed for covering living expenses in Washington. Further, Kármán raised the point that Jerome Hunsaker, chairman of the NACA and head of the Aeronautics Department at MIT, retained his salary even while spending most of his time in Washington working on wartime issues.[22] In the end, he was retained on the salaried roster during the war years. There was no denying that Caltech and Kármán were rewarded by his participation in Arnold's advisory group. Caltech saw continued investment by the Army in meteorology, aeronautics, and rockets over the next three decades. Kármán reaped the rewards of military investment through stock ownership and prestige. Nonetheless, the benefit to the Army Air Forces largely overshadowed these personal and institutional economic issues.[23]

The Scientific Advisory Group

Kármán's first unofficial report was organizational in nature. In it he named Dr. Hugh L. Dryden, longtime head of the National Bureau of Standards (NBS), as his deputy. The month of November 1944 was one of endless conferences and establishment of "relations with the various agencies in the labyrinth of military and scientific aviation."[24] Arnold followed with official written instructions on 7 November. This four-page letter set the boundaries within which the Scientific Advisory Group report was to remain. These boundaries were not very restrictive (see appendix B).

> Except perhaps to review current techniques and research trends, I am asking you and your associates to divorce yourselves from the present war in order to investigate all the possibilities and desirabilities for postwar and future war's development as respects the AAF. Upon completion of your studies, please then give me a report or guide for recommended future AAF research and development programs.[25]

Initially, Kármán's group was called the AAF Consulting Board for Future Research (AAFCBFR), but apparently AAFCBFR was too long an acronym even for the Army. The panel was redesignated the SAG on 1 December 1944, by Headquarters

Office Instruction (HOI) 20-76, and assigned directly to General Arnold.[26]

Germany's last desperate attempt to end the war at the Bulge occurred while the scientists were gathering and anticipating their chance to exploit the work which German scientists had done over the last five to seven years. By January 1945, Kármán's handpicked, scientific team of "thirty-one giant brains" had joined him in Washington and began executing the monumental task. Initially Kármán met internal resistance to a few of his choices for the board. One of these, Sir William Hawthorne, was an Englishman. Col Frederick E. "Fritz" Glantzberg, Kármán's military assistant, voiced his objection to having any "foreigners" on the board. Kármán reminded the colonel that Arnold wanted the best people, regardless where they came from. Glantzberg relented, "The British were, after all, our Allies." Next, Kármán insisted upon adding a naval officer who had also been one of his students, William Bollay. The colonel ground his pencil and insisted that the professor had gone too far. Kármán responded with a simple question, "But Colonel, the Navy are surely our Allies, too?" Glantzberg thought for a moment and finally stated that they were, "not as close as the British, but a damn sight closer than the Russians."[27] For administrative reasons, neither of these served on the board until 1949; but Arnold wanted the best and he didn't care where they came from.

Arnold, now a five-star general, insisted that the group throw conservative thinking to the wind. Kármán then reminded the scientists, in his quiet, Hungarian, "broken-English," that they had to deliver on their promises. Not unexpectedly, the younger members of the team found working in the SAG the "equivalent of a semester of grad school each day."[28] In mid-January, Arnold suffered a severe heart attack and was forced to retreat to Florida for a recovery period. The general described his condition to Lois, his daughter, in mechanical terms. "Apparently one of my cylinders blew a gasket and I had to get down here to have an overhaul job done. . . . While I was here they checked my lubrication, ignition, and gasoline system and they said they were working alright."[29] Fortunately, Arnold had already given Kármán his marching orders.

Meetings were held the first week in February, March, and April during which basic research for individual reports was accomplished and the format for the report finalized. Kármán emphasized that the purpose of these meetings was threefold. First, the group was to search for ways to secure "scientific insight in a standing Air Force." Second, they were to ensure the continued interest of American scientists in the future of the Air Force. Last, the group was to educate the American public in the necessity of maintaining a strong Air Force.[30] These objectives may have seemed remarkably vague, but specifics in design and engineering were not really part of the overall SAG task. This sweeping view had its origins even before America entered the war. In the 24 February 1941 issue of the *Pasadena Star News*, Kármán was quoted by reporters as saying: "So rapid has been the development of military aircraft during the present war, it is impossible to forecast what performance limits will be obtained by warplanes before the war ends."[31] For reasons such as this, a broad approach was always in Kármán's mind.

From February through April, Kármán and Dryden finalized the project design, attempted to make plans which would accommodate Arnold's request that they visit as many foreign countries as possible, and started the messy process of obtaining security clearances for the scientific team. As one might suspect, the process involved in establishing this "secret" organization and planning its itinerary was a paperwork nightmare. After resolving a few security clearance problems which were generated by the diversity of the group's members, the Operation Lusty team waited for the liberation of scientific targets on the continent.

In late April 1945, SAG members departed for Europe to inspect liberated enemy laboratories. Operation Lusty, which Kármán called, "unlikely but pleasant," fulfilled Arnold's insistence that the SAG travel the world and investigate the most advanced scientific and technological aeronautical information available.[32] Lusty was the code name for a much larger operational exploitation expedition of European technologies by the US Army. The SAG was only one small part of the entire task force. Arnold's instructions, via his deputy, Lt Gen Barney Giles, to Gen Carl "Tooey" Spaatz, the European Allied air commander were nonetheless clear. "May I ask . . . in view of the importance of this project that you give it your personal attention."[33] Spaatz, who was already alerted to Arnold's belief in science, did just that. A few months before, while en route to Quebec in September 1944, Arnold had informed Spaatz of his belief in the "value and the importance of these long-haired scientists."[34] Arnold had already secretly established the SAG as proof of his commitment in this area.

Spaatz's immediate cooperation was vital to the success of the SAG portion of Operation Lusty which began with their arrival in Paris on 1 May 1945. One member of the Lusty team, H. Guyford Stever, noted the critical nature of timing during the allied advance. Stever recalled that local looting

Little, Brown and Co.

Camouflaged laboratories were "invaded" by Operation Lusty team members as soon as they were liberated.

was often a problem but the Russians were the real concern. More significantly, Stever mentioned that "until this von Kármán mission, we had to piece the enemy's facts together. Now we had the advantage of actually talking to the German scientists and engineers, seeing their laboratories, and hearing them describe their total programs."[35] Dr. Hugh Dryden, Kármán's deputy, echoed Stever's conclusion. "I think we found out more about what had been going on in the war in a few days conversations with some of these key German leaders, than all the running around and digging for drawings and models . . . could bring."[36] Firsthand rather than second- or thirdhand information made seeing the German scientific picture much easier. Only after Kármán arrived was the totality of the German scientific effort revealed.

To preserve that scientific picture, the American teams boxed up everything they could and immediately shipped it off

Little, Brown and Co.

During Operation Lusty, Kármán caught up with his old professor, Ludwig Prandtl. "H. S." Tsien looks on during one of their conversations.

to Wright Field. In one location, Navy exploitation teams had been the first to arrive after liberation. They quickly boxed up the hardware and technical data in large crates and labeled them, "U.S. Navy." Two days later, Army teams made it to the same location whereupon they crated the Navy boxes in larger crates and relabeled them, "U.S. Army."[37] For these reasons, some good and some apparently ridiculous, immediate access to targets was crucial. Spaatz provided the capability to meet these requirements.[38] His personal involvement in the early days of the SAG helped strengthen his own understanding of its capabilities during his tour as the first Air Force chief of staff. Among the most surprising discoveries during the "scientist's invasion" were a jet-powered helicopter built by Doblhoff, swept-back wings hung in high-speed wind tunnels, hidden assembly locations for V-1 and V-2 "vengeance" weapons, and plans for V-3 (intercontinental) rockets. Of greatest interest were thousands of linear feet of data and documents which accompanied these projects. Upon close examination, many of these confirmed the path that American science had already taken. Some, the jet-powered helicopter for instance, were a total surprise.[39]

Near the end of June, seeing the opportunity to get into Russia, Kármán had asked Arnold if it might be possible for him to attend the 100th anniversary of the Soviet Academy of Science. Arnold granted the request but specified that he not stay long in Moscow and that Glantzberg be made aware of his travel plans. During his month back in Europe, "he was very happy making and renewing friendships and acquaintanceships of people in Europe, and also having something to do with the rebuilding of science in Europe, on the continent."[40] His gregarious nature was paying dividends. While in the Russian capital, he noted the large number of books published by the State Publishing House. He attributed the vast knowledge which many Russian scientists held to this propensity to publish wide varieties of material.[41]

The professor, seeing an opportunity to visit his brother in Budapest from his current location, which he recalled in his autobiography was his intention all along, set out in search of air transportation to his old home. Unfortunately, he neglected to inform his military aides of his changing plans.

AFHRA

Some of the aeronautical treasure found during Operation Lusty. Wind tunnels at the Hermann Göring Institute, mines which housed V-1 and V-2 construction operations, and hardware. Missile test sections, "jet" powered helicopters, and swept-back wing forms hanging in the tunnels.

The following 9 photographs show more aeronautical treasure found during Operation Lusty.

137

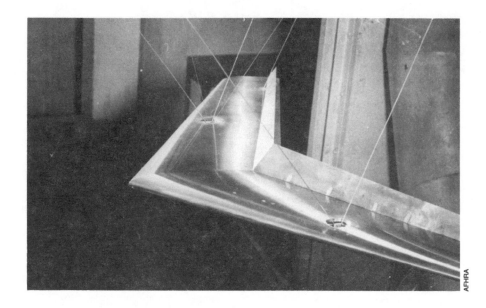

After several futile attempts, Kármán happened upon an old friend of his from Hungary, Dr. Albert Szent-Gyögyi, a prominent biochemist, who was traveling back to Budapest on a military transport plane. Kármán immediately followed him and got on board. Though delayed a day in Kiev because of bad weather, Kármán finally made it to Budapest where his brother still lived.[42] The professor failed to consider the consequences of his unauthorized travel for those assigned to watch over him.

Colonel Glantzberg and Col Godfrey McHugh were those men. Initially, reports of Kármán's disappearance were met with terrible fear. Was he shot? Was he kidnaped? McHugh finally traced the flight Kármán had boarded to Hungary. Glantzberg located him a few days later. Glantzberg and a "rescue" team had flown from Italy to Budapest in a B-25 specifically to retrieve the errant professor. The entire crew was interned in a nearby convent upon landing (fortunately the translator accompanying them was a beautiful young woman or they might have been thrown into a Budapest prison). In fact, the professor was straightening out his brother's banking affairs in Budapest. But the story was not yet over. While in Budapest, Glantzberg's B-25 had been siphoned of fuel. Only emergency fuel remained in the "Tokyo" tank (a carry-over from the Doolittle raid). They were forced to land in Belgrade and were again interned for landing without permission. After some quick talking, the rescue team was given enough gas to make a safe landing in Italy. The "narrow escape" was completed. This incident was a rare instance where Kármán demonstrated a blatant disregard for military policy and, in fact, had endangered himself and those tasked to rescue him.[43] The affair also demonstrated, however, his supreme dedication to his family.

Where We Stand

After six weeks of traveling throughout the devastated European countryside, the professor met Arnold, now recovered from his January setback, in Paris on 13 July 1945, to discuss the team's initial findings. General Arnold was traveling to join President Harry Truman at Potsdam and was pressed for time. He asked the professor to prepare a report summarizing these discoveries. Kármán submitted *Where We Stand* on 22 August, in satisfaction of that request (see appendix B for the report).

Where We Stand, a summary of the exploitation of German science and technology which Kármán's men had unearthed, began by listing a set of eight aspects of aerial warfare which, Kármán believed, had become "fundamental realities." They were

1. that aircraft—manned or pilotless—will move with speeds far beyond the velocity of sound.

2. that due to improvements in aerodynamics, propulsion and electronic control, unmanned devices will transport means of destruction to targets at distances up to several thousand miles.

3. that small amounts of explosive material will cause destruction over areas of several square miles.

143

4. that defense against present-day aircraft will be perfected by target seeking missiles.

5. that only aircraft or missiles moving at extreme speeds will be able to penetrate enemy territory protected by such defenses.

6. that a perfect communication system between fighter command and each individual aircraft will be established.

7. that location and observation of targets, take-off, navigation and landing of aircraft, and communication will be independent of visibility and weather.

8. that fully equipped airborne task forces will be enabled to strike at far distant points and will be supplied by air.[44]

In addition, the report sought to explain why Germany was advanced in some areas and behind in others. Inherent in the title was Kármán's evaluation of US posture in regard to foreign scientific developments.

For example, German achievements in aeronautics were not attributed to superior scientists, rather, German superiority was due to "very substantial support enjoyed by their research institutions in obtaining expensive research equipment such as large supersonic wind tunnels many years before such equipment was planned in this country."[45] These tunnels supported development in the field of transonic and supersonic wing design to the point of "practical application." These ideas were only being discussed in America, and this realization was made by none other than the chief of the leading aeronautics laboratory in the country, the GALCIT. Kármán added a warning, "We cannot hope to secure air superiority in any future conflict without entering the supersonic speed range." Additionally, the report stated that, "The V-2 development was successful not so much because of striking scientific developments as because of an early start, military support, and boldness of execution."[46] An early start, unlimited funding, and bold execution of German scientific plans became a recurring theme throughout the report.

There were also areas where the US held substantial leads over the Axis. The most glaring of these was in radar development. Kármán emphasized the importance of radar development this way.

It must be realized that radar is not a facility of attachment which will occasionally be used under bad conditions. Rather, the Air Force of the future will be operated so that radar is the primary facility, and visual methods will only occasionally be used. . . . Hence, in an all-weather Air Force, radar must be the universally used tool for bombing, gunfire, navigation, landing, and control. The whole structure of the Air Force, the planning of its operations, its training program, and its organization must be based on this premise. The development and perfection of radar and the techniques for using it effectively are as important as the development of the jet-propelled plane.[47]

This realization, today, appears the most prescient of all those made during a period where the Army Air Force's primary doctrine (in Europe certainly), that of precision, strategic bombing, was based primarily on the ability to visually acquire the intended target.[48] He also pointed out that the Germans had failed to keep stride with the rest of the world because, "Most of the development took place in industrial laboratories . . . but the very brilliant group of German physicists in universities were never called in to participate. Consequently, while engineering design was good, imaginative new thinking was lacking." Kármán could always tell where imagination and the element of individual brilliance was missing, be it in his students or in notable scientists. Further, Kármán predicted that, "The ability to achieve Air Force operations under all conditions of darkness and weather contributes more than any other single factor to increasing the military effectiveness of the air forces. Hence, any research program designed to overcome the limitations to flight at night and in bad weather will pay big dividends." Adding a caveat, realizing that the technology behind radar was rapidly being improved, the professor suggested that the Air Force "must be alert in swiftly utilizing any new developments."[49]

By emphasizing radar, Kármán also indirectly assured MIT's future share of military research projects. During the war it had been the MIT Radiation Laboratory (RADLAB) which had worked toward American radar excellence. Generally, much as Caltech held the reins of AAF aeronautical science, MIT directed AAF radar programs. In fact, the addition of Dr. Edward Bowles to Arnold's staff in 1943 linked radar and electronic programs to the AAF much as Kármán's association with the general had linked aeronautics in earlier years. The rivalry which developed between these schools was more friendly than Caltech's rivalry with the NACA because both schools held particular expertise in different areas of technological development, and, for the most part, both respected each other's accomplishments.[50]

Radar was a specific technological device but *Where We Stand* was also broad in its scope. The report addressed the idea of an Air Force school for scientists and engineers, continued relations with the civilian scientific community, continued cooperation with national agencies concerned with scientific research, and made more mundane but important suggestions concerning techniques for measurement taking and data collection during experimentation. Perhaps the most interesting recommendation was not directly related to accomplishment of scientific research or development; it concerned problems of organization.

> It is necessary that the Commanding General of the Air Forces and the Air Staff be advised continuously on the progress of scientific research and development in view of the potentialities of new discoveries and improvements in aerial warfare. A permanent Scientific Advisory Group, consisting of qualified officers and eminent civilian scientific consultants, should be available to the Commanding General, reporting directly to him on novel developments and advising him on the planning of scientific research.[51]

It was this last recommendation which was passed along to Tooey Spaatz by Arnold before he left the scene in February 1946. Spaatz took it to heart and established the Scientific Advisory Board as a permanent group which met for the first time on 17 June 1946. It was not, however, attached to the commanding general but had been relegated to the deputy chief of Air Staff for research and development, Gen Curtis E. LeMay.[52] The SAB had nevertheless survived the end of the war and was established as an organization with the express purpose of providing scientific advice to higher levels of Air Force leadership. The imperfection of the new system would eventually be repaired.

After the initial report was published, Kármán began the arduous task of compiling the SAG's detailed work. Suddenly, the deliberate pace normally associated with scientific research was replaced by a great sense of urgency to complete the project. The war was taking its toll. In mid-September, General Arnold had suffered yet another serious heart attack.

Toward New Horizons

Perhaps fearing the worst, Arnold cabled Kármán, still in Europe, wondering if the report might be finalized by 15 December 1945. To accommodate the ailing general, Kármán canceled his upcoming trip to Japan and sent a few of his team members to the Orient instead. From October through December, work proceeded at a frenetic pace. After many sleepless nights, the draft version of the final report, *Toward New Horizons*, was delivered to Arnold's desk on 15 December 1945.[53] Kármán's summary volume, *Science: The Key to Air Supremacy*, introduced the 12-volume "classified" report (see appendix C for the summary report).[54] In essence, the summary volume amplified the tenets of the August report with a few significant additions. Kármán's three-part volume addressed the problems associated with "research and development from the point of view of the technical requirements which the Air Forces must meet in order to carry out its task, securing the safety of the nation." The third chapter elaborated upon correcting the organizational and administrative problems which had been addressed in *Where We Stand*. Most notable of these elaborations was a plea for government authority to "foster," not "dictate," basic research.[55] This type of long-range, extremely detailed study was the first of its kind ever accomplished in American military history. Along with *Where We Stand*, it was to serve as the blueprint for building the Air Force during the next two decades.

In completing the report, Kármán stuck to his standard methodology. He provided general guidance which, if followed, would result in the eventual supremacy of American airpower. Once the formula had been provided, he moved on to the next pressing problem. "A man will put energy into a certain piece of work and once he gets it done he's very likely to go on to something else and leave it." Dr. Edward Bowles continued, "I think it was true of Kármán, I think that Kármán preferred to be a solo artist."[56] Homerjoe Stewart added that once the new

147

ideas had been generated, "He [Kármán] had young guys to pick them up and run with them."[57]

General Arnold was so interested in the possibilities of future airpower development that, based upon Kármán's preliminary report, he offered his personal perceptions of the SAG's importance to General Spaatz. Arnold reminded the man who became his successor that the Air Forces had no great scientists in their ranks. Military research and development (R&D) labs had stagnated during the war, largely due to increased production requirements and personnel shortages. Outside civilian help had been required during the war to meet development of aircraft power plants and structural design problems. Only through civilians had scientific and technological potential been realized. Arnold reminded Spaatz that: "These men did things that the average Army officer could never have accomplished. We must not lose these contacts."[58]

Notes

1. Dr. Robert Millikan to Henry H. Arnold, letter, 5 September 1945, Murray Green Collection (MGC), roll 12.

2. Henry H. Arnold, *Global Mission* (New York: Harper and Brothers, 1949), 532; and Thomas A. Sturm, *The USAF Scientific Advisory Board: Its First Twenty Years, 1944–1964* (1967; reprint, Washington, D.C.: Office of Air Force History, 1987), 3–4.

3. Theodore von Kármán medical records in folder 1523, Caltech Archives, Beckman Center, Pasadena, Calif.; William Rees Sears, interviewed by author, 8 July 1995, tape; also F. W. Thomas to Kármán, letter, 19 May 1944, Caltech 73.6; Clark Millikan to Kármán, letter, 18 July 1944, Caltech 73.6; Robert A. Millikan to Henry H. Arnold, letter, 3 August 1944, Caltech, Millikan Collection, folder 16.19. Additionally see Theodore von Kármán and Lee Edson, *Wind and Beyond: Theodore von Kármán, Pioneer in Aviation and Pathfinder in Space* (Boston: Little, Brown and Co., 1967), 267–70; and Kármán, interviewed by Shirley Thomas, January 1960.

4. Henry H. Arnold to Theodore von Kármán, telegram, Lake George, N.Y., 4 August 1944, Library of Congress, Arnold Papers, Kármán Folder. Arnold's secretaries addressed Kármán as Carmen, Prof. Kármán, Mr. Kármán, etc.

5. Theodore von Kármán to Arnold, radiogram, 5 August 1944, Library of Congress, Arnold Papers, Kármán Folder.

6. It was obviously sometime in early August that Arnold met with Kármán to discuss the foundations of the SAG, not in September as is generally thought.

7. Kármán and Edson, 268. See also weather analysis in the previous note.

8. Wesley Frank Craven and James Lea Cate, *The Army Air Forces in World War II*, vol. 6, *Men and Planes* (1955; new imprint, Washington, D.C.: Office of Air Force History, 1983), 218–19.

9. Hans Kraft to Kármán, letter, 16 August 1944, Schenectady, N.Y., Caltech 6012.

10. Kármán to Sears, letter, 30 September 1944, Washington, D.C., Caltech 27.44; Millikan to William Knudsen, letter, Caltech, 3 October 1944, Caltech, Millikan Collection, 16.19.

11. Kármán and Edson, 267–68; Millikan to Knudsen, letter, 3 October 1944.

12. Henry H. Arnold to Carl A. Spaatz, letter, 6 December 1945; Arnold to Ira C. Eaker, letter, 22 May 1945, MGC; also Wesley Frank Craven and James Lea Cate, *The Army Air Forces in WW II*, vol. 6, *Men and Planes* (Chicago: University of Chicago Press, 1948), 234; and Thomas A. Sturm, *The USAF Scientific Advisory Board: Its First Twenty Years, 1944-1964* (Washington, D.C.: USAF Historical Division Liaison Office, 1967), 37.

13. Disney Folder, Caltech, 592, Kármán just wanted to give a "little push" to the brain.

14. Arnold, *Global Mission*, 532–33; Reinforced by a cable sent to Spaatz after the war was nearing completion, 15 April 1945, in MGC.

15. On 25 October, in a reply to a letter from Lt Gen George C. Kenney concerning future planning, Hap detailed more than 30 specific actions pertaining to aircraft production and design, but he did not mention the Kármán project which had already been initiated. Arnold only added a brief clue in a postscript, "There is still more that is being prepared now but will not be actuated until the Post-War Period." On 9 November 1944, Arnold spoke to the NACA Aeronautical Research Laboratory where he cryptically told the gathering of scientists and engineers that when the AAF got stuck in a development problem or when looking toward the future of aeronautics, **"normally** we go to the NACA and ask you people to do that work for us [emphasis added]." But Arnold would not go to the NACA this time.

16. Scientific Advisory Board, 1944–45 file, Pentagon, Washington, D.C.

17. Kármán to R. Millikan, 2 October 1944, Caltech 20.28.

18. Brig Gen F. O. Carroll, Chief, Engineering Division, Wright Field to R. Millikan, 12 September 1944; confirmation on 29 September via Western Union, Millikan Papers, Caltech, 16.19.

19. Col Robert Proctor to Kármán, letter, 20 November 1944, and Kármán to Arnold, letter, 20 November 1944. Millikan Papers, 16.19. It should be noted that this exchange is found in Robert Millikan's papers. This certainly increases the chance that Millikan had been informed as to Kármán's impending financial dilemma.

20. E. C. Bowles to G. C. Marshall, letter, 11 August 1944, MGC, roll 12, ref: Library of Congress box 45; and Kármán interview, 12 January 1960, USAFA.

21. Hugh L. Dryden, "Theodore von Kármán: 1881–1963," *Biographical Memoirs* (New York: Columbia University Press, 1965), 356; Michael H. Gorn, *The Universal Man: Theodore von Kármán's Life in Aeronautics* (Washington, D.C.: Smithsonian Institution Press, 1992), 154–57. Kármán died with a net worth value of nearly one-half million dollars. In 1963 this was a fairly large fortune considering that his enormous California home was valued at only $85,000. His will dispersed only a fraction of the money in his portfolio. The rest was dispersed by Edward Beehan, executor of the estate.

22. Kármán to Mr. James R. Page, letter, 22 November 1944, Millikan Papers, 16.19. Kármán traced his entire pay history from his arrival in the US and requested back pay and a substantial raise. He also mentioned that his servants received $100 each month from "Uncle Same [sic]" which was only $50 less than his projected monthly pension. Page was in the hospital and the response was late if it was ever made official at all.

23. In reality it was these very issues, particularly the element of private profit arising from military investment, which defined the "Military-Industrial (and also Academic) Complex" which Aerojet General represented. Although it was not until two decades later that the term was officially used for the first time, the existence of the Military-Industrial Complex as early as the 1940s was undeniable.

24. Kármán's first report for the SAG, 23 November 1944, in MGC; Kármán to Clark Millikan, letter, 4 November 1944, Caltech, 736; and Gorn, 99. Kármán's and Dryden's close association during 1944 and 1945 resulted in a lifelong respect between the two men. Kármán showed his admiration in a letter on the occasion of Dryden's appointment as director of research for the NACA in 1947, replacing George Lewis. "I feel that a new era starts not only in the history of that institution, but also in the history of American Aeronautical research. . . . You know that I not only appreciate your friendship and scientific achievement, but also the splendid way in which you can eliminate difficulties caused by red tape and vanity." Kármán to Dryden, letter, 3 October 1947, Caltech 83.1. The jab at Lewis is unmistakable.

25. Arnold to Kármán, letter, 7 November 1944, Washington, D.C., SAB 1944–45 file.

26. Air Force Scientific Advisory Board, Pentagon, Washington, D.C.; Kármán's first report for the SAG, 23 November 1944, MGC, ref: Library of Congress, box 79; and Gorn, 99–100. H. H. Arnold Papers, HOI 20-76, MGC, Library of Congress, box 40; Arnold to Kármán, letter, 7 November 1944, SAB.

27. Kármán and Edson, 269–70; and William Rees Sears, *Stories from a Twentieth Century Life* (Stanford, Calif.: Parabolic Press, 1993), 219.

28. Kármán, interviewed by S. Thomas; and T. F. Walkowicz, "von Kármán's Singular Contributions to Aerospace Power," *Air Force Magazine*, May 1981, 60–61; Gorn, 47.

29. Arnold to Lois Snowden, letter, 22 February 1945, MGC.

30. Sturm, 5.

31. "No Way to Predict Future of Warplane Performance," *Pasadena Star News*, 24 February 1941, Caltech, 157.2.

32. Kármán, oral history interview, USAFA, Colo.; Chester Hasert, interviewed by author, 10 November 1994, National Academy of Sciences, Washington, D.C.; also Operation Lusty folder, AFHRA. Arnold's heart attack in mid-January did not interfere with the operation of the SAG. He had already given them their marching orders before he was taken ill. He spent the next few months in Florida recuperating before the SAG investigated European scientific laboratories.

33. Lt Gen Barney Giles to Spaatz, letter, 19 April 1945, Caltech 902; Kármán and Edson, 272; Gorn, 103–5; and Kármán, oral history interview, USAF Academy, Colo.

34. In a reply to an earlier letter praising radar developments, Arnold wrote Spaatz on 12 September 1944, affirming his trust in scientists, MGC, roll 12.

35. H. Guyford Stever, interviewed by author, 18 May 1995.

36. Hugh L. Dryden, Columbia University Oral History Review (CUOHR), 24.

37. Homer Joe Stewart, interviewed by author, 21 July 1995.

38. H. Guyford Stever, interviewed by author, 18 May 1995. Dr. Stever was working with the British RADLAB (radiation laboratory) as part of the MIT exchange team when Lusty operations began. He was attached to Kármán's group in the place of Dr. L. DuBridge, who was unavailable. Stever is a former chairman of the SAB from 1962–1964 and a former presidential science advisor.

39. Ibid., tape and transcript, Washington, D.C.; and Dr. Richard P. Hallion, interview for *New World Vistas*, 28 August 1995, tape, Bolling AFB, D.C.; and MGC, roll 12, Summary of memo from Kármán to Arnold, 30 July 1945, which documented the group's travels to that point. *New World Vistas* is the most recent Air Force science and technology forecast completed (in draft) 15 December 1995.

40. Sears, interviewed by author, 8 July 1995.

41. Kármán and Edson, 289.

42. Ibid., 287–89.

43. Godfrey McHugh, interviewed by Murray Green, Washington, D.C., 21 April 1970, MGC, roll 12; and Kármán and Edson, 289.

44. Theodore von Kármán, *Where We Stand: First Report to General of the Army H.H. Arnold on Long Range Research Problems of the Air Forces with a Review of German Plans and Developments, 22 August 1945* (Wright-Patterson AFB, Ohio: Air Force Materiel Command History Office), 12. Sturm has summarized the early efforts of the SAG in *USAF Scientific Advisory Board, Its First Twenty Years*, which includes the evolution and decline of the group through 1964; Alan Gropman has nicely summarized the report itself in "Air Force Planning and the Technology Development Planning Process in the Post-World War II Air Force—The First Decade (1945–1955)," in *Military Planning in the Twentieth Century: The Proceedings of the Eleventh Military History Symposium, USAF Academy, 10–12 October 1984* (Washington, D.C.: Office of Air Force History, 1986), 154–230.

45. Kármán, *Where We Stand*, 5.

46. Ibid., 8, 12, 21.

47. Ibid., 75–76.

48. Maj Gen Haywood S. Hansell Jr. to author, letter, 4 October 1979. Although the AAF did accomplish a limited number of area bombing missions in Europe, these were supplemental to precision attacks in almost every case. American doctrine had been clearly spelled out at the Air Corps Tactical School (ACTS) since 1935 as "the full-blown theory of high-level, daylight precision bombardment of pinpoint targets." Eighth Air Force Commander, Lt Gen Ira C. Eaker, was a 1936 ACTS graduate. Robert T. Finney, *History of the Air Corps Tactical School, 1920–1940* (Washington, D.C.: Center for Air Force History, 1992), 68–70; and Ronald Schaffer, *Wings of Judgment: American Bombing in World War II* (New York: Oxford University Press, 1985), overemphasizes the AAF's use of radar in the European theater and misses altogether the impact of "area bombing" during the war. The *Strategic Bombing Surveys* clearly concluded that morale was not damaged as much as Schaffer implies. For an excellent summary of the report see, *The United States Strategic Bombing Surveys, Summary Volume, 30 September 1945* (reprint; Maxwell AFB, Ala.: Air University Press, 1987), 34–39.

49. Finney, 77–79, 83.

50. Jack H. Nunn, "MIT: A University's Contribution to National Defense," *Military Affairs*, October 1979, 120–25. Nunn emphasized a long relationship which MIT carried on with the Navy, also in the radar and aeronautics field. Dr. Ivan Getting, a member of the MIT RADLAB during these years, recalled that the rivalry is today overplayed. The fact was that, in the 1930s and 40s, travel between east and west in the US was time consuming and inconvenient. MIT and Caltech were separated by distance, not by philosophy. Getting, interviewed by author, 9 November 1994.

51. Ibid., 88.

52. Sturm, 14–15.

53. Kármán and Edson, 290; Gorn, 113–14.

54. Theodore von Kármán, *Toward New Horizons*, vol. 1, *Science: The Key to Air Supremacy*, 15 December 1945, 13.

55. Kármán, *Toward New Horizons*, reprinted version, 69–84. Although future attempts were made to repeat the forecast, none made such a monumental impact on the structure or the vision of the US Air Force. The originals of the Kármán Report are located in both the Arnold and Spaatz Papers in the Library of Congress as well as at the Air Force Materiel Command Archives at Wright-Patterson AFB, Ohio, and the Pentagon Library.

56. Dr. Edward Bowles, interviewed by Murray Green, 6–7 May 1971, Wellesley Hills, Mass., in MGC, roll 12.

57. Dr. Homer Joe Stewart, interviewed by author, 21 July 1995. The ideas ranged from unique approaches to problem solution, normally a not-yet-tried differential approximation, to thoughts on experimental methodology.

58. Arnold to Spaatz, letter, 6 December 1945, MGC.

Chapter 6

Airpower under Construction

By linking up with Kármán, Arnold solved for the Air Force one of America's basic scientific problems, that of dependence upon empirical research. Kármán brought his theoretical and applied aerodynamics ideas to America and Arnold used them as the cornerstone of the infrastructure for future American Air Forces. Even before *Toward New Horizons* was released, Arnold had enacted other programs related to long-term planning for the Army Air Forces (AAF) based on Kármán's first report, *Where We Stand*. The ailing general acted quickly fearing certain postwar budget cuts as well as to defuse the impact of another science and technology forecast authored by Dr. Vannevar Bush, Office of Scientific Research and Development (OSRD) chairman. Bush's report had been released in July 1945 just before *Where We Stand* was completed.

The Bush report, *Science: The Endless Frontier*, recommended a course for scientific research in America. This report, which largely reflected Bush's personal views, would have eliminated the military from performing any form of "long-range scientific research on military problems," just as he had suggested in 1942–43.[1] In fact, there were no military members on the "committees" which compiled Bush's information. The participants were university professors and members of industry. Additionally, the report reemphasized his pessimistic views on rocketry and its applications. What made matters worse, Bush had the president's ear.[2] By 1949 and 1950, Bush's significant government influence apparently contributed to congressional defeat of appropriations large enough to go forward with the Air Force's Atlas rocket, a technology advocated in the first Kármán report.[3]

In 1949, with his publication of *Modern Arms and Free Men*, Bush revealed his true feelings about "military men," views which Arnold may have suspected all along.

> The behavior of man in battle can be soundly estimated only by those who have spent a lifetime in military affairs; the applications that will probably flow out of future science can be soundly estimated only by

153

those who have spent a lifetime developing and utilizing science. Military men have arrived rather generally at the first stage, where they can grasp the value of a device before them; they have by no means arrived at the second, where they can visualize intelligently the devices of the future. Yet military planning for the future that ignores or misinterprets scientific trends is planning in a vacuum. Military men are therefore in a quandary; there is a new and essential element in their planning that they do not understand. To leave it out is obviously absurd. To master it absolutely is impossible.

He continued:

The days are gone when military men could sit on a pedestal, receive the advice of professional groups in neighboring fields who were maintained in a support or tributary position, accept or reject such advice at will, discount its importance as they saw fit, and speak with omniscience on the overall conduct of the war. For one thing, professional men in neighboring fields have no present intention of 'kowtowing' to any military hierarchy, in a world where they know that other professional subjects are just as important in determining the course of future events in the nation's defense as are narrowly limited military considerations. . . . The professional men of the country will work cordially and seriously in professional partnership with the military; they will not become subservient to them; and the military cannot do their full present job without them.[4]

This exposition, a reflection of Bush's perceived experiences with the military since the late 1930s, could only have forced a wide grin from the retired general who knew that he had done the right thing by establishing the Scientific Advisory Group (SAG) in 1944. Kármán agreed with Arnold: "the concept of civilian control (such as advanced by Vannevar Bush) would only injure progress in Air Force research. Such research should be dispersed among all the people and their institutions. The Air Force should feel free to call on anyone who it thinks would be helpful in carrying on its program."[5] Thus, there existed two significant ideological differences between Dr. Bush and Dr. von Kármán: (1) Bush did not believe that military men were capable of "visualizing intelligently the devices of the future," while Kármán was singularly impressed by many Army Air Forces thinkers, particularly Arnold, and (2) Bush insisted that civilian science should direct military long-range planning, while Kármán insisted that military representation was vital to the complete research and development (R&D) process. The differences centered not around who would do the research (civilian scientists were the only qualified individuals at that time) but who would decide what research to pursue, and how specific projects would be decided upon, particularly long-term R&D programs.

In spite of Bush's report, which was geared toward the future of national (rather than uniquely Air Force) scientific development, *Toward New Horizons* (appendix C) and Kármán's earlier report, *Where We Stand* (appendix B), established a long-range forecast and a blueprint for achieving future superiority of the American military airpower system.

SAG to SAB: Evolution

The Army Air Forces witnessed three distinct periods relating to the institutionalization of the Kármán reports. The first of these began in mid-1945 and lasted through Arnold's retirement in February 1946. Both Arnold and Kármán were actively involved, independently and as a team, in establishing the groundwork for institutionalization of science and technology within the AAF. The second period—the Kármán years—were characterized by the professor's active involvement in the follow-up and implementation of major recommendations made in *Toward New Horizons*. The third and most extensive period began with Kármán's resignation as Scientific Advisory Board (SAB) chairman and continues even today. This later period may be characterized by the maturation of the SAB as an institution—the period of independent SAB actions.

During the first period mentioned above, Arnold expanded his multiaxis attack on the problem of long-term scientific and technological planning for the Air Force beyond the establishment of the SAG. In December 1945, while wartime funds were still available, General Arnold created the Office of Scientific Liaison (OSL) in the Pentagon and appointed Col Bernard Schriever as its director. Its purpose was to maintain direct contact with civilian scientists working in industry and at universities throughout the country. Colonel Schriever and Arnold were close despite the difference in rank. Schriever had been married in Arnold's home and the general gave the bride away as a stand-in father. Schriever had flown as a

155

commercial pilot in the exceptionally poor weather conditions of the northwestern United States from 1934 to 1938 and offered Arnold advice on all-weather operations—advice Arnold requested to improve military capability. He was totally dedicated to Arnold as a friend and as a subordinate. Schriever served as director of the OSL for four years and went on to act as the officer most directly responsible for the development of American intercontinental ballistic missiles (ICBM) as the commander of the Western Development Division (also known as the Air Force Ballistic Missile Division [AFBMD]) formed in 1954.[6]

By January 1946, Arnold had allocated $10 million of his military budget to Douglas Aircraft Corporation for a one-year study of future warfare called Project RAND (this blossomed into a three-year, $30 million program). During this first year, a Project RAND mathematician delicately pointed out that not all military problems revolved around math and science. Some problems were best investigated by historians, political scientists, and economists. In 1947, although only 150 were employed there, a "humanities" division was formed at RAND in response to this suggestion. In May 1948, fearing conflict of interest questions between the Air Force and Douglas Corporation, the entire division broke away from Douglas forming the first, nonprofit Research and Development Corporation (RAND) in America.[7]

The stated goal for RAND was to provide a "program of study and research on the broad subject of intercontinental warfare."[8] It was to offer long-term, unbiased, thoughtful research to Air Force planners. By 1950, over 800 men and women were employed in support of that task.[9] In truth, RAND served another purpose in its early days; to act as a counterbalance to Dr. Bush's formulation for the future of American scientific research. Arnold's establishment of Project RAND was the direct result of the general's association with Dr. Edward Bowles and industrial as well as familial ties to Donald Douglas.[10] In the case of RAND, Arnold acted independently of Kármán's direct influence or suggestions.

In addition to Project RAND, Arnold had been busy authorizing technology development programs which looked to future developments, particularly in guided missiles.

Influenced to act by Kármán's initial report *Where We Stand*, the general's vision for the potential of "unpiloted things" for future air forces was reinforced.[11] Although he had officially retired in February, a plan for the April 1946 guided missile program had been determined and approved during his last months in command of the AAF. A total of $34 million had been allocated to 28 different AAF guided missile projects.[12] Arnold's fears concerning the budget were more than accurate. In 1947, the military budget was slashed in typical postwar downsizing and the guided missile budget fell from $34 million to $13 million forcing cancellation of 10 programs already underway. Only short-term projects holding potential for completion in a minimum amount of time were continued. Of the surviving programs only one was a long-range, rocket-propelled missile (ICBM-type)—the MX-774B, which was under contract to Consolidated Vultee Aircraft Corporation (Convair).[13] Thus, although Arnold recognized the need for development in missiles, budget constraints limited Air Force programs in this area until the national political climate was once again altered by an external threat.

Arnold's final official contribution to the incorporation of recommendations made in Kármán's reports was to convince General Spaatz to activate a permanent version of the Scientific Advisory Group as part of his staff.[14] Kármán felt so strongly about this particular recommendation that he immediately pursued action on the subject. Only five days after transmittal of the original *Toward New Horizons* summary volume he sent Arnold a detailed memorandum explaining the importance of the formation of such a group. Kármán wrote,

> It is my strong belief that the necessity for scientific advice will come up frequently in the future and that the Commanding General should have available a permanent group of scientific advisors of high standing, who are familiar with the needs of the AAF, but whose main activities are outside the AAF. . . . It is my belief that such a group would not duplicate any of the work of the office of the Deputy Chief of Staff in charge of Research and Development, since it would not be concerned with any of the current research projects, but would give the Commanding General information and advice on future trends and long-range possibilities.[15]

157

Arnold acted immediately. In a 21 December memorandum to Spaatz, Arnold insisted that *Toward New Horizons* "should be used as a guide for scientific and pre-planning people for many years to come." A meeting was suggested to talk about the formation of a permanent organization. To attend were Lt Gen Ira C. Eaker, deputy commander AAF, and Maj Gen Curtis E. LeMay, deputy chief of staff for R&D, General Spaatz, and Arnold.[16]

By 9 January 1946, the concept of a permanent advisory group was agreed upon but one stumbling block remained. LeMay, who had been selected by Spaatz for the R&D command, wanted control of the new advisors, a suggestion which Kármán rejected.[17] In response to LeMay's attempt to take control of the board, Kármán reiterated his insistence that the "Scientific Advisory Group to the Commanding General AAF, will inform the Commanding General of new developments in science and the results of fundamental scientific research which offer possibilities for the solution of Air Force problems." The words "Commanding General" appeared in eight of 10 paragraphs, a total of 10 times in the brief two-page memo. Also included were definitions of board functions which included personnel structure, meeting schedule, and the possibility for establishing "temporary panels" to participate in "special studies."[18] Arnold, feeling obliged to let Spaatz make the final decision himself, unofficially transferred command to Spaatz in January 1946.

Realizing that his dream of preparing a blueprint for future American Air Forces had been completed, and that his health was rapidly deteriorating, Arnold retired from active service in February 1946 (see appendix A), the same month that the original charter for the SAG expired. The last formal meeting of the AAF Scientific Advisory Group was held on 6 February 1946. Arnold addressed the group and thanked them for their super-human efforts during the past year. He also decorated SAG members with the Meritorious Civilian Service Award and asked that they continue to support the scientific aspects of the Air Forces even, and especially, in times of peace. On 1 March 1946, Kármán resigned his government position as AAF scientific advisor, ending one of the most intellectually active chapters ever written in US Army history.[19]

USAF Photo

Arnold awards Kármán the Meritorious Civilian Service Medal after the SAG's first year. Arnold retired the following year while Kármán continued as SAB chairman for the next decade.

Stagnation

During the second week of February, LeMay had once again initiated actions to put the scientists under his control. Kármán realized what Spaatz and LeMay did not understand. LeMay's research and development organization was concerned with "the over-all program of current projects, the relative priorities assigned, the elimination of unnecessary items, and the possible requirements for new items. Our program is to maintain a strong healthy program of current research and development."[20] Placing Kármán's panel into that type of environment was in direct opposition to its previous function. Times had changed, however, and with Arnold's exit, the forceful LeMay took control of the newly designated Scientific Advisory Board which met for the first time in June.

Kármán, who had accepted the leadership of the SAB despite his misgivings about its attachment to LeMay rather than Spaatz, called the first meeting to order on 17 June 1946. Now facing huge reductions in forces and funds, the SAB had little immediate capability to enact many specific recommendations from *Toward New Horizons*. The new peacetime commander, although he openly supported continued scientific research for the Army Air Forces, lacked the determined, forward-looking drive of the wartime General Arnold. Coupled with the lack of working funds and the less-than-perfect reporting arrangements, the previous year of hard work seemed almost a waste of time.[21]

LeMay's responsibilities as deputy chief of Air Staff for R&D were largely tied to here-and-now requirements. Consequently, the SAB began to stagnate. LeMay's memoirs shed a bit more light on other possible explanations for the failure to utilize the board. "I certainly hadn't been screeching with enthusiasm about my new duties," LeMay recalled, "but it didn't take me long to become mighty interested. It was strictly a management job. I didn't know much about research and development."[22]

USAF Photo

The first Scientific Advisory Board meeting, June 1946. "The Boss" at the head of the table.

Things got so tedious for the SAB that at least one of the original members threw in the towel, quitting the board in 1947. When Kármán asked Dr. Ivan Getting" why he quit the SAB, Getting replied, "Because you weren't doing anything."

Schweinhund!" muttered Kármán.[23]

Getting's disgust confirmed what Kármán had already realized, that there had been no implementation of the SAG's recommendations other than the imperfect establishment of the board itself. Kármán later offered the insightful explanation that "firmness with Russia was not yet elevated into a national policy and national defense was not a matter of deep public concern to a nation in peace and complacent over its A-bomb strength. It seemed to me that only a few of the more conscientious Air Force officers were interested in the long-range future of the Air Force."[24] The newly formed SAB was caught up in the traditional demobilization of the military which had occurred after each American war and national attitudes toward advancement in military technology were muted. Arnold's departure, budget cuts, new leadership, and a major reorganization of the national defense organization—which created the independent Air Force on 17 September 1947—taken together nearly snuffed the SAB out of existence. Lt Gen Donald L. Putt, SAB military director from 1948 to 1952, recalled that the SAB "almost went out of existence in 1948 because nobody was paying any attention to it. It was not being asked to advise which was the reason it was set up in the first place, and it almost disappeared."[25] The traditional Kármán ideological germination period which took place after his initial "seed-sowing" turned out to be a few years longer than the normal one or two years associated with traditional Kármán projects. It was in the face of such adversity that Kármán led the SAB forward without his long-time friend Hap Arnold.

The second period of implementation of Kármán's studies began without the dynamism of General Arnold or the bottomless funding which the Army Air Forces had enjoyed during the previous five years. The newly formed SAB, now reporting to Maj Gen Curtis E. LeMay, forwarded its first set of program recommendations—the results of its June meeting—to General Spaatz on 29 August 1946. Spaatz, although he approved implementation of the proposals, made it clear that any additional funding or restructuring of forces included within these proposals was enough to cancel any recommendation.[26]

Almost as important as lack of funding was the simple fact that the SAB was a new organization within a large, established bureaucracy. The SAG (established in 1944), whose purpose was to produce the Air Force's long-range science and technology blueprint, was disbanded. There were questions which originated in the staff about what function the new board would actually serve. Would they be relegated to immediate issues? Would they have a forecasting function? Some officers, in the face of budget constraints and Air Force reorganization, saw no useful purpose for the SAB at all. Others, although realizing its possible importance in providing advice on scientific matters, were at a loss when deciding just how this might be accomplished. The fledgling SAB was going through growing pains. There existed no organizational precedent for such a permanent group. Kármán and his military staff made up procedures and policies as the need for such arose. And, although Kármán had a "remarkable capacity for picking people who knew the long-term significance of their scientific fields," confusion at all levels of the Army chain of command concerning the possible uses of the SAB hindered its effectiveness.[27]

By May 1947, Kármán began to realize, as did many of the SAB members, that something was wrong. "Crystal gazing" was one appropriate function for the SAB, but the major forecast for the future had already been accomplished. Kármán determined that the SAB function logically entailed not only the future of science in the Air Force, but was also related to the immediate present. "We should also establish a certain procedure," Kármán now emphasized, "which will make it possible for the military establishment to use the services of the individual board members for urgent problems."[28] Kármán also suggested that other administrative changes should include forming specific standing committees for specific Air Force problems, offering SAB help to Air Force field agencies, and clearly defining other roles and missions for the organization. Kármán and the SAB were defining their own function.

An important change, one which allowed greater latitude in self-definition, occurred later that year. General LeMay left for Europe in September 1947 to assume command of the United States Air Forces in Europe (USAFE).[29] He was replaced by Lt Gen Laurence Craigie, commander of the newly established Directorate of Research and Development.

New Vitality

Lieutenant General Craigie, the first American military man to pilot a jet aircraft, had a much greater understanding of the importance of R&D than LeMay. Craigie had been involved with Arnold's XP-59A project from the beginning and was absolutely aware of the importance of R&D to the success of the AAF. Kármán, realizing this, immediately convinced Craigie that the SAB needed to report directly to the chief of staff, as he had recommended in *Toward New Horizons*, rather than through other R&D channels. He also suggested that the board add a military director of sufficient rank to get things done around the Pentagon when necessary. This was not a new approach either. In December 1945, Kármán had emphasized that the successful accomplishment of the SAG's mission was assured because of Arnold's insistence that they disregard current projects, and that they reported directly to the commanding general. The professor had reemphasized the recommendation in 1946 to LeMay who disregarded the advice.[30] Spaatz, following Craigie's careful explanation of the problem, not only supported the recommendations, he enacted them immediately. On 14 May 1948, the Spaatz-Kármán agreement went into effect as Air Force Regulation (AFR) 20-30, the SAB charter. These ups and downs were largely a result of the massive restructuring process which was extricating the Air Force from the Army. The process was finalized in the summer and enacted 18 September 1947.[31] By April 1948, with Craigie's help, initial administrative obstacles had been removed and with Kármán still acting as the chairman, the SAB and the independent Air Force began the real work of attaining and maintaining military air supremacy.

The existence of the SAB was not only the result of Kármán's *Toward New Horizons* recommendations and Arnold's broad support of the document, but also a result of Kármán's tenacity in seeing that his recommendations were implemented properly, even if not immediately.[32] Additionally, help was rendered by individuals who supported Arnold's and Kármán's dedication to the importance of science and technology.

With the SAB poised to function as Kármán had originally visualized, he was now ready to pursue further implementation of recommendations from *Toward New Horizons*. Craigie, who saved the board from extermination, held the military directorship until September 1948 when he was replaced by Maj Gen Donald L. Putt. Putt had studied under Kármán at Caltech and now the two came together again, teacher and student. It was the Kármán/Putt combination which actually assured the utilization of the SAB from November 1948 onward.

During the mid-November SAB meeting Kármán took the opportunity to reemphasize the need for the Air Force to "lay down the leading principles of their own policy and establish the foundation of organized research in their own realm," which he had established in the 1945 report.[33] Gen Hoyt S. Vandenberg's reply reflected the immediate impact of Kármán's November 1948 SAB report. In a 7 April 1949 statement to the SAB, Vandenberg, who had replaced Spaatz as Air Force chief of staff wrote, "I am determined that our research and development activities shall have adequate support in funds, facilities, and properly-trained personnel, and that the USAF shall continually increase the efficiency and effectiveness of our development work on new aircraft, missiles, and air defense systems." His memo finished with a request for the SAB to provide him with the "ultimate plan" for Air Force research and development facilities.[34] A study, however, is not a facility, but in this case it was the first step toward a total reorientation of Air Force R&D policy.[35]

The SAB's first legitimate "special" study was led by Electronics Panel member Louis N. Ridenour, dean of the University of Illinois. His group was immediately dubbed the Ridenour Committee. The committee consisted of two SAB members and seven nonmembers—one of these was Dr.

James H. Doolittle—which established the working standard for SAB ad hoc studies from that time onward. It was also with this committee that Kármán's role in the SAB slowly began to change. Kármán did not sit on the committee itself. Instead he oversaw the SAB as an entity and was involved with establishing committee composition rather than participating in individual committee function. The professor was tending his SAB garden.

Meanwhile, Kármán decided that he could no longer devote adequate time to his California responsibilities. In March 1949 Kármán resigned his position as director of the Jet Propulsion Lab (JPL) and as chairman of the GALCIT although he remained a member of the faculty.[36] The professor was then free to devote time pursuing institutionalization of his 1945 recommendations.

On 11 July 1949 the Ridenour Committee met for the first time and Vandenberg challenged them to "give us a picture of what we ought to be doing but what we are not doing."[37] The Ridenour Committee spent the next two months touring Air Force facilities and contemplating the proper direction for Air Force R&D. In September the report was given to Kármán who approved it and passed it along to General Vandenberg on 21 September 1949. Not surprisingly, Kármán approved the report quickly. It reflected his original recommendations on R&D restructuring now almost five years old. The two major tenets of the report were to reorganize the Air Staff ensuring that R&D functions were isolated from logistics and to establish a separate command for R&D, one not tied to procurement.[38] Kármán's 1945 recommendations read, "In the special case of the Air Forces, two solutions have been proposed: (1) the establishment of one Air Staff section for research and development; and (2) a supervising and directing agency attached to the office of the Chief of Staff."[39] Administrative changes were not addressed in detail because another committee, organized at the Air University was examining those issues at Vandenberg's direction.

The Air University group dubbed the Anderson Committee, delivered similar recommendations to the chief of staff concerning reorganization of the Air Force's R&D establishment. The combination of recommendations generated by these independent yet similar reports, coupled with the smooth salesmanship of Dr. Jimmy Doolittle, convinced Muir Fairchild and Vandenberg that a separate R&D command was the logical next step, something Kármán had advocated since 1945 and the Air Force was now able to direct without Army interference.[40]

On 23 January 1950 the Air Force established the office of the deputy chief of staff for development on the Air Staff and the Air Research and Development Command (ARDC), exactly as Kármán had envisioned the institution in the first place. Less directly, but definitely by design and personal influence, Kármán's initial recommendations concerning scientific ideas and staff organization were finally institutionalized within the Air Force's organizational structure. The first tangible result of this restructuring came in the form of an ARDC study prepared by Maj Gen Gordon SaVille, deputy chief of staff for development, which recommended that a "systems approach" to new weapons be adopted. By that SaVille meant that development of a weapon "system" required development of support equipment as well as the actual hardware itself. This approach, although not the direct result of Arnold's philosophy of airpower, certainly reflected the evolution of the Air Force into a system building organization and "gained immediate acceptance" from the Air Staff.[41] Again, the establishment of ARDC was assisted by a group of followers, dedicated to Kármán's scientific ideology, and their ability to convince others of the importance of his philosophy to the Air Force.[42] Kármán's ideology was slowly being embedded into the science and technology foundation of the Air Force due to his own perseverance as well as the concerted efforts of those who had adopted that ideology.

While the Ridenour/Doolittle Committee findings were being discussed, Kármán was concurrently pursuing the establishment of an Air Force aeronautical research facility. In *Toward New Horizons* he wrote, "The Air Forces must be authorized to expand existing AAF research facilities and create new ones to do their own research and also to make such facilities available to scientists and industrial concerns working on problems of the Air Force."[43] In its first meeting, the SAB had established a standing committee to provide advice on advanced wind tunnel developments but budget constraints loomed large over any possible action recommended by this panel.[44] When the National Advisory Committee for Aeronautics (NACA) learned of the AAF's plan they immediately formulated a wind tunnel plan of their own. The competition between the NACA and the AAF eventually resulted in the formulation of the National Unitary Wind Tunnel Plan.[45] By May 1948 a bill had been introduced to the Congress which would have provided funding for a facility like the one Kármán envisioned in his 1945 report. Adjournment of the 80th Congress, however, preceded a vote on the bill. In essence, the Air Force and the NACA (as well as other organizations, particularly the US Navy) had been at odds over the proposal for an independent Air Force aeronautics center for the last four years. Nonetheless, by early 1949, the combined funding bill was once again ready for congressional approval. At that point, Kármán took an active yet limited role in the proceedings. The professor wrote directly to W. Stuart Symington, secretary of the Air Force, urging a swift activation of the facility to insure American airpower preeminence.

The Arnold Engineering and Development Center (AEDC) was one of the many legacies of SAG recommendations.

Following several months of debate and delay, bill S-1267 passed the Congress in August 1949 authorizing the Unitary Plan (Title I) and the Air Force Plan (Title II). It is interesting to note that the NACA, then headed by Dr. Hugh Latimer Dryden, former deputy of the SAG, testified in favor of the Air Engineering and Development Center (AEDC) portion of the plan marking an overt change in the NACA/Air Force relationship which had existed to that point. For the next year, additional funding requests were authorized and one of Kármán's lifelong pursuits became an Air Force reality.[46] The AEDC was renamed for General Arnold in 1950.

The final approval and establishment of the AEDC was part of an extremely complex set of interactions between people, institutions, and ideas. The origins of the National Unitary Wind Tunnel controversy, however, may be directly linked to Kármán's original SAG report, and subsequent standing committee, which suggested such a facility as early as 1945. Kármán's major actor in this affair was Dr. Frank L. Wattendorf, author of the "Gas Turbine Propulsion" chapter of *Toward New Horizons.* Wattendorf had written a memo to Gen Franklin O. Carroll, chief of the Engineering Division, Air Materiel Command (AMC), dated 19 June 1945, containing a proposal for a new Air Force development center based on his Operation Lusty experiences in Germany.[47] Without the instigation of the SAB, the National Wind Tunnel Facility would likely have been a NACA-dominated institution. As it ended up, the NACA was relegated to serving industrial needs while the Air Force obtained the go-ahead for its planned facility. Despite the House Armed Services Committee's insistence that the military installation was to be used for "evaluation" purposes, there was no doubt that Kármán intended the AEDC to be used as a major research and development center for Air Force aeronautical endeavors.[48]

The AEDC did not come easy. The old story of controversy and bureaucratic posturing which had plagued jet engine development in the early 1940s was at the heart of the wind tunnel debate in this instance as well.[49] The Air Force, however, had finally eclipsed many other institutions in its attempt to maintain its own R&D. The AEDC, in reality, was the manifestation of the NACA's final collapse. The NACA's research philosophy which "valued process over prescience, the team over the individual, experiment over theory, engineering over science, incremental refinement of the existing paradigm over revolutionary creation of new paradigms," had seen the end of its usefulness.[50] Kármán's theoretical approach to scientific and technological applications had been established within the Air Force system and was ready to fill the void.

The decade of the fifties opened with promise for the accomplishment of many more of the challenges set in 1945 by the SAG. Military funding once again became available as the Soviet threat grew and even more so during the Korean War. In fiscal year 1950, the Air Force received $238 million for R&D. In 1951 the total reached a staggering $522.9 million.[51] The reality of an ever increasing role for military aviation technology toppled many skeptic's arguments against continued military research and development. In fact, the SAB received so many requests for studies and investigations during the war that it was impossible to handle them all, even with an increase in staffing provided for by the ballooning budget.[52] Kármán's perseverance had entrenched the SAB in the hierarchy of the Air Force and the crisis of war fertilized its rapidly expanding roots. Germination of Kármán's original SAG report was complete. All that remained was for the professor to move on to some new pursuit as was his usual method.

The establishment of the North Atlantic Treaty Organization (NATO) provided Kármán that opportunity. As far as Kármán's association with the Air Force was concerned, his quest for the formation of an international SAB signaled the transition from the "Kármán years" to the third developmental period—the emergence of the SAB as its own institution.

Throughout the Korean War, Kármán continued to act as SAB chairman but spent less time concerned with SAB matters and more time pursuing the possibility of establishing a Paris-based scientific board in the style of the Air Force's SAB. Kármán named the proposed organization the NATO Advisory Group for Aeronautical Research and Development (AGARD). The concept earned immediate support from William Burden, special assistant for R&D to the Air Force Secretary Thomas K. Finletter. Kármán convinced Maj Gen Gordon SaVille of the potential for such an organization in the face of the developing cold war. Despite stiff opposition from the US Navy (again) the NATO AGARD became a reality on 24 January 1952. For the first two years, the US Air Force was appointed as AGARD's executive agent and Kármán was offered the chair.[53] The professor's belief that scientific ideas were best shared openly and internationally saw the perfect forum in the concept of the AGARD.[54] But he did not immediately resign from the SAB. The Russian's successful detonation of a nuclear weapon in 1949 had provided one last challenge for Kármán—one which he intended to finish.

It was the clamor of ICBM development which finally established the SAB as an independent entity and carried it into its third period of development. From 1950 to 1953, the SAB formed several different committees which evaluated the potential of nuclear power and missile systems. The Nuclear Weapons Panel signified the transition from the Kármán-led organization to a SAB which depended upon other experts to accomplish their tasks. Kármán was only involved as an approving authority to the final reports which these groups offered. Yet his ideas remained a vital part of the organization for many years through the participation of his former students and close associates in SAB matters. By 1953, Kármán was totally satisfied with the structure and philosophical approach taken by board members in discharging their function.[55]

The March 1953 establishment of the Nuclear Weapons Panel was a result of the successful detonation of an American thermonuclear device in November 1952. The "Mike shot" illuminated additional possibilities for the use of nuclear power in a variety of weapons. Kármán selected the committee chair, Dr. John von Neumann, formerly of the Manhattan Project, based upon his expertise in the nuclear field. Also on the committee was Dr. Edward Teller, who was co-credited by many with the development of the theory which enabled the hydrogen bomb, as well as "practically every top nuclear physicist we had in the country."[56] The SAB ad hoc "von Neumann Committee" determined that a 1,500 pound "dry" hydrogen device had become a possibility. The comparatively low weight and increased yield allowed a relaxation of accuracy requirements and thereby lessened the required size of the missile itself. This was remarkable since the first test detonation device had to be loaded aboard a ship as it was too heavy for air transport. General Schriever, the project officer for the ICBM program, recalled that this revelation also meant that a practical, nuclear warhead equipped ICBM was a near-term possibility.[57]

National attention to Soviet nuclear programs coupled with the Eisenhower administration's desire for frugality resulted in the establishment of a committee to study missile organization in America. Trevor Gardner, special assistant for R&D, assigned John von Neumann as the chairman of this group, also known as the Teapot Committee.[58] Armed with the knowledge just gained in the SAB Nuclear Weapons Panel report, von Neumann and his group expanded upon the possibilities for both hardware and organization of national missile programs in America. The February 1954 Teapot Report recommended an immediate increase in the procurement of ICBMs as well as a streamlined organization for obtaining these weapons "with highest national priority."[59] The Soviet's test of its first hydrogen weapon in August 1953 supported the general feeling that the Soviets were further advanced than the US in missile development and added urgency to these recommendations.

The results of von Neumann's report were carried by Gardner to James R. Killian, acting presidential science advisor and president of MIT. Rapid advances in ICBM development were supported by the results of the "Bravo" nuclear test accomplished on 1 March 1954, which proved the potential for lighter, more powerful warheads advocated in the report. By 14 May, the administration had agreed with the findings of the report. The establishment of the Western Development Division (WDD) charged to proceed with utmost speed in establishing an ICBM program was the direct result of the Teapot Committee's recommendations.[60] But General Schriever, first commander of that organization, gave credit to the SAB rather than the Teapot Committee. He said, "To the SAB I give full credit for providing the credibility that we needed to proceed on a program of the magnitude of the ballistic missile program."[61] After the WDD was activated on 2 August 1954, the US proceeded with the development of the Atlas ICBM, the first in a series of ICBMs which were an integral part of every national defense policy which followed.[62] The SAB had demonstrated its importance to both the Air Force and the nation during the early days of nuclear weapons development.

Kármán had witnessed the entire process from his offices in Paris and Washington. He had even approved the initial SAB Nuclear Weapons Panel report in 1954. But his personal involvement in nuclear panel reports after that was basically nil. The independent success of the SAB and its individual members must have given him the reassurance that he needed concerning the standing of the board because he resigned as SAB chairman in September 1954, one month after the establishment of the WDD. Kármán had witnessed the SAB blossom as an Air Force institution. Not only that, the SAB had been utilized by the Air Force and the nation in making critical decisions concerning defense policy in the face of the uncertain challenges of the cold war. For better or for worse, SAB advice had been instrumental in establishing the infrastructure and the mind set within the government which preceded the arms race between the United States and the Soviet Union.[63]

Kármán offered the reason of ill health to Gen Nathan Twining for his resignation. This may only have been partially true as he once used a similar excuse with Robert Millikan immediately after General Arnold had asked him to form the original SAG.[64] The confidence he felt in the success of the SAB as an institution within the Air Force gave him the final impetus he needed to move on, concentrating solely on AGARD.[65] Yet his resignation did not mean an end to his influence. General Twining made him chairman emeritus for as long as he lived to permanently link the name of the SAB's renowned founder to that organization and the Air Force.[66] Additionally, several of Kármán's former students, his closest Guggenheim Aeronautics Laboratory, California Institute of Technology (GALCIT) associate Dr. Clark Millikan being one, remained members of the SAB. Additionally, General Putt was once again its military director. In this way, the professor's ideology was carried forward within the SAB for another decade.[67]

Kármán's direct SAB influence had come to an end, at least temporarily. Even before his resignation went into effect, General Putt asked the professor to chair another long-range forecast for the Air Force. The professor's response was initially negative. He had just arrived back in Paris and was buried in the process of forging the AGARD into an SAB-type organization. This task was particularly difficult because of the international cooperation required to coordinate policies and events. Understandably, he refused to begin such a study in 1954.[68] If nothing else, Putt was persistent. At regular intervals for the next two years he sent Mr. Chester Hasert to Paris in an effort to convince the former chairman to reconsider his 1954 decision. But Kármán felt, at that time, the SAB did not hold the expertise required to perform a broad-based study of the *Toward New Horizons* variety. Advancement in technology had simply come too far for a small panel of experts to tackle as they had in 1945.[69]

By 1957, another study had been planned despite Kármán's reservations about its potential. The Air Force contracted the National Academy of Sciences to complete the work and the SAB was relegated to a participatory, rather than a leadership, role. Kármán had accepted the chair for the study and selected Dr. Hugh Dryden, his deputy for *Toward New Horizons*, and Dr. H. Guyford Stever as his primary assistants during that summer. Although ties to the SAB were fairly strong between individuals, the institution of the SAB itself was basically a nonplayer in the 1957–1958 Woods Hole Summer Study. Making matters worse, many of the non-SAB participants flatly refused to discuss military issues as they pertained to space operations. The report was headed in a lack-luster direction until the launch of *Sputnik* on 4 October 1957. At that point, although the study was not even completed, it was scrapped in the face of public furor over the perceived crisis.[70] This was a clear indication of the importance of public opinion upon the success or failure of scientific forecasts. Dr. Stever recalled that "the significance of space was completely underestimated, not only by our military services but by society in general. As a consequence, when *Sputnik* appeared, we had a crisis of major proportions."[71]

Although a second Woods Hole study was completed in the summer of 1958, it was too late to repair the perceived lack of action within the military concerning space operations and satellites. In essence, it was a failed attempt to "save face."

The Woods Hole Summer Studies had cost the Air Force over $900,000 and had produced nothing of significance—a disappointment for Kármán, but to him not a surprise.[72] The lesson to be learned from the 1957–58 study was that national public opinion actually held a great deal of influence over the success or failure of government studies. In this case, the immediacy of the sputnik crisis cast an extremely dark shadow over the importance of long-range thinking when a perceived national failure existed in the immediate present.

Dr. Hans Mark, secretary of the Air Force from 1980 to 1981, once remarked that "the best way to judge a laboratory is by its junkyard. If the junkyard is too clean, then the laboratory isn't taking any risks. And if it's really too full of junk, you'll recognize that nothing is really coming out."[73] Considered in that fashion, a failure or two was not all bad, particularly in light of the rapid developments on space technology and rapidly expanding national ideology concerning military operations there. With the 1958 study behind him, Kármán returned to Europe and the Parisian café scene where he resided on-and-off until his death in 1963.

Meanwhile, the SAB continued its important work for the Air Force. Throughout the next four decades, successes and a few failures marked the accomplishments of the SAB. One SAB member perceived that over time, "the more advanced technologies were, the more involved the SAB became."[74] From 1955 to 1995 the SAB has accomplished over 350 studies (not all successes). They included such projects as aircraft nuclear propulsion, the "Dyna-Soar" program, wing strengthening and modification of the C-5A Galaxy heavy airlift aircraft and F-111 (TFX) fighter, and remotely piloted vehicles. Recommendations involving arms control, space technology, directed energy weapons, composite materials, and Global Positioning System (GPS) usage and development also highlight SAB accomplishments. The list was diverse, broad in scope, and often international in consequence.[75] These studies fell into one of the three categories—immediate projects, midterm projects, and long-range forecasts—categories which Kármán himself had established in 1948. The nature of the studies continued to reflect Kármán's original charter which emphasized broad-based approaches to

Air Force problems.[76] The emphasis placed upon the importance of these established missions was reemphasized from time to time. Dr. Robert Loewy, SAB chairman 1973–1977, and Dr. Gene McCall, the current (1995) chairman, both reaffirmed the importance of these three missions during their tenure.[77]

Yet attempting to prove that Kármán's ideology is still influential in today's Air Force has remained an interesting challenge. In November 1994, Secretary of the Air Force Dr. Sheila Widnall, and Air Force Chief of Staff Gen Ronald Fogleman, issued a challenge to Dr. Gene McCall and the Air Force SAB at the SAB's 50th anniversary celebration. General Fogleman, who attended graduate school at Duke University where he studied history, spoke first. "Close Air Force operator and scientific community ties are as important today as they were when Hap Arnold and Dr. von Kármán got together. We need scientific visionaries who can look into the future and advise the Chief of Staff and other senior Air Force leaders about technologies which might be relevant ten or twenty years from now."[78] Then Dr. Widnall took the podium and spoke jointly for herself and the chief:

> I want to set a challenge for the SAB. As we celebrate the legacy of General Arnold and Dr. von Kármán, General Fogleman and I would like you to look toward the promises of the future. We want you to rekindle that constant inquisitive attitude toward science. So today, on this fiftieth anniversary of Arnold's challenge to Kármán, I would like to issue a challenge to today's Scientific Advisory Board. I challenge you, once again, to search the world for the most advanced aerospace ideas and project them into the future. Fifty years ago the SAG stepped up to the challenge of writing *Toward New Horizons*. Today, let's begin the search for *New World Vistas*.[79]

New World Vistas, the most recent Air Force science and technology study, and the first one completed under the singular direction of the SAB since *Toward New Horizons*, was presented to the secretary of the Air Force and the chief of staff on 15 December 1995 at the Pentagon—exactly 50 years after the first study was turned over to Arnold.[80] Clearly, Arnold's vision and Kármán's intellectual legacy live on, not only in the minds of today's Air Force leaders, but in their actions as well. Accomplishment of this particular study occupied nearly all of the SAB's working schedule for the better part of an entire

USAF Photo

The 1995 Scientific Advisory Board met at Maxwell Air Force Base in May.

year.[81] As to the ultimate success of *New World Vistas*, time will judge. But if the current national frenzy for technological advancement revolving around computer power continues into the foreseeable future—reflecting national support and acceptance of technological progress—the chances for success and eventual institutionalization of its findings are much greater than they were at the time of sputnik and Woods Hole.

Kármán once ruminated about the idea that reports do not make policy, administrations do.[82] The support which *Toward New Horizons* eventually received, largely a result of his own perseverance, compared with his unpleasant professional experience at Woods Hole, convinced him of the truth in that thought. On 31 January 1996, Dr. Widnall and Dr. McCall held a national press conference releasing *New World Vistas* publicly perhaps in an effort to openly gain public support for the ideas contained within the 2,000-plus page study. That night, on ABC *World News Tonight* with

USAF Photo

The SAB, chaired by Dr. Gene McCall, delivered *New World Vistas*, the most recent science and technology forecast for the Air Force, on 15 December 1995.

Peter Jennings and on Cable News Network (CNN)—over a video segment which demonstrated "brain-wave" aircraft control, advanced unmanned aerial vehicles (UAV), and a smattering of concepts for yet-to-be developed nonlethal weapons—the secretary's words were transmitted to millions of American news-watchers. "I can guarantee you," she stated emphatically, "that this report will not sit on the shelf and gather dust." It seemed that Dr. McCall could not contain his grin.

Notes

1. Vannevar Bush, *Science: The Endless Frontier: A Report to the President* (Washington, D.C.: Government Printing Office, 1945).

2. Ibid. The report also suggested that rockets and long-range missiles were hopelessly expensive and a long way off in the future. As a comparison, *Toward New Horizons* which predicted a 6,000-mile range

missile in its rocketry section (see appendix C); also see Lee Edson, "He Tamed the Wind," *Saturday Evening Post*, 3 August 1957, 24, 76–78; and Theodore von Kármán with Lee Edson, *Wind and Beyond: Theodore von Kármán, Pioneer in Aviation ad Pathfinder in Space* (Boston: Little, Brown and Co., 1967), 271–72.

3. Theodore von Kármán, "Pilotless Aircraft," in *Where We Stand: First Report to General of the Army H. H. Arnold on Long Range Research Problems of the AIR FORCES with a Review of German Plans and Developments*, 22 August 1945 (see appendix B); and Kármán and Edson, 300.

4. Vannevar Bush, *Modern Arms and Free Men: A Discussion of the Role of Science in Preserving Democracy* (New York: Simon and Schuster, 1949), 252–53. It is interesting to note the differentiation Bush makes between "professional" men (men of science), and military men. His tone is also bitter in the extreme which may reflect his disappointment in never breaking the military decision-making barrier. Dr. Bush may be the reflection of civilian scientists and the Manhattan Project. In this, the most expensive and secret R&D program of the war, civilians were particularly dominant both politically and scientifically.

5. Kármán and Edson, 294. Parenthesis are Kármán's.

6. Gen Bernard A. Schriever, USAF, Retired, interviewed by author, tape, 9 November 1994, National Academy of Sciences, Washington, D.C., and telephone interview with author, 12 March 1996, Washington, D.C. General Schriever recalled that the OSL changed names a few times in its short history and its functions were eventually absorbed by other Air Force organizations; also Herbert F. York, *Arms and the Physicist* (Woodbury, N. Y.: American Institute of Physics Press, 1995), 211–12.

7. A. E. Raymond, Columbia University Oral History Review (CUOHR), in Murray Green Collection (MGC), roll 12. The actual decision to give Douglas $10 million was made during a meeting in California in which Ted Conant, Donald Douglas, Edward Bowles, and General Arnold were present; Robert Frank Futrell, *Ideas, Concepts, and Doctrine: Basic Thinking in the United States Air Force*, vol. 1, *1907–1960* (Maxwell AFB, Ala.: Air University Press, December 1989), 478; Kármán and Edson, 302; I. B. Holley, "Jet Lag in the Army Air Corps," 167–73. The Ford Foundation began contributing funds for RAND projects in 1948. By 1959, Advanced Research Project Agency (ARPA) and NASA were also linked to RAND projects. By the mid-1970s RAND was working on projects for state, local, and private organizations, the Air Force being only a small part of the organization represented by the RAND Project Air Force division. Gen Lauris Norstad believed that Dr. Edward Bowles had a great deal of influence over Arnold's decision to form RAND. Lauris Norstad, interviewed by Murray Green, 15 July 1953, MGC, roll 12.

8. "An Introduction to Project Air Force," RAND Publication CP-77 (Santa Monica, Calif.: RAND, June 1990), 1–3.

9. Dr. Courtland Perkins, "Impromptu remarks given at the National Academy of Sciences," transcript, 10 November 1994, on the occasion of the

50th anniversary of the SAB. Differentiated from the SAB, RAND produced studies and research papers while the SAB gave direct advice to the Air Force chief of staff. This role was eventually expanded to include the secretary of the Air Force as well.

10. Martin J. Collins, "Internalizing the Civilian: RAND and the Air Force in the Early Cold War," typed manuscript of speech given at the 1993 Annual Society for the History of Technology (SHOT) meeting; and Mrs. Barbara Arnold, interviewed by author, 6 April 1995. Arnold's son, William Bruce, married Barbara Douglas.

11. Described in Futrell, 205 and 262, note 68. Arnold frequently referred to missiles as unpiloted craft as the term *ICBM* had not yet been officially coined.

12. Jacob Neufeld, *Ballistic Missiles in the United States Air Force, 1945–1960* (Washington, D.C.: Office of Air Force History, 1990), 26–27; also Futrell, 239.

13. Neufeld, 28–33, and 239; also see Max Rosenberg, *The Air Force and the National Guided Missile Program, 1944–1950* (Washington, D.C.: USAF Historical Division Liaison Office, June 1964), 75–85.

14. Theodore von Kármán, *Toward New Horizons,* vol. 1, *Science: The Key to Air Supremacy,* 15 December 1945, 14.12a.

15. Theodore von Kármán to Henry H. Arnold, letter, 20 December 1945, SAB, 1944–45 file.

16. Henry H. Arnold to Carl A. Spaatz, letter, 21 December 1945, SAB, 1944–45 file.

17. Gen Curtis E. LeMay and MacKinlay Kantor, *Mission with LeMay: My Story* (Garden City, N. Y.: Doubleday and Co., Inc., 1965), 395.

18. Theodore von Kármán to Carl A. Spaatz, letter, 9 January 1946, SAB, 1946 file. These "special studies" are the equivalent of today's ad hoc study groups which is a major feature of the SAB's long-term success.

19. Thomas A. Sturm, *The USAF Scientific Advisory Board: Its First Twenty Years, 1944–1964* (Washington, D.C.: USAF Historical Division Liaison Office, 1967), 13; Michael H. Gorn, *The Universal Man: Theodore von Kármán's Life in Aeronautics* (Washington, D.C.: Smithsonian Institution Press, 1992), 118–19.

20. Curtis E. LeMay to Carl A. Spaatz, letter, 3 January 1946, SAB, 1946 file.

21. Dr. Hugh Latimer Dryden, interviewed by Donald Shaughnessy, Air Force Historical Research Agency (AFHRA), Maxwell AFB, K14634-41, 36–37; Sturm, 15–18; Gorn, 118–19; also M. Gorn, *Harnessing the Genie: Science and Technology Forecasting for the Air Force, 1944–1986* (Washington, D.C.: Office of Air Force History, 1988), 2–17; LeMay and Kantor, 395–97.

22. LeMay and Kantor, 396.

23. Dr. Ivan Getting, interviewed by author, tape, 9 November 1994, National Academy of Science, Washington, D.C. *Schweinhund* means

pig-dog in literal translation but, according to Getting was more likely to be used between people who had close or familiar relationships.

24. Kármán and Edson, 298.

25. Lt Gen Donald L. Putt, oral history interview, 1–3 April 1974, AFHRA, Maxwell Air Force Base, Ala., K239.0512-724, 77.

26. LeMay to Spaatz, letter, 29 August 1946; Spaatz to LeMay, letter, 4 September 1946, SAB, 1946 file. Funding was a key issue at this time. The basic structure of the board was, however, protected by this action.

27. Dr. H. Guyford Stever, interviewed by author, 18 May 1995; also see Sturm, 16–19; also Dr. Ivan Getting, interviewed by author, 9 November 1994.

28. SAB meeting minutes, 17–18 March 1948, SAB, 1948 file; also quoted in Sturm, 24. Stated another way, "We shouldn't forget the more remote purposes and the desired projection into the future. . . . But certainly the voice of Minerva should be heard on the current problems." Kármán at 4 February 1947 SAB meeting, SAB, 1947 meeting minutes.

29. LeMay and Kantor, 400–1.

30. Arnold to Spaatz, letter, 21 December 1945, SAB, 1944–45 file. Perhaps Spaatz recalled Arnold's advice, "Attached is a recommendation from Dr. von Kármán concerning the future of his group. I believe that when you have a chance to read the report, you will agree with me that it is an exhaustive report, and one that should be used as a guide for scientific and pre-planning people for many years to come. After you read this over, I would like to have a talk with you about it."

31. Dr. H. Guyford Stever, interviewed by author, 18 May 1995; and Sturm, 25–26.

32. A word must be added about the element of secrecy involving transmittal of *Toward New Horizons*. During the first three months after the release of the document, only a handful of Arnold's most trusted staff were aware of the report's content. It is possible, but impossible to document, that many of those who reacted with indifference to the SAB had not been "read-in." Less than 50 copies of the report were produced and even fewer circulated within the Air Staff in 1946. Dr. Ivan Getting commented that the secrecy of the project limited its impact outside the Air Force. Henry H. Arnold, to Maj Gen Edward M. Powers, letter, 8 January 1946, SAB. This letter discusses the basic distribution of the report. See also Getting interview.

33. Kármán, *Science: The Key to Air Supremacy*, 101; and Theodore von Kármán to Hoyt S. Vandenberg, letter, 15 January 1949, SAB, 1949 file.

34. Gen Hoyt S. Vandenberg, memorandum to the Scientific Advisory Board, 7 April 1949, found in USAF Scientific Advisory Board meeting minutes of 1949.

35. What may be the "real story" behind the 7 April 1949 memo is much more intriguing and instructive than the actual occurrence of events. In his oral history, Lt Gen Donald Putt recounted the "plotting" which occurred within the SAB to get the chief of staff involved in R&D. Putt asked

Vandenberg to address the spring meeting of the SAB as a show of support. Vandenberg agreed as long as Putt provided him with a speech. The SAB team, reflecting Kármán's interest in facilities development, drafted the speech which included the request for the SAB study. Kármán approved the speech and the plan ahead of time. The speech was actually delivered (read) by the deputy chief, Muir S. Fairchild at the board meeting. In essence, Kármán and the SAB had drafted their own study request. The result of that request was the Ridenour/Doolittle Report. Putt, 79–80.

36. Gorn, *Universal Man*, 124.

37. SAB Special Committee minutes, 11 July 1949, SAB.

38. SAB Special Committee minutes, 3 November 1949, SAB.

39. Kármán, *Science: The Key to Air Supremacy*, 142.

40. Futrell, 276–78.

41. Dennis J. Stanley and John J. Weaver, *The Air Force Command for R&D, 1949–1976, The History of ARDC/AFSC* (Washington, D.C.: Office of History, HQ AFSC, 1977), 190; and Futrell, 486.

42. In this case, Putt played an active role but it was Dr. Jimmy Doolittle who spent many hours explaining the value of the Ridenour Report to Vandenberg and Fairchild. For this reason, the report is frequently referred to as the Ridenour/Doolittle Report reflecting his importance to its acceptance. Putt, 81–89.

43. Kármán, *Science: The Key to Air Supremacy*, 102d.

44. Gorn, *Harnessing the Genie*, 46.

45. Alex Roland, *Model Research: The National Advisory Committee for Aeronautics, 1915–1958*, vol. 1 (Washington, D.C.: National Air and Space Administration, 1985), 211–20. The complexities of the debate surrounding the National Unitary Wind Tunnel Plan are described here. One interesting omission in the discussion concerns the relationship of General Arnold and A. E. Raymond of the Douglas Corporation. It was only two months before Raymond's appointment as the NACA chairman of a special panel on supersonic laboratory requirements that $10 million AAF dollars had been earmarked for Douglas Corporation to establish Project RAND. Raymond, Bowles, and Arnold had devised the plan for RAND in mid-1945. This possible connection between establishment of the AEDC and an apparent disregard for Wright Field funding (which is where the $10 million came from) which Arnold had apparently demonstrated might have made perfect investment sense in this light.

46. Raymond W. Jones, "History of Arnold Engineering and Development Center, 1944–1951," typed manuscript, AFHRA, Maxwell AFB, Ala., K215.16, 3–16.

47. Dr. Frank L. Wattendorf, "Historical Aspects of the Oetztal (Modane) Wind Tunnel," typed manuscript, 22 October 1981, AFHRA, Maxwell AFB, Ala., K168.15103. Attachments to this article contain copies of Wattendorf's original reports from 1945; Jones, "History of ARDC," 4. Kármán and Edson, 298; also Stever.

48. Kármán, *Science: The Key to Air Supremacy*, 102d (appendix C) "to expand existing AAF research facilities and create new ones to do their own research." It could not be stated any more clearly; also Roland, 217–21. Roland points out that the NACA, although it had apparently been relegated to a third-ranked position among the military and industry, in actuality was never limited in its use of the Unitary Wind Tunnel facility.

49. Roland, 201–05.

50. Ibid., 98.

51. Futrell, 487.

52. Sturm, 44–45.

53. Gorn, *Universal Man*, 124–29. Dr. Gorn offers an excellent summary of the AGARD formation. This material originated from those pages.

54. Theodore von Kármán, interviewed by Shirley Thomas, January 1960.

55. Minutes of SAB Executive Committee meeting, 30 March 1953, SAB.

56. Ibid.; and Gen Bernard A. Schriever, remarks, "Proceedings of the '50th Anniversary of the SAB' Symposium," National Academy of Sciences, 6 hours, 10 November 1994, videotape. Both Dr. John von Neumann and Dr. Edward Teller were fellow Hungarians who had emigrated during the 1930s. It is from this Nuclear Panel association that author Michael Sherry in *The Rise of American Air Power: The Creation of Armageddon* (New Haven, Conn.: Yale University Press, 1987), 201–3, likely has drawn his discussion concerning a "darker attraction" which these three men shared. "The technology of death itself," as Sherry has described it, is compelling, borders on journalism, and is unsupported. Kármán had very little to do with the state of nuclear affairs in America during the war years.

57. Dr. John von Neumann, "Nuclear Weapons Panel Preliminary Report." US Air Force Scientific Advisory Board, 23 March 1954; General Schriever, interviewed by John Primm, 27 September 1994; and Futrell, 488.

58. The official name of the group was the Air Force Strategic Missile Evaluation Committee. Futrell, 489.

59. Neufeld, 93–94; Sturm, 47–48; and Schriever, "50th Anniversary of the SAB."

60. Dr. H. Guyford Stever, interviewed by author, 18 May 1995; also Stever, US Air Force oral history interview by Dr. Michael Gorn, 20 April 1989; and Dr. Ivan Getting, interviewed by John Primm, 20 September 1994, Coronado, Calif.; and Neufeld, 104.

61. Schriever, "50th Anniversary of the SAB."

62. See Neufeld, for the evolution of the ICBM program during this period.

63. Sherry, 186–89. Sherry's discussion recognizes that the AAF under Arnold were leaders in utilizing civilian scientific advice. He fails to explain how the AAF decided which scientists to believe and why.

64. Theodore von Kármán to Robert A. Millikan, letter, 2 October 1944, Caltech 20.28.

65. Mr. Chester Hasert, interviewed by author, 9 November 1994. Mr. Hasert confirmed that Kármán had looked "tired" during visits he had made to his old professor in Paris from 1952 to 1954. Hasert was an original SAG member and continued service on the SAB as an active duty AF officer; also Sturm, 66–67.

66. Nathan F. Twining to Theodore von Kármán, letter, 31 December 1954, SAB.

67. These students were Dr. Pol E. Duwez, Mr. Chester Hasert, Dr. Homerjoe Stewart, and the most famous, Dr. Clark B. Millikan who remained a member of the board through the following decade. It is interesting to note that Kármán selected Clark Millikan as his successor at GALCIT and the JPL after his resignation of both chairs in 1949. It is likely that Millikan represented the "young talent" to whom Kármán traditionally entrusted projects which he himself had started. Dr. Homerjoe Stewart, interviewed by author, 21 July 1995. The structure of the SAB is laid out in the appendices to Sturm's *Scientific Advisory Board*.

68. Gorn, *Harnessing the Genie*, 60–61.

69. Mr. Chester Hasert, interviewed by author, 9 November 1994; also Hasert to author, letter, 24 May 1995.

70. Gorn, *Universal Man*, 137–43.

71. Dr. H. Guyford Stever, interviewed by Michael H. Gorn, April 1989.

72. Gorn, *Universal Man*, 143–44. It is interesting that in Sturm's history, the Woods Hole report, although not an official SAB project, is never mentioned.

73. Dr. Hans Mark, remarks at the "50th Anniversary of the SAB," 10 November 1994. The collection of speeches given at the 50th anniversary is included in *New World Vistas*, ancillary vol. (Washington, D.C.: SAB, 1996) and should be publicly available by mid-1996.

74. Mr. Harry Hillaker, remarks at the "50th Anniversary of the SAB," 10 November 1994.

75. Dr. Courtland D. Perkins, remarks at the "50th Anniversary of the SAB," 10 November 1994; Mr. Harry Hillaker, remarks at the "50th Anniversary of the SAB," 10 November 1994; Dr. Robert G. Loewy, remarks at the "50th Anniversary of the SAB," 10 November 1994; Dr. Alexander H. Flax, remarks at the "50th Anniversary of the SAB," 10 November 1994; and the USAF Scientific Advisory Board Commemorative History, 9–10 November 1994. A member of the SAB for nearly its entire existence, Dr. Ivan Getting is generally credited with developing the Global Positioning Satellite concept.

76. SAB Meeting Minutes, 17–18 March 1948.

77. Loewy, remarks at the "50th Anniversary of the SAB," 10 November 1994; Dr. Gene McCall, interviewed by author, 20 July 1995, Newport Beach, Calif.

78. Gen Ronald R. Fogleman remarks at the "50th Anniversary of the SAB," 10 November 1994.

79. Dr. Sheila E. Widnall remarks at the "50th Anniversary of the SAB," 10 November 1994.

80. This briefing was given by Dr. McCall in the SECAF conference room. All 12 *New World Vistas* Panel chairs were in attendance as were the Secretary, the Chief, and an array of three-star staff officers. Author in attendance, 15 December 1995.

81. SAB 1994 and 1995 office files.

82. Theodore von Kármán, interviewed by Shaughnessy, 10.

Chapter 7

Conclusion

During the years covered by this examination, the fledgling Army Signal Corps evolved from a service comprised of two pilots and one plane into a complex system of personnel, institutions, and machines. Along the way, powerful personalities and organizations both helped and hindered airpower's technological development. Their sway, whether positive or negative, whether actual or perceived, contributed to the complexity of planning for the future of airpower. Authority wielded by these functionaries did little to simplify the imbroglio inherently resulting from the uncertainties of a rapidly expanding wartime environment, and caused even greater anxiety during the rapid demobilization following the conflict. Yet there were those who realized that the complex problems involved in planning for a powerful Air Force, an Air Force for the future, was not just important but essential. The task of designing that functional blueprint fell to the expertise encompassed within the Scientific Advisory Group, formed by Gen Hap Arnold and directed by Dr. Theodore von Kármán, in 1944.

"Arnold's vision and concern for the future," one historian wrote, "were as important a contribution as his build-up of the Army Air Arm during World War II."[1] Others claimed that it was the blend of Arnold's political acumen and Kármán's unique persona, which combined theoretical brilliance with common-sense application ability, that established the foundation for the research and development bent in the US Air Force.[2] Lt Gen James H. "Jimmy" Doolittle, who chaired the Scientific Advisory Board from 1955 to 1958, offered the unique perspective of a high-ranking military officer who also held a scientific doctor of philosophy (PhD) from MIT.

> General Arnold was unique in his ability to anticipate and prepare for the future, and when he got together with Theodore von Kármán it was a very fortunate thing indeed, because while General Arnold was not a highly technical man he did understand the importance of science and technology, and while Dr. von Kármán was not strictly a

military man he realized the importance to the military of the mobilization of science.[3]

Although their individual and joint contributions were vital, it was the actions which resulted from the collaboration between these men and the impact which those actions had on the evolution of the technological system of airpower which first began molding the fledgling Army Air Forces in 1945 and continues to shape the independent Air Force today.

In the early days, the airplane was simply an object of technological achievement. By 1944, the airplane was only a part of a technological system which Arnold defined as "Air-Power."[4] Thomas P. Hughes, author of *American Genesis: A Century of Invention and Technological Enthusiasm,* described another part of the growing technological system with which Army Air Forces were secretly involved during World War II. In describing the Manhattan Project as "more than just a scientific endeavor," Hughes had really described the state of affairs in the US Army Air Forces. "Thousands of workers, engineers, and managers as well as scientists labored in the heart of the Manhattan Project. [It] was an industrial development-and-production undertaking dependent on scientific laboratories and scientists for essential technical data and theoretical understanding of various processes."[5] Yet it was not possible to separate the Manhattan Project from airpower because the final test required the interaction of both systems to achieve ultimate resolution. In 1995, the complex relationships between systems is even more difficult to unravel. Dr. Eugene E. Covert, SAB chairman from 1982 to 1986, has suggested that "research [itself] as is needed for the Air Force is becoming more and more as a system."[6] While Dr. Michael I. Yarymovych, chairman of North Atlantic Treaty Organization Advisory Group for Aeronautical Research and Development in 1995, has gone one step further. "When we talk about the world bathed in information, or bathed in data that has to be turned into information, the sources to the war fighter are myriad. It's a system of systems—a space system with an aerial system with UAV with ground sources, all of this together provides the picture to the war fighter."[7]

The system Arnold once understood has evolved much further since his retirement in 1946. The complexity of weapon systems interacting with intelligence and communication systems while linked together with information management systems may one day be known as the megasystem of airpower. There is certain irony in the fact that the interrelated systems which Dr. Yarymovych described are the direct result of an explosion of computational power, a development which Kármán and the SAG (and nearly everyone else at that time) missed altogether.[8]

The transition from machine to complex system began even while the airplane was still in its infancy. Arnold's experience with aircraft included both technical aspects and personal ones. His early career, from his West Point days to those spent in Washington, saw the first use of airplanes in combat. Arnold was personally involved in related areas of World War I technological development, like the "Bug," which others in uniform had only heard of by rumor. His involvement with the earliest military utilization of these technologies brought him into contact with the inventors, the designers, the researchers, the teachers, and the supporters of aeronautics. Robert Millikan, Orville and Wilbur Wright, Boss Kettering, Donald Douglas, Larry Bell, Elmer Sperry, Harry Guggenheim, and particularly Theodore von Kármán, were only a handful of these. Through his association with the airplane and aeronautics in general, Arnold became part of a technology/personality circle which provided him with the background and familiarity with both theoretical and applied aeronautics which he used to the benefit of his Army Air Forces.

In retrospect, it seems amazing that Arnold attained a position of high command in the Army. He and his father had protested his first assignment directly to his congressman and senator. He had crashed one brand-new airplane and nearly killed himself in a second when the Army only had a handful of the craft (not totally uncommon in those days). He violated Army regulations, ostensibly on Billy Mitchell's behalf, and was "exiled" for the infraction. He was the recipient of official report cards which called him, among other things, "untrustworthy." He had ample opportunity to "bail out" of the Army and assume the top position for the fledgling Pan Am

187

Airline. Yet, in spite of it all (and because of some behind-the-scenes support from a few high ranking supporters), he stayed with the Army until 1946. His decision to remain a soldier, whatever his reasoning, was essential to the evolution of airpower through and immediately following World War II.

Because Arnold was instrumental in "rowing the Air Force's science and technology boat" while acting as its commander, it is less difficult to understand why his commitment to long-term scientific research changed during wartime. In September 1939, Arnold shifted away from almost every form of research and development which he believed would not immediately (six months to within 2 years) impact the outcome of the war.[9] With few exceptions, Arnold's efforts in production, and production R&D through 1944, provided massive fleets of technically advanced aircraft and weapons which were used by both the Americans and the Allies. The jet airplane, an apparent exception to his rule of "production R&D only" during the war years, held so much potential that he felt obligated to take the risk involved in research and development in that area. Arnold himself saw jet aircraft as a "signpost to the future," rather than a tool for the present.[10] Again, his personal contacts within the industrial sector, his World War I experience, as well as his tour at the Industrial College of the Army were vital to the eventual success of American industrial mobilization efforts. He believed, and expressed his belief to General Spaatz, that it was more important to fight the war with the best weapons at hand, which included technological refinement for those existing systems, than to hang hopes on futuristic weapons which might not make it into the combat zone in time. Arnold himself, during his middle period (fall 1939 to late spring 1944), had shifted back to an approach which favored the American tradition of empiricism. When Arnold felt that the inevitable victory was assured, he once again turned his efforts to long-term planning for the Air Forces. His decisions—which shifted the basic direction of the Air Forces during the "war years," toward, then away, then back toward long-term R&D—were shaped by both internal and external political and economic factors as well as deficiencies in the interwar Army administrative system.

In this regard, the Air Forces acted much like any other social or governmental group and Arnold acted much as any other national leader. He acted within the established guidelines for his service and made decisions based upon his life experiences. Long term, futuristic gazing implied a separation from the "here-and-now" which characterized American scientific activity. It is evident that Arnold did not understand the intricacies of empiricism or theoretical science. But that did not matter. He selected Kármán, who represented the theoretical school, because of previously demonstrated success and a personal bond which had developed over years of informal association. His choice, therefore, insured that the Air Force ended up taking the theoretical—the German approach to science and technology—rather than the purely American approach based upon pragmatic applications of science determined by empirical research.

Theodore von Kármán brought to America a background of European scientific training. His highly disciplined theoretical mind, tempered by a Newtonian ability to apply theory to practical problems, bucked the American tendency toward utilitarianism in problem solution. His rapid climb to excellence assured that his circle of acquaintances included every top European scientist in every discipline by the time he left Aachen in 1930. His work rivaled Prandtl's and, in one famous case, surpassed the accomplishments of his former professor.[11] His high-speed aerodynamics theories were instrumental in the success of the Bell X-1 program.[12] But his defining characteristic was a singular ability to plant intellectual seeds which younger, enthusiastic aerodynamic gardeners tended until scientific or technological fruit had fully ripened. Students, colleagues, and coworkers like Dr. William R. Sears, Dr. Homerjoe Stewart, Dr. Frank L. Wattendorf, Dr. Clark B. Millikan, Dr. H. Guyford Stever, Guggenheim Aeronautics Laboratory, California Institute of Technology staff members, not to mention the SAG and the Army Air Forces, were shaped by this propensity.

Kármán's arrival in America was attributable to world political events. Had the American economy precluded the Guggenheims from establishing an aeronautical trust fund, he would have remained in Europe with many of his German colleagues. Had the nature of German nationalism been less violent or more inclusive, Kármán might have felt secure remaining at Aachen. Had anti-Semitism been kept in check, Kármán might also have remained in Europe. Additionally, Robert Millikan, who had encountered the professor at an international aeronautics conference in 1925, played a pivotal role in both bringing Kármán to America and then introducing him to General Arnold in the early 1930s. This was how Kármán's experience and circle of friends eventually collided with Arnold's.

Arnold's and Kármán's relationship demonstrated the complexities of institutional and interpersonal impact on the evolution of airpower. Arnold's positive relationship over the years with men of Millikan's reputation and influence, directly and indirectly affected the evolution of American military airpower by shaping Arnold's ideas about the importance of science and technology to the Army Air Forces. It is unlikely that a committee of any sort would have nurtured the contacts and earned the trust of the American scientific community that Arnold had achieved individually.

Those who left a negative impression upon both Arnold and Kármán were equally as important as those making a positive one. Dr. Vannevar Bush, although a talented electrical engineer, had proved to both the general and the professor that he lacked intellectual vision. Their impression of Bush undoubtedly influenced the amount of trust which they placed in the National Advisory Committee for Aeronautics (beginning while Bush was in charge there) and the National Defense Research Committee/Office of Scientific Research and Development system, which Bush later chaired. George Lewis, NACA director of aeronautical research, although an adequate administrator, had continually demonstrated shortsightedness in the area of wind tunnel development and high-speed aircraft design. For many years Arnold and Kármán had witnessed firsthand Lewis' tendency toward strict bureaucratic function and research by committee. To Arnold, Lewis had not participated as an integral member of the Army Air Forces' team. To Kármán, Lewis had not demonstrated either the element of individual brilliance or intellectual freedom which the professor considered essential to successful R&D efforts—traits Kármán traditionally passed along to his students, associates, and organizations. It was ironic, at least in the case of Arnold and Kármán, that these negative influences, experienced independently, were instrumental in uniting them as a team. Considering the wide range of influences surrounding them and having similar goals for American airpower, Arnold and Kármán found it comfortable working together in the pursuit of American air supremacy.

"A Close-Run Thing"

Where We Stand and *Toward New Horizons* were the result not only of a general's vision and a scientist's brilliance, but also of many external influences and experiences which both of these men carried with them as decision makers during World War II. The SAG had created a monumental wish list for the Air Force and offered recommendations for the future of airpower. That blueprint was only the first major step. In coming years, after fiscal restraints and national attitudes were forced into a national defense paradigm shift generated by the cold war, functional plans were finally devised and hardware programs funded in an effort to achieve the seemingly "Buck Rogerish" predictions which *Toward New Horizons* had envisioned.

The Arnold/Kármán team, although it existed officially for only 15 months, from November 1944 to February 1946, created the plan which has since evolved into the science and technology infrastructure of today's Air Force.[13] Arnold established Project RAND, the Office of Scientific Liaison, and funded dozens of guided missile programs before postwar demobilization and inevitable budget cuts slowed the procedure. Kármán and the SAG assumed the strenuous task of traveling the world in search of the most advanced technologies, constantly mindful of how these advances might be applied to American airpower. In the end, it was Arnold's realization that such a study was needed and Kármán's unique ability to apply scientific findings to the practical technological needs of the Air Force which—helped along by

191

lifelong associates at opportune times and places—produced a report having great potential for long-term success.

But it was a close-run thing. Success was not guaranteed. After Arnold's retirement, the Air Forces faced monumental obstacles in all facets of its existence, but particularly in the area of science and technology. Funds were initially scarce. Leadership was in a constant flux. The reorganization of the National Military Establishment into the Department of Defense only added to the quagmire. Somehow Kármán was able, by the nature of his association with both officers and scientists, to keep the newly formed SAB from stalling. He nurtured its structure and its function in the face of misunderstanding, other's agendas, and, at times, lack of interest until it was capable of independent growth. By 1954, a decade after the process began, Kármán's vision guided by his own perseverance was directly responsible for the genesis of the SAB. But Arnold's ghost was never far away. During this period Arnold's previous associations with officers, industrialists, and scientists continually surfaced. Among them Gen Bernard Schriever, Lt Gen Laurence Craigie, Lt Gen Benjamin Chidlaw, Larry Bell, Donald Douglas, and Dr. Edward Bowles were all vital to the eventual institutionalization of *Toward New Horizons*.

Only after Kármán was certain that the SAB would thrive did he resign his chair. Similarly, just as Arnold's influence continued in the presence of others, so too did Kármán's. Former students, colleagues, and friends who had been educated by or employed with the professor carried his broad-based, practical applications approach to problem solution as part of their own methodology. Arnold's drive and Kármán's method had become the Air Force's foundation for science and technology matters and were represented by the institutionalized SAB.

Dr. Harold Sorenson, SAB chairman from 1990 to 1993, observed that "the impact of the Scientific Advisory Board for the Air Force is often a very long-term thing. That is, if we point to a specific study, if it's only a year or two old, often it's hard to point to the direct impact it's going to have."[14] The Global Positioning System, the complex avionics suite for the F-22 air superiority fighter, and composite materials are all examples of studies fitting Sorenson's observation.[15] Perhaps it is more appropriate to examine a much broader tenet from Kármán's original report. In *Toward New Horizons* the professor concluded that the Air Force of the future would be required to: (1) reach remote targets swiftly and hit them with great destructive power; (2) secure air superiority over any part of the globe; (3) land, in a very short time, powerful forces of men and weapons any place on the globe; and (4) defend our own territory and bases in the most efficient way.[16] On the occasion of her challenge to the SAB on 10 November 1994, Dr. Widnall reiterated Kármán's words adding, "Does this sound like Global Reach/Global Power?"[17] Global Reach/Global Power is to the Air Force what the Hippocratic oath is to a doctor, it defines the profession. Whether a hard trail of evidence exists as proof linking Arnold and Kármán to the ideological philosophy today's Air Force is largely irrelevant. The fact is that current leadership attributes the Air Force's scientific and technological ideology to Arnold and Kármán and has ordered sweeping actions based upon the belief that the Arnold/Kármán philosophy, manifest in *Toward New Horizons*, has proven itself prophetic. Thus, as the SAB represents tangible evidence of both Arnold's and Kármán's continuous institutional influence, a statement like the comparative one made by the Air Force secretary represents intangible evidence of their continuing ideological influence.

The Essence of the Task

Airpower institutions have evolved erratically since the days of the First World War. In his book, *Ideas and Weapons: Exploration of the Aerial Weapon by the United States During World War I*, I. B. Holley has concluded that, "the postwar [World War I] Air Service made use of only a relatively small portion of the experience of the war regarding the problem of weapons."[18] One lesson which was learned, however, was that quality was better than quantity as far as weapons were concerned. Arnold had internalized that lesson. Unfortunately, the administrative systems which might have assured such high-quality weapons development, or at least a process for their institutionalization, were neglected. Another lesson learned, and perhaps the most significant one, concerned unity of command. According to Holley, "The available evidence shows that after the war the Air Service learned the importance of organization for decision and established channels of command for unified, decisive, and authoritative action in contrast to the dispersed, ill-defined, and overlapping channels which existed during the war."[19] It was this very development which allowed Arnold to act as a stopgap, a committee of one, ensuring that the lessons of the Great War had not fallen on totally deaf ears. Arnold acted as the tangible link between the lost lessons of World War I and the institutionalization of science and technology which became a reality after World War II. Ordering the blueprint which became the scientific and technological cornerstone of American airpower is Arnold's legacy—creating it was Kármán's.

It is accurate to say that the interwar years were not a period during which airpower was "building up." When Arnold took command in 1938, however, he immediately utilized his experience and personal contacts to ensure that his World War I experience was not wasted. He overcame 20 years of institutional neglect in what turned out to be a very short time. Arnold made decisions based upon information provided to him by his circle of scientific and technologically oriented friends, particularly those who had ties to Europe. It was Lindbergh's 1938 letter, for example, which convinced him that faster, more capable planes were necessary if the Army Air Forces were to dominate the air war. Foreign doctrine and weapons, although not examined by a dedicated organization, were examined by Arnold and his staff from the late 1930s through the end of the war. Additionally, Arnold himself acted as the Army Air Forces' "continuing liaison with science." Not only was he familiar with most available technologies, the jet engine being a late addition to that list, but he had earned the respect of many gifted scientists throughout his long career.

The American story of radar, jets, and rocket development, without General Arnold in command, would certainly have proceeded at a slower pace, or in some cases not at all. Arnold's desire for the best available technology of the highest quality, regardless of its source, was instrumental in

Arnold's dream for the future of airpower was manifest in technology like the P-80.

America's acquisition of jet propulsion, guided missiles, intercontinental ballistic missile theory, and advanced aeronautical designs during the closing years of World War II. These acquisitions were made despite the organizational and personal failures of the NACA and the NDRC/OSRD to recognize the potential impact of these technologies on aeronautics. The general's insistence upon finding and using the "best available" people and equipment was also applied to the formation of the SAG in 1944. Although it was true that many functional Army Air Forces scientific and technological research organizations were not formalized until after World War II, it is inaccurate to conclude that lessons from the earlier war did not influence decisions concerning weapons, doctrine, procurement, science, technology, research, and development during the Second World War. Arnold, by his presence alone, ensured that they did, particularly in the fields of science and technology.

What the Army Air Forces lacked in science and technology organization before Pearl Harbor was rectified after V-E Day. Many of the institutional lessons seemingly lost after World War I were finally addressed and incorporated, largely because of the recommendations of Kármán's 1945 reports for General Arnold. During Arnold's command, he carried forth the lessons which he had learned over his career and used them advantageously despite the fact that adequate institutional organizations for incorporating both mundane and "Buck Rogerish" ideas did not yet exist.

"A report does not make a policy," said Kármán, "It depends on the administration."[20] Arnold complemented that statement with one of his own shortly after he retired. "Successful research, being the product of inspiration, cannot

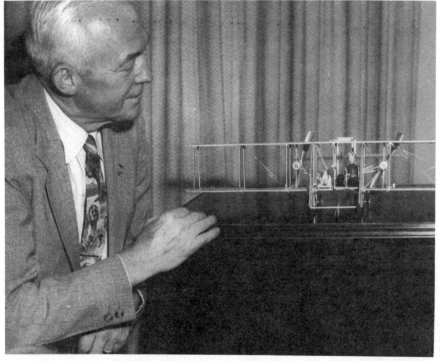

In retirement Arnold remained an active public advocate of airpower. Here he recalls early flying at Simms Station.

"The Elder Statesman of Aeronautics."

be purchased like a commodity. It is the product of the human mind—of intellectual leadership. . . . All of the funds and facilities devoted to research will be wasted unless at the same time America possesses competent intellectual leadership. . . . The proper cultivation of the human mind is the essence of the task."[21] The continued evolution of the Air Force as a technological system within the boundaries of a complex and influential American society has been determined by the realities inherent in those statements during these past five decades.

Notes

1. John W. Huston, "The Wartime Leadership of 'Hap' Arnold," in Alfred F. Hurley and Robert C. Ehrhart, eds., *Air Power and Warfare: The Proceedings of the 8th Military History Symposium, United States Air Force Academy, 18–20 October 1978* (Washington, D.C.: Office of Air Force History, 1979), 181; Gen Bernard Schriever, interviewed by author, 10

November 1994, "He was the most visionary person I've ever seen, yet he was an operator from the word go," 2.

2. Hugh L. Dryden, "Memorial for Theodore von Kármán, 1881–1963" (Memorial Proceedings, US Air Force Academy Special Collections, 28 May 1963), 7; also James H. Doolittle, OHI, 21 April 1969, 9, USAFA, Colorado Springs, Colo.

3. Doolittle.

4. Henry H. Arnold, speech at the NACA laboratories in Cleveland, Ohio, transcript, Murray Green Collection (MGC), roll 12; motion picture, March AFB, Calif. Original film at the Arnold Ranch, Sonoma, Calif.

5. Thomas P. Hughes, *American Genesis: A Century of Invention and Technological Enthusiasm* (New York: Penguin Books, 1989), 383.

6. Dr. Eugene E. Covert, remarks, "Proceedings of the '50th Anniversary Meeting of the SAB' Symposium," National Academy of Sciences, Washington, D.C., 10 November 1994, videotape.

7. Dr. Michael I. Yarymovych, interviewed by author, videotape, 20 July 1995, Newport Beach, Calif.

8. The term *megasystem* was broadly defined in Merritt Roe Smith, and Leo Marx, eds., *Does Technology Drive History? The Dilemma of Technological Determinism* (Cambridge, Mass.: MIT Press, 1994), xi, as "intricately interrelated technical systems—a system of systems." More recently the term was linked to "modern military power" by Eliot A. Cohen, "A Revolution in Warfare," *Foreign Affairs* 75, no. 2 (March/April 1996): 53.

9. Henry H. Arnold and Ira C. Eaker, *Winged Warfare* (New York: Harper and Brothers Publisher, 1941), 238–39.

10. Henry H. Arnold, "Air Force in the Atomic Age," in *One World or None,* ed. Dexter Masters and Katharine Way (New York: McGraw-Hill Co., 1946), 30; also James O. Young, "Riding England's Coattails: The U.S. Army Air Forces and the Turbojet Revolution" (unpublished typed manuscript, Edwards AFB, Calif.: AFFTC History Office, 1995). The debate over whether or not Arnold's staff had kept him as well informed concerning jet development in the US as they could have is a complicated one. His actions in 1940, such as funding the high speed tunnel at Wright Field, seem to indicate that he was aware of the "Kotcher Report" of 1939. Remember, too, that these developments would have taken place during what I call Arnold's early "technological Phase II, Sept 1939–spring 1944," where production and production R&D took precedence over all other projects. The turbojet engine, in the early days, did not show the potential for completion within the two-year restriction which Arnold imposed on R&D projects. Once the Whittle information became available in April 1941, the American timetable moved dramatically forward, hence Arnold's apparently late push into jet propulsion. Actually, this fit well with his wartime R&D restrictions.

11. Dr. William Rees Sears, interviewed by author, 8 July 1995; and Michael H. Gorn, *The Universal Man: Theodore von Kármán's Life in Aeronautics* (Washington, D.C.: Smithsonian Institution Press, 1992), 62–63.

12. For a detailed account of the X-1 project, see Louis Rotundo, *Into the Unknown: The X-1 Story* (Washington, D.C.: Smithsonian Institution Press, 1994); for Kármán's direct contribution I have relied on a personal interview with X-1 test pilot, Brig Gen Charles "Chuck" Yeager, interviewed by author, 10 June 1994, Maxwell AFB, Ala.

13. Schriever interview. He said about Arnold, "There's no question, his greatness was that he created the infrastructure. He visualized the kind of infrastructure that the Air Force needed to really get into the technology age."

14. Dr. Harold W. Sorenson, interview for "50th Anniversary of the SAB," 27 September 1994, Pentagon, Washington, D.C.

15. SAB studies examining the Global Positioning System (GPS) were initiated in the 1960s. Impact upon the commercial market as in cars and portable GPSs was not a consideration when the project began. The F-22, advanced air superiority fighter, incorporates an internal avionics suite which has set the standard for future military systems and has also been influential in commercial designs like the new Boeing-777. Composite studies initiated in 1965 resulted in technology which has revolutionized aircraft construction but also many commercial products like skis and tennis rackets. Dr. Ivan Getting, interviewed by author, 10 November 1994; Dr. Harold W. Sorenson, remarks, "Proceedings of the '50th Anniversary of the SAB' Symposium," National Academy of Sciences, 6 hours, 10 November 1994, videotape; Robert Loewy, remarks at "50th Anniversary of the SAB."

16. Theodore von Kármán, *Toward New Horizons*, vol. 1, *Science: The Key to Air Supremacy*, 15 December 1945, 1.12a-d. This document, Kármán's summary volume, is appendix C.

17. Dr. Sheila E. Widnall, remarks at the "50th Anniversary of the SAB."

18. I. B. Holley Jr., *Ideas and Weapons: Exploitation of the Aerial Weapon by the United States During World War I; A Study in the Relationship of Technological Advance, Military Doctrine, and the Development of Weapons* (1953; new imprint, Washington, D.C.: Office of Air Force History, 1983), 176. The following discussion in the text is based on Dr. Holley's summary and conclusions.

19. Ibid., 177.

20. Theodore von Kármán, interviewed by Donald Shaughnessy, 10.

21. Henry H. Arnold, "Science and Air Power," *Air Affairs*, December 1946, 190. Dr. Gene McCall, the 1995–1996 SAB chairman, has just completed the most recent Air Force science and technology forecast titled, *New World Vistas*. Dr. McCall insisted that the report, to be effective in the long term, must be supported by at least two generations of Air Force military and civilian leadership. The report, without high-level support and funding, would be useless if not institutionalized almost immediately. Perhaps he is also a student of history. Gen Lew Allen, Air Force chief of staff, suggested the long-term impact of the Kármán reports. "The Air Force devoted itself to ensuring that its weapons systems would be at the cutting edge all of the time, and invested wisely in people and in organizational

mechanisms and in the actual projects and developments which allowed those technological advances to occur. The leadership of the Air Force over all those 45 years deserves tremendous credit for being a very major portion of the victory over the Soviet Union by making that technological superiority be clear and unambiguous at all times." Gen Lew Allen, interview for the "50th Anniversary of the SAB," 20 September 1994, Calif.

Appendix A

The Military Career of Henry Harley Arnold (Cadet No. 4596)

Born: 25 June 1886, Gladwyne, Pa.
Died: 15 January 1950, Sonoma, Calif., age 63.

CADET RECORD (all numbers refer to class standing rather than a % grade)				
SUBJECT	*1903/04*	*1904/05*	*1905/06*	*1906/07*
Overall Ranking	82/136	63/119	61/113	66/111
Conduct	25	27	21	52
Demerits (actual)	45	66	36	105
Military/Drill	97	X	70	78
Engineering	X	73	X	47/62
Math	74	49	X	X
English	103	94	X	X
French	98	89	X	X
Spanish	X	94	X	X
Drawing	X	70	51	X
Philosophy	X	X	66	X
Chemistry	X	X	53	X
Hygiene	X	X	94	X
Law	X	X	X	100
History	X	X	X	89
Gunnery	X	X	X	54
Military Efficiency	X	X	X	76
Deportment and Discipline	X	X	X	60

CAREER ASSIGNMENTS	
1 Aug 1903	Entered West Point, the Military Academy
14 Jun 1907	Graduated
5 Dec 1907	Fort William McKinley, P.I.
9 Apr 1908	San Mateo, P.I., and various other temporary locations
18 Jun 1909	En route to US through Asia and Europe
1 Oct 1909	Governor's Island, N.Y.
20 Apr 1911	Aviation School, Dayton, Ohio, Simms Station
15 Jun 1911	College Park, Md. Aviation duty as instructor/supply officer
25 Nov 1911	Augusta, Ga. Same duty
15 Apr 1912	Fort Leavenworth, Kans.
1 May 1912	College Park, Md.
1 Jul 1912	Connecticut maneuvers
5 Aug 1912	College Park, Md.
1 Oct 1912	Fort Riley, Kans. (near fatal spin)
15 Nov 1912	Washington, D.C. Duty in Office of the Chief Signal Officer
1 Sep 1913	Fort Thomas, Ky. Infantry
25 Nov 1913	En route to Philippine Islands
5 Jan 1914	Fort William McKinley, P.I.
5 Jan 1916	En route to Madison Barracks, N.Y.
15 Mar 1916	Madison Barracks, N.Y.
20 May 1916	Aviation School at San Diego, Calif., North Island
5 Feb 1917	Panama Canal Zone
20 Mar 1917	Washington, D.C. Asst. executive and executive officer, Air Division, Signal Corps; board control member; asst. director Military Aeronautics; director of Military Aeronautics

CAREER ASSIGNMENTS	
10 Jan 1919	Rockwell Field, Coronado, Calif. District supervisor, Western District, Air Service
30 May 1919	Crissy Field, San Francisco, Calif. Air Officer, 9th Air Corps Area
17 Oct 1922	Rockwell Field, Calif. Commanding officer, Air Depot
15 Aug 1924	Washington, D.C. Student, Army Industrial College
Mar 1925	Graduated AIC, then assigned to the Office, Chief Air Corps
Mar 1926	Marshal Field, Fort Riley, Kans. ("Exile." Wrote Bill Bruce books.)
Aug 1928	For Leavenworth, Kans. Student, General Service School
12 Jun 1929	Graduated, then to Fairfield Air Depot, Ohio. Commanding officer; chief, Field Service Section, Materiel Division, Air Corps; executive officer, Materiel Division
29 Oct 1931	En route March Field, Calif.
26 Nov 1931	March Field, Calif. Commanding officer
17 Jan 1936	Washington, D.C. Assistant chief of the Air Corps
29 Sep 1938	Chief of the Air Corps
20 Jun 1941	Chief, Army Air Forces
9 Mar 1942	Commanding general, Army Air Forces; Member, Joint Chiefs of Staff; Member, Combined Chiefs of Staff
21 Dec 1944	General of the Army (5 star rank)
9 Feb 1946	Office of the Chief of Staff
3 Mar 1946	End tour
30 Jun 1946	Retired with disability (heart problems), 43 years service
7 May 1949	General of the Air Force

MILITARY RANK PROGRESSION	
1 Aug 1903	Cadet
14 Jun 1907	Second lieutenant, 29th Infantry
10 Apr 1913	First lieutenant of Infantry
20 May 1916	Captain, Aviation Section, Signal Corps
23 Sep 1916	Captain of Infantry
27 Jun 1917	Major, Aviation Section, Signal Corps
5 Aug 1917	Colonel, temporary, Signal Corps
15 Jan 1918	Major, temporary, Infantry
30 Jun 1920	Captain, permanent grade
1 Jul 1920	Major of Infantry (transferred to Air Service 11 August 1920)
1 Feb 1931	Lieutenant colonel, Air Corps
2 Mar 1935	Brigadier general, temporary, Air Corps (one source: 11 Feb)
22 Sep 1938	Major general, chief of Air Corps (30 October, deputy chief of staff Army for air matters)
15 Dec 1941	Lieutenant general
19 Mar 1943	General
21 Dec 1944	General of the Army
30 Jun 1946	General of the Army, Retired
7 May 1949	General of the Air Force

This appendix is compiled from a variety of sources kindly provided by the West Point Archives. For the most part, the assignments and promotions are assembled from the "graduate" update magazine and the *Howitzer*, student yearbook.

Appendix B

Appendix A

The Army Air Forces (AAF) Scientific Advisory Group (SAG) was activated late in 1944 by General of the Army H. H. Arnold. He secured the services of Dr. Theodore von Kármán, renowned scientist and consultant in aeronautics, who agreed to organize and direct the group.

Dr. von Kármán gathered about him a group of American scientists from every field of research having a bearing on airpower. These men then analyzed important developments in the basic sciences, both in the United States and abroad, and attempted to evaluate the effects of their application to airpower.

This volume is one of a group of reports made to the Army Air Forces by the Scientific Advisory Group.

NOTE: The entire set of reports is available to researchers at the Pentagon Library and the USAF Historical Research Agency at Maxwell AFB, Montgomery, Alabama.

Where We Stand

First Report
to
General of the Army H. H. Arnold
on
Long Range Research Problems of the AIR FORCES
with a Review of German Plans and Developments

Theodore von Kármán
Director
Scientific Advisory Group
Army Air Forces

22 August 1945

Contents

I. INTRODUCTION

INTRODUCTION

The present war started on both sides with "conventional" weapons and equipment; "conventional" because their principles of action, design, and performance were fundamentally known to the enemy. During the war both sides produced equipment and weapons of astonishing effects which will certainly change the whole picture of future aerial warfare.

This report is concerned with the main fields in which significant advances have been made and tries to show "where we stand" with some indications as to "where we shall go."

For future planning of research and development, the following new aspects of aerial warfare have to be considered as fundamental realities:

1. that aircraft—manned or pilotless—will move with speeds far beyond the velocity of sound;

2. that due to improvements in aerodynamics, propulsion and electronic control, unmanned devices will transport means of destruction to targets at distances up to several thousand miles;

3. that small amounts of explosive materials will cause destruction over areas of several square miles;

4. that defense against present-day aircraft will be perfected by target seeking missiles;

5. that only aircraft or missiles moving at extreme speeds will be able to penetrate enemy territory protected by such defenses;

6. that a perfect communication system between fighter command and each individual aircraft will be established;

7. that location and observation of targets, take-off, navigation and landing of aircraft, and communication will be independent of visibility and weather;

8. that fully equipped airborne task forces will be enabled to strike at far distant points and will be supplied by air.

It is too early to try to evaluate fully the influence of recent utilization of atomic energy on the conduct of aerial warfare. Therefore, such an evaluation is not attempted in this report. However, the development of this new source of energy will

217

certainly make the supersonic airplane and the automatically-guided pilotless-aircraft even more efficient and will materially extend their range. Hence the progress in utilization of nuclear energy will strengthen and accelerate the trends of aeronautical developments advocated in this report.

Several topics, such as television, weather, medical research, airborne armies, etc., are not mentioned in this report. They will be treated in my final report.

This report was prepared with the collaboration of all members of the Scientific Advisory Group.

II. WHERE WE STAND

Supersonic Flight

Supersonic flight appeared before 1940 as a remote possibility. Supersonic motion was considered as characteristic of artillery shells; level flight supported by wings was thought to be confined to the subsonic speed range. Some people talked of the stone wall against which we were running by trying to fly faster than sound.

One of the main results of bolder and more accurate thinking, and more experimentation in the last few years, is the fact that this stone wall disappeared, at least in our planning, and will disappear in actual practice if efforts are continued.

I believe the first engineering analysis presented in this country was contained in a report by myself and my collaborators early in 1944. It was shown in this report that an airplane of 10,000 lb gross weight, and 80 lb/sq ft wing loading, can climb to 40,000 ft altitude, reach a speed of 1000 mph, and fly at this speed for five minutes. As the propulsion device, a ramjet was considered.

The two main requisites of supersonic flight are the development of air frames which are aerodynamically efficient in the supersonic range and the development of lightweight efficient propulsion units.

The German contribution to the problem of supersonic flight is mainly on the aerodynamic side. No particular advance has been made by them in power plants such as the ramjet and turbojet for extremely high speeds. The Germans tested these power plants only at subsonic speeds. Their main contributions to aerodynamics were as follows:

1. By wind-tunnel testing and by firing of winged missiles, it was shown that the passing of sonic velocity does not entail any stability difficulties if the transition is made in a relatively short time by rapid acceleration.

2. By wind-tunnel testing, it was found that efficient wing forms with high lift over drag ratio and effective control surfaces could be designed for supersonic flight.

221

These German achievements are not the result of any superiority in their technical and scientific personnel, however, but rather due to the very substantial support enjoyed by their research institutions in obtaining expensive research equipment, such as large supersonic wind tunnels, many years before such equipment was planned in this country.

Supersonic Wind Tunnels

There is no doubt that we were slow in recognizing the necessity of supersonic wind-tunnel research. I myself tried to persuade the Chief of Ordnance, after my return from a trip to Europe in 1937, to install a supersonic tunnel at Pasadena. General Barnes decided in 1942 to build such a tunnel at Aberdeen Proving Ground. The design was based on model studies carried out between 1940 and 1942 at the California Institute of Technology. Wright Field and NACA are building supersonic wind tunnels but until recently only one small tunnel with a cross section of 7.5 x 7.5 in was available. As the missile program made the need for supersonic aerodynamic data urgent, the Budget Bureau of the Government ordered hearings with the idea rather of restricting than encouraging the construction of such vital instruments of research under the slogan of "avoid duplications."

The picture of the situation on the other side is given by Figs. 1 and 2, which cover German supersonic wind tunnels in operation and under construction.

It seems to me that the Air Forces have to recognize the fact that the science of supersonic aerodynamics is no longer a part of exterior ballistics but represents the basic knowledge necessary for design of manned and unmanned supersonic aircraft. The Air Forces have to provide facilities and include this field in their research, development, and training programs.

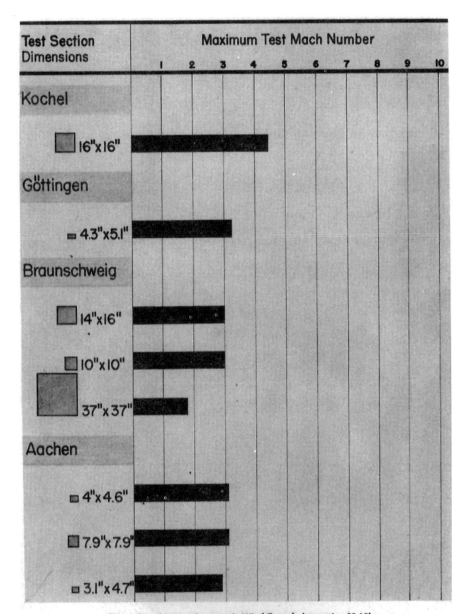

Figure 1 — German Supersonic Wind Tunnels (operation 1945)

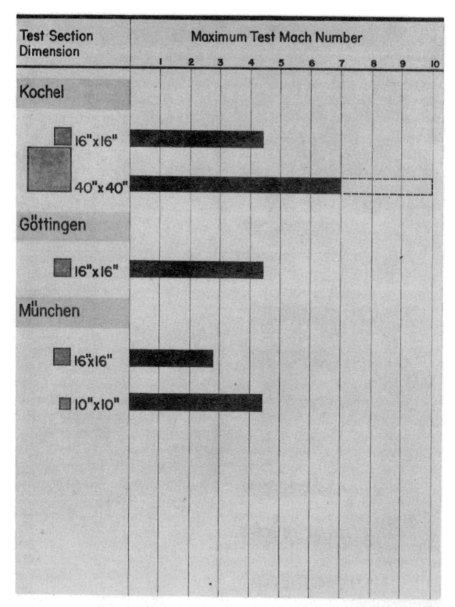

Figure 2 — German Supersonic Wind Tunnels (Construction 1945)

Arrowhead Wing

The main difficulty of flying at speeds near and beyond the velocity of sound is, of course, the extremely low lift-drag ratio of the airplane due to excessive drag. The range of an airplane, for example, is directly proportional to this ratio. Wing theory and wing design for subsonic airplanes were worked out with rather surprising success in this country and we were ahead of the Germans in this field. However, in the field of transonic and supersonic wing design, the Germans developed to the point of practical application ideas which were only in the discussion stage here.

The optimum lift-drag ratio of the wing of a very well designed subsonic airplane, the Mustang, is shown in Fig. 3. It is seen from the same figure that the lift-drag ratio for a rectangular supersonic wing at a Mach number of 2 is less than that of an old-fashioned biplane cell. This is the point where new ideas must step in.

One such idea is that of the arrowhead wing (Pfeilflügel), first suggested in a scientific paper by A. Busemann in 1935. This was a dormant idea until revived with success by German scientists and designers in the period 1942–1945.

The arrowhead wing is based on the thought that sweeping back the wings reduces considerably the effective Mach number of the wing and so lowers the resistance. As a matter of fact, if the sweepback is sufficiently large, the shock wave can be eliminated even at supersonic speeds over the greater part of the wing. I include here two photographs (Fig. 4) which belong to a series of experiments carried out at my suggestion in the Aberdeen supersonic wind tunnel in April, 1945, before I went abroad. These experiments were made at a Mach number of 1.72. It is seen that the straight wing produces a strong shock wave at the leading edge which fails to appear in the case of the swept-back wing. Robert Jones of the NACA announced similar suggestions in a report in June, 1945. The German scientists carried out comprehensive investigations on the problem. The two longer illustrations in Fig. 3 show the improvements of lift-drag ratio which can be realized by proper wing shapes. The Germans found that the reduction of the effective Mach number by sweepback applies also to the transonic range. They found that the critical Mach number at which the compressibility effects increase the drag and cause stability troubles, can be pushed to higher values by large sweepback of the wings. This result was utilized in several of their last airplanes, for example, the Messerschmitt-Lippisch design of their rocket interceptor, the Me-163.

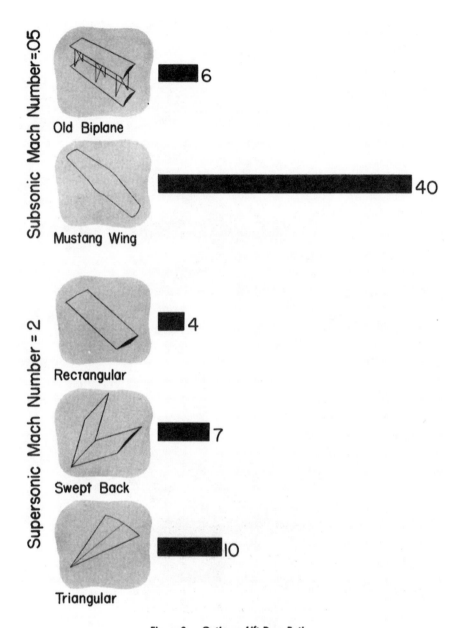

Figure 3 — Optimum Lift-Drag Ratios

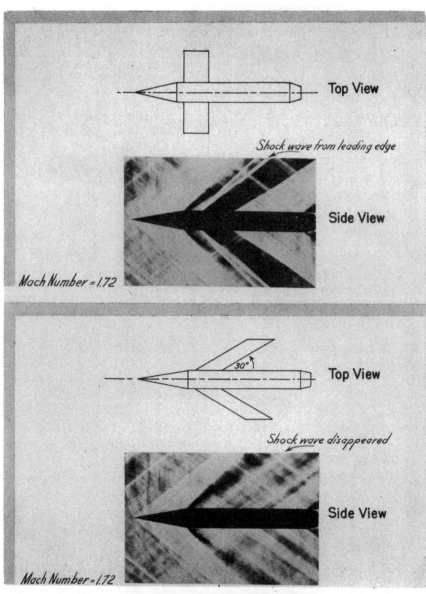

Top View

Shock wave from leading edge

Side View

Mach Number = 1.72

Top View

30°

Shock wave disappeared

Side View

Mach Number = 1.72

Figure 4 — Sweepback Effect on Shock Waves

228

Suggestions for Research

I believe that for the realization of supersonic flight the following engineering researches are indicated:

1. Complete airplane models with actual operating power plant should be tested for performance and detailed improvements in supersonic wind tunnels at supersonic speeds. For this purpose supersonic wind tunnels of large test sections are necessary so that not only the components, such as wing and fuselage, but a whole airplane as well can be studied for optimum design.

2. Since wind-tunnel testing in the speed range in the immediate neighborhood of the sonic velocity is unreliable, research in this speed range should be supplemented by special flying research airplanes in order to obtain performance data as well as flow mechanics data at high speeds. For the success of these tests, a complete, careful instrumentation and flight-testing technique has to be developed so that accurate and detailed flow information can be obtained.

3. Methods of launching the airplane by various auxiliary power plants such as rockets, should be investigated. One promising means of launching is to combine the take-off and climb into one single step by rockets as shown in Fig. 5. The transition through the velocity of sound will be then very fast and the rockets can be dropped when spent. No long runways will be necessary and the main power plant, turbojet, or ramjet, can be designed most efficiently for supersonic operation only.

4. Landing is facilitated by the fact that the fuel consumed is a large percentage of the initial weight. However, to enable landing at a safe low speed, deceleration and lift increase by appropriately directed rocket thrust during the last few seconds of descent may be necessary, as shown in Fig. 5. This method of landing has to be studied.

Only through such a program of research can the problem of supersonic flight be satisfactorily solved. Of course, from the point of view of tactical usage of supersonic aircraft, the result of this research program is only the first step. There still remains the question of working out the best ways of using an aircraft of supersonic speed for the different situations. However, the very new horizon opened up by a velocity higher than sound justifies the intensive research indicated. We cannot hope to secure air superiority in any future conflict without entering the supersonic speed range.

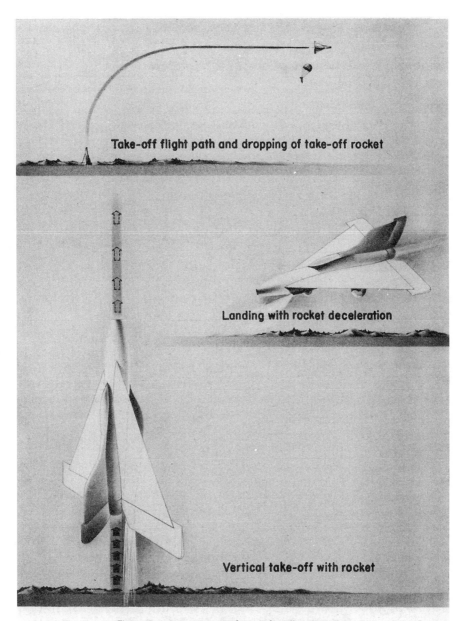

Take-off flight path and dropping of take-off rocket

Landing with rocket deceleration

Vertical take-off with rocket

Figure 5 — Supersonic Airplane: Take-off and Landing

Pilotless Aircraft

German Development of Guided Missiles
and Pilotless Aircraft

The German effort on guided missiles and pilotless aircraft was aimed at three tactical problems: (1) the bombing of Allied ships, both naval and merchant vessels; (2) long-range strategic bombing of England; and (3) defense against Allied bombers. Some thought and effort had also been given to the problem of the long-range strategic bombing of America by unmanned missiles.

Development of high-angle and glide bombs to answer the first problem was started about the end of 1939 or the beginning of 1940 and resulted in the PC-1400-FX and Hs-293 missiles, first used in August and October, 1943. Both missiles were direct-sight radio-controlled and became unusable as soon as air superiority was lost.

The well-known V-1 and V-2 were used to meet the second problem, which arose after the failure of the attempt to bomb England by conventional aircraft because of the efficient British air defense. Although the fundamental scientific research and development work on these missiles had its root in projects initiated for other purposes early as 1935, the focusing of effort on the tactical problem of long-range bombing of England appears to have started in 1941.

The history of development of the buzz-bomb (V-1) is quite interesting. An inventor, Paul Schmidt, had a development contract from the Air Ministry for an intermittent jet motor in 1935. The work proceeded slowly. About November, 1939, Diedrich, of the Argus Motor Company, who had been working for the Air Ministry on exhaust pipe jet-propulsion nozzles, began work on intermittent combustion in an open pipe. In 1940, the Air Ministry brought Schmidt to the Argus Company and combined the developments. The first successful motor was completed in 1941. This motor development itself was intended for use in aircraft. About that time the ground forces development of the large V-2 rocket, which was started at a very early date, was delayed. Since this weapon was considered extremely important for the outcome of the war, an

232

official of the Air Ministry proposed the use of a combination of small airplane with intermittent jet motor as a substitute for the same purpose. The V-l was thus conceived and became a development of the air forces. Its code name was originally Kirschkern (cherry pit) because it was merely to be spit out against England.

Fieseler Aircraft Company was selected to build the air frame. The development tests were made at the Air Ministry laboratory at the Luftfahrtforschungsanstalt Hermann Goering, Braunschweig, in the 2.8-m high-speed wind tunnel. The original model of the V-1 was not very good, the net thrust of the motor being zero at 380 mph. About 60% of the operating time of this wind tunnel was needed for nearly a year to bring the development to its present stage.

The first reconnaissance photograph of the V-l was taken by the British at Peenemünde in April, 1943, and bombing made Peenemünde uninhabitable by August, 1943. The first operational use of the V-l was on 12 June 1944.

The V-2 or long-range rocket was known as A-4 or Apparat 4. The first of the series, A-1, was fired in 1935 at Kummersdorf. It was a small rocket of aluminum construction, 100-kg thrust, intended for use on aircraft.

Dr. von Braun, leader of the Peenemünde group which developed the V-2, was a student of Professor Hermann Oberth, a well-known inventor and writer in the field of rockets, who had published books on interplanetary rocket travel. A group of Oberth's students became interested in rockets and organized an amateur rocket group. All were well-trained scientists. In 1935, Dr. von Braun was employed by the German War Department and sent to Peenemünde. In 1941, von Braun brought Oberth there as head of the Patent Section. By 1941, Peenemünde was an active test station. The Me-163 was brought there in September, 1941 and in October, 1941 flew at a speed of 1,003 km hr (about 623 mph). In October, 1941, the first supersonic wind-tunnel tests were made on a projectile at a Mach number of 4.4. After the bombing of Peenemünde in August, 1943, the activities were decentralized. The wind-tunnel group went to Kochel, where it was in operation in January, 1944. The first use of the V-2 was on 8 September 1944.

Development of guided missile defense against bombers began early in 1943. The missiles were all rocket-propelled and, in their final development, many were to be automatically controlled with homing devices and equipped with proximity fuses. Many of these missiles (X-4, Hs-298, Schmetterling, Rheintochter, Enzian, and Wasserfall) reached their final testing and early production stage but with direct-sight radio control only. The electronic developments, homing devices, and proximity fuses lagged behind the vehicle and propulsion unit developments. The X-4 air-to-air missile was provided with an interesting direct wire control to avoid the possibility of jamming, present with radio control. Two of the wings carry at the tips spools of fine wire long enough to permit a range of three miles while maintaining direct wire connection between the missile and the control aircraft. The wires can be fed out at speeds of more than 400 mph. None of these missiles were used against our bombers. The German situation became so critical indeed that development of complicated guided rockets was stopped in February, 1945, in favor of concentrating on small, unguided rockets to be used in large numbers.

The German military agencies, research institutions, and industrial designers devoted a large effort to guided missiles and considered them very promising weapons. In August, 1944, there were some 25 projects for homing devices under developments. The major research laboratories of the air and ground forces made many wind-tunnel and flight tests, some at high supersonic speeds, and made many theoretical studies of problems related to guided missiles and pilotless aircraft (Fig. 6).

Perhaps the most important result of the German effort in this field was to show that winged missiles are superior in performance to finned missiles. Thus, the next stage in the development of the V-2 rocket was to have been the addition of wing. The necessary wind-tunnel tests had been made in connection with the development of the winged ground-to-air rocket Wasserfall and ballistic computations had shown that this change alone would increase the range of the V-2 rocket from about 250 to about 400 miles. Wind-tunnel models of the winged V-2, known as A-9, are shown in Fig. 7.

The German scientists believed, although some German engineers in industry disagreed, that the ultimate guided missile would be completely automatic in its operation. Although for quick development and for test purposes they favored the use of manual radio control, their long-range plans contemplated first automatic blind tracking of the missile and target, then the connection of the two tracking devices through a computer to the radio control channels, and finally the use of a homing device for the last part of the trajectory and a proximity fuse.

Figure 6 — German "Feuerlilie" Rocket

Original V-2 Rocket

Wasserfall Rocket

V-2 Rocket with Wings

V-2 Rocket with Wings

Figure 7 — Rocket Models for Supersonic Wind-Tunnel Tests

Looking over the great variety of projects one finds that the V-2 rocket was the most outstanding technical achievement and that the Peenemünde group of scientists, working for the ground forces, was the most capable missile research group in Germany. It is important for us to note that one element in their success was the fact that they had under a single leadership in one organization, experts in aerodynamics, structural design, electronics, servomechanisms, gyros and control devices, and propulsion; in fact, every group required for the development of a complete missile. The letters and papers in the files of industrial groups, like Messerschmitt, show rapid progress in the field of vehicle and propulsion, the fields in which the firm itself had qualified people, but delay after delay on controls and electronic devices which had to be secured elsewhere. The Luftwaffe research laboratories made little progress in the actual development of specific weapons, largely because of the absence of electronics experts and their lack of facilities for the construction of experimental missiles.

In addition to the German view that the final guided missile would be completely automatic in operation, the possibilities of long-range strategic bombing were fully understood. There is no question but that the diversion of the efforts of the Peenemünde scientists in 1943 to the development of an antiaircraft guided rocket delayed the introduction of the winged V-2 rocket (A-9) and its successor, the transoceanic rocket (A-9 plus A-10). Drawings and computations had been completed for the A-10, a rocket weighing 85 T with a thrust of 200 T to be used as a launching rocket for the A-9, accelerating it to a speed of 3,600 ft/sec. The motor of the A-9 would accelerate it further to a speed of 8,600 ft/sec, giving it a range of about 3,000 miles. Some consideration was given to the design of one version of the A-9 carrying a pilot. The Scientific Advisory Group agrees that the German results of wind-tunnel tests, ballistic computation, and experience with the V-2 justify the conclusion that a transoceanic rocket can be developed.

The principal German advantage in the field of guided missiles was the lead in time in the development of rockets, which were considered to have serious military applications as early as 1935. Much effort was put into this field and as a result the supporting industrial developments were ready as a foundation for missile designers. They could buy rocket motors and rocket fuels from commercial sources. In this respect they lead us. The V-2 development was successful not so much because of striking scientific developments as because of an early start, military support, and a boldness of execution. In the electronic field, radar in particular, we are definitely one or two years in the lead, although we have not put as much effort in the experimental determination of the limits of application of acoustic and infrared devices.

Pilotless Aircraft from Viewpoint of the Air Forces

The Air Forces have rather thoroughly explored the field of guided high-angle and glide bombs released from aircraft. This program is undoubtedly well known to the Commanding General through the AMC progress reports. It includes preset glide bombs controlled by an automatic pilot, high-angle and glide bombs remotely controlled by radio with and without television repeat-back equipment, and high-angle and glide bombs homing by light, heat, and radar. During the war period there were many projects and the number tended to grow continually. In this early stage of development there was not much possibility for real systematic planning. It should be possible now to reduce the number of projects to those meeting definite military requirements and to standardize on a small number of missiles. These standardized missiles should be used to continue research and development on homing devices.

Our endeavors in pilotless aircraft in the proper sense include, in addition to the successful reproductions of the V-1 type, a few promising beginnings. However, the Air Forces should realize that the task is far beyond the scope of inventing gadgets and trying to make them work. There is urgent need of a systematic analysis of the various tasks which manned airplanes equipped with bombs, guns, and rockets perform, and which now may be performed by pilotless craft.

In other words, two developments have to meet for successful solutions of the problems: The tactical viewpoint must lead to the choice of the types of pilotless aircraft; on the other hand, physical science will proceed to offer more and more extended ranges and improved accuracy.

239

However, beyond that the implications of the accomplishments of the German Pennemünde group and of the recent development of the atomic bomb by United States and British scientists, future methods of aerial warfare call for a reconsideration of all present plans. A part, if not all, of the functions of the manned strategic bomber in destroying the key industries, the communication and transportation systems, and military installations at ranges of from 1,000 to 10,000 miles will be taken over by the pilotless aircraft of extreme velocity. The use of supersonic speeds greatly reduces errors due to wind drift and other atmospheric conditions and the tremendous zone of damage of the atomic bomb diminishes the required precision. Hence, the difficult control problem is made easier.

For the future long-range strategic bomber, the Scientific Advisory Group foresees two types of pilotless aircraft, both with wings, one with a high trajectory reaching far into the outer atmosphere, and the other designed for level flight at high altitudes. The first one can be considered as a further development of the V-2 rocket. In fact, this was planned by the German scientists. By using two or more step-rockets for the acceleration, a very high speed is imparted to a missile, perhaps as high as 17,000 mph or more, to give ranges of several thousand miles. In this case, the wings are required mainly for control purposes, but they also serve to extend the glide path in the lower atmosphere. The German scientists have suggested a second type of trajectory requiring less initial energy, in which the wings are caused to curve the path of the missile when it returns to the region of increasing air density so that it rebounds to great heights. After a number of rebounds the winged missile settles down to a steady glide. Such a trajectory would seem difficult to control accurately (Fig. 8).

The second future strategic bomber is a supersonic pilotless aircraft, flying at altitudes of from 20,000 to say, 60,000 ft. It appears to us now that the speed will be about twice the speed of sound and that the aircraft will be powered by a turbojet motor. An intermediate step might be a pilotless aircraft traveling at high subsonic speeds with a Mach number of about 0.9 about 600 mph at 40,000 ft (Fig. 9).

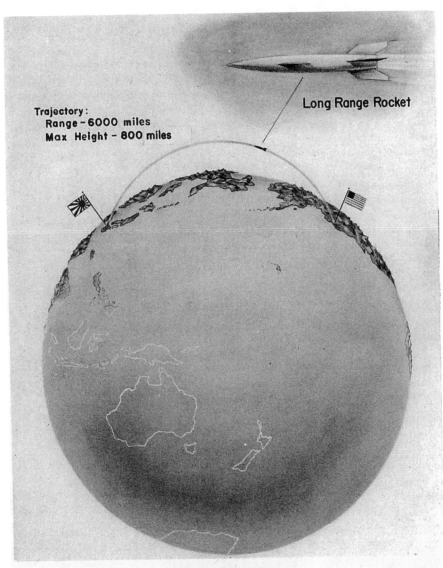

Figure 8 — 6000-Mile Rocket

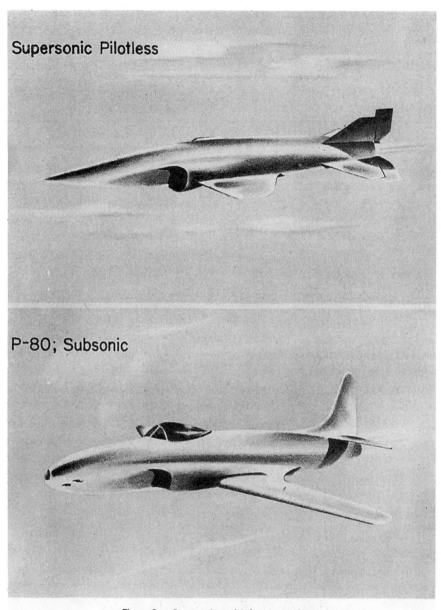

Supersonic Pilotless

P-80; Subsonic

Figure 9 — Supersonic and Subsonic Airplanes

For the future defense against hostile aircraft, it seems clear that supersonic guided missiles will be used, propelled either by rockets or more probably by a ramjet. The fully automatic radar beam guiding methods of control of the type suggested but not experimentally tried, by the Germans will probably be used for guiding, supplemented by simplified heat-homing devices and proximity fuses.

The present facilities and organization for research and development of pilotless aircraft appear inadequate. It cannot be expected that such complex problems can be successfully solved by any group which is specialized in only one of the several fields which are involved.

Leadership in the development of these new weapons of the future can be assured only by uniting experts in aerodynamics, structural design, electronics, servo-mechanisms, gyros, control devices, propulsion, and warhead under one leadership, and providing them with facilities for laboratory and model shop production in their specialties and with facilities for field tests. Such a center must be adequately supported by the highest ranking military and civilian leadership and must be adequately financed, including the support of related work on special aspects of various problems at other laboratories and the support of special industrial developments. It seems to us that this is the lesson to be learned from the activities of the German Peenemünde group.

Propulsion Methods in the Making

Introduction

The following classification embraces the most important novel methods of propulsion emerging from the war years, utilizing atmospheric oxygen:

	Suggested Designation	German Designation
Reciprocating Engine + Ducted Fan	Motor Jet	ML
Gas Turbine + Propeller	Turboprop	PTL
Gas Turbine + Ducted Fan	Turbofan	ZTL
Gas Turbine + Jet	Turbojet	TL
Continuous Jet, Compression by Aerodynamic Ram	Ramjet	L
Intermittent Jet	Pulsojet	IL

These systems are shown schematically in Figs. 10a and 10b.

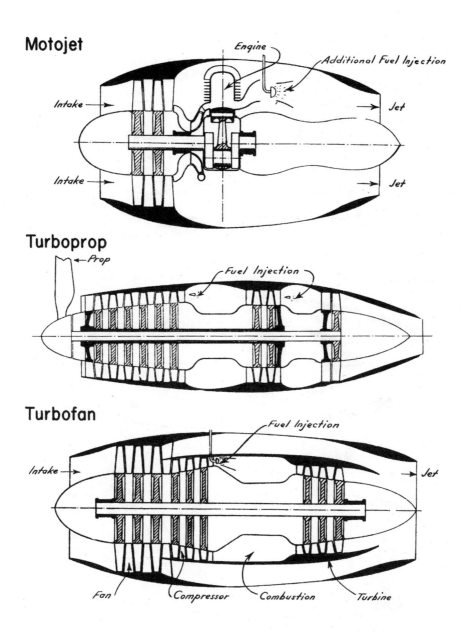

Motojet

Intake →

Intake →

Engine

Additional Fuel Injection

Jet

Jet

Turboprop

← Prop

Fuel Injection

Turbofan

Intake →

Fuel Injection

Jet

Fan

Compressor

Combustion

Turbine

Figure 10-A — Various Propulsion Systems

245

Turbojet

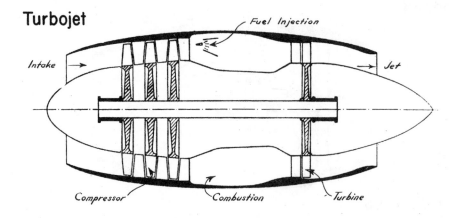

Fuel Injection

Intake

Jet

Compressor

Combustion

Turbine

Ramjet

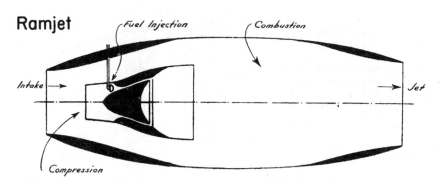

Fuel Injection

Combustion

Intake

Jet

Compression

Pulsojet

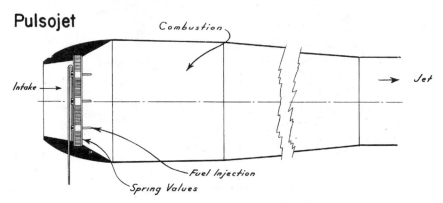

Combustion

Intake

Jet

Fuel Injection

Spring Valves

Figure 10-B — Various Propulsion Systems

The motorjet is widely known as the Campini system. As a matter of fact such a propulsion system was used in the first jet-propelled airplane which was flown in Italy a few years before the war. Probably it will be found heavier and less efficient than some other systems. All elements of the various systems were known long before the war in the patent literature. The fact that they succeeded in becoming practical realities is due to several causes:

1. Fast airplanes and missiles required propulsion systems independent of the use of propellers.

2. Military use justified the design of engines with relatively poor fuel economy, if they are lighter and less bulky than conventional reciprocating engines and/or could offer themselves to simpler manufacturing methods.

3. The science of aerothermodynamics, especially research on combustion in high-speed airflow made great progress in the war years.

4. Metallurgy found new high-temperature-resisting materials.

5. Bold and progressive designers created prototypes of turbines and compressors which conventional engineering considered impossible.

The progress made in combustion technique, lightweight construction, and materials is here to stay and development will continue. In addition, proper scientific study and further research will make at least some of the new propulsion systems equally or more economical than the conventional engines are now. On the other hand it may also happen that the competition of the novel ideas will induce designers of reciprocating engines to produce some radical improvements in their own field. In the following pages, Allied and German developments in the new propulsive devices are compared in some detail. Before discussing the most important types, I include here as a matter of interest a 12-year plan for the period 1938-1950, which the man responsible for engine research in the German Air Ministry published in a secret document in July, 1943, although it does not appear to me as a very well-balanced and far-seeing project.

247

First 4-Year Program (1938–1942). The aim of the first 4-year program was the development of simple turbojet engines for mass production, without particular regard for quality, utilizing readily available material, simple manufacturing methods, and generous tolerances. At the same time studies were to be initiated in preparation for the second period. Results of the first period are shown in mass production of turbojets such as the BMW 003, the Jumo 004, and the Heinkel-Hirth 011.

Second 4-Year Program (1942–1946). This period had the objective of developing the following items:

1. Improved turbojets of higher power, capable of operation at higher altitudes. (Example: BMW 018 for 7700-lb thrust.)
2. Gas turbine + ducted fan units.
3. Gas turbine + propeller combination. (Example: BMW 028 for 12,000 hp at 500 mph at sea level.)
4. Ramjet.
5. Research and design studies on a gas turbine with heat exchanger for long distance flights. This has the German designation GTW.
6. Reciprocating engine + ducted fan units.
7. Research and development on the explosion-type gas turbine. One of the ideas on this subject was the use of a pulsojet, such as the V-1 motor, as a source of gas for operating a turbine.

Third 4-Year Program (1946–1950). Development to a working state of the following items was visualized for this period:

1. Gas turbine with heat exchanger (GTW system).
2. Reciprocating engine + ducted fan units.
3. The intermittent or explosion-type gas turbine.

TURBOPROPELLER AND TURBOFAN

It is general opinion that simultaneously with the development of the jet reaction principle for fast airplanes the gas turbine with propeller or fan drive will have wide applications for airplanes of moderate speed. Jet propulsion has intrinsically low efficiency at low and moderate speeds so that the propeller is superior. On the other hand, it is expected that further research will help the gas turbine attain at least the same efficiency as reciprocating engines now have. It will then have the additional advantages of lighter weight, simpler construction, and absence of the vibrations inherent in reciprocating engines.

The thermal efficiency of existing gas turbines is still considerably lower than that of reciprocating engines at their optimum operating conditions. However, many methods not yet completely developed are available for improvement of the efficiency and associated reduction of fuel consumption of the gas turbine. Heat exchangers help to recover the energy of hot exhaust gases; intercooling between compressor stages and reheating between turbine stages increase the cycle efficiency. Finally, the replacement of the rotating compressor and combustion chamber by a reciprocating system, for example, a free-piston gas generator, allows the use of high pressures and materially lowers the fuel consumption. It is extremely desirable that all of these avenues of further development be thoroughly investigated. An interesting German suggestion, a free-piston gas generator with doughnut-shaped housing for the pistons, is shown in Fig. 11. The arrowhead wing principle applied to the design of high-speed propellers for reducing compressibility effects and increasing efficiency is also shown in Fig.11. Table I outlines German and Allied turboprop and turbofan, and high-speed propeller developments.

Free-Piston Engine

Swept-Back Propeller

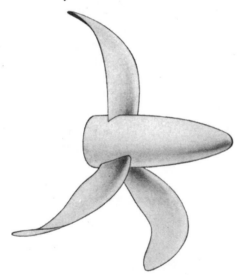

Figure 11 — German Engine and Propeller Developments

TABLE I

Turbopropeller and Turbofan Development

Note: No detailed list of Allied projects is presented since most
of the active projects are Classified

ITEM	GERMAN PROJECTS	REMARKS
Turboprop	BMW 028; Adaptation of BMW 018, 12,000 hp at 500 mph at sea level, wt. 7700 lb. Design stage. Jumo 022; Adaptation of 012, 8000 hp at sea level. Primary design only Daimler-Benz 021; Adaptation of Heinkel-Hirth 011, 4000 hp at 500 mph at 25,000 ft. Design stage only.	U.S. leads Germany in having a low-powered turboprop in experimental operation, namely, the TG-100. Germany leads U.S. in development of high-powered unit, namely the BMW 028. Recommend U.S. push development of larger powered units. U.S. needs greater capacity in compressor and turbine test facilities, and wind tunnels for testing large gas turbine nacelles.
High-speed propellers	Tests of swept-back propeller blades at DVL, Berlin, and AVA Göttingen, show improved efficiency at high-speed flight.	Intensive investigation of swept-back propellers in high-speed wind tunnels recommended for U.S., since it shows possiblity of increasing top speed of propeller-driven aircraft.
Turbofan	Design studies by Junkers, Heinkel, BMW.	Recommend immediate evaluation of this drive for application to U.S. aircraft.
Free-Piston Gas Generator	Junkers reciprocating free piston and LFA rotating free piston.	Rotating free piston shows promise of decreased weight and size over reciprocating free piston. Recommend German development be evaluated whether advantageous for applications in U.S.

The principles and main design characteristics of turbojet engines for airplanes were known before the war in all countries. Endeavors in private industry in England and Germany started at about the same time, in 1935. Our own industry was somewhat discouraged by official studies which were certainly much too conservative, especially concerning the weight of gas turbines and compressors. The German government was perhaps more alert in subsidizing this

251

development than was the English government. The American development started with directives from General Arnold. As far as the centrifugal type of compressor is concerned, the U.S. units were based on Whittle's design, utilizing our own experience with turbosuperchargers. The independent development of the axial-type compressor started about the same time. In the German designs, both centrifugal and axial types are used; with emphasis on the axial. The progress of the actual prototypes in Germany is illustrated by a timetable taken from a German report; dated 2 November 1944, shown in Fig. 12.

The comparative merits of Allied and German turbojet units are shown in Fig. 13. It is seen that the Germans were ahead as far as the sizes of units are concerned; but they were trailing slightly both in specific weight of the engine and in its specific fuel consumption.

In Table II, I am including a list of detailed research problems which may be helpful for planning future research in the field of gas-turbine and jet engines, as well as in the field of turbojets. None of these problems was solved in Germany with decisive success; but most of them were carefully studied in German laboratories. The status of German research is indicated with some remarks concerning the outlook and recommendations.

The present application of turbojet engines is for propelling airplanes at the upper end of the subsonic range. Although the propulsion efficiency of the jet is relatively low at such flying speeds, its application is justified by lightness of weight and simplicity of construction of the jet engine in comparison with reciprocating engines, and because the efficiency of propeller drive decreases somewhat at flight speeds approaching sonic velocity. On the other hand, the propulsive efficiency of jet drive is increasing with increasing velocity; hence, we have to consider the possibility of using the turbojet as a propulsion unit for very high speeds, for example, speeds well beyond the velocity of sound.

Due to the importance of this subject, I initiated a Scientific Advisory Group study of estimated turbojet performance at speeds extending beyond the speed of sound. The results showed that even with the present-day limitations of operating temperatures imposed by materials, the turbojet should outperform the ramjet up to a speed of 1.5 times the speed of sound, and that with increased temperatures still better performance would be obtained. This is in direct contradiction to a widespread belief existing at the present time that a compressor is useless for supersonic speeds, and that the simple ramjet becomes the logical propulsion system. Many other engineers seem to believe that neither the turbojet nor the ramjet is capable of functioning above the speed of sound, and that rocket propulsion is the only possible drive for supersonic flight. We do not believe that this is correct. Our analysis has definitely shown the feasibility of using turbojets for supersonic flying speeds. If the turbojet should be used for supersonic missiles, an expendable type turbojet must be designed in such a way that the manufacturing costs do not become prohibitive. The Scientific Advisory Group several times emphasized the importance of a study of expendable turbojet designs. German reports also include suggestions for the same type of development and at least one project was under way.

The divergence of opinions among various experts on this subject shows the necessity of further fundamental investigations which best can be done in supersonic wind tunnels.

It is our belief that the use of higher speeds will also affect the aerodynamic design of turbines and compressors. The rotational speed of turbomachines is today often restricted by our lack of knowledge of supersonic flow patterns. The development of supersonic turbomachinery may lead to further reduction of the weight and frontal area of jet propulsion units, and materially improve the performance of manned and unmanned airplanes.

	☗ Germany	☲ Britain	☰ U.S.A.
1936	First Design Heinkel jet engine		
1937		First jet engine running	
1938	First run on Heinkel jet engine		
1939	First flight He 178	Contract for jet fighter by RAF	
1940	First run on Ju.004 & BMW 003 jet engines		
1941		First flight "Squirt" ⟹ First airplane	General Arnold directs development to U.S.A.
1942	First flight of Me 262 with two Ju 004 engines	⟹ First engine	to U.S.A. First flight jet plane
1943			
1944	First use Me 262. Start of large scale production	40 jet F's per month 20 Flying Ex. Models Experimental series	20 jet F's per month Experimental series
1945			150 jet F's per month

Data taken from German report dated 2 NOV, 1944

Figure 12

Figure 12 — Timetable of Turbojet Development

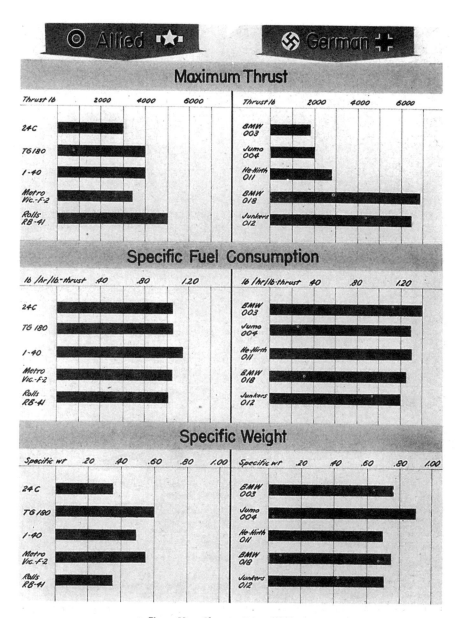

Figure 13 — Characteristics of Turbojets

Table II

Gas Turbine Propulsion Research Problems

Problem	German Projects	Remarks, Outlook, Recommend.
	HIGHER TEMPERATURES	
High Temp. Alloys	DVL and Industry.	U.S. materials superior. Should push research on fatigue improvement.
Ceramic Blades	LFA and AVA.	U.S. not behind. Research on improving brittleness needed.
Cooled Turbine Blades	Air-cooled; BMW, et al. Water cooled; Schmidt, LFA Sodium cooled; Rietz, AVA.	Evaluation of German water-cooled and sodium-cooled technique recommended.
	HIGHER TAKE-OFF THRUST	
Tail Pipe Burning	Used in Jumo 004.	Increased take-off thrust important for turbojets.
Liquid Injection	Experiments with H_2O, HNO_3, N_2O.	Results promising but more thrust increase needed.
Overspeed at Take-off	Not much done.	German units handicapped by materials.
Variable-Area nozzles	Most German jet engines have adjustable tail cones.	Development should also include adjustable stator vanes.
	AERODYNAMIC IMPROVEMENTS	
Compressor Blading	Research at Göttingen, Stuttgart. Little research on increasing stage pressure rise by slots, flaps, and boundary layer suction. Extensive plans for test equipment at Braunschweig, Göttingen, 30,000 hp aerodynamic components laboratory planned at Ötztal.	Germany slightly ahead due to earlier start. German 30,000 hp Ötztal components laboratory exceeds in scope all U.S. plans. Recommend a full scale AAF components test laboratory to supplement basic research of NACA, which should also be expedited.
Nacelle Aerodynamics	Wind-tunnel tests on jet-engine nacelles at Braunschweig, Stuttgart. Ötztal 100,000 hp, 27 ft. Diam, M=1.0 wind tunnel for testing full-scale jet nacelles (80% complete)	Present German and U.S. wind tunnels inadequate in size and speed for jet nacelle tests. Germans had 100,000 hp tunnel under construction. Recommend large high-speed tunnel of similar size be included in plans for AAF equipment.
	CYCLE IMPROVEMENT	
Intercooling and Reheat	Design studies by industry.	German emphasis on mass production of turbojets postponed applied work on cycle improvement. U.S. work should be encouraged.
Regeneration	Design studies by industry; AVA ceramic heat exchanger.	Recommend systematic research on efficient, light-weight, heat exchangers.
Closed Cycle	No evidence of serious consideration.	Recommend Ackeret-Keller system at Escher Wyss, Zurich, be evaluated in terms of aircraft application, especially with use of helium.
	APPLICATION TO MISSILES	
Subsonic Missiles	Design studies of expendable turbojets to replace Argus tube of V-1.	Recommend development of expendable, simple constructed turbojet for missile application.
Supersonic Missiles	No indication of German thought on supersonic turbojet applications	Recommend further studies of supersonic turbojet and construction of experimental model. Supersonic wind-tunnel facilities for testing propulsion units at supersonic speeds urgently needed.

Ramjet

Ramjets and rodsets are the simplest and lightest propulsive devices for aircraft and missiles. The fuel consumption of the ramjet is rather high and, therefore, in the whole field of jet propulsion, it occupies a place between the rocket and the turbojet. Unlike the turbojet, it does not use any mechanical compressor, the compression being obtained only by ram. Therefore, it is indeed a pure aerothermodynamic engine, without mechanical moving parts. Its maximum efficiency occurs naturally at very high flight speed. Hence, it is most suitable for propulsion of aircraft and missiles at transonic and supersonic speeds, especially for short flight durations. This is the reason why the idea of using ramjets, although it was suggested decades ago, lay undeveloped until today, the age of high-speed flight.

For maximum ram efficiency, the design of the entrance diffusers for transonic and for supersonic speeds is somewhat different as shown in Fig. 14.

Due to its promising future, the ramjet is being intensively developed by the Allies; it was earlier developed by the Germans. The situation is outlined in Table III.

A comparison of efforts shows that, although the Germans have run some wind-tunnel tests on their designs, we are not far behind in this initial phase of ramjet development. In fact, part of our effort is wisely directed toward the basic problem of combustion, thus insuring rapid future progress.

For **Transsonic** Speeds

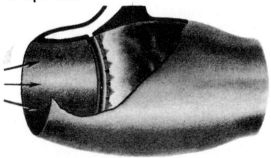

For Supersonic Speeds

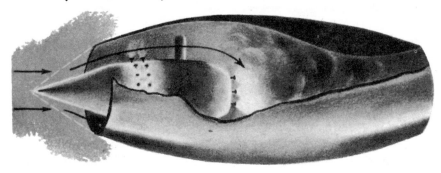

Figure 14 — Ramjets

TABLE III	
Ramjet Development	
GERMANY	**ALLIES**
1943 Fa. Walter Co. of Keil designed a ramjet which was tested at LFA up to M=.85. Fuel consumption 7 lb/hr/lb of thrust.	1943 Combustion research was started at National Bureau of Standards and MIT.
1944 Focke-Wulf Co. designed a short ramjet which was tested at LFA up to M=90. The fuel was first vaporized before burning. Fuel consumption lower than Walter ramjet.	Further Allied development data classified CONFIDENTIAL.
1944 W. Trommsdorf designed a ramjet projectile stabilized by spin. Few initial trials not successful.	
1944 E. Sanger and A. Lippisch suggested use of coal in ramjet as fuel. Combustion research done at Göttingen.	
1944 Supersonic diffuser for ramjet was studied both at Göttingen and LFA.	

Pulsojet

The engine used for the German V-1 flying bombs was the first successful example of a pulsojet. The difference between the pulsojet and the ramjet is that the former utilizes the resonance effect of the duct to obtain higher combustion pressures; there-fore, a better fuel economy is realized in the pulsojet than in the ramjet, which operates without resonance effect and depends on ram compression only. Also, due to this difference in operating principle, the pulsojet can produce a static thrust while the ramjet cannot. However, it is the general belief, substantiated by theoretical analysis, that the advantages of a pulsojet over a ramjet gradually disappear as the speed of flight increases. For supersonic speeds, the ramjet may be the lighter power plant, with the possible further advantage of smooth thrust. However, it seems to me that it is too early to say which power plant is the better one, and this decision should be postponed until more test data on both types of engine are available.

German development of the pulsojet was started by Paul Schmidt, the inventor, as early as 1935. As previously mentioned, its application to the flying bomb, V-1, must be considered as a temporary expedient, used only when the development of the V-2 rocket missile was delayed. The history of the pulsojet is shown schematically in Table IV. It is seen that, although the Germans were the first to have a working pulsojet, their more recent efforts have produced only limited success. The development program in the U.S., while started late, is more thorough and should yield reliable data for judging the comparative merits of the pulsojet and the ramjet in the near future.

TABLE IV

Pulsojet Development

GERMANY	UNITED STATES
1935 P. Schmidt started to develop the pulsojet under the auspices of GAS. Perfected an ignition device for 50 Cycles/sec but found ignition unnecessary once engine was running. Complicated fuel injection.	U.S. projects still classified SECRET
1939 Argus Motor Co., Berlin, also started to work on the pulsojet. They had a cumbersome intake valve shaped like a spiral, but simple fuel injection.	
1940 The simple injection system of Argus was combined with the Schmidt spring air valve. Flight tests made.	
1941 Decision made to apply the Argus engine to the V-1.	
1941 to 1944 Continued research to increase the thrust of the V-1 engine, both by static and wind-tunnel tests. By removing part of the obstruction to the air flow, DFS Group has increased the thrust from 660 to 880 lb. A conical inlet for more air flow by P. Schmidt increased the static thrust to 1500 lb.	

Rockets

Rocket propulsion differs from the jet-propulsion devices hitherto mentioned in that the rocket does not utilize atmospheric oxygen. Its performance is, therefore, practically independent of altitude; in fact, the thrust produced increases somewhat when the outside pressure decreases. It functions best outside of the dense part of the atmosphere. As a matter of fact, it is the only propulsion device for the upper stratosphere and the stellar interspace.

Rocket propellants are either liquids or solid mixtures with moderate or slow rates of burning. Gaseous propellants require bulky containers and are, therefore, impractical. One class of the liquid propellants is called monopropellants; i.e., liquids which under action of igniters or catalyzers decompose and generate a large volume of hot gases. The expansion of the hot gas through the rocket nozzle accelerates the gas and generates the thrust. The bipropellants or the multi-propellants are propellants consisting of two or more components. One component is the oxidizer which, when brought together with the other components in the rocket motor, sustains a vigorous combustion reaction and generates a large quantity of hot gas. The hot gas, in turn, produces the thrust by expansion through the nozzle. The combustion for some propellants has to be started by igniters or catalyzers. But there is a class of bipropellants, such as the combination of nitric acid and aniline, which is spontaneously inflammable when the components are brought into contact in the rocket motor.

One of the important findings of the study on rockets carried out by the Scientific Advisory Group is the fact that, barring the use of atomic energy, the optimum performance of all possible combinations of chemicals used as rocket propellants is not greatly different. Two methods of comparison can be used; comparison can be made on a constant weight-of-propellant basis or on a constant volume-of-propellant basis. The propellant which has the highest impulse per unit weight is the liquid oxygen and liquid hydrogen combination. But the propellant which has the highest impulse per unit volume is the nitric acid and aniline combination. The extremely low density of liquid hydrogen makes very large tanks necessary for its storage and, thus, practically rules out its use in the liquid oxygen and liquid hydrogen propellant. High impulse per unit volume (and, hence, small body and low drag) is very important in guided antiaircraft missiles which have to travel at high speeds in relatively dense atmosphere. The German choice of a nitric acid propellant for such missiles is believed to have been prompted by this advantage.

As a matter of interest, I shall include here the definitions of a few novel terms in German rocket engineering.

Monergol: Monopropellant

Hypergol: Bipropellant or multipropellant that is spontaneously inflammable when the components are brought together in the motor.

Ergol: The inert part of the fuel component in the "Hypergol." For instance, the aromatic gasoline in the mixture with aniline for nitric acid.

Initiator: The active pan of the fuel component of the "Hypergol." For instance, the aniline in the mixture with aromatic gasoline for nitric acid.

Katagol: Monopropellant which is decomposed by catalyzer charged in the motor.

Liquid propellants are generally stored in tanks in the body of a missile and have to be forced into the rocket motor by one of the following methods:

1. Gas, under pressure, acting on the liquid surface in the propellant tanks. The gas can be obtained either from high-pressure storage tanks or from a gas generator, using part of the main propellant itself or a separate solid propellant for this purpose.

2. Liquid pumps. The pump has to be driven by a gas turbine using hot gas from a small combustion "pot" fed by a part of the main propellant supply or by an auxiliary propellant.

At present, the gas-fed systems are generally heavier than the pump-fed systems for durations longer than 30 sec and thrusts larger than 4,000 lb. The gas generator system is, of course, lighter than the gas-under-pressure system due to the saving of the gas-bottle weight. On the other hand, the simplicity of the gas-fed system over the turbine-pump system has many advantages when really large-scale production for expendable weapons is considered.

Rockets as means of propulsion have been developed in the United States with two main applications in mind. The first application is the artillery rocket and the second application is the assisted take-off of heavily loaded airplanes from small airfields and possible short-duration boost to achieve high performance. As actual operational experience was accumulated, it became evident that the requirement for large airfields, for landings by battle-weary pilots, and the power boost of conventional engines by water injection, practically eliminated the necessity for assisted take-off as far as land based bombers are concerned. However, some recent developments indicate a renewed interest in rockets. These developments are:

1. Long-range winged missiles, rising to extreme heights where the rocket is the only power plant which can operate without the assistance of atmospheric oxygen.

2. Guided antiaircraft missiles with a rocket as the main propulsive unit or as the launching device.

3. Launching of supersonic, long-range, pilotless or manned airplanes.

The task of the rocket in launching and take-off of supersonic airplanes and winged missiles is not fully covered by the term assisted take-off. In fact, the rocket will in many cases be the main source of power for take-off of such aircraft.

Both in the U.S. and in Germany, after rocket engineers had succeeded in constructing liquid-fuel rocket motors of several minutes endurance, the idea came up to use rockets as sole power plants on manned airplanes capable of short duration flights. In Germany, such an airplane (the Me-163B) actually was used in combat as an interceptor. However, it is doubtful whether such an airplane will be justified after power plants of almost similar light weight as the rocket motor but with much lower fuel consumption, like the ramjet, become available, and after perfected target-seeking missiles have taken over the task of short duration manned interceptors.

The historical development of rockets by the Germans is summarized in Table V. It is seen that the Germans were forced by the requirements of the war to develop cheap and easily manufactured propellants and to accept the difficulties

263

of handling such propellants as nitric acid and hydrogen peroxide.

There is no doubt that the various applications for rocket motors mentioned above fully justify the statement that rocket research and development have become one of the most important responsibilities of the Air Forces for the future. It is true, of course, that many applications of the rocket concern the ground and naval forces. However, the Air Forces should maintain leadership in rocket development as a main and an auxiliary source of power for manned and pilotless aircraft; they should develop their own facilities for testing rocket propulsion devices; and they should secure a free hand in maintaining the collaboration of the best scientific personnel and the best equipped laboratories in the Nation. Our early perfection of long-duration solid-propellant rockets, and the promising results obtained with nitric-acid aniline and nitro-methane liquid propellants should be further exploited. The propulsion of long-range winged missiles and antiaircraft missiles, and the take-off of supersonic aircraft are important Air Forces applications which call for powerful progress in rocket engineering.

TABLE V
Development of Rockets
GERMANY 1. The German solid propellant for artillery rockets has a wide operating temperature range of from –40° to 140°F.
2. To obtain smooth burning at pressures below the critical pressure of the solid propellant, a spring-loaded regulator valve is fitted to the motor.
3. The handling of 80% concentration of H_2O_2 was relatively safe. Long duration H_2O_2 and methyl alcohol and hydrozine hydrate rocket was perfected for Me-163B. Turbine-pump system functioned well.
4. The difficulty of producing enough H_2O_2 and the advantage of high density of nitric acid-aniline propellant for guided missile application forces the Germans to use the latter. Improvements are made to shorten ignition lag, even after the addition of inert component to the fuel.
5. Film cooling and evaporative cooling was developed, particularly for high performance propellants such as liquid oxygen and alcohol.
6. Early trial on monopropellant not successful. The Schmidding propellant, a mixture of methyl nitrate and methyl alcohol, was not reliable.
UNITED STATES
Projects all still classified SECRET

Atomic Energy for Jet Propulsion

Based upon the published values of the measured heat of fission of U^{235}, it is calculated that the available energy of this material is 3.120×10^{10} BTU per pound. This is more than 1,500,000 times the lower heat value of gasoline, the most powerful fuel generally used today. The study of chemicals suitable for fuels or rocket propellants indicates that no really radical improvements in the BTU per pound ratio can be expected within the frontiers of molecular reaction. It will be possible to produce fuels and propellants more suitable for certain types of engines, increase their safety, improve their handling quality, and lower their costs of production. Nevertheless, no hope for spectacular improvements in range and speed performance of aircraft can be derived from further development of conventional fuels. Use of atomic energy as fuel, however, will radically change this situation.

The question of whether or not and how atomic power can be produced continuously and at a constant rate suitable for propulsion cannot be discussed in this report. Let us transfer our thoughts to an era in which the fundamental aspect of the problem already has been solved.

It appears to me that the application of atomic energy to transportation will probably precede the application to power generation for stationary purposes. In the latter case the cost is the governing factor; in transportation, it is the cost and the weight of the fuel to be carried. In high-speed aerial transportation the importance of weight transcends the importance of cost. Hence, it may be concluded that the extremely expensive atomic agent, now having been developed as an explosive, will be used for propulsion and probably jet propulsion.

In speculating on the possible use of atomic energy for this purpose we have to change our usual concepts. For example, the weight of the fuel proper is certainly negligible. In other words, the available energy is almost unlimited. The problem is how much of this energy we shall be able to utilize in an engine of limited size and limited weight, where the weight of the engine includes all materials which have to be carried in the vehicle besides the atomic fuel proper.

Let us consider, for example, the case of rockets. We shall exclude the use of the disintegration products as working fluid for the rocket. The temperature of the disintegration products alone without dilution would be too high for any known or possible engineering materials to resist. Since temperature is the limit, the most efficient expansion process for the fluid is the isothermal expansion, with the temperature of the gas kept at the maximum allowable value by constant reheating. Inasmuch as one obtains the highest exhaust velocity by using a working fluid with the least possible molecular weight, hydrogen should be used. Then assuming a maximum temperature of 8,000°F, which would require cooling, of course, and a chamber pressure of 100 times atmospheric pressure, we can obtain a specific impulse of 1,365 lb-sec/lb of hydrogen carried in the vehicle. This means that the specific propellant consumption of rockets would be reduced from the present day value of 18 lb/hr/lb of thrust to 2.6 lb/hr/lb of thrust. This is a great reduction, even though the ratio is far below the spectacular figures for the ratio of the effectiveness of atomic and conventional bombs. However, the use of atomic energy would certainly allow the construction of rocket-driven pilotless aircraft which could reach any point of the globe without stop. Even interstellar navigation appears feasible.

As to jet-propulsion devices using atomic energy with atmospheric air as working fluid, the fuel consumption itself again would be negligible. The size and performance of the craft driven by atomic power would depend mainly on the weight of the auxiliary materials like moderators, and devices for cooling and for controlling the rate of energy production. Of course it is difficult today to make any estimate of the bulk and weight of such equipment.

The most interesting feature of such a propulsion system is that the overwhelming part of the weight to be carried by the vehicle is independent of the endurance and only a very small portion of the weight is proportional to the flying time or the range desired. In other words, if one succeeds in reducing the engine weight to the limiting value which makes flight at a certain speed possible, very small further reduction of the weight would increase the range almost without limit.

It seems to me that there are possibilities in the development of nuclear energy for jet propulsion which deserve immediate attention of the Air Forces. To be sure there are problems still to be solved requiring inventive activity of specialists in nuclear physics. However, the main problems are engineering problems requiring inventive genius of the same order but different kind. We have to convert the energy liberated by the nuclear reaction into heat of such temperatures as needed for our propulsive devices. Important problems to be solved are in the nature of heat transfer, resistance of materials to heat, corrosion, etc. It appears necessary to find a way, within the limits of necessary security, for engineering talent which could be used to accelerate the progress in the field of propulsion. It would secure us the conquest of the air over the entire globe without range limitations.

It is my feeling that the Air Forces should, as soon as possible, take the lead in investigating the possibilities of using nuclear energy for jet propulsion.

Jet Propelled Aircraft

Of the novel power plants mentioned in this report, only the turbojet and the liquid-fuel rocket motor have been successfully used on aircraft.

Our Bell P-59 (turbojet), Lockheed P-80 (turbojet), and Ryan FR-1 (reciprocating engine and propeller plus turbojet) are all well known to the Commanding General.

The Germans had developed and used some jet-propelled aircraft in combat and had others under development. This is shown in Table VI.

For future fundamental planning, a very careful choice of propulsion systems is necessary. It is possible to make a basic analysis, computing for various systems the sum of the specific weight of power plant and fuel required to travel at a given speed for a certain endurance. Then the optimum power plant is the one for which this sum has a minimum value. However, it is impossible to decide rigidly from such a simple study which type of propulsive system is best for a certain purpose. Beside the minimum specific weight of the power plant and fuel, many other aspects enter the picture. One important factor is the frontal area of the engine. Then also the structural weight of the airplane is influenced by the choice of power plant. The jet-propelled airplane has the advantages of not requiring a minimum ground clearance for the propeller, and of being comparatively easy to maintain. On the other hand, jet propulsion introduces aerodynamically difficult problems such as the intake and ducting of very large quantities of air.

No one has doubts about the great future propulsion in military aircraft. However, such general statements as "one or two years from now all fighters and bombers will be jet propelled" should be replaced by careful, scientific analysis which secures jet propulsion its proper place, but does not exclude other combinations such as the turboprop or, in the case of extreme ranges, the reciprocating engine and propeller. The choice of the most efficient power plant must not be influenced by any general feeling that the propeller appears obsolete.

I believe that German high-speed wind-tunnel results will prove to be very helpful in our designs in connection with aerodynamic and vibration problems originating from interference between the jet system and the air frame. However, the Air Forces should, in cooperation with aircraft designers, initiate a comprehensive high-speed wind-tunnel test program in order to obtain further information in this field. The ATSC took the first step in such a program by holding a meeting between NACA, industry, the Navy and the ATSC in late summer, 1945. However, any program which is undertaken will be severely restricted and handicapped for a long time by the lack of high-speed wind tunnels of sufficiently large size.

The two rocket airplanes mentioned in Table VI, the Me-163B and the Natter, are of special interest because pure rocket motors were their sole source of power. The Me-163B was more or less conventional in that take-off and climb were accomplished under its own power. However, the Natter was intended to be launched nearly vertically by means of two or four solid-propellant launching rockets. It was to be aimed at a point 2 km behind the point of collision so that attack on a bomber could be made from the rear. This rocket-propelled

CHARACTERISTICS OF GERMAN JET AIRPLANES

Table VI

AIRPLANE	HE-162	ME-262	ARADO-234	ME-163 B	HORTON-229	JU-287	BP-20 'NATTER'
USE	FIGHTER	FIGHTER	BOMBER	TAILLESS FIGHTER	FLYING WING FIGHTER	BOMBER	FIGHTER
ENGINE-NAME & TYPE	BMW-003 E-1 OR E-2	JUMO T-J UNITS TL 109.004 B-1	JUMO-004	BI-FUEL ROCKET MOTOR HWK 509 A-1	JUMO-004	JUMO-004	BI-FUEL ROCKET MOTOR HWK 509 A-2
NUMBER OF ENGINES	ONE	TWO	TWO	ONE	TWO	FOUR	ONE
MAXIMUM THRUST	1,760 LB @ S.L. STATIC	4,000 LB @ S.L. STATIC	3,900 LB @ S.L. STATIC	3,650 LB S.L. STATIC		8,000 LB @ S.L. STATIC	3,750 LB
GROSS WEIGHT	5,940 LB	11,000 LB	20,900 LB NORMAL LOAD	11,500 LB NORMAL LOAD		50,600 LB	4,920 LB
WING LOADING	49.5 LB /SQ FT	40.7 LB /SQ FT	72 LB /SQ FT			81.6 LB /SQ FT	95.5 LB /SQ FT @ TAKE-OFF
MAXIMUM SPEED	522 MPH @ 19,700 FT	550 MPH @ 30,000 FT	500 MPH	590 MPH. @ 25,000 FT	550 MPH @ 20,000-25,000 FT	485 MPH @ 16,400 FT (35,400 LB MEAN WT)	620 MPH @ 16,400 FT
MAX. RANGE OR ENDURANCE	620 MI @ 36,000 FT 85 MIN @ 36,000 FT	945 MI @30,000 FT 80 MIN	600 MI-WITH 1,100 LB BOMBS 900 MI - NO BOMBS	10-12 MIN FULL POWER	1 HR @ 22,500 FT	36 MI AFTER CLIMB 4.36 MIN-500MPH-2800 FT	
TAKE-OFF DISTANCE	2625 FT-NO ASSIST 1,245 FT-WITH ASSIST	3300 FT HARD SURFACE 5000 FT TURF	4,200-4,500 FT	3,600 FT ±			VERTICAL
RATE OF CLIMB	4,230 FT/MIN @ S.L.	4,600 FT/MIN. @ S.L.		10,000 FT/MIN @ 40,000 FT ALT			37,400 FT/MIN @ S.L.
LANDING SPEED	102 MPH	112-124 MPH	APPROX.110 MPH		81 MPH		
STATUS	FLYING EXPERIMENTAL	IN COMBAT	FIGHTER VERSION IN COMBAT	IN COMBAT	DESIGNED	DESIGN STAGE	FLYING EXPERIMENTAL

Table VI — Characteristics of German Jet Airplanes

interceptor was armed with 24 rockets of 7.3-cm caliber. After the rocket ammunition is exhausted, the airplane is caused to disintegrate; the nose section is allowed to fall freely and be expended but the air frame with rocket propulsion motor and the pilot are saved by parachutes. A former Luftwaffe pilot, who had been convicted of some crime, acted as test pilot in the first flight of the Natter and was killed.

Rocket airplanes have, at the present time, intrinsically, only a few minutes of endurance. Their use as interceptors in the future may be made unnecessary by the development of more economical propulsive devices of light weight, and perfection of target-seeking electronic or heat devices which would eliminate the need for a pilot. However, I highly recommend that the rocket-type of airplane be developed at the present time for research purposes. One advantage of rocket drive in this case is the possibility of exact thrust measurement, which is extremely difficult for any other propulsive system. These research airplanes would be very useful for studying performance, flow conditions. and flight mechanics.

Tailless Aircraft

In Germany, tailless aircraft were intensively developed by A. Lippisch and by the Horten brothers. The Junkers' designers did a considerable amount of engineering study on large tailless airplanes but none were actually constructed.

Lippisch worked on the design of tailless airplanes at DFS beginning in 1936. He designed a series of about eight aircraft, before the time when he came in contact with Messerschmitt and developed the Me-163A and Me-163B. Stability problems were encountered at high speeds and the Me-163B was "redlined" at a Mach number of 0.80 (590 mph at 25,000 ft). Satisfactory stalling characteristics were obtained by a special low-drag fixed slot at the wing tips. A vertical tail was found necessary for satisfactory directional stability. Lippisch's latest design was the P-11, a tailless aircraft with two turbojet engines. The critical Mach number was estimated to be 0.92 (about 680 mph at 25,000 ft); wind-tunnel tests indicated a drag coefficient as low as 0.0063.

The Horten brothers flew their first tailless aircraft in 1935. They received no support from the Air Ministry until February, 1945, following the publication of a photograph of a Northrop tailless airplane in "Interavia." Their design was to be powered with two Jumo 004 turbojet engines. Computed high speed was about 600 mph.

The development program for tailless aircraft has been more extensive in the United States than any place abroad.

The Northrop XP-56 was a pusher-type, flying-wing fighter. This airplane was flown only a few times and indications were, from these tests, that the performance was short of expectations and that difficulties in control were encountered. Unfortunately, wind-tunnel tests necessary to trace the basic reasons for these difficulties could not be carried out, because no high priority could be attached to merely experimental projects.

Theoretical studies here and abroad show significant advantages (for example, longer ranges) for tailless aircraft over tailed aircraft, especially in the case of gross weights of 150,000 lb and more. Of course it must be assumed that the tailless aircraft is made stable and maneuverable without measures which would compromise the performance. The recent recognition of the advantage of swept-back wings for very high speeds makes the tailless airplane particularly attractive also for transonic airplanes. It is the opinion of the Scientific Advisory Group that the development of tailless aircraft should be encouraged; however, actual construction should be supplemented by extensive wind-tunnel investigations of methods for improving stability and control at high speeds.

Aerodynamic Miscellanea

By aerodynamic miscellanea, I mean auxiliary items which contribute to the advance of the aerodynamic art. The items which I now consider are:

1. Flow Measurement Techniques,
2. Laminar Flow Wings, and
3. Boundary Layer Control.

A discussion of these miscellanea follows, with a brief review of German developments and comparison with our own.

FLOW MEASUREMENT TECHNIQUES

The average level of German development in wind-tunnel instrumentation appeared somewhat below our own, although in some instances they had surpassed us especially in fields such as supersonic aerodynamics where their basic facilities were more advanced. On the other hand, their electronic equipment was generally inferior to ours.

In high speed air flow, in both the transonic and supersonic range, instruments which project into the air stream cause excessive disturbance of the flow. For this reason, both German and Allied aerodynamic instrument development work was concentrated largely on methods of studying air flow by methods which do not disturb the flow pattern.

Several interesting German developments were:

1. Combination Schlieren and interference methods which show both density gradients and lines of constant density on the same observation screen or photographic plate, as shown in Fig. 15.

2. A novel X-ray method of measuring density, which makes use of the fact that the absorption of an X-ray beam is dependent on the density of the medium through which it passes.

3. A corona method of measuring velocity, which utilizes the fact that the potential of a corona discharge varies with the speed of the air passing by.

4. A spark method of determining local temperature, by measuring the local speed of sound, at which the disturbance, caused by a spark discharge, travels.

A brief comparison of German and Allied developments in measurement technique is given in Table VII.

272

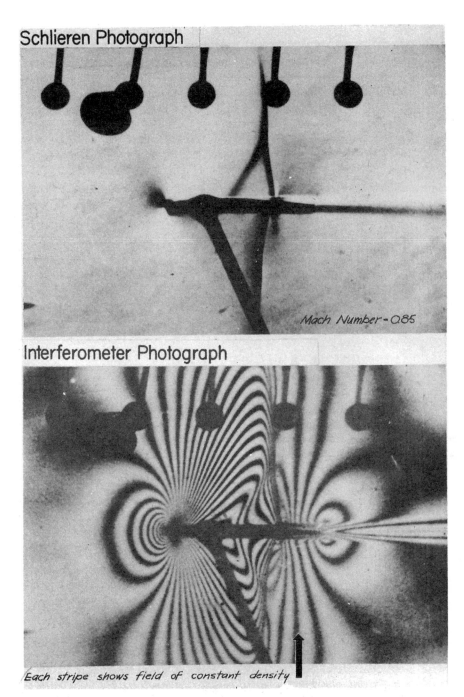

Schlieren Photograph

Mach Number - 0.85

Interferometer Photograph

Each stripe shows field of constant density

Figure 15 — High-Speed Airflow Photographs

273

TABLE VII

Flow Measurement Techniques

Item	German Development	Allied Development
Interfero-meter	Extensive development at LFA, AVA, WVA for measuring density in high-speed air flow; nothing new in principle but considerable development of details. LFA has a system whereby simultaneous Schlieren and interference pictures are recorded on the same photo plate.	U.S. development by Ladenberg, Princeton. Also small project by Dr. Williams, Pasadena. U.S. application lagging German.
X-Ray Method	This method used at Kochel utilizes principle that absorption of X-Ray beam is a function of the density of the medium through which it passes. Ionization meter is calibrated in terms of density.	Unknown to Allies.
Schlieren Method	All supersonic wind tunnels have associated Schlieren equipment. Largest mirrors are 1.2 m in diam, under construction for Kochel, 1m by 1m Mach number 7.0 tunnel.	Used in the few existing Allied supersonic wind tunnels.
Spark Method	A spark creates a disturbance traveling at the speed of sound. Measurement of the local speed of sound determines the local temp. Developed by WVA.	Application to temprature determination unknown to Allies.
Ultrasonic Waves	Generation of high-frequency waves affords another method of determining temperature by means of measuring a local velocity of sound.	Application to temprature determination unknown to Allies.
Hot Wire	Some work at Göttingen but not very advanced.	U.S. Developments, especially by Dryden, NBS; also by Liepmann, CAT; superior to Germans. British work also more advanced than Germans.
Corona	Aachen development of corona for velocity measurement.	Experimental development by Lindvall, CIT, in 1935. Not continued. Some work at MIT.
Doppler Method	Method developed at Fassberg for measuring speed in the jet of rocket by means of the Doppler effect.	This method not used by Allies for measuring speed of rocket discharge.
Electro-magnetic Balances	Used in many of the intermittent wind tunnels, such as, LFA, AVA, WVA, to measure transient forces.	Iin common use in U.S. wind tunnels. Electronic technique in general superior to Germans.
Piczo-electric Capsules	Used at LFA for measuring transient forces.	This method also used by Allies for special purposes.
Half Models	This technique is used at WVA; convenient for measuring pressures, hinge moments, etc.	This technique also used at CIT.
Cavitation	Similarity between cavitation and compressibility phenomena used for qualitative work in water channels on simulated critical compressibility conditions.	Water channels not used by Allies for simulated compressibility effects.
Simulated Turbojets	For wind-tunnel models, small high-speed compressors are used to simulate internal flow, and alcohol is burned to introduce heat.	Not used as yet by Allies for wind tunnel models of jet aircraft.
Flexible Walls	In some supersonic wind tunnels, continuous flexible walls of the test section are used to change Mach number. Some tunnels use fixed nozzles and variable diffuser.	Flexible walls have been ordered for Aberdeen, Wright Field, and Ames supersonic wind tunnels. Flexible walls have been used for several years by NACA and in England.
Half-Open Jets	In some supersonic tunnels the test section is partly closed and partly open. This is said to decrease wall interference, especially through transonic range.	This technique is not yet used by the Allies for supersonic flow.

LAMINAR FLOW WINGS

In this field we were far ahead of the Germans. In the following paragraphs, the German development status will first be given, followed by our own.

German Developments

According to the German dynamicist Schlichting, German work on laminar flow airfoils did not start until about the end of 1938. By 1940, Schlichting considered that the fundamentals were known. Drag coefficients as low as 0.0027 were reached at a Reynolds Number of 5×10^6, but the German scientists were unable to retain the low drag at higher Reynolds Numbers. They were handicapped by lack of suitable low-turbulence wind tunnels. On one occasion, Prandtl reported: "Suitable wind tunnels for the conduct of airfoil investigations at sufficiently high Reynolds Number and at low turbulence are lacking in Germany. On the other hand, it is known that in the U.S.A. particular installations created for this purpose are working exceptionally vigorously in this field."

Tests were made on a Japanese laminar flow airfoil, on three airfoils derived from one member of an obsolete NACA Series 27215 (which was described in a captured French secret report), and on a few airfoils designed by Schlichting. The Germans also had some information on a Russian laminar flow airfoil obtained from a captured report.

The Germans never used laminar flow airfoils on aircraft. They were astonished and mystified by the performance of the Mustang and made many wind-tunnel and flight tests. They gave the following tabulation of wing profile drag coefficients (obtained by momentum method) for a number of airplanes at lift coefficient of 0.2:

He 177	0.0109
Me 109B	0.0101
Ju 288	0.0102
FW-190	0.0089
Mustang	0.0072

The German comment is: "The drag of this only foreign original airfoil tested up till now is far below the drag of all

275

German wings tested in which it should be remembered that it was tested without any smoothing layer."

Another writer says: "A comparison of flight measurements shows quite unmistakably that the Mustang is far superior aerodynamically to all other airplanes and that it maintains this superiority in spite of its considerably greater wing area."

Allied Developments

The NACA began investigations of laminar flow airfoils in a low-turbulence wind tunnel in the spring of 1938, and the encouraging nature of the results obtained (without details) were described in the Wilbur Wright Lecture of the Royal Aeronautical Society on 25 May 1939, and in the NACA Annual Report for 1939. In June, 1939, an advance confidential report by Jacobs was released. A summary was published in March, 1942 in confidential form. The most recent summary was released in March, 1945, and this summary has been kept up to date by supplementary sheets.

As indicated in the summary of German developments, the Allies are far ahead in low-turbulence wind-tunnel equipment and in knowledge of laminar flow airfoils and their application to aircraft. Drag coefficients as low as 0.003 at a Reynolds Number of 20×10^6 have been obtained.

A summary of the present state of knowledge is given in the NACA restricted report L5C05, "Summary of Airfoil Data," by Abbott, von Doenhoff, and Stivers, March, 1945.

BOUNDARY LAYER CONTROL

In this field the Germans had an advanced start and had just about reached a practical state. A discussion of German and Allied developments follows.

German Developments

Considerable work was done on boundary layer control at AVA, Göttingen, starting in 1925. The first airplane with boundary layer control was built and flown in 1932.

From about 1942 on, work was intensified. Schwier obtained a maximum lift coefficient of 4.3, using pressure jet boundary layer control in wind tunnel tests. In July, 1943, Stüper obtained a maximum lift coefficient 3.8 in full-scale flight tests with boundary layer control by suction. The maximum lift coefficient on his airplane without boundary layer control was 1.9. About the same time, a maximum lift coefficient of 3.4 with boundary layer control was reported in wind-tunnel tests of a four-motored airplane which was to be developed by Junkers. A unique suction and pressure-jet boundary layer control system was used. Air was sucked in over the inboard portion of the wing, just ahead of the flaps, and blown out over the outboard portion of the wing, just ahead of the ailerons. In November, 1943, Wagner outlined work which was done at Arado, shoving a maximum lift coefficient of 4.0 to be possible.

All German investigators noted that the internal wing ducting required and the power required to drive the boundary layer control equipment constituted serious obstacles to the successful, practical application of boundary layer control. However, it was felt that these obstacles could be successfully met. At the end of the war, an Arado transport airplane, having low landing and take-off speeds because of boundary layer control, was in service in the German Air Force.

United States Developments

An L-1 airplane was equipped with boundary layer control by suction. The maximum lift coefficient was 3.5 without boundary layer control and 3.6 with boundary layer control. The landing speed of the modified L-1 was considerably higher than that of the original airplane due to the weight of the boundary layer control equipment.

Boundary layer control has an important application in making low landing speeds possible on high-speed aircraft. It also appears that the potentialities of boundary layer control in the transonic speed range have never been systematically evaluated. We found that some interesting work was done by Ackeret at the Institute of Technology in Zurich, Switzerland. The Scientific Advisory Group recommends that an intensive research program on boundary layer control be undertaken by the Army Air Forces.

The Art of Radar

INTRODUCTION

The last four years of war-stimulated research have resulted in the development of equipment and techniques in the radar and electronics field which offer possibilities of profoundly affecting the whole concept of future air force operations. These devices have already passed the laboratory stage, and nearly $3,000,000,000 worth of radar equipment is now in actual combat use in the Army, the Navy, and the Air Forces. Thus, the fundamental ideas in the field have been thoroughly proven and are definitely here to stay.

In spite of the rapid progress made in a relatively short time, the technique in this field is still in its infancy. Enormous possibilities lie ahead, and additional research, both on the technical and on the operational side, will pay huge dividends in more effective air force operations.

At the same time, the rapid introduction of new and miraculous devices has led to the feeling among the uninitiated that anything is possible by the use of electronics. It is, therefore, of greatest importance to understand thoroughly the limitations as well as the possibilities of radio, radar, and electronic equipment in order to avoid raising impossible hopes and in order to eliminate unnecessary and ill-conceived research and development programs.

Fundamentally, radar is a device which enormously extends the range, power, capabilities, and accuracy of human vision. For example:

1. The human eye cannot see in darkness or through fog, clouds, and rain. Radar is not at all limited by darkness or by fog, and to only a slight extent by heavy clouds and rain.

2. The human eye determines only roughly and with difficulty the distance to an object which it sees. Radar determines the distance rapidly, accurately, and continuously.

3. The human eye can pick up or see objects such as airplanes only at distances of a few miles. Suitable radar can see airplanes at distances up to 200 miles.

4. The human eye, aided by optical instruments, can get accurate data on bearing, elevation, and range of only one

distant object at a time, and considerable time is required for such determinations. Radar can determine and display these data within a few seconds for all objects in view over an enormous area, in the best cases up to a radius of 200 miles.

These features of radar open up many possibilities, such as: all-weather day and night air operations; an increase in accuracy and versatility of bombing, gunfire, and navigation; the control from the ground or from the air of major air force operations; provision of information and controls to relieve the overburdened pilot, both in navigation and in combat; and, the accurate remote control of pilotless aircraft.

Furthermore, it must be realized that radar is not a facility or attachment which will occasionally be used under bad conditions. Rather, the air force of the future will be operated so that radar is the primary facility, and visual methods will be only occasionally used. Bad weather or darkness are normally prevalent from 60 to 90% of the time, and predictions of good weather at remote points fail to be realized from about 25 to 50% of the time. Hence, in an all-weather air force, radar must be the universally used tool for bombing, gunfire, navigation, landing, and control. The whole structure of the air force, the planning of its operations, its training program, and its organization must be based on this premise. The development and perfection of radar and the techniques for using it effectively are as important as the development of the jet-propelled plane.

GERMAN RADAR DEVELOPMENTS

Broadly speaking, the radar art in Germany at the end of the war was in about the same state as it was in this country and England in early 1942. The Germans did not realize the possibilities of microwave radar, for example, until they inspected equipment shot down in British and American airplanes. Furthermore, they were forced, during the latter years of the war to concentrate their efforts on defensive measures and hence, never developed a concept of the offensive use of radar. Finally, the British and American jamming and countermeasures techniques were so effective that over half of the German radar development talent was forced into the task of developing anti-jamming measures, to protect their own existing radar equipment. This did much to stop progress in the development of new radar techniques.

The beginnings of German radar took place at as early a date (1936) as the corresponding developments in the United States and England. By the beginning of the war the Germans had an early warning system of good design and were making progress on equipment for control of fighter aircraft and for antiaircraft artillery. The German scientists felt that 50 to 60 cm was about the shortest wavelength that could be practically employed in radar and concentrated very considerable engineering talent on the development of a variety of equipments at this wavelength. Their engineers considered the development of microwave techniques, but discarded this possibility as impractical because no adequate transmitter at such frequencies was known to them. The equipment they had in use at 50 to 60-cm wavelengths, however, was excellent in its engineering design and very large quantities were in actual use.

Germany suffered seriously through the lack of a good organization of their radar and electronics development effort. Most of the development took place in industrial laboratories such as those of Teietunken, but the very brilliant group of German physicists in universities were never called in to participate. Consequently, while engineering design was good, imaginative thinking was lacking. The industrial engineers complained that they received no intelligent and understanding cooperation from any of the military agencies. They believed that the top military commands had no conception of the importance of radar and electronic equipment. On the other hand, the university scientists did not take the initiative to mobilize their efforts themselves as was done in the United States and England. The close coordination which existed in this country between both technical and operational military officers, the industrial laboratories, and the university scientists was completely lacking in Germany. Some attempt to remedy this situation was made in late 1944, but the effort never got going before the end of the war. The development work was scattered widely throughout the country, largely due to the disruptive effects of Allied bombing, and the various agencies and laboratories worked independently and without adequate coordination.

The only German radar put into extensive tactical use was that designed for air warning and air defense. Early warning stations, ground-controlled interception stations, antiaircraft fire control equipment, and airborne aircraft interception equipment were all in effective use. The techniques used by the Germans for navigational assistance to bombers on offensive missions during the Battle of Britain did not utilize radar, but employed elaborations of the United States airway navigational aids. Ingenious radio beam techniques were employed and in some cases these were made to operate bomb computing devices in the aircraft. However, the British jamming of these radio beams was very effective, in spite of strenuous efforts continuously made by the Germans to change frequencies and otherwise alter their techniques to avoid jamming. The concept of using microwave airborne radar for bombing and attack on shipping apparently did not come until British and American planes carrying such equipment were shot down over German-occupied territory. The capture of this equipment created a considerable sensation among German scientists and military experts. A large effort was immediately undertaken to copy this equipment. However, no sooner had a start been made on copying 10-cm equipment than 3-cm equipment appeared in American planes. Rumors that even shorter wavelengths were being developed by the Allies caused the Germans to start work on 1-cm and shorter wavelength devices. Their efforts became so scattered thereby that apparently no microwave equipment at all was ever put into production. In addition, the efforts of the engineers were also diverted to improving their air-defense equipment and to finding methods of avoiding Allied countermeasures, so that the positive efforts to develop radar for new offensive uses were greatly retarded. The concept of using radar for the ground control of tactical and strategic air operations, so successfully employed by the U. S. 8th and 9th Air Forces, apparently never occurred to the Germans, even though some of their ground equipment could have been adapted to this purpose.

The development of rockets and other unmanned missiles was far more actively pursued in Germany than the development of electronic equipment. As a result, apparently no advanced electronic or radio control methods for their missiles comparable with Allied developments ever got beyond the paper or laboratory stage. Had the Germans had an active coordinated electronic development program comparable to that built up by the Allies and had this been combined with their missile work, some dangerous weapons might have resulted. Various ideas were reported by individual workers for the control of missiles but the aerodynamics laboratories apparently did not have adequate electronic talent and the electronic engineers were largely cut off from contact with the aerodynamic work. Only the most successful missile development organization, the Peenemünde group, had a qualified electronic engineering section.

RADAR FROM THE VIEWPOINT OF THE AIR FORCES

The ability to achieve air force operations under all conditions of darkness and weather contributes more than any other single factor to increasing the military effectiveness of the air forces. Hence, any research program designed to overcome the limitations to flight at night and in bad weather will pay big dividends.

Radar has already done much to overcome visibility limitations, and is of the greatest importance in the problems of traffic control in and near airports and of landing under conditions of bad or zero visibility. Although there is room for great technical development of the radio and radar aids to landing and traffic control, one of the chief problems is the development of a system in which all conceivable aids will be properly integrated and used together. This can only come as a result of extensive experience and a comprehensive program of trials.

Radar has revolutionized methods of air navigation. The development of microwave radar, which permits the use of narrow beams, enables the continuous presentation to the navigator of a more or less recognizable map of the surrounding country. In its earliest and crude form little more than cities, towns, and coastlines could be distinguished; but modern developments give sufficient resolution to identify many features of the landscape such as rivers, streams, bridges, and rail lines and make feasible the use of ordinary maps. In addition, heavy storm clouds make themselves evident on the radar screen. Over the sea, radar contact flying is restricted to areas within sight of identifiable land, but radar "sees" at distances up to 50 or 100 miles.

The possibilities of direct radar navigation are greatly extended by the use of strong, readily identifiable, artificial echoes provided by radar beacons, the radar equivalent of optical beacons or lighthouses. Radar permits the measurement of distance to the beacon and its bearing within the inherent accuracy of the radar equipment carried on the aircraft. By measurements on two beacons, the position of the aircraft can be determined.

Microwave systems give essentially short-range navigation. For long ranges the pulse techniques of radar are applied to longer waves, for example, in the Loran system. Here two pairs of ground stations emit synchronized pulses. In the aircraft the pulses are received and the time difference between the arrival of the pulses from the members of a pair is measured. This locates the aircraft on a hyperbolic line of position and two such lines give a fix. The airplane carries only a receiver and the traffic capacity is unlimited.

The use of radar in strategic bombing operations has proven itself in this war. Suitable radar equipment can allow the carrying on of such operations under the many conditions where visual bombing is not possible. Only a beginning has been made in the development of radar bombsights and much remains to be done to improve their precision, their versatility, and over-all operational usefulness.

Tremendous improvement in the control and marshaling of air forces appears possible through the medium of airborne radar. Control of air operations includes military functions, involving radar surveillance of movements of friendly and enemy aircraft, and the guidance of our own planes on their missions.

The future development of control radar falls into two categories: radar for the defense of this country, and radar for attack. It is not necessary to say more about the defensive possibilities of ground control radar. The problem of the future is chiefly an economic one; to install sufficient stations to surround the country completely is possible and necessary. Since these stations can be easily integrated into the airlines navigational net, the investment will be of great peacetime value. While in peacetime the network will be extremely valuable, in war it will be our protection against sneak attacks and against air raids of all descriptions. Control radar for offensive warfare will undoubtedly develop to the point where a unified command of air operations is possible throughout the whole operation. The commanding general will see the disposition of his own and enemy forces, whether piloted or pilotless, and be able to instantly modify his plans.

Radar also has been used in aerial fighting for aircraft interception, for range finding, for tail warning, and for fire control, particularly in the defense of heavy bombers. Future developments of radar equipment for fighters are largely dependent on the extent to which it is found desirable to control fighters by ground equipment of increased range and resolving power. Fire control and associated radar equipment for heavy bombers can be made indefinitely more and more complex. An analysis to determine whether one should abandon such air battleships seems in order, before developing more complicated equipment which may only slow down the airplane to the point where still more and more complexity and fire power is needed.

The radically altered military situation produced by the development of guided missiles has been discussed previously. The development of radar and other detection and navigation devices has provided a wealth of technical means for locating and guiding missiles. The essential problems which radar can solve are those of locating the missile, locating the target, and transferring intelligence to and from the missile. The present fundamental limitation is that the missile cannot be followed over the horizon. This limitation has to be circumvented by providing one or more relay stations, putting the controlling radar in an aircraft, or by shifting the location problem to the missile itself. Long-range guidance will be combined with homing devices for attack against certain targets, for example, ships.

The application of radar to guided missiles brings in new problems because of the large scale on which missile warfare must be planned. Radar components of much simpler design must be developed.

Most of the problems mentioned above require, before all, engineering skill and talents for clever adaptation and combination of recently developed principles and methods. However, the art of radar is so new that limitations which appear today may soon disappear because of novel discoveries. The Air Forces must be alert in swiftly utilizing any new developments.

Infrared Developments

The military applications of infrared and heat radiation are for (1) signaling, (2) identification, (3) detection, (4) communication, and (5) guiding of heat-homing missiles.

GERMAN DEVELOPMENTS

At the onset of the war, the Germans assumed that the Allies would employ infrared equipment and consequently produced in limited quantity a simple phosphor infrared detector as a countermeasure. These instruments were very insensitive compared with the U.S. phosphor developed somewhat later in the war. Although work continued in Germany, apparently it did not lead to improved instruments.

Very intensive work was done in Germany on the development of electron image tubes. However, this work was not unified and there appears to have been considerable duplication of effort and lost motion due to a lack of full interchange of information. The performance of the tubes was quite good but none of the designs was suitable for large quantity production. Furthermore, instead of concentrating on the manufacture of one type, they attempted to produce four or five different types. The telescopes used with the image tubes were elaborate and complex in the extreme; for example, one driving and gun sighting telescope had 17 glass elements mounted in a structure weighing more than 25 pounds. Because of this, German production was only just getting started at the close of the war. A total of 1,000 to 3,000 units was built, but almost none of these ever saw combat duty.

The Germans appeared not to have developed a signaling and identification system using tholofode cells. In the field of infrared communication equipment (optiphones), the Germans were somewhat ahead of the Allies in that they had at least 3,000 units in field service. These units are not technically superior to the developmental model built in the United States.

The German work in the far-infrared field (heat) was not very extensive, the only work reported so far being a number of ship-detecting units for detecting and determining the range of ships off shore.

ALLIED DEVELOPMENTS

The British concentrated work on a simple electron image tube suited primarily for signaling and identification, although it was used experimentally for such purposes as driving, gun aiming, etc. Production started about 1941 and the instruments were used on the British Isles throughout the war. For security reasons, few were used on the Continent but some, together with a few U.S. instruments, were used in North Africa.

U.S. production of image tubes and telescopes was not started until 1942 and they were not produced in quantity until a year later. Their first use in large numbers was by the Navy for signal communications. Later the Army put into the field a gun-sighting and reconnaissance unit. These were used almost exclusively in the Pacific.

Airborne applications have been found practical but the various technical difficulties were overcome too late for field use. Detection of aircraft by infrared telescopes was found not to be feasible.

No communication systems for speech transmission were put into production.

Very intensive work has been done on heat sensitive elements for guided missiles, the production in some instances running into fairly large figures. Recent tests of the VB6, a heat-homing missile developed by NDRC Division 5 in collaboration with ATSC, have been very successful.

The possibilities of infrared and heat-seeking devices are certainly not yet fully explored. It will be one of the important research fields of the Air Forces. The importance of this branch of physical research will be enhanced by the fact that many industrial and military establishments still try to obtain relative safety by going under ground.

III. PROBLEMS OF ORGANIZATION

Problems of Organization

The following problems relating to the long range research and development program of the Air Forces deserve consideration:

1. **Scientific Planning**: It is necessary that the Commanding General of the Air Forces and the Air Staff be advised continuously on the progress of scientific research and development in view of the potentialities of new discoveries and improvements in aerial warfare. A permanent Scientific Advisory Group, consisting of qualified officers and eminent civilian scientific consultants, should be available to the Commanding General, reporting directly to him on novel developments and advising him on the planning of scientific research. The scientific material collected by the organizations for military intelligence (G-2 and A-2) should be made available to this group for evaluation. Correspondingly, the scientific branch of G-2 and A-2 should be greatly strengthened by qualified personnel and facilities.

2. **Research and Development within the Air Forces**: It is necessary to organize a broad training program for officers in scientific and engineering fields, not merely to impart information on scientific and technical matters but to accustom them to working in cooperation with scientific institutions and scientists.

Officers with engineering training on engineering duty should not be handicapped as regards promotion because of long tenure of the same assignment or time spent in acquiring advanced education. An officer in charge of a laboratory or proving ground can be really useful only if he holds the position for a sufficient time to become thoroughly acquainted with the subject matter and personnel.

The position of rank of officers responsible for research and development in the Technical Services should be made commensurate with the importance of their work and achievement and should not depend on the size of the organization under their command.

Methods of appointment, compensation, and management of scientific personnel should be freed from those restrictions of the Civil Service regulations which make government service unattractive to first-rate scientists.

Specific comments and proposals in regard to the organization of research in the AAF will be made in my final report.

3. **Securing the Interest and Collaboration of Scientific Institutions and Individual Scientists**: The Air Force should have access to the best qualified scientific talent and the best equipped laboratories of the nation for collaboration on their problems.

Experimental investigations desired by the scientific leaders of the Air Forces to be carried out in any laboratory should be obtained by direct contract for the services desired.

It is recommended that the interest of scientists in classified problems be cultivated by sponsoring a society for military sciences whose membership and publications would be restricted in conformity with security regulations. AAF personnel shall be given membership in this society and permission to discuss and publish the results of their endeavors in the classified publications of the society.

Interchanges of military and civilian personnel of the Air Forces should be made with civilian scientists working in other institutions. Temporary assignment of AAF personnel to civilian laboratories and civilian scientists to Service Laboratories and proving grounds would serve this purpose. Also by this method, the AAF would be able to develop a scientific reserve corps familiar with current military problems as a pool for active service in war time.

4. **Cooperation with National Agencies Involved in the Planning of Scientific Research**: There are in existence several national agencies concerned with scientific research having a bearing on aerial warfare. These are the National Advisory Committee for Aeronautics, the Research Board for National Security, and the Office of Scientific Research and Development. There has been proposed a National Research Foundation to continue and supplement the work of the Office of Scientific Research and Development in peace time.

These agencies fulfill important functions in the national research picture. We believe, however, that it would be a mistake to assign complete responsibility for the long range development of new weapons to civilian agencies, leaving to the Air Forces only the functions of service testing of new weapons and the improvement of existing weapons. Since the Air Forces have knowledge of the strategic and tactical requirements, they should carry the primary responsibility for long range planning, with all possible advice and cooperation from other agencies.

For a fuller utilization of the research talent and facilities of the country, I propose the establishment of an Aeronautical Research Board, composed of representatives of the Army Air Forces; the Bureau of Aeronautics; Navy Department; the Civil Aeronautics Administration; the National Advisory Committee for Aeronautics; the aircraft industry; the air lines; and the aeronautical sciences. The primary function of the Board should be the making of recommendations on research contracts to the contracting agencies, and on needed research facilities to be built at government expense, on their operation and location; and to serve as a clearing house for aeronautical research information.

IV. LIST OF TABLES

List of Tables

V. LIST OF FIGURES

List of Figures

VI. INDEX OF
TOWARD NEW HORIZONS

Index of *Toward New Horizons*

A Report to General of the Army H. H. Arnold by the AAF Scientific Advisory Group

306

Appendix C

SCIENCE: The Key to Air Supremacy

TOWARD NEW HORIZONS

A Report to
General of the Army H.H. Arnold
Submitted on behalf of the
A.A.F. Scientific Advisory Group

by
TH VON KÁRMÁN
Science, the Key to Air Supremacy

15 December 1945

313

CONTENTS

HEADQUARTERS, ARMY AIR FORCES
WASHINGTON

7 November 1944

MEMORANDUM FOR DR. VON KÁRMÁN:

Subject: AAF Long Range Development Program

1. I believe the security of the United States of America will continue to rest in part in developments instituted by our educational and professional scientists. I am anxious that Air Forces postwar and next-war research and development programs be placed on a sound and continuing basis. In addition, I am desirous that these programs be in such form and contain such well thought out, long range thinking that, in addition to guaranteeing the security of our nation and serving as a guide for the next 10–20 year period, that the recommended programs can be used as a basis for adequate Congressional appropriations.

2. To assist you and your associates in our current concepts of war, may I review our principles. The object of total war is to destroy the enemy's will to resist, thereby enabling us to force our will on him. The attainment of war's objective divides itself into three phases: political, strategic and tactical. Political action is directed against the enemy's governing power, strategic action against his economic resources, and tactical action against his armed forces. Strategical and tactical actions are our main concern and are governed by the principles of objective, surprise, simplicity, mass, offensive, movement, economy of forces, cooperation and security.

3. I believe it is axiomatic that:

a. We as a nation are now one of the predominant powers.

b. We will no doubt have potential enemies that will constitute a continuing threat to the nation.

c. While major wars will continue to be fought principally between the 30th and 60th parallels, north, global war must be contemplated.

d. Our prewar research and development has often been inferior to our enemies.

e. Offensive, not defensive, weapons win wars. Counter-measures are of secondary importance.

f. Our country will not support a large standing army.

g. Peace time economy requirements indicate that, while the AAF now receives 43% of current War Department appropriations, this allotment or this proportion may not continue.

h. Obsolete equipment, now available in large quantities, may stalemate development and give Congress a false sense of security.

i. While our scientists do not necessarily have the questionable advantage of basic military training, conversely our AAF officers cannot by necessity be professional scientists.

j. Human-sighted (and perhaps radar or television assisted) weapons have more potential efficiency and flexibility than mechanically assisted weapons.

k. It is a fundamental principle of American democracy that personnel casualties are distasteful. We will continue to fight mechanical rather than manpower wars.

l. As of yet we have not overcome the problems of great distances, weather and darkness.

m. More potent explosives, supersonic speed, greater mass offensive efficiency, increased weapon flexibility and control, are requirements.

n. The present trend toward terror weapons such as buzz bombs, phosphorous and napalm may further continue toward gas and bacteriological warfare.

4. The possibility of future major wars cannot be overlooked. We, as a nation, may not always have friendly major powers or great oceanic distances as barriers. Likewise, I presume methods of stopping aircraft power plants may soon be available to our enemies. Is it not now possible to determine if another totally different weapon will replace the airplane? Are manless remote-controlled radar or television assisted precision military rockets or multiple purpose seekers a possibility? Is atomic propulsion a thought for consideration in future warfare?

5. Except perhaps to review current techniques and research trends, I am asking you and your associates to divorce yourselves from the present war in order to investigate all the possibilities and desirabilities for postwar and future war's development as respects the AAF. Upon completion of your studies, please then give me a report or guide for recommended future AAF research and development programs. May I ask that your final report also include recommendations to the following questions:

a. What assistance should we give or ask from our educational and commercial scientific organizations during peacetime?

b. Is the time approaching when all our scientists and their organizations must give a small portion of their time and resources to assist in avoiding future national peril and winning the next war?

c. What are the best methods of instituting the pilot production of requited nonrevenue equipments of no commercial value developed exclusively for the postwar period?

d. What proportion of available money should be allocated to research and development?

6. Pending completion of your final report, may I ask that you give me a short monthly written progress report. Meanwhile, I have specifically directed the AC/AS, OC&R (General Wilson) to be responsible for your direct administrative and staff needs. Also, as I have already told

you, I welcome you and your associates into my Headquarters. May I again say that the services of the AAF are at your disposal to assist in solving these difficult problems.

Signed

H.H. Arnold

HEADQUARTERS, ARMY AIR FORCES
WASHINGTON

IN REPLY REFER TO:

15 December 1945

General of the Army H. H. Arnold
Commanding General, Army Air Forces
Washington 25, D. C.

Dear General Arnold:

In your basic memorandum of the seventh of November 1944, you directed me to prepare a report as a guide for recommended future Army Air Forces research and development progress.

In cooperation with a group of selected associates, experts in various branches of the sciences involved, I have tried to review the scientific requirements involved in the functions of the future Air Forces, and I submit herewith the results of our study.

The first volume contains a discussion of the relation between science and aerial warfare; an analysis of the main research problems of the air forces, from the point of view of its functions; and recommendations on organization of research. The twelve volumes which follow contain thirty-two scientific monographs, with detailed research programs in specific fields.

The general conclusions of this study may be summarized as follows:

1. The discovery of atomic means of destruction makes a powerful Air Forces even more imperative than before. This subject is discussed in Chapter I of the first volume.

2. The scientific discoveries in aerodynamics, propulsion, electronics, and nuclear physics, open new horizons for the use of air power.

3. The next ten years should be a period of systematic, vigorous development, devoted to the realization of the potentialities of scientific progress, with the following principal goals: supersonic flight, pilotless aircraft, all-weather flying,

perfected navigation and communication, remote-controlled and automatic fighter and bomber forces, and aerial transportation of entire armies.

4. The research problems, as analyzed in Chapter I of the first volume, should be considered in their relation to the functions of the Air Forces, rather than as isolated scientific problems.

5. Therefore, development centers should be established for new types of equipment and for making novel methods suggested by scientific discoveries practical. Such development centers for definite tasks are more efficient than separate laboratories for certain branches of science.

6. The use of scientific means and equipment requires the infiltration of scientific thought and knowledge throughout the Air Forces and, therefore, certain organizatory changes in recruiting personnel, in training, and in staff work. Pertinent suggestions are made in Chapter III of the first volume of this report.

7. A global strategy for the application of novel equipment and methods, especially pilotless aircraft, should be studied and worked out. Full application of air power requires a properly distributed network of bases within and beyond the limits of the continental United States.

8. As new equipment becomes available, experimental pilotless aircraft units should be formed and personnel systematically trained for operation of the new devices.

9. According to the outcome of a practical testing period, a proper balance between weapons directed by humans, assisted by electronic devices, and purely automatic weapons should be established.

10. The men in charge of the future Air Forces should always remember that problems never have final or universal solutions, and only a constant inquisitive attitude toward science and a ceaseless and swift adaptation to new developments can maintain the security of this nation through world air supremacy.

In your basic memorandum, you also desired recommendations on the following questions:

a. What assistance should be given or asked from our educational and commercial scientific organizations during peacetime?

b. Is the time approaching when all our scientists and their organizations must give a small portion of their time and resources to assist in avoiding future national peril and winning the next war?

c. What are the best methods of instituting the pilot production of required nonrevenue equipments of no commercial value developed exclusively for the post war period?

d. What proportion of available money should be allocated to research and development?

Recommendations on the first three points are included in the sections of the report dealing with cooperation between science, industry, and the Air Forces. I am somewhat reluctant to give a definite answer to your fourth question. I prefer to submit the following consideration. The money to be allocated for research and development should be related to the cost of one year's aerial warfare. It appears that spending for research in peacetime five percent of one war year's expenditures, in order to be prepared for or avoid a future war, is not an exaggerated drain on the nation's pocketbook. A quick inquiry showed that our large industrial concerns spend a percentage of this order of the total sum involved in their year's business for research. If in peacetime 15–20 percent of the sum spent in a war year were allowed for total expenditures of the Air Forces, the amount required for research and development should constitute 25–33 percent of the total Air Forces budget.

Respectfully yours,

Signed

TH. VON KÁRMÁN
Director
AAF Scientific Advisory Group

AAF Scientific Advisory Group

The AAF Scientific Advisory Group was activated late in 1944 by General of the Army H. H. Arnold. He secured the services of Dr. Theodore von Kármán, renowned scientist and consultant in aeronautics, who agreed to organize and direct the group.

Dr. von Kármán gathered about him a group of American scientists from every field of research having a bearing on air power. These men then analyzed important developments in the basic sciences, both here and abroad, and attempted to evaluate the effects of their application to air power.

This volume is one of a group of reports made to the Army Air Forces by the Scientific Advisory Group.

Dr. Th. von Kármán
Director

Colonel F. E. Glantzberg
Deputy Director, Military

Dr. H. L. Dryden
Deputy Director, Scientific

Lt Col G. T. McHugh, Executive
Capt C. H. Jackson, Jr., Secretary

CONSULTANTS

Dr. C. W. Bray	Dr. A. J. Stosick
Dr. L. A. DuBridge	Dr. W. J. Sweeney
Dr. Pol Duwez	Dr. H. S. Tsien
Dr. G. Gamow	Dr. G. E. Valley
Dr. I. A. Getting	Dr. F. L. Wattendorf
Dr. L. P. Hammett	Dr. F. Zwicky
Dr. W. S. Hunter	Dr. V. K. Zworykin
Dr. I. P. Krick	Col D. N. Yates
Dr. D. R. MacDougall	Col W. R. Lovelace II
Dr. G. A. Morton	Lt Col A. P. Gagge
Dr. N. M. Newmark	Lt Col E. W. Williams
Dr. W. H. Pickering	Major T. F. Walkowicz
Dr. E. M. Purcell	Capt C. N. Hasert
Dr. G. B. Schubauer	Mr. M. Alperin

325

Dr. W. R. Sears   Mr. I. L. Ashkenas
              Mr. G. S. Schairer

LAYOUT & ILLUSTRATION

Capt M. Miller   Capt T. E. Daley

Chapter I

Science and Aerial Warfare

Introduction

1.1 There have been two wars on a world scale in our time, in which the pendulum of victory seemed at first to swing far out in the direction of our enemies before indicating the final decision. In the First World War, victory or defeat was decided mainly by human endurance. Science and technology played an important but to some extent a secondary role. It is true, of course, that the superiority of the Allies in the design and production of tanks, as well as the paralyzing effect of the complete blockade on all branches of German industrial production, contributed very essentially to Germany's defeat in 1918. However, the complete exhaustion of human endurance on the German side was the main factor in the decision. The second war had, from the beginning, a technological character. The overwhelming technological preparation of Germany secured her first brilliant successes on the European continent. The shortcomings of the Luftwaffe in strategic bombing and the lack of experience of the German Army and its consequent poor preparation for amphibious operations, caused the attack against England to be stillborn. The mounting tide of Allied, especially American, air power became finally the main factor in Germany's defeat. Even in the East, although the bravery and endurance of the Russians were perhaps the most important factors in stopping the German Army, the Russian march of victory to the West could not have been achieved without technological superiority, due partly to Russian and partly to American production. An interesting sign of the technological character of this war is the fact that the time in which superiority in aircraft could be achieved was predicted, based on figures of industrial potential, at the beginning of the war. The predictions were fairly well verified by the actual events.

1.2 In addition to the technological character of this war, a new aspect became evident, which did not appear so obviously

327

in the war of 1914–1918. This new element was the decisive contribution of organized science to effective weapons. Of course, scientific discoveries have been used in all wars since ancient times; it is related, for example, that Archimedes concentrated the heat of the sun by means of large mirrors to destroy enemy ships. However, never before have such large numbers of scientific workers been united for planned evaluation and utilization of scientific ideas for military purposes. Outstanding results of such planned cooperative research are, on our side, radar and atomic bombs, and on the German side, jet-propelled missiles.

1.3 The recognition of the growing technological character of modern war partly emerged from the experiences of the First World War, and the scientific character of any future warfare becomes obvious in the light of the war which has just ended. In this report an attempt is made to formulate some of the consequences of this conception for the program of the Air Forces.

The Position of the Air Forces in a Scientific Warfare

1.4 Until recently it was not generally recognized that destruction from the air is the most efficient method for defeating an enemy. This fact has now been proved by the results obtained in Germany and Japan. However, after the use of the atomic bomb, a strange change of opinion took place. Many leaders of public opinion seem to believe that destruction by means of a few airplanes or missiles carrying atomic bombs is the only method of future warfare, making a strong air force superfluous. Others say that international control of atomic energy will make war impossible for time to come.

1.5 We believe that all possible aspects of the complex problem introduced by this new scientific achievement must be considered:

First, we must consider the possibility that international control of atomic energy cannot be achieved in such a manner

328

that the use of atomic destruction by potential enemies is impossible.

Second, the case has to be considered that international control of atomic energy will be achieved by agreement; it must be recognized, however, that such control will probably have to be supported by force.

Finally, we must also assume that, in spite of the international control of atomic energy and the outlawing of war by international organizations, the possibility of desperate attacks against the United States or its vital interests somewhere on the globe cannot be excluded.

1.6 The first assumption (international control of atomic energy cannot be achieved) means total war, with full use of atomic energy on both sides. Atomic energy will be used in the form of explosives, and, in all probability, as a means for jet propulsion. Atomic engineering and atomic industry will be simply a part of the war-making potential of a nation, perhaps the most important one. Consequently, one of the first aims of warfare will be the destruction of this potential. Fortunately, at least at present, production of atomic energy requires rather extensive plants, which can hardly be completely hidden and made safe against destruction. Of course, great effort will be expended upon keeping secret the places of research, development, and production. Hence, it will be one of the fundamental problems of the intelligence service to gather the most accurate information possible concerning these potential targets and evaluate it from the scientific, technological, and military points of view.

1.7 It can be assumed that the first attack in any war will be against targets connected with the production of atomic devices for destruction and propulsion. It is evident that such an attack will be the primary responsibility of the Air Forces. The places of research and production will certainly be removed as far as possible from the land and sea frontiers. An attempt will be made, of course, to annihilate the enemy's installations by bombs carried by piloted and pilotless airplanes. However, because of intricate defense measures by the enemy, who will probably put the most important installations underground, it may be necessary to land troops and to occupy certain territories. Thus, all aspects of modern aerial warfare may enter into the picture; strategic bombing, air superiority, and airborne armies.

1.8 It is evident that preparations must be made for strategic bombing of enemy targets involved in atomic work, by proper location of bases, especially bases for pilotless airplanes. In the past, systems of fortification, communication lines, and transportation facilities were built according to the strategic requirements of warfare on land and on sea. Today's strategic considerations refer to the three-dimensional space surrounding the globe. They must be worked out with the same imagination and thoroughness displayed by old-time strategists in solving the problems of attacking and defending certain lines extending on the surface of the earth, or certain points which controlled traffic on the seas.

1.9 It may be argued that the devastation and loss of life caused by atomic bombs is so tremendous that total atomic warfare will never occur. I believe the answer is the following: No man in the past centuries could, by any stretch of the imagination, foresee the devastation and loss of life produced by two consecutive wars in our time. Humans adjust themselves rapidly to new concepts. What is considered an incredibly large loss of life today may appear inevitable in years to come. I believe we must agree with Dr. Einstein's view that, even in case of total atomic warfare, humanity and human civilization will not disappear. The number of lives lost in the two wars, which were separated by a relatively short interval, appears to us certainly disastrous. However, there is no proof that economic pressure and human passion cannot produce conflicts which lead to the annihilation of one-half or two-thirds of the population of a country. Preparedness certainly has to make provisions for such possibilities.

1.10 The second assumption (that international control of atomic energy will be achieved but will require support by force) seems to be the most probable solution of the atomic problem within the next decades. Then, the main responsibility of the Armed Forces will be the enforcement of international agreements. Here again the nation must rely on a powerful air force. It will be necessary to strike at any arbitrary point of the globe, to strike swiftly and forcefully. History shows that international agreements have not protected the signatories and have not prevented wars, either because there were no means available for swift and forceful action, or because political reasons prevented their use. No branch of the Armed Forces except the Air Forces can perform the required action in time to be effective.

1.11 The same requirements as in the second case apply to the third assumption (unexpected treacherous attacks cannot be excluded in spite of international agreement). However, in the latter case the matter of efficient defense must be emphasized. It must be realized that a one hundred percent safe defense is impossible. It is easier to make offensive action efficient by scientific means than defensive action. The high speed of pilotless airplanes and missiles makes them almost safe against a hit; no effective means is yet known for stopping such missiles, once they are launched, and, the fact that one single airplane or missile is able to drop a bomb of immense destructive power puts an almost impossible task on the air defense. All that we can hope is that absolute air superiority, combined with highly developed and specialized warning and homing devices, will help us to erect an impregnable aeroelectronic wall, which will reduce to a minimum the possibility of any enemy device slipping through undetected and undestroyed.

The main conclusion of these considerations is the necessity for a powerful air force, which is capable of:

a. Reaching remote targets swiftly and hitting them with great destructive power.

b. Securing air superiority over any region of the globe.

c. Landing, in a short time, powerful forces, men and firepower, at any point on the globe.

d. Defending our own territory and bases in the most efficient way.

1.13 It is evident that only an air force which fully exploits all the knowledge and skill which science has available now and will have available in the future, will have a chance of accomplishing these tasks. Aerodynamics, thermodynamics, electronics, nuclear physics, and chemistry must reunite their efforts. In the following section, a short review is given of the most important scientific facts. These facts are important elements to be considered in selecting and training personnel and developing equipment for the future Air Forces.

Science's Main Contributions

1.14 The development of aviation is a struggle against the limitations imposed by nature upon man, created to live on the ground, but nevertheless endeavoring to move in the unlimited space surrounding our globe.

1.15 As the problem of heavier-than-air locomotion was solved in principle by the discovery of the airplane, speed and range were confined to narrow limits. Weather and night appeared as insurmountable obstacles, and human skill seemed to be an indispensable element for diverse uses of the airplane in peace and war.

1.16 Science has already removed many of these limitations:

a. By gradual improvement in aerodynamic design, the velocity and economy of the airplane have been greatly increased. Airplane designers have continuously endeavored to eliminate all possible drag which impairs economy, i.e., the parasite drag, by attempting to make the aircraft essentially into a flying wing; the turbulent friction of the air by creating laminar flow around the wing. In recent years our knowledge of supersonic phenomena has increased the velocity of the airplane and brought it closer and closer to the speed of sound, which for a long time appeared as a natural upper limit. This knowledge has opened the door for winged aircraft, both piloted and pilotless, to the threshold of velocities faster than sound. Until now only unmanned ballistic devices have attained such speeds.

b. Novel propulsive systems, using the reaction or jet principle, have facilitated the reaching of high speeds, because of their reduced weight and increasing efficiency with increasing speed. These systems replace the conventional engine and propeller at high speeds because the efficiency of a propeller decreases greatly when very high speeds are attained. The rocket principle makes propulsion independent of the use of the atmospheric air and rocket-driven aircraft are able to reach extraordinary attitudes [sic] in an extremely short time.

c. By gradual improvement, both in aerodynamic design and in engine construction, the performance and economy of airplane transportation have been tremendously increased. The spectacular increase in the range of our military aircraft and in the carrying capacity of our cargo aircraft is an indication of improved economy. Although essential improvements in aerodynamic and engine design can be expected to increase airplane economy further, the amount of heat which can be released by combustion of our most efficient fuels per unit weight or per unit volume, imposes a serious limitation on any large increase in range with conventional fuels. The use of nuclear energy, however, may radically change this situation and help to reach almost unlimited ranges, at least in the case of aircraft which do not carry human beings.

d. Navigation and instrument flying were greatly aided by use of the radio even in its early stages of development. The recent extension of the spectrum of radiation down to centimeter and millimeter wavelengths, and the application of the pulse and echo principles of radar, opened fundamentally new possibilities in the struggle of aviation against weather, clouds, and darkness. Blind landing, blind bombing and location of remote and invisible objects (aircraft or targets) are paramount examples of the contributions of radar technique. Seeing through darkness by night and seeing through clouds by day became routine facts in military aviation. Fighter control from the ground became an important element in warfare. It appears that a wide-open field exists for progress in communication and other applications of radio and electronics which are discussed at length in "Radar and Communications," by other members of the AAF Scientific Advisory Group.

e. Gradual improvements in gyroscopic devices led to the automatic pilot, which materially relieves the human pilot. In addition, the development of gyro and servomotor devices made possible a great variety of remote control systems. Since we are able to transfer optical impressions by television devices, aircraft or missiles can be piloted to distant points from the ground or from the air by remote control. Radar location devices similarly can be applied to the remote control of aircraft.

f. The progress in electromagnetic radiation techniques made automatic homing (target seeking) possible and effective. A radar homing bomb was in use by the U.S. Navy in the Pacific at the close of the war. Infrared (heat) radiation proved to be one of the most promising methods. Radio, infrared, and radar have been applied to the problem extremely useful in automatic fire control. Along with automatic homing, the design of automatic computers became a great practical domain of military engineering.

g. Combination of methods of automatic and remote control with homing devices will lead to a complete solution of the problem of pilotless aircraft, having tremendous speed, extraordinary range and ability to hit targets accurately. Although pilotless aircraft will never completely eliminate manned aircraft, they obviously will take over certain missions. Both in the German and in the Japanese theaters, our strategic bombing forces brought utter destruction to our enemies with the clocklike accuracy of a great machine. The future aim is to build up, for this purpose, a war machine in the proper sense of the word, consisting of technical devices only, and yet directed in all details by the mind and staff of some master strategist of the air.

Plan of Analysis

1.17 The abundance and variety of applications of scientific ideas and devices in aerial warfare, sketched very briefly above, put a tremendous task before the men responsible for the future Air Forces. For the most part the scientific foundation of the applications mentioned has already been laid, and other applications will emerge as scientific research continues to be productive of new knowledge.

1.18 The scientific-technological questions are only a small part of the whole problem. We are fully aware that a report prepared by men of science can contribute only a small part of the solution.

1.19 Chapter 11 of this volume analyzes the problem of research and development from the point of view of the technical requirements which the Air Forces must meet in order to be able to carry out its task, securing the safety of the nation. It appears that the main requirements in which scientific methods, scientific research and development play an important role, may be listed as the abilities to:

    a. Move swiftly and transport loads through the air.

    b. Locate targets and recognize them.

    c. Hit targets accurately.

    d. Cause destruction.

    e. Function independently of weather and darkness.

    f. Defeat enemy interference.

    g. Perfect communications from ground to air and from air to air.

h. Defend home territory.

1.20 Chapter III contains recommendations of an organizatory character as follows:

a. Fundamental principles for organization of research.

b. Cooperation between science and the Air Forces.

c. Cooperation between industry and the Air Forces.

d. Adequate facilities in the Air Forces for research and development.

e. Induction of scientific ideas into command and staff work.

f. Scientific and technological training of Air Forces personnel.

1.21 Further volumes of this general report contain individual studies prepared by members and collaborators of the Scientific Advisory Group on the main scientific topics. They may be used as a kind of guide for the direction of future research, starting from the present state of the art toward the realm of the unknown to be revealed in the years to come.

Chapter II

Analysis of Research Problems

Move Swiftly and Transport Loads Through the Air

2.1 This fundamental problem can also be described as the problem of the aerial vehicle. It includes the design and construction of manned and unmanned aircraft, subsonic and supersonic.

2.2 Looking back to the past, the aeronautical engineer certainly can be proud of the performance of the present day airplane. Speed, rate of climb, and range have been multiplied by factors of considerable magnitude in the twenty-seven years since the end of the First World War. A great portion of the progress was achieved during the last decade in the six years of conscious preparation by the Army Air Forces and in the four years of actual warfare. However, if the problem of war in the future is considered, we conclude that our best present type airplanes are still far from doing the job which they will have to achieve.

Range vs. Speed

2.3 The two great problems of aerial locomotion are range and speed. The ideal solution is a combination of both.

2.4 Range is imperative because of the global character of aerial warfare. We have to reach enormous ranges, distances as great as half of the length of the equator, in order to be able to attack and occupy points located anywhere on the globe. With the possible exception of an airplane driven by atomic energy, the design of aircraft to carry very heavy loads to shorter ranges is essentially the same problem, because of the interchangeability of fuel and pay load.

2.5 Speed is imperative for effective action, safety against enemy countermeasures from the ground, and superiority over enemy aircraft.

2.6 Hence, it appears that for the crystallization of our ideas concerning the desired performance of future aircraft, we have to see clearly the fundamental relations between range and speed. The range of an airplane depends on three factors: (1) ratio between drag and lift, (2) fuel consumption per unit thrust horsepower, and (3) ratio between the weight of the fuel and the total weight of the airplane, at the beginning of the flight. The first factor is determined by aerodynamics of the airplane, the second, by aerothermodynamics of the propulsive system, and the third, by construction and material.

2.7 The critical factor is the lift-drag ratio, which decreases abruptly at the approach to sonic velocity and in the supersonic range never again attains the favorable values realized in the subsonic regime. Even if we are very optimistic as to the future developments of our supersonic aerodynamics, it is improbable that the extreme ranges possible for subsonic airplanes can be realized for supersonic planes. On the other hand, the belief that supersonic flight is restricted to extremely short ranges is too pessimistic. For instance, if atomic energy can be used for propulsion, the range of jet and rocket planes will increase to unprecedented values. However, even with present fuels, improvements can be expected in the design of jet propulsion units which would bring the range of supersonic planes to 1500–2000 miles in the substratosphere and 3000–3500 miles in the stratosphere.

2.8 In the example represented by the diagram, the ranges are shown for two values of the ratio between fuel and initial weight, 0.5 and 0.7. For the lift-drag ratio and the thermal propulsive efficiency of the propulsive system, best current values are used, and the flight is assumed to be carried out at the optimum values. The ranges given for level flight at 20,000 ft altitude; fuel for take-off and climb is not considered.

2.9 The ranges realized or realizable with present engineering methods are discussed in detail in the report, "The Airplane-Prospects and Problems" by W. R. Sears and I. L. Asbkenas, in the SAG report Aerodynamics and Aircraft

Design. The attainment of the values shown in the diagram, page 15, necessitates considerable improvements in aerodynamics, both in the subsonic and supersonic ranges, and radical changes in the propulsion units used in the supersonic range. At supersonic speeds the frontal area of the engine required for given thrust is the greatest impediment and must be greatly reduced. The ranges given in the diagram should be considered as goals of a systematic effort of the next decade to be achieved by close cooperation between airplane and engine research groups.

Air Plane Types

2.10 No attempt is made to write the specifications for the aircraft of 1965; however, it appears possible to indicate certain general functional requirements of future aircraft. The following classification is based on the analysis of the functions of the Air Forces given in paragraph 1.12.

2.11 The first function of the Air Forces is to reach swiftly, and hit with great destructive power, remote targets. Two classes of aircraft will be used for this function:

a. An aircraft which carries the means of destruction to the target and returns to its base or lands at some other predetermined base. This is the bomber in the proper sense of the word.

b. An aircraft which is expendable and hits the target by means of remote control or automatic homing, i.e., a pilotless bomber.

2.12 The development of bomber aircraft, in the proper sense of the word, will probably continue for a few years the trend followed in recent years. However, it is not envisioned that bombers will continue to grow in size. Increase of size cannot continue to increase speed and range indefinitely, but may be necessary to permit carrying sufficient defensive armament. Such armament in the future would include radio-controlled high-speed missiles, launched from the bomber, which would serve as fighter cover in case of necessity. The greatest increase of speed and range must be accomplished by improvements in aerodynamics and propulsive methods.

2.13 In the field of pilotless bombers the goal is the intercontinental missile. We assume a system of bases distributed in such a way that all possible target areas in the world can be reached by such missiles. Two types of pilotless bombers should be developed for this purpose. The first type should be a high-altitude, pilotless, jet-propelled bomber, with a speed equal to about twice the velocity of sound. This pilotless bomber will carry either atomic or conventional bombs. Launched by rockets or lifted to high attitude by piloted airplanes, it will be capable of level flight up to a range of 2500 to 3000 miles. The second type aimed for should be an ultrastratospheric pilotless bomber, equipped with wings, but not designed for level flight in the atmosphere. It should be endowed with extreme velocity during the acceleration period. The wings will be used for two purposes: (1) to increase the length of the trajectory, and (2) to secure a controllability which is not possible with the pure V-2 type projectile. The propulsion of this type of pilotless bomber will be accomplished by the rocket principle.

2.14 Atomic energy may be used for propulsion in both types of pilotless bombers, thus increasing their ranges to an unprecedented extent. (Cf. 2.51 to 2.56)

2.15 To secure air superiority various types of combat aircraft will be needed. Tactical requirements will determine their design. The two principal categories will always be bombers and fighters, although there will be overlapping of the duties of these, as at present, and some bombers and fighters will also be developed for highly specialized auxiliary tasks, such as photo reconnaissance. The very large battleship of the air, bristling with defensive armament, seems destined to give way ultimately to smaller bombers having superior performance, fighter control, etc.

2.16 An important problem is the development of special aircraft for airborne armies. These aircraft must be capable of cruising at comparatively high speeds, while still retaining the ability to land and take off at safe, low speeds from small fields. Vigorous application of jet-assisted take-off, boundary layer control, high-lift devices, and deceleration devices on troop-carrier aircraft can make this possible. Troop-carrier airplanes must also be specially designed for rapid and easy loading and unloading of bulky items of ground equipment.

2.17 Every item of equipment in the Army (naturally, with the exception of railway guns, heavy seacoast defense guns, and the like) must be air-transportable. However, the number of different types and sizes of troop-carrier airplanes developed must be kept down to a practical minimum. There is immediate need for an over-all study of the weight and dimensional characteristics of every item of equipment in the Army. Only a complete study can show what types and sizes of future troop-carrier aircraft are required to move the Army by air with greatest possible efficiency. However, the entire burden of making the Army air-transportable must not be allowed to fall solely on the aircraft designer. There must be established a means of control over the weights and dimensions of Army equipment to insure that future equipment will be capable of being carried in future aircraft. This can be done and must be done without compromising battlefield requirements in any way. The cargo airplane and ground equipment development programs must be coordinated at frequent intervals by an agency charged with the specific responsibility of making the Army capable of movement by air.

2.18 Gliders were used on a large scale (and with great effectiveness) for the first time in the airborne operations of World War II. The development of gliders and glider techniques must be continued since, at the present time, this is the safest, cheapest, most acceptable method of landing heavy equipment during the assault phase of an airborne operation. New glider developments should stress the following: adequate crash protection for crew and cargo; low landing speeds and use of deceleration devices for shortening the length of landing ground roll; rapid unloading through wide, rear-loading doors; adequate protection against small-arms fire for pilot and copilot; greater aerodynamic and structural efficiencies through the use of high-lift devices and metal construction; and the use of assisted takeoff techniques for decreasing the length of take-off run required by glider-towplane combinations. New gliders (towed-aircraft) must be and can be easily designed for rapid conversion to low-powered transports. This will eliminate some of the major shortcomings of gliders because ferrying to combat theaters and use as short-haul transports between airborne missions will be possible. The advantage of having such a transport, which can be easily and rapidly loaded and unloaded, for shorthaul work immediately behind the lines cannot be overemphasized. Promising new techniques for the assault landing of heavy equipment must be developed and evaluated tactically. Important among these are the assault transport, the method of dropping heavy equipment by means of parachutes and decelerating rockets, aircraft with jettisonable cargo compartments, and rotary-wing aircraft. Stable (nonoscillating) parachutes with lower opening-loads must be developed for paratroopers.

2.19 The possibility of attacks by single aircraft with disastrous effects makes the defense of our frontiers, industrial equipment, and bases one of the most important tasks of the Air Forces. Piloted and pilotless interceptors are envisaged as the main instruments of defense. Speed and controllability are the main requirements for this type of aircraft.

Aerodynamic Problems

2.20 Improvements in the lift-drag ratio proportionately increase the range of an airplane. Therefore, efforts should be concentrated to attain such improvements. In 1935, an eminent American aerodynamicist, who, ironically enough, later became instrumental in the development of the laminar wing, declared that in his opinion no more major progress can be expected in aerodynamic science. He referred to the fact that with the discovery of the wing theory, lift and drag became calculable quantities, and the performance of the airplane could be fairly exactly predicted. Also, the designer learned the rules of streamlining and methods of eliminating superfluous drag by "cleaning up" the airplane. By use of systematic and detailed wind-tunnel tests, this cleaning up process became almost perfect, so that further improvements can be expected only in exceptional cases. However, even in the fairly well explored subsonic speed range, new possibilities appeared with the discovery of the laminar wing section and the efforts to design an efficient flying wing.

2.21 The concept of the laminar wing is based on the fundamental fact that when the flow in the boundary layer of a surface moving in air is laminar, the surface friction is very much less than in the case when turbulent motion takes place in the same layer. The laminar wing sections which we are using in the present-day design, endeavor to keep the boundary layer laminar over a portion of the wing surface by means of an appropriate shape of the section. This method was applied in the design of quite a few of our modern airplanes, with considerable success. The proposal was first received with skepticism. Several objections were raised: that the expected effects of drag reduction could only be obtained if the wing surface is extremely smooth, and that the beneficial effect could only be attained for small values of the lift coefficient, thus restricting the benefit of the reduced friction to certain flight attitudes. Nevertheless, it appears that the initial successes of the laminar wing are so encouraging that in future research we should strive to go the whole way, i.e., to try to secure laminar flow in the boundary layer by positive measures along the entire wing and in a large range of angles of attack. It is known that theoretically this aim can be attained by the so-called boundary layer control. Results along this line are already available, for example, in the tests carried out by Professor J. Ackeret and his collaborators at the Technical University at Zurich. It is true that the process requires extremely smooth surfaces with relatively narrow slots extending spanwise along the wing. This might cause practical difficulties (for example, in the case of icing). However, looking into the future, extreme smoothness might be realized by materials now in the making, and it will certainly be worth-while to put in a great amount of research work to eliminate other possible practical obstacles. There is even the possibility of eventual elimination of conventional movable control surfaces, by use of boundary layer control to effect changes in lift and moment.

2.22 The same principle can be applied also to reductions of the drag of airplane; for example, bodies with circular cross sections. In the case of wings, it will be bodies, if necessary to subdivide the wing into a number of compartments with individually regulated boundary layer control. In the case of bodies, it might be sufficient to apply the control at a few critical cross sections.

2.23 The fundamental idea of the flying wing is the elimination of the parasite drag contributed by such parts of the airplane as do not produce lift. The tailless airplane is an even more controversial subject than the laminar wing. As does every unorthodox type, it introduces some new problems. The fact that the longitudinal control is placed in the wing involves control force characteristics which are different from those occurring in conventional airplanes. Much discussed problems are the proper method of securing directional stability, and the best arrangement for sweepback. As a matter of fact, the designs which have been produced up to now have not yet brought a final decision concerning the relative advantages and disadvantages of the flying wing and the tailless airplane. However, as the global character of aerial transportation, and especially aerial warfare, becomes more and more evident, it is apparent that our present airplanes are inadequate to meet the demand for range. Therefore, the two methods promising essential aerodynamic progress, namely boundary layer control and tailless design, should be explored with adequate facilities.

2.24 The large decrease in the value of the lift-drag ratio at the Mach number of about 0.8 is due to the rather sudden increase of the drag of the airplane. This increase is essentially due to the fact that the relative velocity of the air

344

locally becomes larger than the velocity of sound. Simultaneously with the increase of the drag, difficulties are encountered, in most cases, in the stability and control of the airplane. Generally these phenomena are designated as compressibility effects; we prefer to use the designation "transonic problem." Obviously, in order to extend the speed limit of highspeed airplanes, a thorough investigation of the aerodynamic phenomena in the transonic range is needed. As a matter of fact, the aerodynamics of both the subsonic and supersonic ranges are better known than that of the transonic range, which extends approximately between the Mach numbers of 0.8 and 1.2. One reason is that the mathematical analysis is extremely difficult, since the flow around the airplane is partly subsonic and partly supersonic. Another great difficulty is caused by the unreliability of wind-tunnel tests in this range. Flight tests, dropping tests, and measurements on models carried by rockets are the main sources for experimental information.

2.25 Fighters and interceptors now in the making operate actually at the border of the transonic range. Hence, every method which is able to raise the limit of the rapid drag increase is of great importance. German scientists observed that increase of drag of the wing can be postponed to higher Mach numbers by sufficient sweepback. This method is generally used now in the design of fast fighters and interceptors. Designers are seeking means to reduce the excess weight and the difficulties in stability and control connected with the swept-back wing shape. However, this solution is not necessarily a final one. When our knowledge of aerodynamic phenomena in the transonic range has been more firmly established, we may find methods for eliminating the separation of the flow behind the shock wave, and the fundamental trouble, namely the occurrence of shock waves. In the subsonic range aerodynamic research brought rich returns. It can be expected that the same process will repeat itself and will lead to the solution of the transonic problem.

2.26 One of the main questions in the supersonic speed range is the feasibility of long-range flight. The supersonic airplane necessitates very high wing loading with small size of the wing. Hence, in most cases, the volume available in the wing for fuel or pay load is very small, and a disproportion appears between the sizes of the wing and the fuselage. In other words, the resistance of the body in comparison with the resistance of the wing is much greater than in the case of the conventional subsonic airplane. It appears that the best solution is offered by a fuselage of large fineness ratio. A rather thorough investigation of the problem was made by the Scientific Advisory Group on this question. These investigations suggest that, assuming a given ratio between fuel and total weight and a certain space required in the fuselage, the range is essentially a function of the altitude at which the supersonic flight takes place. The diagrams on pages 347 and 348 show an example of the variation of range with altitude. The ideal application of such a supersonic airplane is the pilotless bomber (Cf. 2.13). Similar types of supersonic airplanes will serve as pilotless interceptors (Cf. 2.19). The best speed range for the latter device may be between 1.2 and 1.5 times sound velocity.

Ranges Attainable at 1,000 MPH at Various Altitudes

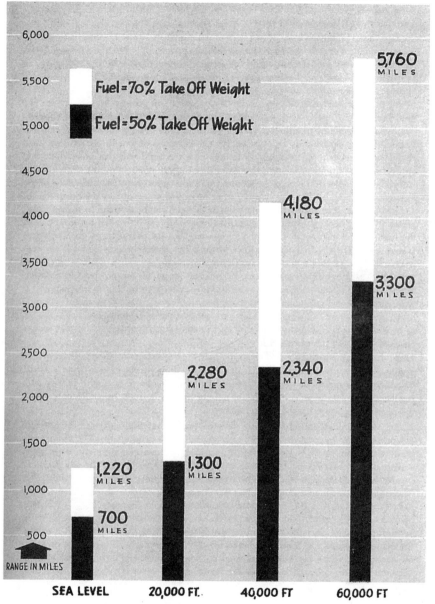

Ranges Attainable at Various Speeds

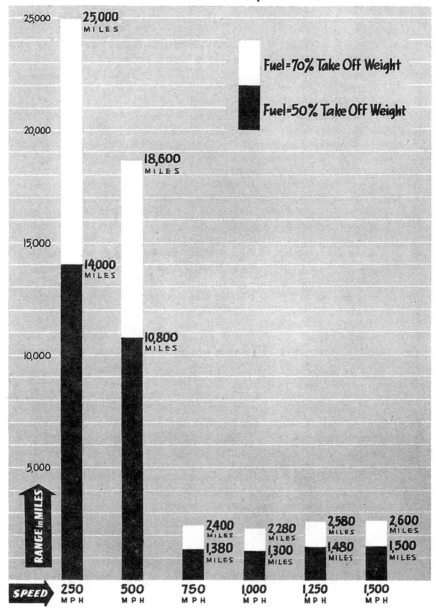

Fuel=70% Take Off Weight

Fuel=50% Take Off Weight

25,000 MILES

18,600 MILES

14,000 MILES

10,800 MILES

2,400 MILES

1,380 MILES

2,280 MILES

1,300 MILES

2,580 MILES

1,480 MILES

2,600 MILES

1,500 MILES

RANGE in MILES

SPEED

250 MPH

500 MPH

750 MPH

1,000 MPH

1,250 MPH

1,500 MPH

2.27 The fact that in the case of the supersonic airplane, the body resistance contributes a relatively larger portion to the total drag than in the case of subsonic planes calls for study of an all-wing design. However, supersonic flight requires wings with small thickness-chord ratio. Hence, one can create sufficient space only by using a wing shape of very small aspect ratio. It is fortunate that, in the supersonic range, triangular-shaped wings give relatively high lift-drag ratios in comparison with other plan forms. Hence, for manned interceptors a series of all-wing airplanes should be tried, eventually with a small cockpit for a pilot. Such a series should extend from a tailless airplane similar to the Me-163 to pure triangular-shaped airplanes.

2.28 Besides the lift and drag properties, the questions of stability and control are the most important. The change of the flow regime introduces difficulties in the transonic range. But also in the pure supersonic range, very little is known about the efficiency of aerodynamic control surfaces and control forces. This field needs thorough exploration by all means available, starting with wind-tunnel tests and ending with flight tests. Possibly in addition to conventional means, displacements of weights or direct control of the pressure distribution by modification of the flow, as in the case of boundary layer control, are necessary.

2.29 The difficulties of landing are much more serious for supersonic than for subsonic airplanes because of their high-wing loading. The wing loading decreases with altitude and supersonic airplanes designed for stratospheric flight may land without special devices. However, systematic investigations are necessary of high-lift devices suitable for use on the thin, sharp-nosed airfoils that are desirable for supersonic flight. This must include the problem of raising the maximum lift of triangular, low-aspect-ratio wings, and particularly of reducing the extremely large angles at which such wings now attain their maximum lift. In addition, devices such as rockets, which produce simultaneously deceleratory thrust and increase of lift for the short period of landing should be studied.

Propulsive Problems

2.30 All our airplanes actually used in the war were propelled by propellers driven by reciprocating engines. However, the progress made in the field of jet propulsion and gas turbines and the experience gathered in Great Britain and Germany, and also with our own experimental jet-propelled airplanes, enable us to choose the best propulsion system for any future project. In broad lines, the merit of a propulsive system is determined by two figures: the weight which has to be installed in the airplane for unit thrust-horsepower, and the fuel consumption per thrust-horsepower-hour. It is evident that for flight of short duration, small engine weight has the determining influence; for long duration flight, low fuel consumption is more essential. Fuel consumption per thrust-horsepower is determined by the efficiency of the engine and the propulsive efficiency of the system. At the present moment the reciprocating engine is still more economical than the gas turbine, and at subsonic speeds the propeller has higher propulsive efficiency than the jet. However, looking into the future, the following considerations appear important.

2.31 It appears to be rather difficult to attain radical improvements in the efficiency of reciprocating engines, whereas a wide open field is available for improvements in the case of the gas turbine. Hence, efforts should certainly be concentrated on developing the gas turbine for propeller drive, in order to secure the advantages of light weight, freedom from vibration, and reduction of nacelle drag connected with this system. Between the various engine systems, an intensive competition can be expected, to reach the best fuel economy at the lightest possible weight and the smallest space requirement.

2.32 The pure gas turbine has the advantage of simplicity, light weight and small dimensions. The reciprocating engine has at present an advantage over the simple gas turbine chiefly due to its utilization of higher pressures. However, it should be pointed out that the advantage of the reciprocating engine holds for the cruising condition only, but maximum power output the gas turbine equals or surpasses the reciprocating engine in fuel economy.

2.33 There are many ways of improving the performance of the pure gas turbine, for instance:

a. Higher combustion temperature.

b. Higher pressure ratio.

c. Improving the aerodynamic efficiency.

d. Intercooling between compressor stages.

e. Reheating the air between turbine stages.

f. Use of separate turbine for propeller drive.

g. Regeneration by the use of a heat exchanger to extract heat from the turbine exhaust, and utilize this heat to warm the air entering the combustion chamber.

These improvements involve partly metallurgical problems in search of better materials, partly aerodynamic problems, finally design problems to avoid undue penalties in size, weight, and complexity.

2.34 Improvement of reciprocating engines appears possible by utilization of somewhat higher pressure ratios, but in the pure reciprocating engine this tends to be offset by loss of heat in the exhaust. A promising development is the so-called compound engine in which the exhaust of a reciprocating engine drives a gas turbine which feeds back into the drive shaft. In this way the pistons of a reciprocating engine are used partly to drive a crankshaft and partly to serve as a gas generator for driving a gas turbine. The free piston-type of engine represents the extreme in this compounding principle. In this system the pistons are used solely as gas generators, and the products of combustion are used entirely to run a gas turbine. Both the compound engine and the free piston engine have not been explored enough to judge their ultimate possibilities.

2.35 With the practical realization of the gas turbine, the entire field of propulsion, aerial, maritime, and ground transportation came into a revolutionary stage. Science and industry are feverishly working on the analysis of related aerodynamic and thermodynamic phenomena, improvement of materials and construction. Undoubtedly in this field the Air Forces will receive in the next decade the benefit of many developments initiated by others. However, it will be necessary to give industry orientation in the direction of requirements of the Air Forces. Many of these requirements involve special problems in which industry in any case might not be primarily interested, for example, performance at extreme altitude and large excess power for short duration.

2.36 Jet propulsion will be generally used for transonic and supersonic speeds, i.e., in the speed range where the propulsive efficiency of the jet is superior to that of the propeller. However, the light weight of jet devices may justify their use also at lower speeds. For example, combined propeller and jet drive enables an airplane to cruise economically with the propeller drive at lower speed and reach high speeds for short duration by means of additional jet propulsion.

2.37 The various jet-propulsion systems utilizing hydrocarbon fuels in the atmosphere are listed in the SAG report *Where We Stand*, by Theodore von Kármán, as follows:

Reciprocating engine + ducted fan + jet	Motorjet
Gas turbine + ducted fan + jet	Turbofan
Gas turbine + jet	Turbojet
Continuous jet, compression by aerodynamic ram	Ramjet
Intermittent jet	Pulsojet

2.38 The chief limitations of the motorjet are those associated with the reciprocating engine. Since the reciprocating engine has a large frontal area in comparison with the gas turbine, units of large power become difficult to accommodate in the duct. The motorjet is considered a transition stage between the conventional engine-propeller combination and the turbofan. It is not considered, therefore, an important item in a long-range propulsion program. It is interesting to note that the Japanese also had a motorjet which they considered an interim jet motor pending development of the gas turbine.

2.39 In the turbofan the gas turbine drives, besides its own compressor, a larger compressor or fan in a duct. It appears to be a promising development for filling the speed range between the turbopropeller and turbojet. It has the advantage of greater efficiency over the turbojet in the high subsonic or transonic speed range because it moves a larger mass of air. It also has the advantage over the turbopropeller in the same range because the use of shrouded fans avoids the tip losses which propellers have at high Mach number. There has been very little development on this system up to the present, and much applied research is needed; for example, wind-tunnel testing at transonic speeds on gas turbine-ducted fan combinations in various duct arrangements.

2.40 The turbojet development of the last five years proved the practicability of the system beyond doubt, and realized considerable progress both in the size of units and in fuel economy. On the other hand, many problems are unsolved and call for intensive research. In addition to the problems related generally to gas turbines and discussed above, two methods of producing excess thrust are under investigation: afterburning in the tail pipe, and fluid injection. At present requirements of high thrust for a given frontal area and of fuel economy are conflicting, which constitutes a difficulty for the application of current turbojets to supersonic aircraft. However, possibilities for further improvement show definite promise of eliminating this difficulty and should make future turbojets applicable to supersonic flight provided sufficient development is concentrated on the subject. Since turbojets

353

have an excellent propulsion efficiency at supersonic speeds, the effort of adapting them to this speed range should bring valuable returns. Supersonic aerodynamics applied to the blade design of compressors and gas turbines also should bring worth-while gains. For use in pilotless airplanes, expendable turbojets should be developed to have an endurance only slightly greater than that required by their mission.

2.41 With increasing flight velocity, the inlet air pressure to a turbojet compressor increases due to ram compression. When the aircraft is flying at sonic velocity, the ram pressure is approximately twice the atmospheric pressure and an efficient duct design is able to utilize a high percentage of this pressure. For supersonic velocities beyond Mach number 2, the air pressure due to ram compression can be many times the astrospheric pressure and we can well dispense with the mechanical compressor and hence the turbine of the turbojet. The unit will then consist of an entrance air diffusor, the combustion chamber, and the exit nozzle. This is the ramjet. The ramjet is thus essentially a supersonic propulsive power plant. Its practicability at supersonic velocities is already demonstrated. The present theoretical calculation shows that for flight Mach numbers exceeding 2, the specific fuel consumption of the ramjet could be as low as two pounds per hour per pound-thrust. This is comparable with the specific fuel consumption of the turbojet. However, the ramjet has the further advantage of light weight due to much simpler construction and higher thrust per unit frontal area due to the higher combustion temperature permitted by the absence of highly stressed moving parts.

2.42 It seems then that the ramjet is the logical power plant for supersonic flight with speeds greater than twice the speed of sound. Of course for short duration boost, even applications at subsonic or transonic speeds may be considered. However, here the fuel consumption of the ramjet is high. Furthermore, the drag of the duct when not in use is very large. Therefore, if a turbojet or turbofan is the main power plant of the aircraft, then a wiser plan is perhaps to inject fuel into the tail pipe of the main engine for obtaining a short burst of large thrust.

2.43 For supersonic application, it is essential to reduce the frontal area of the duct for low drag. This means a small combustion chamber cross section and high flow velocity. Efficient and intense heat release at high flow velocity is one of the most urgent problems in ramjet development. This problem and the problem of efficient diffusor and exit nozzle design have to be solved by concentrated efforts with the help of high speed wind tunnels.

2.44 The high fuel consumption of ramjets at subsonic velocities is due to the low pressure in the combustion chamber obtainable by ram. By carrying out the combustion in a confined chamber, like an explosion, the pressure at the end of combustion can be raised. This is the pulsojet. Its feasibility was first demonstrated by the engine of the German V-1 flying bomb. This type of engine in its present form has a fuel consumption between the ramjet and the turbojet in the subsonic and transonic range. Thus, its advantage in simplicity compared with the turbojet is counterbalanced by the high fuel consumption. Therefore, the answer to the question of whether it will be used for propelling pilotless aircraft in these speed ranges depends on two factors: (1) the development of simple expendable turbojet units, and (2) the possibility of improving the fuel economy by improved injection and combustion methods.

2.45 At supersonic speeds, the present type of pulsojet with the spring valve is definitely inferior to the ramjet. However, theoretical considerations show the possibility of removing the valve and depending on the inertia of the air column for valve action. If this could be done, then the performance of pulsojet would be comparable with that of the ramjet. Here the choice between pulsojet and ramjet is difficult because of present meager knowledge of these power plants. Only continued experiments can answer this question.

2.46 Jet-propulsion devices using chemical propellants without the benefit of the atmospheric air are called rockets. The combustion in the rocket motor is made possible by having the oxidizer and fuel contained either in a single compound or in separate compounds. In the first case, we have the monopropellant; in the second case, the multi propellant. Since the oxidizer is carried in the propellant, where as for the thermal jets, the oxidizer, oxygen, is supplied by the atmosphere, the specific consumption of propellant is much higher for rockets than for thermal jets. For rockets, this value is generally 14 to 16 lb/hr/lb-thrust. However, the rockets have two distinct advantages when compared with other types of jet-propulsion devices: First, the installed weight per pound of thrust of the power plant, excluding the propellant, is extremely small. For instance, the power plant weight for the V-2 rocket is only 0.03 lb/hr/lb of thrust. The second advantage is that the thrust of the rocket is independent of the forward motion and the altitude. In fact, the thrust of the rocket even increases slightly with increase in altitude. These characteristics of the rocket motor immediately indicate that their most efficient applications must be either (1) for short operating duration so that the total weight of the power plant plus the fuel is small in spite of the heavy consumption, or (2) at extremely high altitudes so that no other power plant can produce sufficient thrust.

2.47 As far as chemical energy is concerned, no great advance can be expected in increasing the heat value of the propellant so as to reduce specific consumption. The future development must rely on detailed improvement of the characteristics of the propellant so that a more compact and efficient power plant can be designed. Since gas propellants require bulky containers, they are impractical for use in aircraft. Therefore, we are restricted to solid and liquid propellants. The solid propellant may be the lightest unit if the application calls for very short duration, for example, one to 30 seconds. Such applications are: assisted take-off, launching of pilotless aircraft, and boosting of aircraft during flight. Such boosting may be necessary when the aircraft has to pass through the sonic range of velocity. For short-time solid-propellant rockets are able to develop a very high thrust. If the application calls for somewhat longer duration, the liquid-propellant rocket will be, in general, more desirable. There are three methods of feeding the liquid propellant into the rocket motor, namely: by use of a pressurized gas, by means of a gas generator which produces the necessary gas pressure, and by pumping. The first method can be applied only for very short duration. For longer duration, one of the two other methods must be applied where the gas generator may be simpler in design and construction than the pump.

2.48 If the rocket is to operate in the dense atmosphere of lower altitudes, as in the case of antiaircraft missiles, the drag of the missile is of primary importance. We wish to reduce the frontal area and, hence, the volume of the missile. Then the propellant should have the highest impulse per unit volume. At present, the best propellant in this respect is the nitric acid-aniline combination. If the rocket is to operate in the rare upper atmosphere, for example V-2 rockets, the drag of the missile is of secondary importance. Then, the propellant should have the highest impulse per unit weight. At present, the best propellant in this respect is the liquid oxygen and liquid hydrogen combination. The extremely low temperature of the liquid hydrogen may cause difficulties in the design. A more practical choice may be the combination of liquid oxygen and liquid hydrazine.

2.49 For more efficient design of the liquid-propellant rockets, improvements can be expected when we have a better understanding of the combustion and the flow in the motor. The cooling of the motor should be particularly studied for building long-duration rockets.

2.50 In case of solid propellant rockets, our aim in research and development should be a more versatile propellant or a series of propellants which can cover the range of applications as to operating duration and operating ambient temperature. Much reduction of the unit weight can be achieved by reducing the pressure in the motor during burning without causing unstable combustion.

2.51 Since the end of the war, the importance of atomic energy has become more and more evident. Without doubt extensive research will be done in all countries with the goal of using atomic energy as a source of power. From the point of view of aircraft propulsion the problem is centered on the question: Can we replace the combustion chamber of a rocket or a thermal jet by a nuclear reaction chamber? In the case of the rocket we have to transfer the heat released by the nuclear reaction to an appropriately related working fluid, in the case of the thermal jet, to the air.

2.52 The nuclear process in a system containing fissionable atoms, for example, a uranium pile, is characterized by the so-called multiplication factor. This factor indicates the increase of the number of neutrons produced by nuclear fission for every free neutron present in the system at a given time. If the multiplication factor is larger than unity, a chain reaction occurs. The number of neutrons, the number of atomic fissions, and the amount of released energy increase exponentially with time. If the multiplication factor is larger than unity, a chain reaction occurs. The number of neutrons, the number of atomic fissions, and the amount of released energy increase exponentially with time. If the multiplication factor is smaller than unity, the process stops. The first case corresponds to an explosion in a combustion chamber; the second case is analogous to an expiring flame. Hence, in order to substitute release of atomic energy for steady fuel combustion, one needs a system in which the multiplication factor is exactly one. One needs a method which regulates the process in such a way that the multiplication factor is kept with sufficient accuracy at a value equal to unity.

2.53 As a matter of fact, such systems are already operating, for instance, in the manufacturing process of plutonium. However, they operate at the present time at low temperatures and are relatively heavy. At the level they now operate, they would be prohibitive for any aircraft or propulsive device. To be sure, the consumption of material per kilowatt hour is negligible, practically zero. However, the initial weight is large. By use of concentrated fissionable material the weight can certainly be reduced and one can imagine that the present difficulties of increasing the temperature at which the release of heat takes place will be overcome. However, two great impediments would remain: (1) The amount of fissionable material required for the process represents a very high cost and investment in comparison to the power used in any mission of a pilotless aircraft. (2) The strong neutron and gamma radiation makes the application in a piloted aircraft difficult if not impossible.

2.54 However, atomic engineering is at the beginning of its history and it can be expected that if the problems are clearly recognized they will also be solved. Evidently the first stage of development is finished: We have systems with a tremendous ratio between energy available for release and weight. However, we have no possibility, as yet, of releasing energy at any reasonable rate without using a minimum amount of material which represents an immense reservoir of energy out of all proportion to the energy actually needed for one flight, with the exception of the case in which the same fissionable matter is used both for propulsion and warhead. Assuming that the problem of energy release is solved, the following situation would be realized as far as aircraft propulsion is concerned.

2.55 In the case of the rocket ship, which does not use air, a working fluid has to be carried in the rocket. One will choose the lightest gas, i.e., hydrogen, since for the same energy released, hydrogen will give the greatest exhaust velocity and, therefore, the greatest thrust per unit weight of material consumed. It is estimated that if we are able to produce sufficiently high temperatures and high pressures, the thrust produced per unit weight of consumed material could be made about six times the present value. This would increase more than thirty times the range of V-2 type rockets using chemical propellants and would make rocket navigation possible up to the highest altitude beyond the stratosphere. The "satellite" is a definite possibility.

2.56 If the substitution of nuclear reaction chambers for fuel combustion chamber in ramjets and turbojets, is feasible, the question of range would automatically be solved. In other words, if a jet-propelled aircraft with atomic combustion chamber could carry itself in the atmosphere, it would have practically infinite range, since its fuel consumption is practically zero. For this purpose an atomic engine weighing as much as eight or nine pounds per brake-horsepower would be acceptable for use in large bombers for subsonic flight, but for greater performance, such as supersonic speeds, a better specific engine weight would be necessary. This weight must include all moderators and regulating devices, and radiation shielding.

2.57 The application of atomic energy to the propulsion of manned airplanes will probably be out of the question for a very long time because of the difficulty of protecting efficiently the personnel from the disastrous effects of radiation. The necessary shielding, at least at present, implies prohibitive weight. However, for a pilotless airplane there are definite possibilities. The problem should be attacked urgently and with adequate personnel and means.

Problems in Materials

2.58 Aircraft materials have been perfected continuously and new materials studied with much promise. Nevertheless, it can be stated that we do not yet have the ideal material which would fulfill both the requirements for strength and for aerodynamic behavior. Whereas, for slow airplanes it was sufficient that the elastic limit of the material be not surpassed, for high-speed airplanes it is essential that the aerodynamic shape of wing and body be maintained with a minimum of deformation, avoiding any local waviness. Also, a perfectly smooth surface is necessary, and the possibility of keeping the surface smooth in service. These requirements call for improvement in properties of known materials or discovery of new materials of low specific weight, as well as development of methods of fabrication and production to take full advantage of the material properties.

2.59 Another equally important requirement is the development of high-temperature materials for gas turbines and jet propulsion devices. Great advances have been achieved during the past five years. However, the investigations were generally made by purely empirical methods, without consideration of the fundamental character of the solid state of metals from the physicist's point of view. This more fundamental approach will definitely open ways to new horizons in a field where old concepts and methods seem to yield diminishing returns. For application to individual design, a closer understanding of the particular requirements in each case will also aid greatly in material development. We must choose among the multitude of material properties (such as elasticity, plasticity, yield characteristics, impact strength, fatigue strength, etc.) the most important ones for a given design, and not require the optimum in every aspect. This means a closer analysis of the stresses of machine parts, especially under dynamic and high thermal stress conditions.

2.60 An entirely new possibility is the introduction of ceramics as a construction material. Ceramics are particularly heat resistant, as the melting points of these materials are generally much higher than those of the metals. However, the strength of the ceramics now known is usually too low to be used for high stressed parts. On the other hand, ceramics have not been developed for such purposes before, and much remains to be learned. Two points need to be mentioned particularly: (1) The cost per pound of the ceramic material for machine parts could be many times that of the industrial ceramic materials now used, and thus the possible choice of basic components is much wider. (2) The ceramics can be used as a coating on metallic parts, and thus the temperature resisting property could be combined with the high strength property.

2.61 A different approach to the problem of increasing the inlet gas temperature in turbines consists of cooling the parts of the engine exposed to high temperatures. The cooling problem brings up new requirements for the material. Thermal conductivity and thermal extension may become more important than creep at high temperatures. The recently proposed method of cooling by injecting the coolant through a porous material will promote the development of new alloys.

2.62 In rocket motors the need for high temperature resisting material has grown with the increasing demand for longer duration of operation. In view of the very high temperature involved in the combustion of rocket fuels, liquid-cooled chambers and nozzles have been used for long-duration units. The erosion of the nozzle has been a very difficult problem from the material point of view. It seems, however, that erosion occurs only if the temperature of the surface reaches some critical value. Nozzles made of very soft material (aluminum) have been used successfully when properly cooled. It appears that the conditions the material should satisfy to operate properly in a liquid cooled unit are different from those required for an uncooled unit. In the first case, metals can be used almost exclusively. Thermal conductivity, thermal extension, and machinability are the essential factors in this case. In the second case, most metals will not stand the combustion chamber temperature, and the use of high melting point metals (tungsten, molybdenum, tantalum) and of ceramic materials seems to be justified.

2.63 In the design of nuclear reaction chambers, quite different characteristics of the material must be considered, especially the absorption of neutrons, alpha particles, and radiation, combined with high temperature.

Rotary-Wing Aircraft

2.64 No mention has been made so far of aircraft different from the airplane type. Certainly rotary-wing aircraft, in spite of serious limitations, have military applications in airborne operations, as well as a host of special duties such as rescue, liaison, etc. The application of jet propulsion to rotary-wing aircraft is worthy of further investigation, and other forms of rotary-wing aircraft, such as the cyclogyro and gyrodyne, should be more fully explored. A somewhat fantastic idea is a helicopter driven by atomic energy which could serve as an observation station for a very long period of time at considerable altitude, reporting data to the ground or to an airplane.

Airships

2.65 The airship is in principle a slow-velocity aerial vehicle, with the advantage of large cargo carrying capacity. Aerodynamic development and development in propulsion may considerably increase the speed of the airship. Since the greatest portion of the drag of an airship consists of skin friction, laminar boundary layer control may cause a very essential reduction of the drag. Another less important improvement could be derived from a rear propeller drive, consisting of shrouded propellers located in the stern of the ship. Boundary layer control, of course, would probably require a construction material suitable for forming a smooth surface with sufficient local strength.

Locate Targets and Recognize Them

3.1 In order to accomplish its mission the Air Forces must not only be able to move swiftly and transport loads through the air but the movement must be directed to bring the aircraft or missile and its means of destruction from a base to the vicinity of a military target which may be anywhere on the globe. The target must then be recognized. The technical problem is one of locating two objects, the aircraft or missile, and the target, with respect to some frame of reference and of bringing the two locations in coincidence by guiding the aircraft or missile. It is convenient to consider the problem in three successive phases: (1) reconnaissance, or obtaining advance knowledge of where targets are to be found so that an attack may be planned; (2) navigation, or guiding the aircraft or missile from the base of operations to the vicinity of the target; and (3) recognition of the target immediately prior to its attack.

Reconnaissance

3.2 The basic frame of reference for locating targets is an accurate and precise survey map of the earth's surface, but before targets can be located on a map, we must first know that they exist. The first procedure will undoubtedly be to make factual surveys of enemy industry, transportation systems, and military installations by the usual methods involving agents traveling within enemy territory, study of prewar economic data, and similar methods. The next step is to obtain information by reconnaissance flights of aircraft or missiles using every known method of aiding the senses of man, including aerial photographs, radar, heat detectors, detectors of radioactive materials, etc. The enemy will try to disguise his main factories and other installations by camouflage and decoy targets and will try to interfere with the operation of our scientific aids, for example, by providing smoke screens and by electronic jamming. We must, therefore, employ a variety of means, comparing the results of one against the others. This problem of determining precisely where the target is located in the first place requires the judgment which can only be supplied by the human brain, and cannot be entrusted wholly to any single mechanism as may perhaps be possible in the navigation and attack problems.

Aerial Photography

3.3 If accurate maps of the enemy's territory are not already available they must be provided by our own forces and the most feasible method is by means of aerial photography. Methods of aerial photography have been highly developed and will continue to be useful even if aircraft fly faster and higher. It may happen that difficulty is experienced with clouds and haze in which case radar methods can be used as discussed in the next section. Maps made from aerial photographs may or may not show the actual location of all possible targets but they will show the shape and location of cities, important rivers, coastlines, mountains, and other natural features and they will serve as the basic frame of reference for location of strategic and other fixed targets.

3.4 Aerial photography is also used for detailed surveillance of enemy territory and for the detection of specific military targets. The long period of time which is available for the study of reconnaissance data usually enables the detection of decoys and camouflage and permits exact location of the target. Concealment by camouflage can generally be defeated by color photography or stereoscopic photography, both of which have been highly developed. Few pigments useful for optical camouflage match the colors of the surrounding territory so perfectly that they cannot be detected by color photography with suitable selected filters. Stereoscopic photography enables the detection of the relative heights of objects in the field of view which cannot be changed by application of paint.

Radar Surveys

3.5 Useful maps can be made by photographing the indicator scope of an airborne radar and the detail is greater the narrower the radar beam, i.e., the shorter the wave length for a given antenna size. It is, in fact, desirable to provide special reconnaissance radar equipment in a special aircraft whose express function is to provide large and clear map-like presentations of the terrain suitable for photographing. Such records are useful not only for making the usual line maps but as guides to bombardiers when radar methods of bombing are used. Radar reconnaissance can be made at night and through clouds. It penetrates the nets and cloths commonly used as camouflage materials, and may even penetrate natural cover like forests under certain conditions.

3.6 Cities and large industrial installations are usually easily detected in radar photographs. Smaller targets can be detected under suitable background coordinations. Objects surrounded on one or more sides by water such as bridges, piers, ships, etc., are easily detected by modern radar equipment.

Heat Surveys

3.7 Underground installations cannot be detected either by aerial photography or by radar, and other means must be sought. Any large industrial plant uses considerable amounts of power which is eventually turned into heat by friction in the machines, losses in electric motors, electric lights, air compressors, etc. In an underground plant the heat must be conveyed to the surface through a suitable ventilating system except in very unusual circumstances. The hot air exhaust pipe may be detected by sensitive heat meters carried in reconnaissance aircraft. The same equipment is effective in detecting optically camouflaged industrial plants and in differentiating between real and decoy targets.

Acoustic Methods

3.8 The present war saw the development of sonobuoys for detecting the presence of submarines. These devices dropped from aircraft into the sea contain microphones to pick up underwater noise and a radio transmitter to relay the information to the reconnaissance aircraft. It is practicable to use similar devices against surface and underground targets which give off considerable noise as is the case for many types of industrial plants.

Magnetic Methods

3.9 The present war has also brought the development of magnetic methods of detecting submerged submarines. In principle the same methods should be applicable to the detection of underground factories. Because of their short range of detection these devices are not at present highly practicable for this purpose.

Atomic Power Plants

3.10 Plants engaged in the manufacture of materials for atomic bombs or atomic power plants may be detected not only by the heat given off but by the special types of radiation from them which penetrates considerable thickness of earth. Suitable airborne equipment can probably be designed for the detection of such radiation.

Navigation

3.11 Having fixed the geographical location of the enemy targets the next step is to bring the aircraft or missile to the vicinity. The central problem of navigation is to determine quickly and accurately the geographical position of an aircraft. The ideal situation is to have available continuously the position of the aircraft regardless of weather conditions, preferably in the form of a plot on a map showing the history of the flight up to the present moment. As the speed of the aircraft increases, the time required to obtain the position must be reduced. For example, an aircraft flying at 1200 miles per hour traverses 20 miles in one minute, and it would be necessary to reduce the time to less than three seconds if an accuracy of one mile were desired. It is obvious that automatic observing and computing devices are required.

Position Finding

3.12 The methods available for locating the position of an aircraft may be classified in various ways. They will be discussed here under the headings visual methods, dead reckoning, and radio and radar methods, the greatest emphasis being placed on the radar methods because they seem to offer the greatest possibilities of attaining the ideal.

Visual Methods

3.13 When the ground is visible, the position of the aircraft may be obtained by referring to visible landmarks such as cities, railroads, rivers, mountains, lakes, lighthouses, etc., and comparing them with a map. This simplest method of navigation, known as air pilotage or piloting, is useful primarily over land in clear weather and over territory for which maps are available.

3.14 Over the oceans, also over land and above clouds when celestial objects are visible, the methods of celestial navigation may be used. This procedure amounts fundamentally to a determination of the position of the aircraft relative to the geographical position of one or more celestial bodies which is known if the time is known. Much ingenuity has been exercised in developing aids for converting the observed data into position of the aircraft in the shortest possible time.

Attention should be given to the problem of automatic celestial navigation of pilotless aircraft.

Dead Reckoning

3.15 Dead reckoning is the method of estimating position by keeping an account, or reckoning, of the course and distance from a previously known position. The basic observed data are the air speed and the compass course, but suitable corrections must be made for air temperature and pressure to give true air speed, for declination and deviation to give the true heading, and for the wind.

3.16 Much of the human labor involved in this method has been removed by the development of the flux-gate compass and of instruments for measuring true air speed in conjunction with a device known as an air position indicator. In this device, the compass heading is combined with true air speed automatically to give latitude and longitude, starting from an initial setting at a known position. The mechanism takes account of the fact that a degree of longitude is of varying length at different latitudes and functions accurately except at very high latitudes. The compass corrections may be set in manually from time to time.

3.17 When science has perfected a satisfactory ground speed indicator not dependent on ground stations, the mechanized dead-reckoning system, or ground position indicator, will be a most effective navigational aid. Its weakness is that the errors are cumulative and that it must have been in operation continuously from some known position. Its advantage is that the equipment is all on the aircraft and operation is not dependent on receiving radio transmission over long distances. The method of dead reckoning is the one method that is always available.

3.18 The navigation employed in the V-1 and V-2 long-range missiles was essentially that of dead reckoning. In the case of V-1, the altitude was automatically controlled, the heading was determined by a magnetic compass which monitored the directional gyro of the autopilot, and the distance was measured by an air log. At the preset distance the bomb was made to dive on the target. In the case of V-2, the navigation occurred during the burning period of the rocket motor. The vertical heading was controlled by an elevation gyro, the azimuth by a radio beam, and the propulsion was cut off when a fixed speed was reached as determined by an integrating accelerometer.

3.19 The accuracy obtainable by dead-reckoning methods is of the order of from two to five percent of the range from the last known position, the exact value depending not only on the type of measuring instruments and computers but also on atmospheric conditions. For example, the accuracy of current air position indicators is such that the error infrequently exceeds four percent and averages about two percent. The errors of measurement and computation can probably be reduced below one percent with continued improvement in instrument design. The principal source of error is the variability and uncertainty of the wind. This error decreases as the speed of the missile or aircraft increases.

Radio and Radar Methods

3.20 Prior to the introduction of radar techniques, many radio aids to navigation had been developed. Two-way radio telephone communication and the broadcasting of meteorological information are of incalculable assistance to navigators. For regular air routes the system of radio beams radiating from radio-range beacons and the radio marker beacons enable navigation under conditions of zero visibility. This system has been highly developed for commercial air transport in the United States. The beam defines a specific track in space, enabling correction to be made for wind drift. The information is independent of any transmission from the aircraft and the number of aircraft which can receive the information simultaneously is unlimited. However, there are technical difficulties at the radio frequencies used by the present system associated with the effects of the terrain and of the ionosphere on radio transmission at those frequencies.

The trend is toward the use of higher frequencies and to methods dependent on microwaves and pulse transmission.

3.21 Before radar, there was extensive development of aircraft radio direction finders, and homing devices, and of systems of aircraft location by direction finding from ground stations. Information so obtained was used for occasional computation of position as a fix in connection with navigation by dead reckoning. The most highly developed form of radio direction finder is the automatic radio compass which gives direct readings of the bearing relative to the axis of the aircraft of any radio station to which it is tuned. Indicators are available which combine this indication with that of a flux-gate magnetic compass. The same technical difficulties are encountered as for the radio-range system at the frequencies commonly used because of the effects of terrain and ionosphere on the transmission giving rise to night effects, multiple and bent courses, etc. In any system based on direction finding the errors increase with the range. Perhaps the most elegant beam system is the modern German "Sonne" system which allows an observer to determine his bearing relative to a land station with an accuracy of the order of 10 at ranges up to 1000 or 2000 miles.

3.22 Radar has developed many new techniques which are described in greater detail in the reports of the radar consultants, Radar and Communications. The development of microwave radar makes it possible for the navigator to "see" the terrain under blind-flying conditions and to use the simplest of all methods, air pilotage. In X-band and shorter wavelengths, the resolution is sufficient for identification of rivers, streams, bridges, rail lines, and other surface features. In addition, the range of radar vision is greater than that of the eye, so that over the sea, land may be "seen" at ranges of from 50 to 100 miles. When over land, or at sea with the aid of radar buoys, drift may be determined and combined with an air position indicator to give a ground position indication. An accuracy of the order of two percent of the distance traveled since the last fix is attainable. This method of radar navigation requires no ground stations.

3.23 The pulse techniques of radar have given rise to the development of a new technique of position finding based on measuring distances rather than directions to known points, hence called telemetric. The known points may be marked by radar beacons which provide strong identifiable artificial echoes. When "interrogated" by receiving a signal from a microwave transmitter in the aircraft, the beacon transmits an echo, and the time interval from pulse emission to receipt of echo is a measure of the distance. Even a single beacon enables a fix within the accuracy set by the width of the radar beam. Much greater precision is obtained by measuring simultaneously the distance from two beacons, the procedure used in the British "H" system and Shoran. The traffic capacity of this type of system is limited.

3.24 Another telemetric method is the hyperbolic method in which pairs of ground stations emit synchronized pulses. The pulses are received in the aircraft and the time difference between the arrival of pulses from the member of a pair is measured. This locates the aircraft on a hyperbola and two such hyperbolas give a fix. The aircraft requires only a receiver and the traffic capacity is unlimited.

3.25 The range of microwave systems extends to the optical horizon or only slightly beyond. For long ranges a relatively low radio frequency must be used. The hyperbolic system of navigation operating at frequencies of two megacycles per second or lower is known as Loran. The standard system now in use has a range over water of 700 nautical miles by day and 1400 miles by night with errors of from 0.1 to 10 miles depending on the geometry of the lines of position. A system under development is expected to have a range of 1200 miles by day and 2000 by night with errors of from one to two miles at 1000 miles. Laboratory techniques of pulse comparison indicate the possibility of improving the accuracy by an order of magnitude.

3.26 The process of hyperbolic navigation may be compared with that of celestial navigation. The determination of lines of position is essentially similar except that the mathematics is more complicated. However, the unchanging character position obtained from fixed reference stations in contrast to the moving stars permits precomputation. Charts may be prepared in advance for pairs of stations and the results are permanently useful so long as the stations are maintained because the lines of equal time difference are fixed with respect to the surface of the earth.

3.27 There is no technical obstacle to a complete mechanization of the receiver so that the output is either in the form of dial counters giving Loran coordinates or a plotting board which will plot the position continuously on a Loran chart. It is then a short step to connect the output to the rudder so that a predetermined track may be followed automatically.

3.28 Since hyperbolic navigation requires only a receiver on the aircraft or missile, and the traffic capacity is unlimited, it is the most promising system for the control of large numbers of long-range ground-to-ground pilotless aircraft. As now visualized, special ground stations would be adjusted so that the hyperbolic line of position corresponding to a fixed time difference for which the missile receivers are set passes through the target. Aircraft could be launched from many points in a large area, all following a preset course until they intercepted the line of position through the target. They would then change course and follow the line of position to the target. The attitude would be controlled independently and the dive to the ground would be initiated by reaching the appropriate position line of a second pair of ground stations. This type of attack could be operated without close coordination between control group and launching crews; their operations would be practically independent.

Magnetic Methods

3.29 The use of the compass for determining direction on the earth's surface is well known. It has been repeatedly suggested that additional measurements on the earth's magnetic field may yield another method of navigation. Thus,

372

in theory, measurements of the magnetic dip and of magnetic field strength give two numbers which could serve as coordinates of position to be related to ordinary geographic coordinates by suitable surveys. The principal weakness of the method is that a recent survey over the territory to be traversed is necessitated by the secular variation of magnetic properties. In addition, the accuracy would be severely limited by diurnal variations and magnetic storms as well as by the lack of suitable airborne instruments. The method may be worthy of some further study.

3.30 It is probable that no single method will answer all of the navigation problems of piloted and pilotless aircraft. However, there are available scientific methods and techniques in rich variety which make possible continuous knowledge of position independent of adverse meteorological conditions.

Recognition of the Target

3.31 As the aircraft or missile approaches the general vicinity of the target, the bombardier, gunner, operator, or the mechanism of the pilotless missile (if of the target seeking type) must find and recognize the target preparatory to the attack. Most of the methods useful for reconnaissance are also useful for recognition with the exception of photography which takes too much time.

3.32 In the case of large and extended targets such as cities, factories, or other major installations above ground, when the visibility is adequate, there is no difficulty. The eye may be aided by a suitable telescope, and the mind may be assisted by suitable aerial photographs and maps. The photographs, maps, or sketches may be constructed in relief to show the appearance when approached at the normal approach altitude and thus facilitate recognition.

3.33 Photographs of radar indicator scopes obtained on reconnaissance missions may be used in the same manner as aerial photographs as an aid to recognition.

3.34 Skilled operators have no difficulty in recognizing many types of targets directly on the radar indicator. Cities, bridges, piers, ships, islands, beaches at the coast line, and aircraft can all be recognized without difficulty. Special techniques are available for detecting moving targets which are especially useful for aircraft detection but which are also applicable to ground targets under some conditions.

3.35 If agents are available in the enemy territory, they may mark targets otherwise invisible by portable radar beacons or, in special cases, such marking beacons may be dropped from the air.

3.36 Radar methods may be used to follow the aircraft or missile from ground control stations and to direct the pilot or actually remotely control the aircraft to a target whose map location is known by previous reconnaissance.

3.37 The reconnaissance methods using heat detectors, detectors of special types of radiation from radioactive materials, magnetic measurements, or acoustic radiosondes dropped on the ground may find application in recognition of special targets. These methods as well as radar are applicable to the homing control of missiles. In fact any target possessing any peculiarity as to physical properties which set it off from its background can be recognized by a suitable homing intelligence device.

3.38 Especially in the case of pilotless aircraft, the operation of recognition and control may be carried out at a remote point by the aid of radio repeat-back of information from a television camera or a radar search set.

See further reports of the Scientific Advisory Group:

Guided Missiles and Pilotless Aircraft
Guidance and Homing of Missiles and Pilotless Aircraft
Radar and Communications

Hit Targets Accurately

4.1 The degree of accuracy required for successful strategic bombing is one of the most discussed topics of aerial warfare. Visual bombsights were designed for so-called pin-point bombing. However, war experiences show that this type of bombing is applicable only to a limited extent, because of weather and enemy interference. Hence, in most cases pin-point bombing has to be replaced by area-bombing, i.e., by bombing with an accuracy obtainable by radar blind aiming, by dropping the bombs simultaneously from a large formation, or by missiles equipped with automatic pilot. In the future, bombing in large formations will probably be prevented by improved antiaircraft devices. It will be necessary to revise bombing equipment in the light of future methods of strategy, including the use of atomic bombs.

4.2 The ability to hit targets accurately is dependent on the aerodynamic performance of the bombs, meteorological conditions, the accuracy of the bombsight, and the abilities of the bombardier. The study of the aerodynamic characteristics of bombs at low speeds has been well developed, but further research is needed in the transonic region. A considerable loss in accuracy of bombing from high altitude, originally attributed to the effect of high speed on the aerodynamic characteristics, was finally traced to structural failure of the fins. However, there is some evidence of an adverse effect of high speed on stability for certain types of bombs.

4.3 Bombers require bombsights in order to hit the target. In general, it can be said that the faster an airplane travels the less accurately it can drop its bombs. If bombers are actually going to fly at speeds around 1000 mph it cannot be said with certainty that present bombing precision can be improved upon or even maintained in spite of ever increasing complexity of the bombsights. Errors in the release mechanism and ballistic trajectories become important at high speeds. The reaction time of the bombardier will have a significant effect on precision.

4.4 Any self contained bombsight has two parts, the sighting means and the computer. In optical bombsights the sighting means is a telescope; in radar bombsights it is a radar. There are only trivial differences in computer design in the two cases.

4.5 The faster the bomber flies, the farther ahead the sighting means must see; above 400 or 500 mph only radar can see far enough and there is no sense in trying to develop optical bombsights for such aircraft.

4.6 But a fundamental difficulty with radar is that in order for it to see far and also clearly, its antenna must be wide; this is a tendency in flat contradiction to aerodynamical trends for high-speed aircraft.

4.7 The design of bombsight computers aims not only at accuracy but at decreasing the time required for manipulation after the target is recognized. This has a profound effect on what is required of the associated radar since the more time required to adjust the computer the farther away the target has to be recognized, and there is a practical limit to this. The recent war has seen the beginning of the development of computers suitable for use in dive and glide bombing as well as for offset bombing, i.e., sighting at some more easily recognizable point whose position relative to the target is known. These developments give greater freedom of flight path to the bomber.

4.8 Pilotless bombers whose range is limited to less than approximately 100 miles may be entirely directed by means of precision ground-based devices employing radar principles. Extensions of the Shoran equipment to automatically control such aircraft can be perfected.

4.9 For longer ranges, studies should be made of the use of airborne relay stations such as airplanes, rotary-wing aircraft, or missiles, and of combinations of ground based directors with a homing device in the vehicle. In order to achieve long range the ground stations must operate on relatively long wavelengths such as are employed by the Loran system; this connotes low precision. Such means must thereby be employed to bring the missile to the vicinity of the target, whereupon the homing device may take over control.

4.10 Studies of the optimum locations of Loran stations for this purpose should be undertaken; the possibility of mounting such stations on submarines should be explored. The possibility of long-range guiding by automatic celestial navigation should also be investigated.

4.11 The homing devices used may react to any radiation emitted from the target or may, radar-like, themselves illuminate it. Radio waves, thermal radiation, light, and certain of the high-energy radiations from nuclear reactions may be considered as practical for homing purposes; if the device homes on radiation emitted from the target, then to a certain extent it can automatically recognize the target. Thus, a device made to home only on gamma rays would only home on unshielded atomic power plants, whereas one made to home on radio waves would neglect atomic power plants in favor of radio transmitters. This advantage is not so favorable as it sounds however, since the possibility of erecting decoy targets always exists, even for atomic energy plants.

4.12 For extremely high-speed missiles like V-2 the homing problem is made very difficult by the extremely long range required of the detecting device.

4.13 Magnetic airborne devices are not regarded as offering good prospects for guiding pilotless aircraft. It is to be doubted whether devices sensitive to sound will be of any use either.

4.14 Means for guiding missiles may be ground-based or air-based regardless of whether the missile itself is launched from ground or air. The particular tactical need will determine which of the four possible combinations should be used. It may prove upon further study that the guiding and launching means should be similarly based.

4.15 The most difficult problem in launching missiles from the air is to launch them in the proper direction, if the target is nearby, so that they will require a minimum time of flight. The proposed defense of very heavy aircraft by this means may prove particularly difficult for this reason.

4.16 While use is made of all available aerodynamic knowledge in the design of pilotless bombers, especially in the field of transonic and supersonic aerodynamics, there are many special problems introduced by the use of homing devices which must be solved if high accuracy is to be attained. For greater accuracy the missile should look in the direction of travel of its center of gravity except as corrections for wind and target motion are introduced by a course computer. An aircraft of conventional design operates at a variable angle of attack dependent on load and speed, and boresight errors would arise as discussed by Dr. H. L. Dryden in "Present State of the Guided Missile Art, " Part I of the SAG report Guided Missiles and Pilotless Aircraft.

4.17 Perhaps the major problem in the design of a pilotless bomber is the coordination of all elements to give stable operation without excessive hunting, i.e., systems coordination. The tag characteristics of the intelligence device and of the autopilot and associated servomechanisms are perhaps the most important factors, but the stability and accuracy are dependent on many other factors including the aerodynamic characteristics of the missile.

4.18 In addition to bombs released from manned airplanes or carried by guided pilotless bombers, guns and rockets play an important role in aerial warfare. Rockets, stabilized either by tail fins like a bomb or by spin like a shell, are one of the important new developments of the present war. Comparatively large missiles may be fired and continually improved with better knowledge of the aerodynamics of rockets and with the development of rocket-sighting devices. Their effectiveness by the application of proximity fuses has greatly increased.

4.19 The development of fire-control equipment has had little difficulty in keeping ahead of the development of guns. The range, accuracy, and rate of fire of the guns are not at all of a magnitude commensurate with the needs of aircraft traveling at supersonic speeds. Problems which must receive increased attention are the adaptation of guns and aircraft so that neither the aerodynamic performance of the aircraft nor the effectiveness of the gun is impaired. One typical engineering problem is the elimination of vibration which impairs the accuracy. It will do very little good to make superior gunsights if the guns are not also improved.

4.20 Many of the present computers for antiaircraft fire are based on the assumption that the two aircraft are traveling in straight lines. This assumption does not give sufficient accuracy. A fundamental study should be made of the types of paths usually followed by aircraft in combat and gunsights should be redesigned on the basis of the results of the study.

4.21 As the speed of airplanes increases to the supersonic range, a further limit on accuracy is imposed by the unalterable reaction time of the human operator. In principle, this difficulty can be overcome by making machines which are more and more automatic. Some progress had been made in this direction in the experimental radar-controlled guns which could be locked on any desired aerial target and thereafter would automatically keep the guns pointed at it. If such devices can be developed of sufficiently low weight, the man would be called upon only for the will to fight, a trait which so far has not been built into any automatic device.

4.22 It is certain that instruments of control will become more complicated in structure as they are required to perform more and more functions formerly carried out by men. The problem of instrumental reliability and satisfactory operation then becomes urgent.

4.23 Reliability can only be assured by a continuing program of development not only of the instruments themselves but also, and equally important, of the component parts of which they are made. Such development of improved components may not be adequately supported by the ordinary economic forces of peacetime competition and heavy financial support by the Air Forces may be necessary.

4.24 Satisfactory operation can only be assured by careful selection and training of personnel and above all by careful designing of instruments in accordance with the psychological and physiological needs of the men who are supposed to operate them. A special staff of persons trained both in engineering and psychology may be needed to carry out this kind of development. It would be the prime purpose of this group to insure that the design of aircraft, of the offensive armament, and of the instruments meant to control them are coordinated so that one integrated fighting machine comes out. The present tendency to design an airplane and then hang on guns, rockets, bombs, radar, and sighting devices as a multitude of accessories must cease.

Ability to Cause Destruction

5.1 The war which just ended was the first one in which aerial bombing played a decisive role. An immense amount of work was put into the development of bombs, bombing instruments, and bombing tables. Much of the present knowledge of the results of bombing and the effectiveness of bombs was obtained by systematic observation and analysis. A new branch of terminal ballistics developed, dealing with the effect of bombs on their targets. Since the heat released by our present molecular explosives is near the possible upper limit, great attention was paid to the most efficient use of the limited amount of energy. Then with the appearance of the atomic bomb, the destructive power of one bomb was made equal to the effect of 20,000 tons of explosive. The question arises, should the efforts for further improvement in construction and use of conventional bombs be continued, or should the whole material available be worked up for the archives and further study be concentrated on the atomic phase of the problem.

5.2 It is true that after the discovery of the gun, archery gradually became a sport instead of a military art. This process of substitution was slow; however, analogous processes in our age may become very rapid. Hence, we might argue that atomic bombs are the future means of destruction and we may forget about conventional bombs. The arguments against this theory are the following:

(1) Production facilities of atomic bombs may be limited, so that their use will be restricted to the most important actions. (2) In many cases of future warfare we shall not be willing to use means of utter destruction. (3) Economic and political reasons may suggest the use of conventional explosives as an alternative to atomic explosives.

5.3 Fundamental features of nuclear processes involved in the functioning of the present atomic bomb do not permit making them of considerably smaller power than those which have been used against Japan. The answer to the question whether the development of conventional bombs should be continued depends to a great extent on whether the developments of nuclear science will produce a variety of bombs in a range of sizes, adaptable to various missions. The gap between the effect of the largest conventional and the present atomic bomb is immense. Warfare is directed primarily to securing the safety of our nation and not to the indiscriminate destruction of others. Hence, it appears that the most reasonable channel for development of atomic weapons is to investigate the possibility of smaller capacities. No one can tell today whether and to what extent this is possible. Since there is no guarantee that atomic bombs can be substituted completely for conventional bombs, the work on development and improvement of conventional weapons must be continued.

5.4 I believe the Air Forces should concentrate its effort upon: (1) getting full information about the destructive power of the present atomic bombs; (2) studying the possibilities of the adaptation of atomic bombs to various missions which proved to be effective against the war potential of the enemy in the last war; (3) studying the possibilities of developing smaller size nuclear bombs perhaps by using nuclear reactions other than fission; and (4) making comparative studies of efficiency and costs of past methods of strategic bombing and future methods using pilotless bombers loaded with either atomic or conventional explosives.

5.5 Special study should be made of the problem of destruction of underground establishments. In the last war submarine berths were attacked with bombs, but with practically no success. It must be anticipated that a considerable portion of the key industries of possible enemies will be located underground in order to escape bombardment. Probably attack on communications leading to the underground factories and depots gives the best possibility of successful neutralization of such underground establishments.

5.6 The destruction of air targets, i.e., aircraft and missiles, has received comparatively little scientific study. Recent tasks by the War Department have shown that one pound of high explosives exploding within the wing of an airplane will cause sufficient damage to produce a crash or at least make return from a mission improbable. However, additional study is needed of the damage from blast and fragmentation at distances within the range of proximity fuses. In this application of fragmentation as a means of destruction, considerable progress has already been made by the application of scientific principles to develop controlled fragmentation, controlled both as to size and general direction of travel of the fragments. The theory of blast is now well developed; from this theory, for example, it has been estimated that 20,000 tons of TNT, which is said to be the equivalent as regards blast, of the atomic bomb, will destroy an aircraft one to two miles away. The efficient design of warheads for air to air missiles and ground to air missiles is dependent on accurate information on the destructive effects of both ordinary and atomic explosives when used either for blast or for hurling fragments.

5.7 The destruction of ships offers many new problems in terminal ballistics. The penetration of the armor of battleships and other men-of-war is essentially the same problem as penetration of the armor tanks. A scientific curiosity of the first decades of this century, the so-called Monroe effect, has been applied in this last war to the development of hollow or shaped charges which have remarkable powers of penetration. Ships are more easily destroyed by underwater explosions.

5.8 "Terminal Ballistics and Destructive Effects," by Dr. N. M. Newmark (Part III of Explosives and Terminal Ballistics) describes the present state of knowledge of destructive effects of explosives. This report also contributes suggestions for completing our information on the subject. It is believed that such a program should be carried out because (1) in a transition period such information is certainly needed, and (2) the final picture concerning the relation between the atomic and the conventional explosive is yet uncertain.

5.9 The following conclusions regarding the selection of conventional weapons for attack of various ground targets appear to be generally accepted:

a. The most effective high explosive bomb for attack of light industrial buildings is a GP bomb fused to burst between the roof and the floor. Greater damage is produced to the building and to its contents with this fusing than with instantaneous fusings, or with cratering bombs.

b. Against heavy industrial buildings and heavy machinery, large cratering bombs or penetrating bombs are required to produce severe damage.

c. Against relatively combustible construction, either residential or industrial, incendiary bombs were several times as effective, weight for weight, as any other type of bomb, except possibly air burst of very large blast bombs.

d. Small bombs, blast bombs, and incendiary bombs had virtually no effect on submarine pens and heavy fortifications. Penetrating bombs or large general purpose bombs are required.

e. Against brick wall-bearing construction and against light wood-frame construction, blast bombs are most effective, and air burst at the proper height produces more damage than ground burst or cratering bombs.

5.10 Improvements needed in present conventional weapons depend on the availability in quantity and size of atomic bombs. Since it must be assumed, in the immediate future at least, that only a relatively small quantity of present-type atomic bombs will be available, conventional bombs must be capable of being used effectively against all possible types of targets.

5.11 The following requirements seem to be most urgently needed:

a. Bombs designed specifically for the attack of massive underground installations including shaped-charge bombs, rocket-assisted bombs, and follow-through bombs. Possibly the required improvement in penetration performance can be obtained by developing bomb cases of increased strength.

b. Development of large blast bombs with extremely light cases, to be used with proximity fuses for air burst, as a weapon against targets vulnerable to blast.

c. Development of fragmentation bombs with more adequately controlled fragmentation.

d. Development of fuses with more accurate control of timing, to permit bombs to burst after penetrating the roof of a building and before striking the floor or penetrating the earth beneath. (See SAG report, *Explosives Terminal and Ballistics*.)

Function Independently of Weather and Darkness

6.1 The goal of the Air Forces is an all-weather air force, i.e., complete independence of weather, both for flying and carrying out offensive and defensive missions. Flying independently of weather includes take-off, landing, and traffic operations without visibility, navigation without contact and minimum influence of the weather situation and wind on the flight path and flying time. The main requirement for carrying out offensive missions in any weather is the replacement of visual bombing and visual fire control by radar methods. The same methods and equipment which are needed to carry out flight bombing and combat operations in cloudy weather serve the same purposes on dark nights.

Blind Landing

6.2 There are two aspects to the problem of blind landing, the actual blind landing or blind approach of a single aircraft, and the problem of traffic control in the neighborhood of a landing area, which is in many ways more difficult than traffic control along cross-country airways. The first problem mentioned has been attacked from two different directions, represented by the glide-path-localizer system, and the more recent GCA (ground-controlled-approach) system. In the glide-path-localizer system a direction of approach, and a glide path, are defined in space by fixed radio beams. Through a suitable receiver and indicator the pilot is apprised automatically of his position relative to this path. In the GCA system the position of the aircraft is determined by a precision radar set on the ground and instructions are given to the pilot over any available communication channel. Each system has its advantages and disadvantages and both are certainly susceptible to technical improvement. The radar method is inherently flexible, and it requires no special equipment in the aircraft; however, its traffic handling capacity is now rather restricted and it does require fairly elaborate ground equipment and a highly trained crew. We cannot regard either method as a universal solution of the problem. There may be in fact several future systems, or combinations of systems for different types of airports, ranging from permanent commercial air bases to temporary landing strips at advanced military bases. What is needed, in addition to technical improvements, is extensive experience and a comprehensive program of trials aimed at an integrated combination of all useful aids.

Traffic Control

6.3 Traffic control near an airfield is peculiarly difficult because of the congestion which exists at such a focal point and the necessity of orderly approach to the landing path. Microwave search radar, on the ground, is a powerful aid and is an essential adjunct of the GCA system. It does not, however, solve all the critical problems, which include communication and identification. It ought to be possible for a ground controller not only to know the position and altitude of any aircraft in the vicinity, but to talk directly to any selected one. This requires a multiplicity of channels, and a degree of flexibility and reliability not approached by any existing communication equipment. However, the voice communication techniques available at microwave frequencies are very promising and should be exploited. Incidentally the heavy investment in existing types of equipment is exerting a retarding influence on this development, which we consider extremely important for the future Air Forces.

6.4 Going even further, one can envisage means by which some of the information available on the ground could be relayed to each pilot in the vicinity, almost completely breaking down the barriers of overcast and darkness.

Instrument Flying

6.5 Navigation without contact involves, first, instrument flying, that is, controlling the aircraft in a condition of reasonably steady flight on a given course, and second, determining as frequently as necessary the position of the aircraft in ground coordinates. We have to consider also obstacle detection or collision prevention.

6.6 Automatic pilots have been in use since about 1933. In the present form one or more gyroscopes are used to detect rotations of the aircraft; the resulting relative motion is translated into a signal which is amplified and operates the controls. Means are provided to make various adjustments of sensitivity and to prevent self-oscillation. The automatic pilot must be adjusted to the particular type of aircraft and the best adjustment often depends on the roughness of the air. Automatic pilots for pilotless aircraft must be designed to operate without the necessity of manual adjustments in the air.

6.7 Instrument flying in all weather conditions requires a solution of the icing problem which is still a great obstacle to continuous operation of pilotless as well as piloted aircraft.

6.8 An aircraft flying blind can keep track of its position by the sort of aided dead reckoning provided by the ground-position-indicator for some time after a fix in ground coordinates has been obtained. Even with further improvements in instrumentation there will remain the inherent limitation due to lack of precise knowledge of the wind. Airborne radar of reasonably high resolution permits, over land at least, contact flying or direct radar pilotage, which may be used on occasion as the sole means of navigation or may more usually serve to establish frequent fixes for an automatic dead-reckoning instrument. Not all aircraft will be able to afford the space for this facility, and, since the radar picture must be interpreted by a human observer, pilotless aircraft would be required to relay such a picture back to the controlling base.

6.9 A very important means of blind navigation is provided by the long range hyperbolic system, Loran, which has come into wide use. A detailed discussion of the future possibilities of this and related systems is included in the report of the consultants on radar. (See the SAG report, *Radar and Communication*.) We should call particular attention to the possibility of increasing the accuracy of such systems at very long range, which has an important bearing on the problem of guiding pilotless aircraft far beyond the horizon.

Obstacle Detection

6.10 Military operations require the simultaneous operation of large numbers of aircraft under blind conditions. The problem arises of avoiding collision. Any airborne radar with 360° view is capable of performing this function within the limitations imposed by its minimum range and resolving power. The minimum range is fundamentally limited by the pulse length; it is about 125 feet for a 1-microsecond pulse. Hence, while the airborne radar search set suffices to warn of the approach of other aircraft, it cannot be used to guide formation flying in blind conditions in the tight formations employed in clear weather. However, there seems to be no good reason for close formations in bad weather.

6.11 It would be possible to devise systems smaller and less elaborate than a complete search radar to perform solely the function of warning of obstacles. Whether these would be worthwhile in themselves depends on the type of formation flying, and the type of aircraft, which develop in the future.

Weather

6.12 Long range flights in general will be carried out at altitudes "over the weather" thus avoiding most disturbances caused by the weather situation. For this purpose it is generally sufficient to fly at 40,000 feet altitude at moderate latitude and at 50,000 feet altitude in the equatorial zone. Altitude flying involves certain equipment, especially supercharged engines and supercharged cabins. Problems occurring at high altitudes in gas turbine and jet engine operation have to be solved. Furthermore, problems of aeromedicine related to high altitude flying have to be pursued. (Cf. 7.11 to 7.15) The influence of wind will be automatically minimized by the high speed of future aircraft.

6.13 The age of the "All-Weather Air Force" is drawing nearer. However, it will never be possible to ignore the forces of weather. The key to all-weather flying lies in knowing what the weather will be, understanding its dangers, and circumventing them. Circumvention can be achieved through the development of special equipment (radar, new electronic aids, television) and through careful selection of flight paths. Use of equipment, choice of procedures, and determination of flight paths must be based on the weather forecast. The weather forecast is vital also to ground force operations. Fire control necessitates corrections for atmospheric conditions, chemical warfare cannot be conducted with precision when a weather forecast is lacking, soil trafficability is a function of the weather, and tactics and planning demand an evaluation of what future weather will be. No military operation is wholly freed from the weather; many are bound closely to it.

6.14 Wartime researches led to marked advances in upper aid analysis, weather forecasting, weather observation, and the application of weather information to military problems. Particularly noteworthy progress was made in upper air researches. Unprecedented quantities of upper air observations from all over the world provided the fundamental data. Researches led to the formulation of new methods of upper air analysis and to the extension and development of fundamental theories concerning the dynamics and structure of the upper air. Major advances were also made in long-range forecasting. Several long-range forecasting methods were developed and submitted to rigorous trial, using specially devised mathematical techniques to test their validity. The best methods were then utilized to prepare weather advice for pending military operations. The development of new scientific devices, for example, radar, made possible the development of new and improved instruments which extended the range and accuracy of meteorological measurements. In turn, the effective use of radar required additional meteorological studies.

6.15 Future research must be directed towards improving weather forecasting, obtaining vital knowledge concerning the upper atmosphere and ionosphere, and achieving all-weather flight. The theories and data obtained during the war must be carefully checked and sifted to develop new forecast tools. The advent of new weapons, such as the atomic bomb, guided missiles, robot planes, and very high ceiling aircraft makes it necessary to obtain observational data for the upper atmosphere and ionosphere and to develop theories that will make forecasting practicable for these high regions. This involves research in highly specialized branches of physics and meteorology, for such factors as cosmic rays, terrestrial magnetism, ionization, and special radiation effects become important in the high atmosphere. In the achievement of all-weather flight, the weather obstacles to be overcome in flight must be described and measured in detail if equipment and procedures to overcome the weather are to be successfully devised. The atmosphere is of ever-increasing importance as the medium through which the instruments of war are launched. Meteorology, the science of the atmosphere, is of ever-increasing importance to the military. To keep abreast of modern military developments, research in meteorology must be vigorously pursued.

6.16 The conditioning of weather over large territories has not been seriously considered in the past, however, the progress of meteorological science and the possibility of introducing in the air large amounts of energy by nuclear methods, might bring this aim into the realm of possibility. For example, the amount of energy required for forced local release of atmospheric instability in the case of convective storms and for the dissipation of fog should be within the limits of available energy from atomic sources. The general problem consists essentially of three parts: (1) exact knowledge of the weather parameters in the domain in which we want to produce changes, including both instantaneous values and their tendency of variation; (2) methods of computing the future weather, as dependent on the presence or absence of available control measures; and (3) means of applying the controls, such as adding energy in certain regions, modifying the reflection coefficient of certain areas, etc. It seems possible, with the aid of electronic computers, to produce a model of a certain region of the earth's surface and the existing weather situation, which can be used not only for fast weather prediction, but also for direct rapid experimentation, on a mode scale, with various control methods. (See the SAG report, *Weather*, by I. P. Krick.)

Defeat Enemy Interference

7.1 The fight for air superiority includes the annihilation of all the means the enemy has to take the air and the neutralization of his ground defenses. Hence, strategic bombing and the fight for air superiority are intimately interwoven; bombing missions promote air superiority, and the gain of air superiority increases the effectiveness of bombing missions. However, the possibility has to be envisaged that concentrated battles of air power against air power will be fought for control of the air, as battles were fought for superiority on land and on sea. Then, of course, superior experience, superior skill, and superior equipment will decide the outcome.

Armament vs. Speed

7.2 It is possible to develop large battleships of the air which would depend for protection on powerful, defensive armament including target-seeking missiles. It must be kept in mind, however, that they will be opposed by fighter airplanes with superior speed and maneuverability, of both the piloted and remotely-controlled variety. This suggests that a more effective method of defense against such attacks will be obtained by increasing the speed, the ceiling, and the maneuverability of the bomber to avoid the inevitable decrease in performance inherent in reliance on complex and necessarily heavy defensive armament. The problems are somewhat similar to those encountered in the past in building up sea power, and the future strategists of the air will have to decide on the relative merits of the different schools of thought which will probably develop.

7.3 As far as the technical problems are concerned, speed, maneuverability, rate of climb, and altitude, appear as the main requirements. Improvements in speed and rate of climb are determined by improvements in aerodynamics, propulsion, and lightweight construction. One particular difficulty with jet-propelled airplanes occurs when fast climbing from the ground is required. Although the rate of climb is excellent, the total time of reaching a certain altitude is handicapped by the fact that the best speed of climbing is relatively high, near the maximum speed. Consequently, considerable time is needed for acceleration of the plane near the ground. Probably means of assisted take-off will be needed to reduce the time of acceleration.

7.4 Present jet-propelled, fast airplanes lack, in some respects, the maneuverability of earlier fighter airplanes. This is a natural consequence of higher flying speeds, but steps must be taken to counteract it insofar as possible, in order to produce interceptors capable of pursuing successfully the fastest and most maneuverable enemy bombers. This requires the maintenance of lift to as large angles of attack as possible without stalling, particularly at high Mach numbers, and the use of as low wing loadings as are consistent with the requirements of high speed and range. In piloted aircraft this problem also involves the black out limit of the pilot, which must be maintained as high as possible by use of pressure suits and other aero-medical techniques, and probably by use of the prone position in very fast interceptors.

High Altitude

7.5 To secure air superiority it is necessary to reach equal or higher altitudes than the enemy. Rocket-driven airplanes are especially suitable for extreme altitudes, because their propulsion is independent of atmospheric air, although their flight duration is inherently limited. Hence, it will be necessary to use every possible means to adapt other types of jet propulsion to high altitudes. Improvements in combustion and improvements in compressor design are the main requirements, especially the elimination of difficulties which are encountered in compressor efficiency when supersonic flow occurs in the machine.

Human Limitations and Capabilities

7.6 The human element, both on the ground and in flight, is of paramount importance in global operations directed toward attaining air supremacy. The study of this element is the concern of aviation medicine which includes: (1) the initial selection of personnel on the basis of those human qualities which make for efficient combat airmen with emphasis on vision, hearing, reaction time, neuropsychiatric normality, cardio-respiratory efficiency, physical prowess and psychologic adaptability; (2) the training of aircrews in the technique which will enable them to perform efficiently, independently of weather and darkness, under the unusual stresses produced by high speed, high altitude, great maneuverability, rapid changes in barometric pressure with changing altitude, and instrument right and contact with the enemy; (3) the effect of flight on the human organism; (4) the maintenance of health, efficiency, and safety of flying personnel under all environmental conditions; and (5) a detailed consideration of human requirements and limitations in the design of aircraft, so that the airman-aircraft complex will be made into an efficient fighting element.

7.7 Inasmuch as human tolerance does not change, the steadily progressive increase in speed, ceiling, and potential maneuverability of aircraft has resulted in a progressively smaller margin between psycho-physiological requirements and human tolerance. Once supersonic speed is exceeded this margin will be of paramount importance in the operation of the aircraft. Hence, it is essential to determine under all conditions of flight the human tolerance as given by nature and the limits which can be attained as the result of selection, training, and the use of special protective devices, such as a G-suit, in order to utilize fully new aircraft in combat operations. Of necessity, the performance of present and future aircraft will be based in part on human limitations and capabilities.

7.8 An additional human factor is that once an aircraft is damaged and must be abandoned, the aeronautical engineer's problem is over but the problem of survival of the crew, wherever they may happen to be in the world, is just beginning.

7.9 High-speed flight and maneuverability result in certain hazards and stresses on the flyer. At the comparatively slow speed of 600 mph, 880 ft are traversed every second. Between the time the pilot receives an impulse to act and action by the pilot 0.2 sec elapses for simple reactions and he has traveled 176 ft without anything happening. For discriminative reactions the reaction time may be 0.4 sec or more. These times require that the controls be immediately at hand and that the flyer be alert. If the situation requires a change in the course of the airplane, aiming and firing a gun or carrying out other mechanical tasks, the total time lag increases (reaction time and mechanical lag). To keep this reactionless period at a minimum requires that pilots be selected who have the shortest possible reaction time. When two aircraft are approaching head on at a speed of 2000 mph there will be an extremely short interval of time from the instant when the crews of the two aircraft first see the other aircraft until the aircraft are passing. Obviously radar aids are essential. Danger of collision will be a real possibility.

7.10 When flying at very high speed, quick turns with resultant high acceleration of short duration may be a method of eluding guided missiles. Therefore, studies to determine the effects of comparatively high acceleration of from 1 to 5 sec duration on flying personnel is of vital importance. Also, the effects of exposure to negative acceleration immediately after exposure to positive acceleration and vice versa should be carefully investigated. The effect on acceleration tolerance of such factors as anoxia, cold, heat, febrile and post-febrile state and intake of food and fluids is virtually unknown. All acceleration suits should be incorporated into the flying suit. Determination of the maximum acceleration that can be tolerated when the pilot is in the prone position (approximately 10–12 g from the chest to the back) and still allow manipulation of the controls will allow the aeronautical engineer to design such aircraft to withstand higher acceleration than ever designed before. However, the tolerance of a man in the prone position to acceleration from the head to feet on take-off and feet to head on landing is known to be quite low.

7.11 Flight at high altitudes requires the use of oxygen by the crew. The oxygen equipment, now used by the Army Air Forces, gives flyers complete protection against anoxia up to altitudes of 37,000 ft. For continued flying efficiency above 37,000 ft, some form of added pressure must be used to protect the flyer. Pressure breathing (6in. water pressure) can increase the ceiling 2,000–3,000 ft. Pressure breathing used in connection with counterpressure pneumatic clothing can give protection for a few minutes as high as 60,000 ft. Pressure suits and pressure cabins, however, give the only complete protection at extreme altitude.

7.12 Aeroembolism (or bends) is a serious human limitation in high altitude flights and becomes increasingly significant above 30,000 ft. For one hour's exposure 35,000 ft, one person in ten would be incapacitated; one in four at 40,000 ft. Very few individuals can stay more than 20 min above 40,000 ft without suffering from aeroembolism. Prebreathing of oxygen for from ½ to 1 hr before flight can delay very considerably the onset of aeroembolism. On the other hand, exercises at altitude increases the danger of its onset.

7.13 Of the mechanical effects of altitude, the most serious is the rapid expansion of body gases, especially above 30,000 ft, which, if they exist, can cause painful abdominal discomfort. Extreme rates of decompression are well tolerated but compression rates above 1 psi/min are increasingly difficult to withstand except for specially trained and selected personnel.

7.14 All aircraft designed for extreme high-altitude flights (ten miles and up) must be equipped with pressure cabins and ideally should be maintained at an absolute pressure of 4.4 psi or over. Pressure suits have been built that satisfy this requirement but have proved to be extremely cumbersome and awkward.

7.15 Experiments on human subjects have shown that the human body can tolerate a relative expansion of internal gases of 2.3 during any explosive decompression of a pressure cabin or a pressure suit. Above 50,000 ft, however, it is virtually impossible to protect a pilot by proper choice of cabin pressure condition from both the dangers of anoxia and expanding internal gases. Loss of cabin pressure at any altitude above 50,000 ft will place the pilot in sufficient danger to require emergency protection from some form of pneumatic clothing, a practical version of which has yet to be developed.

7.16 Emergency escape from an aircraft, while traveling at extremely high speeds (transonic and supersonic), and at high altitudes (10–50 miles) will require many special considerations. A parachute must be developed that will relieve the very high expected opening shock and will be free of oscillation. For this purpose, the Germans developed the ribbon parachute. Emergency oxygen must be carried, probably in the parachute, and for bailouts above 50,000 ft, some protection must be provided against severe anoxia and aeroembolism. Methods must be provided to eject the flyer free of his damaged ship. Ejection seats as an escape method are only practical for subsonic speeds. Full-face oxygen masks will protect the face from wind blast and cold. The concept of an ejectable cockpit, properly pressurized, is at present the best probable solution to escape at extreme altitudes. For such a cockpit, a stabilizing parachute is required as the speed drops through the transonic range. Larger parachutes free of severe opening shocks will be required to reduce descent to a safe value for striking the ground. Alternately, the cockpit could be unsealed automatically below 50,000 ft and allow a conventional parachute descent. Automatic opening devices should be used throughout the sequence of events.

7.17 The high skin temperature of supersonic aircraft will require special protection for the pilot against heat prostration. Air-cooled flying clothing will be a requirement. Proper choice of insulation on the cabin will be a factor. As the speed of the aircraft drops to subsonic levels, protection against the cold for the pilot must be considered.

7.18 Since some rocket-propelled aircraft may use liquid oxygen as one of the fuel components, this liquid could be used as a source of cabin pressurization, as a source of oxygen for the pilot, and as a method of cooling an air ventilated duct for protection against excessive cabin heat. For rocket propulsion, using toxic liquids or atomic energy sources, protection must be given the pilot against noxious gases or radiation.

Countermeasures

7.19 High speed, maneuverability, and high altitude are the means of escaping interference from ground defenses. However, we must attribute to the enemy the same highly developed weapons of defense which we try to develop. Hence, it appears imperative to have in our airplanes means for detection and deflection of target-seeking devices aimed at them. This is one of the many problems which concern countermeasures against new remote-controlled or homing devices.

7.20 A technically competent enemy will try to thwart our operations by countermeasures directed at our own electronic devices for the collection of information and the transmission of intelligence and control. The vulnerability of a target-finding radar to jamming is no less important than the vulnerability to fighter attack of the vehicle which carries the radar and the bomb. We have seen in the war just past a lively battle of weapon and counter-weapon in the fields of radio and radar. At certain times we enjoyed the advantage of a new technique, temporarily unknown to the enemy, and hence, of a period when a new device (for example, microwave ASV radar) could be used with impunity. It would not be wise to count on many such advantages in the future, and it is, therefore, important to assess the vulnerability of new devices at an early stage of their development. In the reports of the individual consultants on radar, communications, infrared, and guided missiles, the specific problems of countermeasures are taken up. It is worthwhile to present here certain broad conclusions which emerge from these studies:

a. The fact that an electronic device can, in principle, be jammed (and most of them can) does not necessarily mean that it will be jammed so as to impair seriously its military value. The problem of jamming, realistically considered, is not merely one of ingenuity, of which we must assume that the enemy has an unlimited supply, but of electric power and energy and well-known physical laws. It may be made uneconomical for the enemy to interfere with some device of ours, even though he regards it as a serious threat.

b. The developments in radar and related fields which promise the most in freedom from enemy interference are the use of a diversity of frequency channels, rapid tuning from one channel to another, higher power, and where consistent with other requirements, more directive beams of radiation. The opening up of the microwave region of the spectrum has, on the whole, made the task of the would-be jammer much more formidable.

c. Radio links used for remote guiding and control, or for transfer of intelligence from and to unmanned aircraft, will probably make more and more use of the "combination-lock" type of security, exemplified by electronic pulse coding and decoding in contrast to the "concealed-button" type of security, which involves the dangerous assumption that the enemy cannot readily discover what we are doing.

d. Concealment and camouflage against detection by radar and other means have been developed vigorously and will continue to develop. We must keep active and alert in this field, if only to be able to anticipate the countermeasures to which our devices may fall victim.

e. In general, electronic warfare puts a premium on ingenuity, speed, adaptability, and alertness. Against the countermeasures of a determined and technically advanced enemy our only permanent military assets are well-informed, resourceful, scientific personnel, and a flexible production organization.

Perfect Communication from Ground to Air and From Air to Air

8.1 The preceding discussion has assumed accurate and reliable communication between the airplanes involved, and between the airplanes and their base. Present aviation communication, while fairly satisfactory, still lacks a good deal in reliability and ability to make contact. However, if the present rate of development continues, the requirements of the projected Air Forces can be met in a relatively few years.

8.2 At present the communication problem is divided into two parts:

a. Liaison communication for the long-range transfer of information between individual airplanes or flights of airplanes and their base, distances from a few hundred miles to several thousand miles.

b. Command communication between the members of a group or formation of planes.

8.3 Future aviation communication will undoubtedly retain these two subdivisions, and will probably include a third, namely short-range communication between air bases and airplanes, for the purpose of guiding offensive operations, traffic direction, and landing control. This may include visual presentation by television and instrument indication, as well as voice communication.

8.4 The liaison system must operate on frequencies between one and ten megacycles. This is because radiations at higher frequencies follow essentially line-of-sight paths, while lower frequencies, such as are used for transoceanic communication, require antenna lengths which cannot be accom-modated, even in the largest bombers. In order to obtain communication at a distance in the frequency range available for liaison work, it is necessary to depend upon ionospheric reflection, and to obtain reliability it is essential to select from among eight or ten bands in this region. Because of these limitations, liaison communication is limited to between five and ten speech channels. This means communication must be very highly organized in order to economize the needed channels.

8.5 The use of teletype systems and special voice coding can greatly reduce the frequency bandwidth required for a communication channel. By adopting these means, a great many more channels become available. This may become an important part of liaison.

8.6 Long-distance communication of the liaison type may be supplemented by a high-frequency relay system. This will make available a large number of channels, which can be used for liaison. However, the longer wavelength direct liaison channels must be retained in the event the relay chain is broken.

8.7 Command communication allows a much greater latitude in the selection of the frequency at which it can operate, since only line-of-sight is required. In practice it will be carried on at as high a frequency as possible, in order to make available a maximum of communication channels, limited only by the state of technical development, antenna considerations, and the molecular absorption of the air.

8.8 At present, command systems operate at frequencies around a hundred megacycles. In the immediate future the frequency should be increased by a factor of at least ten, and perhaps much more. There will be available a large number of communication channels at these upper frequencies, so that each airplane in the group or formation can be assigned individual channels, in addition to general and emergency channels shared by the whole group.

8.9 The channel space available can be used not only to give a large number of bands, but also to protect the system from jamming, interference, and interception, by using special forms of modulation, multiple channels, or other refinements.

8.10 With the large number of channels to be employed in this type of operation, it is imperative that the individual units be integrated into a closely knit practical system. This can be done following practices similar to those employed in ordinary telephone systems. Each airplane in the formation would be assigned a frequency or pair of frequencies on which he would communicate with anyone calling him. In order to call another airplane, the calling transmitter and receiver would be tuned to the frequency of the station being called, simply by manipulating a numbered dial similar to a telephone dial. While certain problems connected with frequency stability remain, steps have already been taken toward their solution in the use of a single stabilized oscillator to control the frequency of both transmitter and receiver, various feedback systems, and similar measures. In such a network it would be essential that certain master channels be kept open at all times for the reception of general commands and emergency instruction. Since these channels must be available whether or not a station is calling another airplane, this arrangement may require some duplication of equipment. This will not be seriously objectionable, because short-range, high-frequency radio equipment can be made relatively small.

8.11 Certain command operations may be aided by highly directional transmission. Communication of this type can be carried out very efficiently in the microwave portions of the radio spectrum. Laboratory models of receivers and transmitters are at present in existence, and the technical availability of this equipment is assured.

8.12 The extremely high-frequency portion of the radio spectrum, that is 60,000 megacycles or more, has certain properties which may be of value for short-range command systems. Here the molecular absorption of the atmosphere begins to be important. This means that the signal is attenuated very rapidly with distance. Thus, it would be possible to carry on communication between airplanes in a formation and yet maintain radio silence as far as ground detector or more distant airplanes are concerned. However, before such equipment becomes available for practical aviation application, it must go through a long period of research and development.

8.13 For single-seat fighters and other aircraft where one man must perform a great many operations, as well as act as radio operator, it may be necessary to supplement voice communication with an indicating system, with a semipermanent record of the message. Developmental equipment of this type has already been produced in the form of the British "Beechnut" and American "Volflag." These units not only give an annunciator presentation of the message, to be read by the pilot, but also give an automatic answer-back when the equipment correctly records the signal. This type of equipment can be made highly selective and jam-proof.

8.14 Facsimile may also serve as an adjunct to voice communication. It allows the transmission of large amounts of information over a relatively narrow channel. Furthermore, this information is in the form of a permanent record. The information which can be transmitted may be in the form of maps, pictures, or charts, in addition to written words, which in itself can be of considerable value. Because the bandwidth required is somewhat greater than is needed for speech transmission, it probably will not be used as liaison equipment, but will be operated at command frequencies and on radio relay chains.

8.15 In order to carry out successfully large-scale aerial operations under all weather conditions, it is necessary to provide very complete contact between the air base and airplanes leaving or approaching the base. When large numbers of airplanes are involved, voice communication will not be adequate, but must be supplemented by some form of visual aid. A modification of the "Teleran" system can provide the required contact. With this system, the location and altitude of all airplanes in the neighborhood of the base are determined by radar equipment at the ground station. This information is electronically plotted on maps of the terrain, dividing the space above the air base into a predetermined number of levels. A picture of the map and the airplanes at a given level is transmitted by television to the airplanes at the level. Thus, the pilot of every airplane at each level knows the whereabouts of every other airplane at his altitude, and the danger of collision is greatly reduced. The transmitted map carries with it appropriate meteorological information and any instructions that may be necessary. Blind landing and take-off aids are also provided for airplanes at the lowest level.

8.16 This system gives the ground station complete control of the airplanes in the vicinity and makes possible the concentration of large numbers of aircraft with relatively little danger. It also makes it possible for the air station to direct the grouping of large airplane formations and perform other functions necessary in carrying out air activities on a large scale.

8.17 The three classes of communication described will provide for the interchange of information required for integrated air activity on a large scale. In its present state of development, the radio art is in a position to supply most of the technical means for liaison, command, and air-base control. However, radio research should be encouraged in order to improve present means and develop new equipment giving better performance. (See the report, *Aircraft Radio Communication Equipment*, Part III of the SAG report, *Radar and Communications.)*

Defend Home Territory

Detection and Warning

9.1 The first problem of defense is detection and warning. The successful defense of England was attributed largely to long-wavelength, early warning radar, installed at the time of the Munich agreement. This equipment could detect aircraft at a range of 150 miles at normal cruising altitudes, although its resolution was so low that it could not separate as distinct indications two aircraft 10 or 15 miles apart. Aircraft at low altitudes could not be detected. Had the Germans known the limitations of the equipment, they could have defeated its use.

9.2 These early types of equipment, operating on wavelengths of ten and three meters, were succeeded by microwave equipment of much greater resolution. The range of all types is essentially limited by the optical horizon. It is possible to build equipment capable of detecting all aircraft flying below any given altitude and above the optical horizon with a resolution and position accuracy of the order of 150 feet, under normal atmospheric conditions. It is possible to eliminate from the indicator all targets which are not moving. Hence, the area covered will be determined by the height of the set and the screening by surrounding hills. The height can be increased by using airborne sets, but the size of the available aircraft limits such equipment to lower weight and power, which in turn limits the range to about 200 miles.

9.3 Identification of the detected aircraft as friendly or hostile is a major problem. Identification beacons have been found to be only a partial solution. Reliance has to be placed in large measure on knowledge of the flight plan and of the progress of the flights of all friendly aircraft, identifying unfriendly aircraft by a process of elimination. Advances in communication techniques will probably supply additional aid in identification.

9.4 Unsolved problems in detection and warning are the ability of aircraft to fly low, so that they remain below the optical horizon until very close, and the problem of detecting missiles like V-2, coming in from the stratosphere at steep angles outside the angles covered by present radar warning sets. The first may be solved by the use of airborne search radar sensitive only to moving targets. The second requires only additional engineering development to improve the high-altitude coverage.

9.5 The provision of warning alone, without methods of defeating the attack, is useless. The warning network must be integrated with the control of fighter and missile squadrons.

Countermeasures Against Missiles

9.6 The second great problem of defense of home territory is countermeasures against missiles. We shall not here discuss passive measures, such as dispersion of industry, underground location of key targets, etc., but only the active measures against the missile in flight. So far as known at present, the possible active measures against atomic bombs do not differ from those against missiles carrying ordinary explosives. Such measures will be directed to deflect the attack by electronic disturbances, to produce premature explosion, and finally to hit or destroy the missiles by blast or fragmentation from warheads of defensive missiles.

9.7 Any missile using remote radio control, electronic homing devices, or proximity fuses, can in theory be jammed. In practice it is necessary to know something of the method of operation and to adapt jamming equipment to the particular enemy device. The information may be obtained either by intelligence methods, by continuous search of the electromagnetic spectrum, or by examination of captured equipment. There is no blanket over-all method of jamming which would defeat any and all types of electronic apparatus. This method of defense requires extremely close cooperation between intelligence officers, special reconnaissance patrols, and electronics specialists engaged in development of jamming equipment.

9.8 Missiles using homing devices may be deceived by decoy targets. Thus a missile using heat radiation could be decayed by artificial targets. This device is of limited application, since techniques of target selection are known, and the enemy must be assumed to possess them. It would be difficult, if not impossible, to locate a decoy target within the field of view if a missile were directed toward the real target and yet far enough away to be outside the radius of destruction of an atomic bomb.

9.9 Many persons have suggested the possibility of producing premature explosion or otherwise incapacitating missiles by means of some form of ray. If the missile carries a proximity fuse, it may indeed be possible to operate it by a suitable electronic jammer and thus explode the bomb, whether it consists of atomic or ordinary explosive. In the absence of a proximity fuse or of a system for remote electronic control of detonation, science offers no prospect of detonation at a distance. The interaction of electromagnetic radiation with matter has been thoroughly investigated from long radio waves through microwaves, infrared, visible light, ultraviolet, X rays, gamma rays, to cosmic rays. Our ability to concentrate radiant energy at a distant point is limited by a fundamental property of wave motion in an unbounded medium, i.e., the tendency of the waves to spread. Even if twice the total electric power of the United States were placed in a single beam from a reflector 50 feet in diameter, the intensity at one mile would just reach the sparking voltage in air. Furthermore, shielding is relatively easy, because of the high inductivity of metals. The very shortest rays cannot be focused, and the energy decreases as the inverse square of the distance. Thus, present scientific knowledge offers no hope for, but on the contrary distinct evidence against, the possibility of detonating bombs at a distance.

9.10 No serious attempt has yet been made to hit a projectile or missile moving with, say, twice the velocity of sound. However, by adapting the target-seeking principle to winged rocket projectiles, it should be possible to accomplish this aim, provided location and warning occur sufficiently in advance. Another principle would be that of a barrage of aerial mines; however, it does not appear possible to increase the density of the barrage to such an extent that the missile would not slip through. Certainly both methods should be studied.

9.11 Against aircraft, manned or unmanned, moving with sonic or slightly higher velocity, target-seeking automatic interceptors seem to give most promise. The German project Wasserfall, the British CAP project, and some of our own undertakings move in this direction. Ramjet propulsion seems to be the most efficient way to reach the necessary speed and flight duration.

9.12 Manned interceptors will be developed, as well as automatic devices. For this purpose both rocket and jet propulsion drive should be considered. For extreme altitudes, the rocket may be the only method of propulsion which promises success. Because of human limitations, manned interceptors probably cannot be used against extremely high-speed unmanned missiles.

Offense is Best Defense

9.13 One possibility in the future may be the rocket barrage with atomic warhead. This could be used against aircraft or missiles traveling at high altitude. If the range of the effect of the atomic explosion is exactly known (estimated as about two miles for the present atomic bomb) and atomic explosion is possible in devices of reduced size, damage on our own territory can be avoided. Especially, attack from the high seas could be prevented by projecting the barrage at a sufficient distance out to sea.

9.14 While it is profitable to develop as effective means as possible for both active and passive defense against enemy action, it must be remembered that a purely defensive attitude is defeatist. A nation which relies solely on defense for its security is inviting disaster. England might well have become untenable if only defensive measures had been relief [sic] on to stop the V-2 attacks. These attacks were only stopped after use of the launching sites had been denied the enemy. Japan's defeat was assured when she failed to deny us access to air bases from which we could attack the homeland itself. The best defense is adequate preparation for a strong offense.

Chapter III

Problems of Organization with Recommendations

Fundamental Principles for Organization of Research

10.1 The spectacular innovations in technological warfare which appeared with ever increasing momentum in World War II have made us extremely conscious of the necessity for continuous scientific research to insure maintenance of our national security. The legislative and executive branches of the government, industry, and science are now intensively engaged in finding the best form of organization and the most efficient scheme for uniting all efforts to create the best facilities and utilize all the available scientific talents. Many of the fundamental questions of organization will be decided after the legislative work has been done. However, it is of the utmost importance that the Air Forces lay down the leading principles of their own policy and establish the foundation of organized research in their own realm.

10.2 The basic principles of the responsibilities of the Air Forces in the scientific domain may be formulated as follows:

a. The Air Forces have the fundamental responsibility for insuring that the nation is prepared to wage effective air warfare. This responsibility cannot be delegated to any other government agency or scientific body.

b. The Air Forces must be able to call on all talents and facilities existing in the nation and sponsor further development of facilities and creative work of scientists and industry.

c. The Air Forces must have the means of recruiting and training personnel who will have full understanding of the scientific facts necessary to procure and use equipment which is more advanced than that used by any other nation.

d. The Air Forces must be authorized to expand existing AAF research facilities and create new ones to do their own research and also to make such facilities available to scientists and industrial concerns working on problems of the Air Forces.

10.3 During World War II, the Air Forces enjoyed the fruits of research work being done by several scientific bodies organized or called upon for the duration of the war. Moreover, the whole scientific manpower of the nation was available to the services, and a great portion of it to the Army Air Forces. How to secure the cooperation of science and industry during peacetime is a very difficult problem.

10.4 Unfortunately it is not possible to establish the necessary link between science and industry on one side and the Air Forces on the other, by establishing contact and agreement at the top level only. It would be simple to establish an office of organized science and agree to allot scientific problems to such an office and military problems to the Air Forces. However, scientific results cannot be used efficiently by soldiers who have no understanding of them, and scientists cannot produce results useful for warfare without an understanding of the operations. The following sections present certain recommendations which may have some value for the solution of the problem.

Cooperation Between Science and the Air Forces

11.1 It is generally recognized that an adequate national program for extending the frontiers of knowledge in various fields of basic science is a necessary adjunct to the maintenance of military security of the nation. Every scientific development eventually finds its way into the field of military applications. However, basic research requires time. Wars are fought with weapons based on fundamentals discovered during the preceding years of peace. Discovery of fundamental results is dependent on an atmosphere of freedom from immediate specific goals and time tables.

11.2 For these reasons government authorities, military or civilian, should foster, but not dictate, basic research. The successful conduct of such research requires freedom and continuity of effort and cannot be accomplished by intermittent contacts for small tasks. Research staffs cannot be assembled and dispersed at short intervals. In addition, parallel competitive attacks on research problems do not constitute wasteful duplication. Coordination should take the form of exchange of information, rather than centralized dictatorial control of projects, funds, and facilities.

11.3 The Air Forces do not desire to do basic scientific research in their own organizations; however, they wish to encourage and sponsor such research as they deem necessary for the defense of the nation.

11.4 At the present time there is a tendency to concentrate the direction of scientific research activities in one controlling organization and make this organization responsible for the production of scientific results needed by the services, for the development of new weapons and equipment. Such centralization can be detrimental to American science, if it means exclusion of independent individuals and small groups of research men whose contributions are vital to the maintenance of an abundant scientific life within a nation.

11.5 Generally it may be said that the conception and initial development of new ideas often come from men and groups which are widely dispersed and not directly connected with central organizations and planned research. Jet propulsion and atomic energy are good examples of this thesis. In both fields individual initiative, not dictated by any preconceived plan, played an important part, both in this country and abroad. If free enterprise and initiative are necessary for maintaining a sound economy within a nation, certainly they are even more necessary in scientific life.

11.6 It is imperative from this point of view that the Air Forces continue and expand their present direct relations, spiritual and contractual, with various universities, research laboratories, and individual scientists. None of the central organizations existing now and to be established should be the only source of information and the sole intermediary agency between science and the Air Forces. The Air Forces should have the freedom to call on institutions and individuals whose assistance they deem to be of the greatest benefit for their program.

11.7 The ideal goal is, on one side, the creation of a scientific atmosphere in the Air Forces, on the other side, the maintaining of a permanent interest of scientific workers in problems of the Air Forces. The handling of research on applications of nuclear physics by some military authorities gives an interesting example of how scientific people can be antagonized by too much command.

11.8 The physical attributes of scientific life are libraries, laboratories, publications, society meetings. The main impediment to high-grade cooperative scientific activity in the past has been the conflicting philosophy of scientists and soldiers in handling scientific matters. An unavoidable difficulty is introduced, of course, by the security restrictions necessitated by the character of military research. However, it is believed that this problem can be successfully solved.

11.9 The first requirement for successful scientific collaboration is an efficient method of making the material contained in the archives of the Air Forces and other military bodies accessible to those scientific workers who are cleared for classified information and whose cooperation is desired. The lack of such an organized library service has in the past been one of the great impediments to scientific work. The Air Documents Division, established recently at Wright Field, may be the nucleus for the development of an efficient library and information service.

11.10 Concerning the laboratory work, it is recommended that Army Air Force personnel be assigned to civilian laboratories, in order to acquire an intimate knowledge of scientific research to permit them to evaluate correctly scientific facts and effectively direct and supervise research in the Air Forces laboratories. However, the personnel assigned to civilian laboratories should not be there as supervising or liaison officers, but merely to learn. On the other hand, it is recommended that the Air Forces develop a scientific reserve corps familiar with current military problems, as a pool for active service in wartime. Younger scientists, who were working on projects in various civilian organizations during the war, would constitute admirably fit candidates for this reserve corps.

11.11 The employment of civilian consultants, which was authorized for the duration of the emergency, should be continued in peacetime. The wide variety of research and development problems facing the Air Forces definitely requires that the Air Forces be able to call upon specialists from time to time and for limited periods, in order to obtain the best advice and comprehensive reports on selected topics of current interest.

11.12 During the war several laboratories, established by the services and the NDRC, in close connection with universities and directed by scientists belonging to the universities, made important contributions. This favorable result suggests the establishment of cooperative laboratories, in which the administrative and financial responsibility and management would remain with the government, and the scientific direction would be undertaken by faculty members. This method would solve the security problem and yet have the advantages of the geographical and spiritual connection with a place of scientific learning.

11.13 In the field of publications and meetings, it is recommended that the interest of scientists in military problems be cultivated by sponsoring a society for military sciences, whose membership and publications would be restricted in conformity with security regulations. Air Forces personnel should be given membership in this society and permission to discuss and publish the results of their endeavors in the classified publications of the society.

11.14 The following recommendations are therefore made:

a. Direct research contracts between the Air Forces and scientific institutions.

b. Library of classified material, to be made available to scientists who have been cleared.

c. Exchange of personnel between the Air Forces and civilian laboratories.

d. Authorization for temporary employment of scientific consultants.

e. Cooperative laboratories in close connection with universities.

f. Scientific society for military sciences, with membership requiring clearance, and classified publications.

Cooperation Between Industry and the Air Forces

12.1 This report does not deal with problems of procurement. Thus the analysis and recommendations are restricted to the problems of research and development to be done cooperatively by the Air Forces and industry.

12.2 The main field in which industry and the Air Forces will work in close cooperation is applied research and development. It is imperative that the Air Forces separate funds and management of development contracts from procurement contracts. In the past, much time and effort have been wasted by lack of a clear line between procurement and development. Development contracts should also be based on competition, since the competitive spirit probably produces the best solution in the shortest time. However, competition in scientific and development work is different in its nature from pure commercial competition.

414

12.3 The main objective in separating research and development from procurement is to make it possible for industry and the talent available in the industry to carry on applied research, which is absolutely necessary for rapid progress in the articles to be produced. Some industrial companies own facilities and funds for this purpose, as for example, the large companies producing electrical equipment, automobiles, and chemical products. These companies practice mass production and have a wide market for their products; therefore, they are able to do applied (in some cases even basic) research for the purpose of improving their products or of reducing the cost of production. In the case of the aircraft industry, it is generally recognized that the government must at least partially support the costs of applied research, because many of the problems refer solely to military applications and the costs of development cannot be recovered by the sale of the product. It is believed that it is more advantageous for the Air Forces to pay for the research needed than to pay higher prices for the products which would include the costs of development.

12.4 Supersonic flight and pilotless airplanes will undoubtedly create a gap between aircraft used in civilian life and in aerial warfare. Consequently certain parts of the aircraft industry will be engaged in developments which have no commercial value and will not result in large orders from the government during peacetime. It is then necessary that promising developments of this type be carried through the pilot-plant stage with the financial support of the Air Forces. These pilot plants should be able to furnish the quantity necessary for tactical evaluation of the equipment. In addition, all preparations must be made for securing a rapid expansion of production of both materials (such as special fuels and propellants) and devices (like missiles, electronic equipment, etc.).

12.5 Many problems require facilities which are only available to the government. In the past NACA, at the request of the armed services, carried out most of the tests necessary to improve the characteristics of experimental airplane types. It is believed that it would be more advantageous for the general progress if the NACA were relieved of the duty of testing and improving experimental types and could concentrate on forward-looking investigations on questions of basic and applied science. The testing and research for immediate improvement of experimental types should be taken over by the Air Forces and new facilities should be created which allow the carrying out of such tests on a large scale. The design of new facilities should take into account the probable development in the next decades.

12.6 The air lines will be an important factor in any future warfare, since their equipment and experienced personnel constitute a valuable reserve for organized transportation between the mainland and bases distributed over the world. Hence, a close connection between the air lines and the Air Forces is necessary. In the operational field, as in the field of airplane and engine development, the natural development is that the facilities of the Air Forces should be used for perfecting operational methods, such as traffic control, landing aids, etc.

12.7 The following recommendations are therefore made:

a. Separation of funds and management of research and development contracts from procurement contracts.

b. Design of Air Forces facilities for applied research and development, both in the field of technology and operations, on such a scale that they can be made available to the industry producing equipment and the companies engaged in air transportation, to carry out the research necessary for the development desired by the Air Forces.

c. Promising developments of the nonrevenue-producing type should be placed in pilot plant production to such an extent that the Air Forces can obtain a sufficient number for tactical evaluation of the special equipment and devices to be used in case of war.

d. Rapid expansion of production facilities for such items should be adequately provided for by the development contracts.

Adequate Facilities in the Air Forces for Research and Development

13.1 Scientific research in the Air Forces embraces not only the application of the physical sciences for production of efficient equipment, but should refer to all phases of aerial warfare which require scientific thought and analysis. For example, it should include problems of a physiological and psychological nature, as well as the scientific analysis of operations and methods of prognosis of the effects of planned operations.

13.2 In the past, especially in the last prewar years and during the war, the Air Forces developed research and testing equipment at Wright Field for aircraft, engines, armament and other equipment, materials, and also for aeromedicine and physiology. At Eglin Field a proving ground was established for equipment to be tested under field conditions and for the study of effects of means of destruction. These facilities, in the light of future development, appear definitely inadequate, even from the purely technical viewpoint of producing and testing efficient equipment.

13.3 There is no doubt that electronic devices will play an increasingly important part in all future Air Forces operations. In the past, the history of electronic applications has usually been that a device was developed for ground use, and then, some time later, its value to the Air Forces was realized, and after suffering severe and prolonged redesigning, it finally becomes useable in the air. Almost invariably this process of redesign was carried out by engineers with no real knowledge of the special problems of aircraft. In other words, the aeronautical engineers have had no appreciation of the possible value of electronics in solving their problems, and the electronic engineers have had no knowledge of the difficulties their equipment would experience on aircraft. Electronic equipment has been added to planes as an afterthought, with consequent difficulties of installation and operation. Even in the case of radar, it was not until 1944 that a group of radar scientists and aeronautical engineers conferred for the

417

purpose of studying the uses of radar and discussing the problems of installing radar equipment in planes.

13.4 Future controlled missiles are completely dependent on electronic devices. They must be designed by electronic and aeronautical engineers working in close cooperation. Instrument flying requires that the electronic equipment be designed by persons familiar with aeronautical problems.

13.5 In the age of moderate speed airplanes with conventional engine-propeller drive, it was possible to carry out development work on separate components. Supersonic airplanes and pilotless aircraft cannot be developed successfully by such methods. Questions of aerodynamics, structures, propulsion, and control are closely interconnected. The component parts of a guided missile cannot be made to function independently any more than can any one organ of the human body. Based on these considerations, it is proposed that the Air Forces create new facilities, under one command, entirely separated from procurement and supply, with the objective of developing supersonic and pilotless aircraft.

13.6 The Center for Supersonic and Pilotless Aircraft Development (SPAD) should be equipped with adequate wind-tunnel facilities to attain speeds up to three times the velocity of sound, with large enough test sections to accommodate models of reasonable size, including jet propulsion units, and one ultrasonic wind tunnel for exploration of the upper frontier of the supersonic speed range. Ample facilities for the study of combustion and other characteristics of propulsion systems at very high altitudes should be provided. Electronic engineers should be given the necessary facilities to study control methods, servo-mechanisms, and homing devices in close cooperation with aerodynamicists and propulsion experts. The Development Center should also provide facilities for investigations of the human aspects of flight at supersonic speed and extreme altitudes. The facilities for experimental launching, flight research, and flight analysis should be integral parts of the Development Center.

13.7 It is believed that the Air Forces program in the field of supersonic and pilotless aircraft urgently needs the establishment of such a central organization to lead the activities of the scientific institutions and industrial companies to new horizons; and, to make facilities available for research and development work, necessary, beyond a doubt, for maintaining our supremacy in the air.

13.8 It is proposed that research and development in the field of aircraft operations, communications, and weather service be consolidated into a Center for Operational Aircraft Development (OAD), with the objective of approaching the ideal of the all weather Air Forces, solving the problems of traffic control, fighter control, and of warning and location. This Center should be equipped with adequate laboratory facilities for applications of radar television technique. Experimental bases for testing control and communication devices should be integral parts of this Center. It should cooperate closely with the air lines and the weather service.

13.9 It is believed that the proving ground at Eglin Field should be put in charge of development of bombing devices and procedures, and study of bombing survey and analysis methods.

13.10 It is proposed that a Center for Nuclear Aircraft Development (NAD) be initiated, dealing with problems arising in connection with atomic bombs and the use of atomic energy for aircraft propulsion.

13.11 The organizations and facilities suggested in this chapter cannot be created in one year, but must be developed gradually in coordination with the work of other interested military and civilian agencies. On the other hand, it is my conviction that unless the Air Forces begin systematically building up development centers with competent personnel and adequate testing facilities, they will unavoidably lose the lead and initiative in fields which in a few years will constitute the domains of their most vital responsibilities.

Summary of Recommendations

13.12 The following recommendations are therefore made:

a. Research and development in the field of aerodynamics, propulsion, control, and electronics should function as one entity.

b. A Center for Supersonic and Pilotless Aircraft Development (SPAD) should be established, with adequate wind-tunnel, propulsion, control, and electronic research facilities.

c. A Center for Operational Aircraft Development (OAD) should be established for research and development in the operational field, such as all-weather flight problems, communications, and fighter control.

d. A Center for Nuclear Aircraft Development (NAD) should be initiated.

e. Eglin Field should be developed into a research and development center for bombing technique, research on blast effects, and bombing survey and analysis methods.

Induction of Scientific Ideas in Staff and Command Work

Long-Range Planning

14.1 Scientific planning must be years ahead of the actual research and development work. Long-range planning should be the responsibility of the Commanding General of the Air Forces. I believe there is general agreement throughout the nation that in the past decades the direct interest of the Commanding General in long-range planning has been one of the most important assets of the former Air Corps and the present Air Forces. This philosophy should be preserved in the future. From this point of view, it is advisable that a permanent Scientific Advisory Group, consisting of qualified officers and eminent civilian scientists, should be available to the Commanding General, reporting directly to him on

420

important new developments and advising him on the planning of scientific research. It is considered that the advice and contributions of persons who, although thoroughly familiar with the work and the needs of the Air Forces, have their main activity outside of the Army, would be of considerable value. This group should contain experts with broad experience in the various branches of science involved, who would represent a cross section of our scientific thought. Their reports to the Commanding General would be used to effect continuous revision of the Air Forces research and development program.

Management of Research and Development

14.2 The problem of the best organization of management and development is a very difficult one. It cannot be expected that unanimous agreement can be reached on this question. The plan for management of research and development is a sore point in all large organizations or companies. It mostly undergoes periodic changes, which emphasize one or the other side of the question, ranging from separate and almost independent research laboratories to decentralization of research and development into the operating units. In the special case of the Air Forces, two solutions have been proposed: (1) the establishment of one Air Staff section for research and development; and (2) a supervising and directing agency attached to the office of the Chief of Air Staff. Both solutions have advantages and disadvantages. Obviously it would be extremely difficult to remove the actual operation of all research and development facilities from all the various existing staff sections and concentrate them in one new section. On the other hand, the central supervising and directing agency would have a hard task introducing new ideas into the operation of a large number of dispersed sections and commands engaged in research and development.

14.3 Independently of the special form of management of research and development, the office in charge of direction and supervision of research should establish panels consisting of representatives of other agencies engaged in aeronautical and related research, for example, the National Advisory Committee for Aeronautics, the National Bureau of Standards, the Civil Aeronautics Administration, the aircraft industry, the air lines, scientific institutions, and individual scientists. These panels should assist in formulation of the detailed research program and the choice of the agency, institution, or individual best fitted and available to carry out the desired research work.

Scientific Intelligence

14.4 Scientific intelligence is one of the important requirements for the future Air Forces. In the recent past the necessity for an organized scientific intelligence service became more and more evident as the war proceeded, and it became an urgent necessity as Germany collapsed. Fortunately, at that time a great number of scientists and technicians could be made available to the Air Forces on a voluntary basis. In this way the information gained from Germany could be worked up in an appropriate manner. However, at the present time, only a few months later, no more such personnel is available. The supervision of future German scientific work, for example, is still lacking scientific help.

14.5 Scientific intelligence starts at home. The example of the atomic bomb show that scientific discoveries of prominent military importance were made by pure scientists who had no connection with any military office or establishment; as a matter of fact, they were not interested in military applications. Hence, it will be necessary for the Intelligence Service to employ scientific personnel with broad interest and knowledge, who have the ability to recognize the military aspects in the scientific production of our theoretical and experimental scientists, university, and industrial laboratories. The screening of patents and inventive ideas presented to the military agencies, as it has been done in the past, will not be sufficient. The Intelligence Service needs permanent collaborators who pursue the scientific literature, attend meetings, visit scientific establishments, and report their findings and suggestions periodically. In peacetime much tact will be necessary to accomplish such efficient intelligence service, because of the commercial interests involved and the natural inclination of scientific men not to talk about their results before the final rounding up of their work.

14.6 Scientific intelligence in foreign countries is, of course, a much more difficult matter. One can distinguish between scientific intelligence on subjects which are open to discussion and on subjects which are classified. I believe that all knowledge of scientific life in a foreign country is of great importance since, after all, the same scientific personalities who create the peacetime science of a country will be called upon to help their country in wartime. Therefore, it is strongly recommended that the Air Forces: (1) have scientific attachés in embassies and legations in various countries; (2) send scientifically trained officers, engineers, or consultants of the Air Forces to scientific meetings and congresses abroad; and (3) send personnel connected with the Air Forces for longer periods to study at foreign institutions.

14.7 The intelligence services concerned with subjects which a foreign country does not want us to know, will use the methods which were successful in general military intelligence. However, it is imperative to have a scientific section in the Intelligence Service which will direct the search for and exploit the results of scientific data. It is imperative that we have knowledge, in advance, of all potential targets which could be of importance in scientific warfare, unless a complete exchange of scientific and technical data, as proposed recently by Great Britain, extends over the whole world.

Science In Plans and Operations

14.8 The Air Forces entered into World War II with quite inadequate preparation as far as the prognosis and analysis of the results of missions were concerned. Analysis groups were assembled during the war, and opinions concerning the relative importance of targets were widely different. We now have the experience of a long war. The work done by organizations such as the U.S. Strategic Bombing Survey gives material for discussion and for planning future applications. Of course, in a future war bombs, missiles and atomic energy involve radical changes and bombers will be different; however, it cannot be sufficiently emphasized that it would be a great mistake, after dissolving the groups which worked on analysis of operations, to discontinue the analytical work itself. It is believed that the staff sections dealing with planning and operations should be equipped with adequate scientific personnel to be able to continue studies on methods of target analysis, operational analysis, and the like. It is necessary to have in peacetime a nucleus for scientific groups such as those which successfully assisted in the command and staff work in the field during the war. In these studies experts in statistical, technical, economic and political science must cooperate.

Personnel Policy

14.9 It is believed that many shortcomings of research and development in the Air Forces originate from a lack of appreciation, at higher levels, of the qualifications necessary for successful direction of a laboratory or a proving ground. The theory that an intelligent officer is able to direct any organization, military, technical, or scientific, is certainly obsolete. An officer in charge of a laboratory or proving ground can be really useful only if he holds the position for a sufficient time to become thoroughly acquainted with the subject matter and personnel. Officers with engineering training on engineering duty must not be handicapped, as regards promotion, because of long tenure of the same assignment or time spent in acquiring advance education.

14.10 The position and rank of officers responsible for research and development must be made commensurate with the importance of their work and achievement and must not depend on the size of the organizations under their command.

14.11 The level of civilian personnel engaged in research and development work must be raised by authorizing the Air Forces to hire or dismiss civilian scientific personnel outside of the Civil Service. Also, methods of appointment, compensation, and management of civilian scientific personnel under the Civil Service must be freed from those restrictions of the Civil Service regulations which make the government service unattractive to first-rate scientists. In this connection, a separate branch of the Civil Service for scientific personnel would be of value.

Summary of Recommendations

14.12 The following recommendations are therefore made:

a. A permanent Scientific Advisory Group should be available to the Commanding General, to advise him on questions of long-range scientific planning.

b. The office in charge of research and development should establish research panels for coordination of Air Forces research with that of government agencies and other scientific institutions.

c. Scientific intelligence at home and abroad should be strengthened by including scientific personnel in the Intelligence Service, appointing scientific attaches abroad, and frequently sending scientifically-trained officers or civilians to meetings and for study in foreign countries.

d. Operational analysis and target studies should be continued in peacetime, with adequate scientific personnel.

e. Officers in charge of laboratories should keep such positions long enough to be really useful, without being handicapped in promotion by long tenure of such assignments.

f. Position and rank of officers responsible for research should be determined by the importance of their work and not by the size of the organizations under their command.

g. Appointment and compensation of civilian scientific personnel should be freed from Civil Service regulations, to enable the Air Forces to employ first-class scientists and engineers.

Scientific and Technological Training of Air Forces Personnel

15.1 The discussion in this section refers only to the scientific and technological training of Air Forces officers. The specific training of mechanics, radio operators, electronics technicians, and the like, is not considered. It is believed that in addition to utilizing civilian consultants in various advisory capacities and civilian scientists and engineers in the Civil Service, the Air Forces must organize a broad training program for officers in various fields of science and engineering. New scientific discoveries will continually have a profound influence on the concepts of air warfare, and the Air Forces must be flexible and capable of adjusting themselves to these new concepts. This requires, above all, that the Air Forces be permeated by officers who have the training which will make them capable of evaluating scientific facts with good technical judgement and vision.

Training for Air Staff Work

15.2 Practically all sections of the Air Staff are confronted with problems involving the application of science. Therefore, it is desirable that future Air Staff officers have an understanding of the capabilities of science and an appreciation of scientific thought. Therefore, it is proposed that a certain number of young officers be selected and given scientific training for future Air Staff work. Two years of special training at scientific institutions should be given these officers, in a branch of science chosen by them. The aim of this education should be training of the mind and acquaintance with scientific results, rather than specialized knowledge and routine skill. At intervals of about five years, one-year refresher courses should be inserted. The scientific training would be in addition to military training for staff duties, which is given at such places as the Army War College, the Command and General Staff School.

Training for Research and Development

15.3 A certain number of officers should be given specialized scientific technological training in the branches of mathematics, physical sciences, and engineering, which are of vital interest for development of equipment and operational methods. This training should be accomplished at scientific institutions. Its main objective should be not so much the education of research men in the proper sense, as to give future officers engaged in, or in charge of, research and development an intimate knowledge of the capabilities and limitations of science and accustom them to working in cooperation with scientists and scientific institutions. It is very important that in the future scientific training, a broad variety of sciences which have applications to Air Forces problems be taken into account. A proper balance must be established between aeronautics proper, thermodynamics, electronics, nuclear physics, meteorology, aeromedicine, economics, etc. These officers can best be recruited through the Air Forces ROTC. Exceptionally brilliant students (about 20 percent of the total number taken) should be permitted to continue their scholastic training until they have an M.S. degree and then be put on active duty for about three years. This will give them an opportunity to orient themselves in the type of work they are best suited for in the Air Forces. After that, they should return to college for a period of two years, or long enough to get a Ph.D. degree. This would produce a supply of officers with an intimate knowledge of several fields of science. This is essential to finding the best compromises when military requirements produce conflicting design problems involving more than one field of science. The remaining 80 percent of those students selected through ROTC would go on active service after obtaining a B.S. degree and would return to college, after about three years of active service, long enough to obtain an M.S. degree.

15.4 All officers engaged in research and development must be given repeat scientific training for a period of one year at intervals of about five years. This training can be given at scientific institutions, or by assigning the officer to work as an engineer at one of the research laboratories working on Air Forces problems.

15.5 Every effort should be made to retain in the Air Forces those research and development officers who have already received added scholastic training at government expense during the war. Flying training in grade should be provided for those who are not pilots at the present time, but who desire flight training and can qualify for it. Training a pilot is a much simpler job than training an engineer. It does not appear reasonable to concentrate on trying to make engineers out of pilots at the Air Forces Engineering School, while at the same time refusing to give good engineers a chance to become pilots because they have not been members of combat aircrews.

Technical Schools in the Air Forces

15.6 The main objective of the technical schools in existence or to be established in the Air Forces should be training for procurement, maintenance, and operation of equipment. While these schools should give a short review of the fundamentals of the sciences involved, they should concentrate their efforts on the transmittal of practical knowledge and skill. Exceptionally brilliant graduates of the Air Forces technical schools should be selected for further scientific training in civilian schools.

Summary of Recommendations

15.7 The following recommendations are therefore made:

a. A certain number of young officers should be selected and given special training at scientific institutions in preparation for future scientific Air Staff work.

b. Technical officers recruited throughout the Air Forces ROTC should be given advanced scientific training up to the level required for an M.S. degree, in a broad variety of sciences which have applications to Air Forces problems.

c. Additional training should be given 20 percent of the officers referred to in the preceding recommendation, to qualify them for a Ph.D. degree.

d. All future Air Staff and technical officers who receive scientific training should be given one-year refresher courses at intervals of five years.

e. Every effort should be made to retain in the Air Forces those research and development officers who received scholastic training at government expense during the war.

f. Flying training should be opened immediately to those officers with scientific training who, regardless of combat experience, otherwise qualify.

g. The AAF Engineering School shall be built up in such a way, that fundamentals of the sciences involved in AAF problems shall be included in the curriculum. Exceptionally able graduates shall be selected for further scientific training in civilian educational institutions.

Glossary

AAC	Army Air Corps
AAF	Army Air Forces, US Army
ACM	air chief marshal
AEDC	Arnold Engineering and Development Center
AFBMD	Air Force Ballistic Missile Division
AFFTC	Air Force Flight Test Center
AFHRA	Air Force Historical Research Agency, Maxwell AFB, Alabama
AFIT	Air Force Institute of Technology
AFR	Air Force regulation
AFSC	Air Force Systems Command
AGARD	NATO Advisory Group for Aeronautical Research and Development
AIC	Army Industrial College
Air Corps	Army air branch, 1926–1941
Air Service	Army air branch, 1920–1926
AMC	Air Materiel Command
Aphrodite	Project using radio-controlled bombers to crash into German targets
AR	Army regulation
ARDC	Air Research and Development Command
AWPD-1	Air War Plans Division/Plan Number 1 (1941)
BLC	boundary layer control
Caltech	California Institute of Technology, Pasadena, California
CEP	circular error probable
CG	commanding general
CNN	Cable News Network
CO	commanding officer
COA	Committee of Operations Analysis
Convair	Consolidated Vultee Aircraft Corporation
Crossbow	German V-1 and V-2 launches against Britain
ETO	European theater of operations

FAI	*Federation Aeronautique Internationale*
FDR	Franklin Delano Roosevelt
GALCIT	Guggenheim Aeronautics Laboratory, California Institute of Technology
GE	General Electric
GHQ	General Headquarters, Air Force (1935)
GPS	Global Positioning System
HOI	Headquarters Office Instruction
ICAF	Industrial College of the Armed Forces
ICBM	intercontinental ballistic missile
JATO	jet assisted takeoff
JCS	Joint Chiefs of Staff
JPL	Jet Propulsion Laboratory
Lusty	**LU**ftwaffe **S**ecret **T**echnolog**Y**, project to investigate German scientific laboratories as they were liberated after D day
MIT	Massachusetts Institute of Technology
Mike Shot	First US thermonuclear test detonation, November 1952
MPH	miles per hour
NACA	National Advisory Committee for Aeronautics
NAS	National Academy of Sciences
NASA	National Aeronautics and Space Administration
NASM	National Air and Space Museum
NATO	North Atlantic Treaty Organization
NBS	National Bureau of Standards
NDRC	National Defense Research Committee
NRC	National Research Council
OCAC	Office of the Chief of the Air Corps
OCAS	Office of the Chief of the Air Service
Octagon	Second Quebec Conference, September 1944

ORDCIT	Ordnance, California Institute of Technology
OSRD	Office of Scientific Research and Development
Overlord	Cross-channel invasion from Britain to Normandy Beaches, 6 June 1944
R&D	research and development
RADLAB	Radiation Laboratory, MIT
RAND	Research and Development Corporation
SAB	Scientific Advisory Board, 1946–present
SADU	sea-search attack development unit
SAG	Scientific Advisory Group, 1944–1945
TFX	tactical fighter (experimental)
UAV	unmanned aerial vehicle
USAF	United States Air Force, 1947–present
USAFA	United States Air Force Academy, Colorado Springs, Colorado
USAFE	US Air Forces in Europe
USC	University of South Carolina
USMA	US Military Academy, West Point, New York
USSTAF	US Strategic Air Forces in Europe
WDD	Western Development Division
Weary Willie	Project to send automated (pilotless) war-weary bombers against Germany

Bibliography

Manuscript Collections

California Institute of Technology, Institute Archives, Pasadena, Calif.

> The Theodore von Kármán Collection.
> Millikan, Robert A. Papers.

Jet Propulsion Laboratory, Archives, Pasadena, Calif.

> Various papers covering the early days of the GALCIT were used from this archive. Additionally, the photo collection was very helpful in the compilation of photo essays for this work.

The Johns Hopkins University, Milton S. Eisenhower Library, Baltimore, Md.

> Dryden, Hugh L. Papers, 1898–1965.

Library of Congress, Manuscript Division, Washington, D.C.

> Andrews, Gen Frank M. Papers.
> Arnold, Gen Henry Harley. Papers.
> Bush, Dr. Vannevar. Papers.
> Doolittle, Gen James H. Papers.
> Eaker, Lt Gen Ira C. Papers.
> Foulois, Maj Gen Benjamin D. Papers.
> Guggenheim, Harry F. Papers.
> LeMay, Gen Curtis E. Papers.
> Millikan, Robert A. Papers.
> Mitchell, William "Billy." Papers.
> Spaatz, Gen Carl Andrew. Papers.
> Wright, Orville and Wilbur. Papers.

Harry S Truman Library, Independence, Mo.

> Truman, Harry S. Papers.

435

University of South Carolina, Caroliniana Library, Columbia, S.C.

Montgomery, John K. Papers.

US Air Force Academy Library, Special Collections, Colorado Springs, Colo.

"HAP" Arnold. The Murray Green Collection.
Hansell, Maj Gen Haywood S. Papers.
Kármán, Theodore von. Papers.
Kuter, Gen Laurence S. Papers.
Victory, John F. Papers.

US Air Force Historical Research Agency (AFHRA), Maxwell AFB, Ala.

The system used at the AFHRA centers around two antiquated research tools, IRIS and the card catalog. Collections are named by call number only. Oral history interviews are listed separately in this section. A new computer system is currently being installed to simplify research in this facility.

US Air Force Materiel Command History Office, Dayton, Ohio.

Original volumes of *Toward New Horizons* are located here.

US Air Force Museum, Wright-Patterson AFB, Ohio.

Arnold, Henry H. Papers.
Ercoupe Folder.
The Kettering Bug Folder.

Approximately 50 folders containing technical information on many aircraft designations were consulted in preparing this manuscript.

US Air Force Scientific Advisory Board, Washington, D.C.

Early SAG files contain many of the organizational documents missing in other locations. Additionally, the papers of Floyd Sweet, former SAB secretary, are on file there.

US Army Military History Institute, Carlisle, Pa.

A variety of collections were consulted in pursuit of Arnold letters and photographs.

US Military Academy Library, West Point, N.Y.

A variety of sources were used to piece together Arnold's cadet life.

Public Records and Documents, Unpublished

National Air and Space Museum Archives (NASM).

NASM, Washington, D.C.

Arnold, Henry H. Folder.
Bush, Vannevar. Folder.
Jet Engines, General and 1920–1945.
Kármán, Theodore von. Folder.
Lewis, George W. Collection.
Munk, Max. Folder.
Prandtl, Ludwig. Folder.

NASM, Silver Hill, Md.

Hunsaker, Jerome Clarke. Papers.

A microfiche copy of the Kármán Papers are located here, however, there are substantial amounts of personal information, and photos which were not copied from the originals at Caltech.

US National Archives and Records Administration.

National Archives, Washington, D.C.

Record Group 18. Records of the Office of the Chief of the Air Corps.

National Archives, College Park, Md.

Record Group 255. NACA Executive Committee Meeting Minutes.
Record Group 111. H. H. Arnold Photo Collection.

Public Records and Documents, Published

US Official Histories

Craven, Wesley Frank, and James Lea Cate, eds. *The Army Air Forces in World War II.* 7 vols. 1948–1958. New imprint, Washington, D.C.: Office of Air Force History, 1983.

Vol. 1: *Plans and Early Operations, January 1939 to August 1942.*
Vol. 2: *Europe: Torch to Pointblank, August 1942 to December 1943.*
Vol. 3: *Europe: Argument to V-E Day, January 1944 to May 1945.*
Vol. 4: *The Pacific: Guadalcanal to Saipan, August 1942 to July 1944.*
Vol. 5: *The Pacific: Matterhorn to Nagasaki, June 1944 to August 1945.*
Vol. 6: *Men and Planes.*
Vol. 7: *Services Around the World.*

Maurer, Maurer, ed. *The US Air Service in World War I.* 4 vols. Washington, D.C.: Office of Air Force History, 1978–1979.

Vol. 1: *The Final Report and a Tactical History.*
Vol. 2: *Early Concepts of Military Aviation.*
Vol. 3: *The Battle of St. Mihiel.*
Vol. 4: *Postwar Review.*

US Army in World War II Series

The War Department

Cline, Ray S. *Washington Command Post: The Operations Division.* Washington, D.C.: Center of Military History, United States Army, 1951.

Coakley, Robert W., and Richard M. Leighton. *Global Logistics and Strategy, 1943–1945.* Washington, D.C.: Center of Military History, United States Army, 1968.

Fairchild, Byron, and Jonathan Grossman. *The Army and Industrial Manpower*. Washington, D.C.: Center of Military History, United States Army, 1959.

Leighton, Richard M., and Robert W. Coakley. *Global Logistics and Strategy, 1940–1943*. Washington, D.C.: Center of Military History, United States Army, 1955.

Matloff, Maurice, and Edwin M. Snell. *Strategic Planning for Coalition Warfare, 1941–1942*. Washington, D.C.: Center of Military History, United States Army, 1953.

Matloff, Maurice. *Strategic Planning for Coalition Warfare, 1943–1944*. Washington, D.C.: Center of Military History, United States Army, 1959.

Smith, R. Elberton. *The Army and Economic Mobilization*. Washington, D.C.: Center of Military History, United States Army, 1959.

Watson, Mark S. *Chief of Staff: Pre-War Plans and Preparations*. Washington, D.C.: Center of Military History, United States Army, 1950.

Special Studies

Holley, Irving Brinton, Jr. *Buying Aircraft: Matériel Procurement for the Army Air Forces*. Washington, D.C.: Center of Military History, United States Army, 1964.

Jones, Vincent C. *MANHATTAN: The Army and the Atomic Bomb*. Washington, D.C.: Center of Military History, United States Army, 1985.

Treadwell, Mattie E. *The Women's Army Corps*. Washington, D.C.: Center of Military History, United States Army, 1954.

US Government and Air Force Reports

"An Air Force Command for R&D, 1949–1976: The History of ARDC/AFSC." 1976. K243.04-39, AFHRA.

Arnold, H. H. "First Report of the Commanding General of the Army Air Forces to the Secretary of War." 4 January 1944.

———. "Second Report of the Commanding General of the Army Air Forces to the Secretary of War." 27 February 1945.

———. "Third Report of the Commanding General of the Army Air Forces to the Secretary of War." 12 November 1945.

Bush, Vannevar. *Science: The Endless Frontier: A Report to the President.* Washington, D.C.: US Government Printing Office, 1945.

"Case History of Whittle Engine." Historical Study 93. Air Force Logistical Command History Office, n.d.

"Global Presence, 1995." Washington, D.C.: Department of the Air Force, 1995.

"Global Reach/Global Power: The Evolving Air Force Contribution to National Security." Department of the Air Force, 1992.

"History of Arnold Engineering and Development Center, 1944–1951." 1951. K215.16, AFHRA.

Kármán, Theodore von. *Where We Stand: First Report to General of the Army H.H. Arnold on Long Range Research Problems of the Air Forces with a Review of German Plans and Developments.* 22 August 1945.

———. *Science: The Key to Air Supremacy.* The Executive Summary from, *Toward New Horizons.* 15 December 1945.

New World Vistas, Ancillary Volume. Washington, D.C.: USAF Scientific Advisory Board, 1996.

"Proceedings from the USAF Scientific Advisory Board 50th Anniversary Symposium, 9–10 November 1994." Washington, D.C.: USAF/SAB, 1995, draft copy.

The Rand Corporation, The First Fifteen Years. Santa Monica, Calif.: RAND, 1963.

Russell, Robert R. *Expansion of Facilities Under Army Air Force Auspices, 1940–1945.* USAF Historical Study. Maxwell AFB, Ala.: Air University, 1946.

"Toward New Horizons: SCIENCE, the Key to Air Supremacy, Commemorative Edition, 1950–1992." Wright-Patterson AFB, Ohio: Headquarters Air Force Systems Command History Office, 1992.

"United States Air Force Scientific Advisory Board 50th Anniversary, 1944–1994, Commemorative History, 9–10 November 1994." Washington, D.C.: USAF/SAB, 1994.

The United States Strategic Bombing Surveys, Summary Volume, 30 September 1945. Reprint. Maxwell AFB, Ala.: Air University Press, 1987.

Dissertations

Grumelli, Michael L. "Trial of Faith: The Dissent and Court Martial of Billy Mitchell." PhD diss., Rutgers, The State University of New Jersey, 1991.

Nye, Roger H. "The United States Military Academy in an Era of Educational Reform, 1900–1925." Diss., Columbia University, 1968.

Articles

Primary

Arnold, Henry H. "Air Force in the Atomic Age." In *One World or None.* Edited by Dexter Masters and Katharine Way. New York: McGraw, Hill Co., 1946.

———. "The New Army Air Force." *Army Magazine,* 29 July 1940, AFHRA, 168.3952-122, 1939–1940.

———. "Science and Air Power." *Air Affairs,* December 1946, 184–195.

———. "Tomorrow." In James H. Straubel, ed. *Air Force Diary: 111 Stories from the Official Service Journal of the USAAF.* New York: Simon and Schuster, 1947.

———. "Tradition Can't Win Wars." *Collier's,* 15 October 1949, 13, 65–66.

Kármán, Theodore von. "The Next Fifty Years." *Interavia* 10, no.1 (1955): 20–21.

Kotcher, Ezra. "Our Jet Propelled Fighter." *Air Force,* March 1944, 6–8, 64.

Kuter, Gen Laurence S. "The General vs. The Establishment: Gen. H. H. Arnold and the Air Staff." *Aerospace Historian,* September 1973, 185–189.

———. "How Hap Built the AAF." *Air Force Magazine* 56, no. 9 (September 1973): 88–93.

Mitchell, Col William. "Lawrence Sperry and the Aerial Torpedo." *US Air Service,* January 1926.

Walkowicz, T. F. "Von Kármán's Singular Contributions to American Aerospace Power." *Air Force Magazine*, May 1981, 60–61.

————. "USAF Scientific Advisory Board: Hap's Brain Child." *Air Force Magazine*, June 1955.

Whittle, Frank. "The Birth of the Jet Engine in Britain." In *The Jet Age: Forty Years of Jet Aviation.* Edited by W. J. Boyne and D. S. Lopez. Washington, D.C.: Smithsonian Institution Press, 1979.

Secondary

Bry, Ilse, and Janet Doe. "War and Men of Science." *Science* 122 (11 November 1955): 912–13.

Cohen, Eliot A. "A Revolution in Warfare." *Foreign Affairs* 75, no. 2 (March/April 1996): 37–54.

Edson, Lee. "He Tamed the Wind." *Saturday Evening Post*, 3 August 1957, 24, 76–78.

Ford, Daniel. "Gentlemen, I Give You the Whittle Engine." *Air and Space*, October/November 1992, 88–98.

Grier, Peter. "New World Vistas." *Air Force* 79, no. 3 (March 1996): 20–25.

Hall, R. Cargill. "Shaping the Course of Aeronautics, Rocketry, and Astronautics, Theodore von Kármán, 1881–1963." *Journal of Aerospace Sciences* 26, no. 4 (October/December 1978): 369–86.

————. "Theodore von Kármán, 1881–1963." *Aerospace Historian*, Winter 1981, 252–58.

Hallion, Richard P. "Pioneer of Flight: Doolittle as Aviation Technologist." *Air Power History* 40, no. 4 (Winter 1993): 9–15.

Hunley, J. D. "The Enigma of Robert H. Goddard." *Technology and Culture* 36 (April 1995): 327–50.

Infield, Glenn. "Hap Arnold's WWI Buzz Bomb." *Air Force Magazine*, May 1974, n.p.

Nunn, Jack H. "MIT: A University's Contribution to National Defense." *Military Affairs*, October 1979, 120–25.

Nye, Joseph S., and William A. Owens. "America's Information Edge." *Foreign Affairs* 75, no. 2 (March/April 1996): 20–36.

Reich, Leonard S. "From the *Spirit of St. Louis* to the SST: Charles Lindbergh, Technology and Environment." *Technology and Culture*, April 1995, 351–93.

Roland, Alex. "Science, Technology, and War." *Technology and Culture*, supplement to 36, no. 2 (April 1995): S83–S99.

Schaffer, Ronald. "American Military Ethics in World War II: The Bombing of German Cities." *Journal of American History* 67, no. 2 (September 1980): 318–34.

Shiner, John F. "The Air Corps, the Navy, and Coast Defense, 1919–1941." *Military Affairs*, October 1981, 113–20.

Sturm, Thomas A. "Organizational Evolution." *Air Force*, September 1970, 68–84.

"A Technological High Command." *Fortune*, April 1942, 13–16, 67, 191–96.

"The Triple Alliance: Millikan, Guggenheim, and von Kármán." *Engineering and Science*, April 1981, 23–25.

Tunner, William H. "Technology or Manpower." *Air University Review* 5, no. 3 (Fall 1952): 3–21.

"U. S. Making Rocket War Plane." *Washington Post*, 7 January 1944.

Vaughan, David K. "Hap Arnold's Bill Bruce Books." *Air Power History* 40, no. 4 (Winter 1993): 43–49.

Ward, John W. "The Meaning of Lindbergh's Flight." *American Quarterly* 10, no. 1 (Spring 1958): 3–16.

Watson, George M., Jr. "A 5-Star Leader." *Airman Magazine* (June 1986): 29–32.

Wolk, Herman S. "Renaissance Man of Aviation." *Air Power History* 40, no. 4 (Winter 1993): 4–8.

Memoirs, Biographies, and Published Personal Papers

Ambrose, Stephen E. *The Supreme Commander: The War Years of General Dwight D. Eisenhower.* New York: Doubleday and Co., 1969.

Arnold, Henry H. *Global Mission.* New York: Harper and Brothers, 1949.

Various drafts of this work are available in the Library of Congress in the Arnold Papers and are valuable to review.

Citations used in this work are from the book only rather than from the original manuscript.

————, and Ira C. Eaker. *Army Flyer*. New York: Harper and Brothers, 1942.

Blumberg, Stanley A., and Gwinn Owens. *Energy and Conflict: The Life and Times of Edward Teller*. New York: G. P. Putnam's Sons, 1976.

Bush, Vannevar. *Modern Arms and Free Men: A Discussion of the Role of Science in Preserving Democracy*. New York: Simon and Schuster, 1949.

Coffey, Thomas M. *HAP: The Story of the US Air Force and the Man Who Built It, General Henry H. "Hap" Arnold*. New York: Viking Press, 1982.

Davis, Richard G. *Carl A. Spaatz and the Air War in Europe*. Washington, D.C.: Center for Air Force History, 1993.

Dryden, Hugh L. "Theodore von Kármán: 1881–1963." *Biographical Memoirs*. New York: Columbia University Press, 1965.

Dupre, Flint O. *Hap Arnold: Architect of American Air Power*. New York: MacMillan Co., 1972.

Frisbee, John L., ed. *Makers of the United States Air Force*. Washington, D.C.: Office of Air Force History, 1987.

Glines, Carroll V. *Jimmy Doolittle: Master of the Calculated Risk*. New York: Van Norstrand Reinhold Co., 1972.

Golley, John. *Whittle: The True Story*. Washington, D.C.: Smithsonian Institution Press, 1987.

Goodstein, Judith R. *Millikan's School: A History of the California Institute of Technology*. New York: W. W. Norton and Co., 1991.

Gorn, Michael H. *The Universal Man: Theodore von Kármán's Life in Aeronautics*. Washington, D.C.: Smithsonian Institution Press, 1992.

Groves, Leslie R. *Now It Can Be Told: The Story of the Manhattan Project*. New York: Harper and Brothers, 1969.

Hanle, Paul A. *Bringing Aerodynamics to America*. Cambridge, Mass.: MIT Press, 1982.

Hurley, Alfred F. *Billy Mitchell: Crusader for Airpower*. Bloomington, Ind.: Indiana University Press, 1964.

Kargon, Robert H. *The Rise of Robert Millikan: Portrait of a Life in American Science*. Ithaca, N.Y.: Cornell University Press, 1982.

Kármán, Theodore von, and Lee Edson. *The Wind and Beyond: Theodore von Kármán, Pioneer in Aviation and Pathfinder in Space*. Boston: Little, Brown and Co., 1967.

———. *The Collected Works of Theodore von Kármán*. 4 Vols. London: Butterworths Scientific Publications, 1956.

Kenney, George C. *General Kenney Reports*. Reprint, Washington, D.C.: Office of Air Force History, 1987.

Larabee, Eric. *Commander in Chief: Franklin Delano Roosevelt, His Lieutenants and Their War*. New York: Harper and Row, Publishers, 1987.

LeMay, Gen Curtis E., with MacKinlay Kantor. *Mission with LeMay: My Story*. Garden City, N.Y.: Doubleday and Company, Inc., 1965.

Leslie, Stuart W. *Boss Kettering*. New York: Columbia University Press, 1983.

Lindbergh, Charles A. *Charles A. Lindbergh: Autobiography of Values*. New York: Harcourt Brace Jovanovich, Publishers, 1976.

Meilinger, Phillip S. *Hoyt S. Vandenberg: The Life of a General*. Bloomington, Ind.: Indiana University Press, 1989.

Mets, David R. *Master of Airpower: General Carl A. Spaatz*. Novato, Calif.: Presidio Press, 1988.

Mitchell, William. *Memoirs of World War I: From Start to Finish of our Greatest War*. New York: Random House, 1960.

Parrish, Thomas. *Roosevelt and Marshall: Partners in Politics and War*. New York: William Morrow and Co., Inc., 1989.

Parton, James. *"Air Force Spoken Here" General Ira C. Eaker and the Command of the Air*. Bethesda, Md.: Adler and Adler, Publishers, Inc., 1986.

Pogue, Forrest C. *George C. Marshall: Ordeal and Hope, 1939–1942*. New York: Viking Press, 1966.

———. *George C. Marshall: Organizer of Victory, 1943–45*. New York: Viking Press, 1973.

Powers, Thomas. *Heisenberg's War: The Secret of the German Bomb*. New York: Alfred A. Knopf, 1993.

Sears, William Rees. *Stories from a Twentieth Century Life.* Stanford, Calif.: Parabolic Press, 1993.

Sherwood, Robert E. *Roosevelt and Hopkins: An Intimate History.* New York: Harper and Brothers, 1950.

Shiner, John F. *Foulois and the US Army Air Corps, 1931–1935.* Washington, D.C.: Office of Air Force History, 1983.

Trimble, William F. *Admiral William A. Moffett: Architect of Naval Aviation.* Washington, D.C.: Smithsonian Institution Press, 1994.

Whittle, Frank. *Jet: The Story of a Pioneer.* London: Frederick Muller, 1953.

Monographs and Secondary Sources

Arnold, Henry H., and Ira C. Eaker. *Winged Warfare.* New York: Harper and Brothers, Pub., 1941.

Baxter, James P., III. *Scientists Against Time.* Cambridge, Mass.: MIT Press, 1968.

Beyerchen, Alan D. *Scientists under Hitler.* New Haven: Yale University Press, 1977.

Bilstein, Roger E. *Orders of Magnitude: A History of the NACA and NASA, 1915–1990.* Washington, D.C.: National Aeronautics and Space Administration, 1989.

Biographical Register of the Officers and Graduates of the USMA at West Point, New York. West Point, N.Y.: USMA Printing Office, 1900–1910.

Borden, Norman E., Jr. *The Air Mail Emergency: 1934.* Freeport, Maine: Bond Wheelwright Co., 1968.

Borowski, Harry R. *Military Planning in the Twentieth Century, Proceedings of the Eleventh Military History Symposium, USAF Academy, 10–12 October 1984.* Washington, D.C.: Office of Air Force History, 1986.

Charters, David A., Marc Milner, and J. Brent Wilson, eds. *Military History and the Military Profession.* Westport, Conn.: Praeger, 1992.

Constant, Edward W., II. *The Origins of the Turbojet Revolution.* Baltimore: Johns Hopkins University Press, 1980.

Crouch, Tom D. *A Dream of Wings: Americans and the Airplane, 1875–1905*. Washington, D.C.: Smithsonian Institution Press, 1981.

Cutcliffe, Stephen, and Robert Post. *In Context: History and the History of Technology-Essays in Honor of Melvin Kranzberg*. Bethlehem, Pa.: Leheigh University Press, 1988.

Dawson, Virginia P. *Engines and Innovation: Lewis Laboratory and American Propulsion Technology*. Washington, D.C.: National Aeronautics and Space Administration, 1991.

Dupree, A. Hunter. *Science in the Federal Government: A History of Policies and Activities to 1940*. Cambridge, Mass.: Belknap Press, 1957.

Emme, Eugene M. *The Impact of Airpower: National Security and World Politics*. Princeton, N.J.: D. Van Norstrand Co., Inc., 1959.

Finney, Robert T. *History of the Air Corps Tactical School, 1920–1940*. Washington, D.C.: Center for Air Force History, 1992.

Futrell, Robert F. *Ideas, Concepts, and Doctrine*, vol. 1, *Basic Thinking in the United States Air Force, 1907–1960*. Maxwell AFB, Ala.: Air University Press, 1989.

Gilbert, Felix. *The End of the European Era, 1890 to the Present*. New York: W. W. Norton and Co., Inc., 1970.

Gorn, Michael H. *Harnessing the Genie: Science and Technology Forecasting for the Air Force, 1944–1986*. Washington, D.C.: Office of Air Force History, 1988.

———, ed. *Prophesy Fulfilled: "Toward New Horizons" and Its Legacy*. Washington, D.C.: Air Force History and Museums Program, 1994.

Greer, Thomas H. *The Development of Air Doctrine in the Army Air Arm, 1917–1941*. Maxwell AFB, Ala.: Historical Division, Research Studies Institute, Air University, 1955.

Hallion, Richard P. *Legacy of Flight: The Guggenheim Contribution to American Aviation*. Seattle: University of Washington Press, 1977.

Hansen, James R. *Engineer in Charge: A History of the Langley Aeronautical Laboratory*. Washington, D.C.: National Aeronautics and Space Administration, 1987.

Hennessy, Juliette A. *The United States Air Arm: April 1861 to April 1917*. Washington, D.C.: Office of Air Force History, 1985.

Herzstein, Robert E. *Roosevelt and Hitler: Prelude to War*. New York: Paragon House, 1989.

Holley, I. B., Jr. *Ideas and Weapons: Exploitation of the Aerial Weapon by the United States During World War I; A Study in the Relationship of Technological Advance, Military Doctrine, and the Development of Weapons*. 1953. New imprint. Washington, D.C.: Office of Air Force History, 1983.

Howitzer: The Yearbook of the United States Military Academy Corps of Cadets. West Point, N.Y.: US Military Academy Printing Office (USMA), 1903–1907.

Hughes, Thomas P. *American Genesis: A Century of Invention and Technological Enthusiasm*. New York: Penguin Books, 1989.

Hurley, Alfred F., and Robert C. Ehrhart, eds. *Air Power and Warfare: The Proceedings of the 8th Military History Symposium, United States Air Force Academy, 18–20 October 1978*. Washington, D.C.: Office of Air Force History, 1979.

Johnson, David. *V-1, V-2: Hitler's Vengeance on London*. New York: Stein and Day, 1981.

Kelsey, Benjamin S. *The Dragon's Teeth: The Creation of US Air Power, World War II*. Washington, D.C.: Smithsonian Institution Press, 1982.

Kennett, Lee. *The First Air War, 1914–1918*. New York: Free Press, 1991.

Kevles, Daniel J. *The Physicists: The History of a Scientific Community in Modern America*. New York: Vintage Books, 1979.

Maurer, Maurer. *Aviation in the US Army, 1919–1939*. Washington, D.C.: Office of Air Force History, 1987.

McFarland, Stephen L. *America's Pursuit of Precision Bombing, 1910–1945*. Washington, D.C.: Smithsonian Institution Press, 1995.

McNeill, William H. *The Pursuit of Power: Technology, Armed Force, and Society since A.D. 1000.* Chicago: University of Chicago Press, 1982.

Messenger, Charles. *"Bomber" Harris and the Strategic Bombing Offensive, 1939–1945.* London: Arms and Armour Press, 1984.

Morrow, John H., Jr. *The Great War in the Air: Military Aviation from 1909–1921.* Washington, D.C.: Smithsonian Institution Press, 1993.

Neufeld, Jacob. *Ballistic Missiles in the United States Air Force, 1945–1960.* Washington, D.C.: Office of Air Force History, 1990.

————, ed. *Reflections on Research and Development in the United States Air Force.* Washington, D.C.: Center for Air Force History, 1993.

Official Resister of the Officers and Cadets of the USMA. West Point, N.Y.: USMA Printing Office, June 1904.

Overy, R. J. *The Air War, 1939–1945.* New York: Stein and Day, 1981.

Pursell, Carroll W., ed. *Technology in America: A History of Individuals and Ideas.* Cambridge, Mass.: MIT Press, 1981.

Reynolds, Quentin. *The Amazing Mr. Doolittle.* New York: Appleton-Century-Crofts, 1953.

Rhodes, Richard. *The Making of the Atomic Bomb.* New York: Simon and Schuster, 1986.

Roland, Alex. *Model Research: The National Advisory Committee for Aeronautics, 1915–1958.* 2 vols. Washington, D.C.: National Aeronautics and Space Administration, 1985.

Rosenberg, Max. *The Air Force and the National Guided Missile Program, 1944–1950.* Washington, D.C.: USAF Historical Division Liaison Office, June 1964.

Rotundo, Louis. *Into the Unknown: The X-1 Story.* Washington, D.C.: Smithsonian Institution Press, 1994.

Sapolsky, Harvey M. *Science and the Navy: The History of the Office of Naval Research.* Princeton, N.J.: Princeton University Press, 1990.

Schaffer, Ronald. *Wings of Judgment: American Bombing in World War II.* New York: Oxford University Press, 1985.

Schlaifer, Robert. *The Development of Aircraft Engines.* Bridge, Mass.: Harvard University Graduate School of Business Administration, 1950.

Sherry, Michael S. *Preparing for the Next War: America Plans for Postwar Defense, 1941–45.* New Haven: Yale University Press, 1977.

———. *The Rise of American Air Power: The Creation of Armageddon.* New Haven: Yale University Press, 1987.

Smith, Merritt Roe, ed. *Military Enterprise and Technological Change: Perspectives on the American Experience.* Cambridge, Mass.: The MIT Press, 1985.

———, and Leo Marx, eds. *Does Technology Drive History? The Dilemma of Technological Determinism.* Cambridge, Mass.: MIT Press, 1994.

Smith, Perry McCoy. *The Air Force Plans for Peace, 1943–1945.* Baltimore: Johns Hopkins University Press, 1970.

Stanley, Dennis J., and John J. Weaver. *The Air Force Command for R&D, 1949–1976, The History of ARDC/AFSC.* Washington, D.C.: Office of History, HQ AFSC, 1977.

Staudenmaier, John M. *Technology's Storytellers: Reweaving the Human Fabric.* Cambridge: MIT Press, 1985.

Sturm, Thomas A. *USAF Scientific Advisory Board: Its First Twenty Years, 1944–1964.* Washington, D.C.: USAF Historical Division Liaison Office, 1967.

———. *The USAF Scientific Advisory Board: Its First Twenty Years, 1944–1964.* 1967. Reprint, Washington, D.C.: Office of Air Force History, 1987.

Underwood, Jeffery S. The *Wings of Democracy: The Influence of Air Power on the Roosevelt Administration, 1933–1941.* College Station, Tex.: Texas A&M University Press, 1991.

Van Creveld, Martin. *Technology and War: From 2000 B.C. to the Present.* New York: Free Press, 1989.

Walker, Lois E., and Shelby E. Wickam. *From Huffman Prairie to the Moon: The History of Wright-Patterson Air Force Base.* Dayton, Ohio: Air Force Logistics Command, 1986.

Watts, Barry D. *The Foundations of US Air Doctrine: The Problem of Friction in War.* Maxwell AFB, Ala.: Air University Press, 1984.

Wolk, Herman S. *Planning and Organizing the Post War Air Force, 1943–1947.* Washington, D.C.: Office of Air Force History, 1984.

Wolko, Howard S. *In the Cause of Flight: Technologists of Aeronautics and Astronautics.* Washington, D.C.: Smithsonian Institution Press, 1981.

Wright, Monte D., and Lawrence J. Paszek, eds. *Science, Technology, and Warfare: The Proceedings of the Third Military History Symposium, United States Air Force Academy, 8–9 May 1969.* Washington, D.C.: Office of Air Force History, 1970.

York, Herbert F. *Arms and the Physicist.* Woodbury, New York: The American Institute of Physics, 1995.

Young, James O., ed. *Supersonic Symposium: The Men of Mach One.* Edwards AFB, Calif.: Air Force Flight Test Center History Office, 1990.

Unpublished Material

Daso, Dik A. "Events in Foreign Policy: The End of American Neutrality, 1917–1918." Typed manuscript. University of South Carolina, 1994.

Collins, Martin J. "Internalizing the Civilian: RAND and the Air Force in the Early Cold War." For the 1993 Society for the History of Technology (SHOT) Annual Meeting, typed manuscript. Department of Space History, National Air and Space Museum, 1993.

Dryden, Hugh L. "Memorial Ceremony for Theodore von Kármán, 1881–1963." Memorial Proceedings. USAF Academy Special Collections, 28 May 1963.

Komons, Nick A. "Science and the Air Force: A History of the Air Force Office of Scientific Research." Typed manuscript. Historical Division, Office of Information, Office of Aerospace Research, Arlington, Va., 1966.

Young, James O. "Riding England's Coattails: The U.S. Army Air Forces and the Turbojet Revolution." Edwards AFB, Calif.: AFFTC History Office, 1995.

Letters to the Author from:

Eaker, Ira C. 1 October 1979, and 7 December 1979.

Getting, Ivan. 17 October 1994.

Green, Murray. 18 November 1993, 9 February 1994, and 20 June 1994.

Hansell, Haywood. 4 October 1979, and 9 December 1979.

Hasert, Chester N. 24 May 1995.

Huston, John W. 13 December 1993, 19 August 1994, and 22 February 1996.

Roland, Alex. 4 May, 5 August 1994, and 15 February 1996.

Interviews and Oral Histories

Interviews by the Author

Arnold, Mrs. Barbara. 6 April 1995.

Arnold, Mr. Robert. 14–16 July 1995.

Charyk, Dr., and Mrs. Joseph. 9 November 1994.

Flax, Dr. Alexander. 9 November 1994.

Getting, Dr. Ivan. 9 November 1994.

Hallion, Dr. Richard P. 28 August 1995.

Hasert, Mr. Chester. 9 November 1994.

Schriever, Bernard A. 9 November 1995, 12 March 1996.

Sears, Dr. William Rees. 8 July 1995.

Stewart, Dr. Homer Joe. 21 July 1995.

Stever, Dr. H. Guyford. 18 May 1995.

Yarymovych, Dr. Michael I. 20 July 1995.

USAF Academy Oral History Interviews

Doolittle, Lt Gen James H. 21 April 1969, 22 December 1977.

Eaker, Lt Gen Ira C. 19 October 1978.

Kármán, Dr. Theodore von. Number 212. 27 January 1960.

Twining, Gen Nathan F. Number 206, 206A. November 1965, 3 November 1967.

Victory, John F. Number 210A. October 1962.

Murray Green Collection Interviews

Arnold, General of the Air Force, H. H. Interviewed by T. A. Boyd. 19 October 1949.

Arnold, Col H. H., Jr., Retired. 29–30 August 1972.

Arnold, Mrs. H. H. n.d.

Bowman, Brig Gen H. W. 23 August 1969.

Carroll, Maj Gen Franklin. 1 September 1971.

Chidlaw, Gen Benjamin. 12 December 1969.

Conant, F. W. CUOHR.

Craigie, Lt Gen Laurence. 19 August 1970.

Dean, Lt Gen Fred. 20 February 1973.

Gardner, Grandison. CUOHR.

Keirn, Maj Gen Donald J., Retired. 25 September 1970.

Kelsey, Benjamin S. 9 June 1971.

McHugh, Brig Gen Godfrey. 21 April 1970.

Milling, Thomas D. n.d. CUOHR.

Raymond, A. E. n.d. CUOHR.

Viccellio, Lt Gen Henry, Jr. 13 May 1970.

Reminiscences of Friends and Family, on file at USAF Academy

Arnold, Mrs. H. H.

Spaatz, Gen Carl A.

Air Force Historical Research Agency Oral History Interviews

Cook, Orvil R. K239.0512-740, 836.

Craigie, Laurence. K239.0512-637, 647, 695, 1397, and 146.33-34.

Doolittle, James H. K239.0512-1405, 623, 625, 793, 998, 1152, and 146.34-39.

Dryden, Dr. Hugh Latimer. K146.34-41.

Eaker, Ira C. K239.0512-626, 627, 799, 829, 868, 918, and 142.052.

Hunsaker, Jerome C. K146.34-53.

Kármán, Theodore von. K146.34-59.

Knerr, Hugh. K239.0512-616, 1012.

Lindbergh, Charles A. K146.34-64.

McHugh, Godfrey T. K239.0512-1458.
Norstad, Lauris. K239.0512-1116, 1473.
O'Donnell, Gen Emmett "Rosie." K239.0512-1476.
Peabody, Hume. K239.0512-867.
Putt, Lt Gen Donald L. K239.0512-724.
Seamans, Robert C. K239.0512-866.
Symington, Stuart. K239.0512-932, 1039, 1343.
Twining, Nathan F. K239.0512-635, 636.
Whittle, Sir Frank. K239.0512-931.

Miscellaneous Interviews

Allen, Gen Lew, Jr., USAF, Retired. Interviewed for *5 Decades of Progress: Toward New Horizons*, by John Primm, videotape, USAF Television, 20 September 1994.

Kármán, Theodore von. Interviewed by Shirley Thomas, tape, January 1960.

Sorenson, Harold. Interview for 50th Anniversary SAB, Pentagon, Washington, D.C., 27 September 1994.

Video Recordings

Primm, John. *5 Decades of Progress: Toward New Horizons.* USAF Television, Pentagon, Washington, D.C., 30 min., 1994.

———. *New World Vistas.* USAF Television, 54 min., 15 December 1995.

Sears, William Rees. "Oral History Interview, 9 July 1995, Tucson, AZ." USAF Television, 1995.

Young, John O. *Lighting the Flame.* USAF Flight Test Center, 36 min., 1995.

"Proceedings of the '50th Anniversary of the SAB' Symposium." 10 November 1994, National Academy of Sciences. 6 hours, 1994.

Index

Atlas ICBM: 171

B-17: 38, 82
B-24: 82
B-29: 38
Baker Board: 55
"Barling" bomber: 38
Bell Aircraft: 73
Bell, Alexander Graham: 24
Bell X-1: 189
Bell XP-59A: 75
Bell, Larry: 73
"Black Hand": 9
Bollay, William: 132
boundary layer control (BLC): 116
Boushey, Homer: 67
Bowles, Edward L.: 81, 145
Bowman, H. W.: 53
Browning Board: 56
Browning, William S.: 56
Bush, Vannevar: 59, 86–87, 116, 153, 178

Caltech: 48, 66, 100, 129
Carroll, Franklin O.: 7, 92–93, 149, 168
cavalry: 40–41, 55
charged particle experiments: 43
Charyk, Joseph: 118
Chidlaw, Benjamin: 73
Civil War: 9
Committee on Air Corps Research: 59
Consolidated Vultee Aircraft Corporation (Convair): 157
Covert, Eugene E.: 186, 198
Craigie, Laurence: 74–75, 163
Curtiss B-2 "Condor" bomber: 43
Curtiss JN-3: 24

DH-4 aircraft: 33
Doolittle, James H. "Jimmy": 165, 185
Douglas DC-3: 111
Douglas, Donald: 40, 49, 53, 178, 187, 192
Douglas O-38: 42
Drum Board: 55, 57

jet assisted takeoff (JATO) system: 59, 66, 117
jet engine: 76
Jet Engine Facility: 95
jet plane: 75
Jet Propulsion Committee: 92
Jet Propulsion Laboratory (JPL): 60
Jouett, Jack: 41

Kármán:
    Kármán, fillets: 111
    Kármán, Helen von: 97, 101
    Kármán, Maurice von: 97
    Kármán, Pipö von: 101, 123
    Kármán, Theodore von: 4, 47, 59, 97, 101, 125, 127, 150, 153,
        157, 160, 165–66, 172–73, 185, 189
Kawanishi Company: 102
Keirn, Donald J.: 74
Kettering, Charles: 31, 81
Kettering Flying Bug: 26, 81
Kilner Board: 61, 70
Klien, Arthur, "Maj": 102
Knudsen, William S.: 149
Kobe, Japan: 102, 105
Kraft, Hans: 127
Kuter, Laurence S.: 3

LaGuardia meeting: 126
Langley Field: 59, 63
LeMay, Curtis E.: 146, 158–59
Lewis, George W.: 70, 115, 117
Liberty engine: 33, 84
Lindbergh, Charles: 61, 70

Mackay Trophy: 16, 45
Malina, Frank: 60, 67, 112, 115
Manhattan Project: 186
March Fiield, CA: 43–45, 47, 55, 67
Mark, Hans: 174
Marshall, George C.: 23, 61, 88
Martin B-10: 45
Massachusetts Institute of Technology (MIT): 80, 145
    MIT Radiation Laboratory (RADLAB): 81, 145

McCall, Gene: 175–77, 183–84, 199
Menlo Park: 6
Millikan:
   Millikan, Clark B.: 69, 108, 116–17, 172, 183
   Millikan, Robert: 29, 43, 59, 89, 101, 109, 125, 128
Milling, Thomas DeWitt "Tommy": 2, 13, 16
missile programs: 171
Mitchell, William "Billy": 36, 40
Modern Arms and Free Men: 153, 178
Montgomery, John K.: 41
MX-774B: 157

National Academy of Sciences, U.S. (NAS): 59, 173
National Advisory Committee for Aeronautics (NACA): 24, 33, 72,
   115, 117, 168
   NACA Main Committee: 63
National Defense Research Committee (NDRC): 80
National Unitary Wind Tunnel Plan: 167
National Wind Tunnel Facility: 168
NATO Advisory Group for Aeronautical Research and Development
   (AGARD): 169
Neumann, John von: 170–71
New World Vistas: 175–76
Newton, Sir Isaac: 107, 122
nuclear power: 170
Nuclear Weapons Panel: 170

O'Donnell, Emmett "Rosie": 3
Office of Scientific Liaison (OSL): 155
Office of Scientific Research and Development (OSRD): 86, 116, 153
Operation Lusty: 129, 133

P-51: 127
Pan Am Airlines: 41
Panama: 24, 26, 65
Patrick, Mason: 39
Pentagon: 49, 125–26, 152, 155, 163, 175
Pershing, John J.: 24, 31, 39, 51
Philippines: 11
Pool, Eleanor: 20
Portal, Sir Charles: 73
Prandtl, Ludwig: 48, 97

supersonic wind tunnel: 116, 144
Symington, W. Stuart: 167
systems: 6, 8, 164, 166, 186–88, 193, 198–99

Tacoma Narrows Bridge: 107
Teapot Committee: 171
technology: 21, 70, 156
Teller, Edward: 5, 170, 182
Toward New Horizons: 147, 180
Treaty of Trianon: 105
Twining, Nathan F.: 3

V-1: 84, 136
V-2: 84, 136
Vandenberg, Hoyt S.: 164

Walt Disney Productions: 128
War for Independence: 9
War Production Board: 87
Warner, Donald F. "Truly": 73
Washington, D.C.: 2, 16, 26, 53
Wattendorf, Frank L.: 112, 168
Weary Willy: 82, 94
Welsh, Al: 13, 16
West Point: 48
Western Development Division (WDD): 171
Westover, Oscar: 58
Where We Stand: 143, 147
"Whittle" jet engine: 70, 72
Widnall, Sheila: 175
Willy Orphan: 94
Wilson, Woodrow: 26, 64
wind tunnel: 101, 103, 115, 117
Wood, Leonard: 26
Woods Hole Summer Studies: 174
World War II: 6
Wright Brothers' flying school: 13
Wright, Orville: 29
Wright, Wilbur: 16

Yarymovych, Michael I.: 186

Zook, George F.: 105